ŚRĪMAD BHĀGAVATAM

Third Canto
"The Status Quo"

(Part Two—Chapters 9–16)

With the Original Sanskrit Text,
Its Roman Transliteration, Synonyms,
Translation and Elaborate Purports

by

His Divine Grace
A.C. Bhaktivedanta Swami Prabhupāda
Founder-*Ācārya* of the International Society for Krishna Consciousness

THE BHAKTIVEDANTA BOOK TRUST

Readers interested in the subject matter of this book are invited by the International Society for Krishna Consciousness to correspond with its Secretary at one of the following addresses:

ISKCON Reader Services
P. O. Box 730
Watford, WD25 8ZE, United Kingdom
Tel: +44 (0)1923 857244
Website: www.iskcon.org.uk

Karuṇa Bhavan
Bankhouse Road, Lesmahagow
Lanarkshire, ML11 0ES
Scotland, United Kingdom
Tel: +44 (0)1555 894790
Fax: +44 (0)1555 894526
E-mail: karunabhavan@aol.com
Website: www.gouranga.cc

The Bhaktivedanta Book Trust
P. O. Box 380
Riverstone, NSW
Australia 2765
Tel: +61 (0)2 96276306
Fax: +61 (0)2 96276052

The Bhaktivedanta Book Trust
Hare Krishna Land
Juhu, Mumbai 400 049, India
Tel: +91 (0)22 26202921
Fax: +91 (0)22 26200357
E-mail: bbtmumbai@pamho.net
Website: www.bbtindia.net

www.krishna.com

ISBN 0-89213-406-2
ISBN 0-89213-430-5 (30-volume set)

Printed in India

Table of Contents

CHAPTER FOURTEEN
Pregnancy of Diti in the Evening   219

CHAPTER FIFTEEN
Description of the Kingdom of God   267

Preface

We must know the present need of human society. And what is that need? Human society is no longer bounded by geographical limits to particular countries or communities. Human society is broader than in the Middle Ages, and the world tendency is toward one state or one human society. The ideals of spiritual communism, according to *Śrīmad-Bhāgavatam*, are based more or less on the oneness of the entire human society, nay, of the entire energy of living beings. The need is felt by great thinkers to make this a successful ideology. *Śrīmad-Bhāgavatam* will fill this need in human society. It begins, therefore, with the aphorism of Vedānta philosophy *janmādy asya yataḥ* to establish the ideal of a common cause.

Human society, at the present moment, is not in the darkness of oblivion. It has made rapid progress in the field of material comforts, education and economic development throughout the entire world. But there is a pinprick somewhere in the social body at large, and therefore there are large-scale quarrels, even over less important issues. There is need of a clue as to how humanity can become one in peace, friendship and prosperity with a common cause. *Śrīmad-Bhāgavatam* will fill this need, for it is a cultural presentation for the respiritualization of the entire human society.

Śrīmad-Bhāgavatam should be introduced also in the schools and colleges, for it is recommended by the great student-devotee Prahlāda Mahārāja in order to change the demoniac face of society.

kaumāra ācaret prājño
dharmān bhāgavatān iha
durlabhaṁ mānuṣaṁ janma
tad apy adhruvam arthadam
(*Bhāg.* 7.6.1)

Disparity in human society is due to lack of principles in a godless civilization. There is God, or the Almighty One, from whom everything emanates, by whom everything is maintained and in whom everything is merged to rest. Material science has tried to find the ultimate source of creation very insufficiently, but it is a fact that there is one ultimate source of everything that be. This ultimate source is explained rationally and authoritatively in the beautiful *Bhāgavatam*, or *Śrīmad-Bhāgavatam.*

Śrīmad-Bhāgavatam is the transcendental science not only for knowing the ultimate source of everything but also for knowing our relation with Him and our duty towards perfection of the human society on the basis of this perfect knowledge. It is powerful reading matter in the Sanskrit language, and it is now rendered into English elaborately so that simply by a careful reading one will know God perfectly well, so much so that the reader will be sufficiently educated to defend himself from the onslaught of atheists. Over and above this, the reader will be able to convert others to accepting God as a concrete principle.

Śrīmad-Bhāgavatam begins with the definition of the ultimate source. It is a bona fide commentary on the *Vedānta-sūtra* by the same author, Śrīla Vyāsadeva, and gradually it develops into nine cantos up to the highest state of God realization. The only qualification one needs to study this great book of transcendental knowledge is to proceed step by step cautiously and not jump forward haphazardly like with an ordinary book. It should be gone through chapter by chapter, one after another. The reading matter is so arranged with its original Sanskrit text, its English transliteration, synonyms, translation and purports so that one is sure to become a God-realized soul at the end of finishing the first nine cantos.

The Tenth Canto is distinct from the first nine cantos because it deals directly with the transcendental activities of the Personality of Godhead Śrī Kṛṣṇa. One will be unable to capture the effects of the Tenth Canto without going through the first nine cantos. The book is complete in twelve cantos, each independent, but it is good for all to read them in small installments one after another.

I must admit my frailties in presenting *Śrīmad-Bhāgavatam*, but still I am hopeful of its good reception by the thinkers and leaders of society on the strength of the following statement of *Śrīmad-Bhāgavatam* (1.5.11):

tad-vāg-visargo janatāgha-viplavo
yasmin prati-ślokam abaddhavaty api

nāmāny anantasya yaśo 'ṅkitāni yac
chṛṇvanti gāyanti gṛṇanti sādhavaḥ

"On the other hand, that literature which is full with descriptions of the transcendental glories of the name, fame, form and pastimes of the unlimited Supreme Lord is a transcendental creation meant to bring about a revolution in the impious life of a misdirected civilization. Such transcendental literatures, even though irregularly composed, are heard, sung and accepted by purified men who are thoroughly honest."

Oṁ tat sat

A. C. Bhaktivedanta Swami

Introduction

"This *Bhāgavata Purāṇa* is as brilliant as the sun, and it has arisen just after the departure of Lord Kṛṣṇa to His own abode, accompanied by religion, knowledge, etc. Persons who have lost their vision due to the dense darkness of ignorance in the age of Kali shall get light from this *Purāṇa*." (*Śrīmad-Bhāgavatam* 1.3.43)

The timeless wisdom of India is expressed in the *Vedas*, ancient Sanskrit texts that touch upon all fields of human knowledge. Originally preserved through oral tradition, the *Vedas* were first put into writing five thousand years ago by Śrīla Vyāsadeva, the "literary incarnation of God." After compiling the *Vedas*, Vyāsadeva set forth their essence in the aphorisms known as *Vedānta-sūtras*. *Śrīmad-Bhāgavatam* is Vyāsadeva's commentary on his own *Vedānta-sūtras*. It was written in the maturity of his spiritual life under the direction of Nārada Muni, his spiritual master. Referred to as "the ripened fruit of the tree of Vedic literature," *Śrīmad-Bhāgavatam* is the most complete and authoritative exposition of Vedic knowledge.

After compiling the *Bhāgavatam*, Vyāsa impressed the synopsis of it upon his son, the sage Śukadeva Gosvāmī. Śukadeva Gosvāmī subsequently recited the entire *Bhāgavatam* to Mahārāja Parīkṣit in an assembly of learned saints on the bank of the Ganges at Hastināpura (now Delhi). Mahārāja Parīkṣit was the emperor of the world and was a great *rājarṣi* (saintly king). Having received a warning that he would die within a week, he renounced his entire kingdom and retired to the bank of the Ganges to fast until death and receive spiritual enlightenment. The *Bhāgavatam* begins with Emperor Parīkṣit's sober inquiry to Śukadeva Gosvāmī: "You are the spiritual master of great saints and devotees. I am therefore begging you to show the way of perfection for all persons, and especially for one who is about to die. Please let me know what a man should hear, chant, remember and worship, and also what he should not do. Please explain all this to me."

Śukadeva Gosvāmī's answer to this question, and numerous other questions posed by Mahārāja Parīkṣit, concerning everything from the nature of the self to the origin of the universe, held the assembled sages in rapt attention continuously for the seven days leading to the King's death. The sage Sūta Gosvāmī, who was present on the bank of the Ganges when Śukadeva Gosvāmī first recited *Śrīmad-Bhāgavatam*, later repeated the *Bhāgavatam* before a gathering of sages in the forest of Naimiṣāraṇya. Those sages, concerned about the spiritual welfare of the people in general, had gathered to perform a long, continuous chain of sacrifices to counteract the degrading influence of the incipient age of Kali. In response to the sages' request that he speak the essence of Vedic wisdom, Sūta Gosvāmī repeated from memory the entire eighteen thousand verses of *Śrīmad-Bhāgavatam*, as spoken by Śukadeva Gosvāmī to Mahārāja Parīkṣit.

The reader of *Śrīmad-Bhāgavatam* hears Sūta Gosvāmī relate the questions of Mahārāja Parīkṣit and the answers of Śukadeva Gosvāmī. Also, Sūta Gosvāmī sometimes responds directly to questions put by Śaunaka Ṛṣi, the spokesman for the sages gathered at Naimiṣāraṇya. One therefore simultaneously hears two dialogues: one between Mahārāja Parīkṣit and Śukadeva Gosvāmī on the bank of the Ganges, and another at Naimiṣāraṇya between Sūta Gosvāmī and the sages at Naimiṣāraṇya Forest, headed by Śaunaka Ṛṣi. Furthermore, while instructing King Parīkṣit, Śukadeva Gosvāmī often relates historical episodes and gives accounts of lengthy philosophical discussions between such great souls as the saint Maitreya and his disciple Vidura. With this understanding of the history of the *Bhāgavatam*, the reader will easily be able to follow its intermingling of dialogues and events from various sources. Since philosophical wisdom, not chronological order, is most important in the text, one need only be attentive to the subject matter of *Śrīmad-Bhāgavatam* to appreciate fully its profound message.

The translator of this edition compares the *Bhāgavatam* to sugar candy—wherever you taste it, you will find it equally sweet and relishable. Therefore, to taste the sweetness of the *Bhāgavatam*, one may begin by reading any of its volumes. After such an introductory taste, however, the serious reader is best advised to go back to Volume One of the First Canto and then proceed through the *Bhāgavatam*, volume after volume, in its natural order.

This edition of the *Bhāgavatam* is the first complete English translation of this important text with an elaborate commentary, and it is the first widely available to the English-speaking public. It is the product of the scholarly and devotional effort of His Divine Grace A. C. Bhaktivedanta Swami Prabhupāda, the world's most distinguished teacher of Indian religious and philosophical thought. His consummate Sanskrit scholarship and intimate familiarity with Vedic culture and thought as well as the modern way of life combine to reveal to the West a magnificent exposition of this important classic.

Readers will find this work of value for many reasons. For those interested in the classical roots of Indian civilization, it serves as a vast reservoir of detailed information on virtually every one of its aspects. For students of comparative philosophy and religion, the *Bhāgavatam* offers a penetrating view into the meaning of India's profound spiritual heritage. To sociologists and anthropologists, the *Bhāgavatam* reveals the practical workings of a peaceful and scientifically organized Vedic culture, whose institutions were integrated on the basis of a highly developed spiritual world-view. Students of literature will discover the *Bhāgavatam* to be a masterpiece of majestic poetry. For students of psychology, the text provides important perspectives on the nature of consciousness, human behavior and the philosophical study of identity. Finally, to those seeking spiritual insight, the *Bhāgavatam* offers simple and practical guidance for attainment of the highest self-knowledge and realization of the Absolute Truth. The entire multivolume text, presented by the Bhaktivedanta Book Trust, promises to occupy a significant place in the intellectual, cultural and spiritual life of modern man for a long time to come.

—The Publishers

CHAPTER NINE

Brahmā's Prayers for Creative Energy

TEXT 1

ब्रह्मोवाच
ज्ञातोऽसि मेऽद्य सुचिरान्ननु देहभाजां
न ज्ञायते भगवतो गतिरित्यवद्यम् ।
नान्यत्त्वदस्ति भगवन्नपि तन्न शुद्धं
मायागुणव्यतिकराद्यदुरुर्विभासि ॥ १ ॥

brahmovāca
jñāto 'si me 'dya sucirān nanu deha-bhājāṁ
na jñāyate bhagavato gatir ity avadyam
nānyat tvad asti bhagavann api tan na śuddhaṁ
māyā-guṇa-vyatikarād yad urur vibhāsi

brahmā uvāca—Lord Brahmā said; *jñātaḥ*—known; *asi*—You are; *me*—by me; *adya*—today; *sucirāt*—after a long time; *nanu*—but; *deha-bhājām*—of one who has a material body; *na*—not; *jñāyate*—is known; *bhagavataḥ*—of the Personality of Godhead; *gatiḥ*—course; *iti*—so it is; *avadyam*—great offense; *na anyat*—none beyond; *tvat*—You; *asti*—there is; *bhagavan*—O my Lord; *api*—even though there is; *tat*—anything that may be; *na*—never; *śuddham*—absolute; *māyā*—material energy; *guṇa-vyatikarāt*—because of the mixture of the modes of; *yat*—to which; *uruḥ*—transcendental; *vibhāsi*—You are.

TRANSLATION

Lord Brahmā said: O my Lord, today, after many, many years of penance, I have come to know about You. Oh, how unfortunate the embodied living entities are that they are unable to know Your personality! My Lord, You are the only knowable object because

there is nothing supreme beyond You. If there is anything supposedly superior to You, it is not the Absolute. You exist as the Supreme by exhibiting the creative energy of matter.

PURPORT

The highest peak of the ignorance of the living entities who are conditioned by material bodies is that they are unaware of the supreme cause of the cosmic manifestation. Different people have different theories regarding the supreme cause, but none of them are genuine. The only supreme cause is Viṣṇu, and the intervening impediment is the illusory energy of the Lord. The Lord has employed His wonderful material energy in manifesting many, many wonderful distractions in the material world, and the conditioned souls, illusioned by the same energy, are thus unable to know the supreme cause. The most stalwart scientists and philosophers, therefore, cannot be accepted as wonderful. They only appear wonderful because they are instruments in the hands of the illusory energy of the Lord. Under illusion, the general mass of people deny the existence of the Supreme Lord and accept the foolish products of illusory energy as supreme.

One can know the supreme cause, the Personality of Godhead, by the causeless mercy of the Lord, which is bestowed upon the Lord's pure devotees like Brahmā and those in his disciplic succession. By acts of penance only was Lord Brahmā able to see the Garbhodakaśāyī Viṣṇu, and by realization only could he understand the Lord as He is. Brahmā was extremely satisfied upon observing the magnificent beauty and opulence of the Lord, and he admitted that nothing can be comparable to Him. Only by penance can one appreciate the beauty and opulence of the Lord, and when one is acquainted with that beauty and opulence, he is no longer attracted by any other. This is confirmed in *Bhagavad-gītā* (2.59): *paraṁ dṛṣṭvā nivartate.*

Foolish human beings who do not endeavor to investigate the supreme beauty and opulence of the Lord are here condemned by Brahmā. It is imperative that every human being try for such knowledge, and if anyone does not do so, his life is spoiled. Anything that is beautiful and opulent in the material sense is enjoyed by those living entities who are like crows. Crows always engage in picking at rejected garbage, whereas the white ducks do not mix with the crows. Rather, they take pleasure in transparent lakes with lotus flowers, surrounded by beautiful orchards. Both crows and ducks are undoubtedly birds by birth, but they are not of the same feather.

TEXT 2

रूपं यदेतदवबोधरसोदयेन
शश्वन्निवृत्ततमसः सदनुग्रहाय ।
आदौ गृहीतमवतारशतैकबीजं
यन्नाभिपद्मभवनादहमाविरासम् ॥ २ ॥

rūpaṁ yad etad avabodha-rasodayena
śaśvan-nivṛtta-tamasaḥ sad-anugrahāya
ādau gṛhītam avatāra-śataika-bījaṁ
yan-nābhi-padma-bhavanād aham āvirāsam

rūpam—form; *yat*—which; *etat*—that; *avabodha-rasa*—of Your internal potency; *udayena*—with the manifestation; *śaśvat*—forever; *nivṛtta*—freed from; *tamasaḥ*—material contamination; *sat-anugrahāya*—for the sake of the devotees; *ādau*—original in the creative energy of matter; *gṛhītam*—accepted; *avatāra*—of incarnations; *śata-eka-bījam*—the root cause of hundreds; *yat*—that which; *nābhi-padma*—the navel lotus flower; *bhavanāt*—from the home; *aham*—myself; *āvirāsam*—generated.

TRANSLATION

The form which I see is eternally freed from material contamination and has advented to show mercy to the devotees as a manifestation of internal potency. This incarnation is the origin of many other incarnations, and I am born from the lotus flower grown from Your navel home.

PURPORT

The three deities Brahmā, Viṣṇu and Maheśvara (Śiva), the executive heads of the three modes of material nature (passion, goodness and ignorance), are all generated from Garbhodakaśāyī Viṣṇu, who is described herein by Brahmā. From the Kṣīrodakaśāyī Viṣṇu, many Viṣṇu incarnations expand at different ages in the duration of the cosmic manifestation. They are expanded only for the transcendental happiness of the pure devotees. The incarnations of Viṣṇu, who appear at different ages and times, are never to be compared to the conditioned souls. The *viṣṇu-tattvas* are not to be compared to deities like Brahmā and Śiva, nor are they on the same level. Anyone who compares them is called a *pāṣaṇḍī*, or infidel. *Tamasaḥ*, mentioned herein, is the material nature, and the spiritual nature has a completely separate existence from *tamaḥ*. Therefore, spiritual nature is called *avabodha-rasa*, or *avarodha-rasa*. *Avarodha* means "that which completely nullifies." In the Transcendence there is no chance of material contact by any means. Brahmā is the first living being, and therefore he mentions his birth from the lotus flower generated from the abdomen of Garbhodakaśāyī Viṣṇu.

TEXT 3

नातः परं परम यद्भवतः स्वरूप-
मानन्दमात्रमविकल्पमविद्धवर्चः ।
पश्यामि विश्वसृजमेकमविश्वमात्मन्
भूतेन्द्रियात्मकमदस्त उपाश्रितोऽस्मि ॥३॥

nātaḥ paraṁ parama yad bhavataḥ svarūpam
ānanda-mātram avikalpam aviddha-varcaḥ
paśyāmi viśva-sṛjam ekam aviśvam ātman
bhūtendriyātmaka-madas ta upāśrito 'smi

na—do not; *ataḥ param*—hereafter; *parama*—O Supreme; *yat*—that which; *bhavataḥ*—of Your Lordship; *svarūpam*—eternal form; *ānanda-mātram*—impersonal Brahman effulgence; *avikalpam*—without changes; *aviddha-varcaḥ*—without deterioration of potency; *paśyāmi*—do I see; *viśva-sṛjam*—creator of the cosmic manifestation; *ekam*—one without a second; *aviśvam*—and yet not of matter; *ātman*—O Supreme Cause; *bhūta*—body; *indriya*—senses; *ātmaka*—on such identification; *madaḥ*—pride; *te*—unto You; *upāśritaḥ*—surrendered; *asmi*—I am.

TRANSLATION

O my Lord, I do not see a form superior to Your present form of eternal bliss and knowledge. In Your impersonal Brahman effulgence in the spiritual sky, there is no occasional change and no deterioration of internal potency. I surrender unto You because whereas I am proud of my material body and senses, Your Lordship is the cause of the cosmic manifestation and yet You are untouched by matter.

PURPORT

As stated in *Bhagavad-gītā* (18.55), *bhaktyā mām abhijānāti yāvān yaś cāsmi tattvataḥ:* the Supreme Personality of Godhead can only be partially known, and only by the process of devotional service to the Lord. Lord Brahmā became aware that the Supreme Lord Kṛṣṇa has many, many eternal, blissful forms of knowledge. He has described such expansions of the Supreme Lord, Govinda, in his *Brahma-saṁhitā* (5.33), as follows:

advaitam acyutam anādim ananta-rūpam
ādyaṁ purāṇa-puruṣaṁ nava-yauvanaṁ ca
vedeṣu durlabham adurlabham ātma-bhaktau
govindam ādi-puruṣaṁ tam ahaṁ bhajāmi

"I worship Govinda, the primeval Lord, who is nondual and infallible. He is the original cause of all causes, even though He expands in many, many forms. Although He is the oldest personality, He is ever youthful, unaffected by old age. The Supreme Personality of Godhead cannot be known by the academic wisdom of the *Vedas;* one has to approach the devotee of the Lord to understand Him."

The only way to understand the Lord as He is, is by devotional service to the Lord, or by approaching the devotee of the Lord who always has the Lord in his heart. By devotional perfection one can understand that the impersonal *brahmajyoti* is only a partial representation of the Supreme Personality of Godhead, Lord Kṛṣṇa, and that the three *puruṣa* expansions in the material creation are His plenary portions. In the spiritual sky of the *brahmajyoti* there is no change of various *kalpas* or millenniums, and there are no creative activities in the Vaikuṇṭha worlds. The influence of time is conspicuous by its absence. The rays of the transcendental body of the Lord, the unlimited *brahmajyoti*, are undeterred by the influence of material energy. In the material world also, the initial creator is the Lord Himself. He brings about the creation of Brahmā, who becomes the subsequent creator, empowered by the Lord.

TEXT 4

तद्वा इदं भुवनमङ्गल मङ्गलाय
ध्याने स्म नो दर्शितं त उपासकानाम् ।
तस्मै नमो भगवतेऽनुविधेम तुभ्यं
योऽनादृतो नरकभाग्भिरसत्प्रसङ्गैः ॥ ४ ॥

tad vā idaṁ bhuvana-maṅgala maṅgalāya
dhyāne sma no darśitaṁ ta upāsakānām
tasmai namo bhagavate 'nuvidhema tubhyaṁ
yo 'nādṛto naraka-bhāgbhir asat-prasaṅgaiḥ

tat—the Supreme Personality of Godhead, Śrī Kṛṣṇa; *vā*—or; *idam*—this present form; *bhuvana-maṅgala*—O You who are all-auspicious for all the universes; *maṅgalāya*—for the sake of all prosperity; *dhyāne*—in meditation; *sma*—as it were; *naḥ*—unto us; *darśitam*—manifested; *te*—Your; *upāsakānām*—of the devotees; *tasmai*—unto Him; *namaḥ*—my respectful obeisances; *bhagavate*—unto the Personality of Godhead; *anuvidhema*—I perform; *tubhyam*—unto You; *yaḥ*—which; *anādṛtaḥ*—is neglected; *naraka-bhāgbhiḥ*—by persons destined for hell; *asat-prasaṅgaiḥ*—by material topics.

TRANSLATION

This present form, or any transcendental form expanded by the Supreme Personality of Godhead, Śrī Kṛṣṇa, is equally auspicious for all the universes. Since You have manifested this eternal personal form upon whom Your devotees meditate, I therefore offer my respectful obeisances unto You. Those who are destined to be

dispatched to the path of hell neglect Your personal form because of speculating on material topics.

PURPORT

Regarding the personal and impersonal features of the Supreme Absolute Truth, the personal forms exhibited by the Lord in His different plenary expansions are all for the benediction of all the universes. The personal form of the Lord is also worshiped in meditation as Supersoul, Paramātmā, but the impersonal *brahmajyoti* is not worshiped. Persons who are addicted to the impersonal feature of the Lord, whether in meditation or otherwise, are all pilgrims to hell because, as stated in *Bhagavad-gītā* (12.5), impersonalists simply waste their time in mundane mental speculation because they are addicted more to false arguments than to reality. Therefore, the association of the impersonalists is condemned herewith by Brahmā.

All the plenary expansions of the Personality of Godhead are equally potent, as confirmed in the *Brahma-saṁhitā* (5.46):

dīpārcir eva hi daśāntaram abhyupetya
dīpāyate vivṛta-hetu-samāna-dharmā
yas tādṛg eva hi ca viṣṇutayā vibhāti
govindam ādi-puruṣaṁ tam ahaṁ bhajāmi

The Lord expands Himself as the flames of a fire expand one after another. Although the original flame, or Śrī Kṛṣṇa, is accepted as Govinda, the Supreme Person, all other expansions, such as Rāma, Nṛsiṁha and Varāha, are as potent as the original Lord. All such expanded forms are transcendental. In the beginning of *Śrīmad-Bhāgavatam* it is made clear that the Supreme Truth is eternally uncontaminated by material touch. There is no jugglery of words and activities in the transcendental kingdom of the Lord. All the Lord's forms are transcendental, and such manifestations are ever identical. The particular form of the Lord exhibited to a devotee is not mundane, even though the devotee may retain material desire, nor is it manifest under the influence of material energy, as is foolishly considered by the impersonalists. Impersonalists who consider the transcendental forms of the Lord to be products of the material world are surely destined for hell.

TEXT 5

ये तु त्वदीयचरणाम्बुजकोशगन्धं
जिघ्रन्ति कर्णविवरैः श्रुतिवातनीतम् ।
भक्त्या गृहीतचरणः परया च तेषां
नापैषि नाथ हृदयाम्बुरुहात्स्वपुंसाम् ॥५॥

ye tu tvadīya-caraṇāmbuja-kośa-gandhaṁ
jighranti karṇa-vivaraiḥ śruti-vāta-nītam
bhaktyā gṛhīta-caraṇaḥ parayā ca teṣāṁ
nāpaiṣi nātha hṛdayāmburuhāt sva-puṁsām

ye—those who; *tu*—but; *tvadīya*—Your; *caraṇa-ambuja*—lotus feet; *kośa*—inside; *gandham*—flavor; *jighranti*—smell; *karṇa-vivaraiḥ*—through the channel of the ears; *śruti-vāta-nītam*—carried by the air of Vedic sound; *bhaktyā*—by devotional service; *gṛhīta-caraṇaḥ*—accepting the lotus feet; *parayā*—transcendental; *ca*—also; *teṣām*—for them; *na*—never; *apaiṣi*—separate; *nātha*—O my Lord; *hṛdaya*—heart; *ambu-ruhāt*—from the lotus of; *sva-puṁsām*—of Your own devotees.

TRANSLATION

O my Lord, persons who smell the aroma of Your lotus feet, carried by the air of Vedic sound through the holes of the ears, accept Your devotional service. For them You are never separated from the lotus of their hearts.

PURPORT

For the pure devotee of the Lord there is nothing beyond the lotus feet of the Lord, and the Lord knows that such devotees do not wish anything more than that. The word *tu* specifically establishes this fact. The Lord also does not wish to be separated from the lotus hearts of those pure devotees. That is the transcendental relationship between the pure devotees and the Personality of Godhead. Because the Lord does not wish to separate Himself from the hearts of such pure devotees, it is understood that they are specifically dearer than the impersonalists. The relationship of the pure devotees with the Lord develops because of devotional service to the Lord on the authentic basis of Vedic authority. Such pure devotees are not mundane sentimentalists, but are factually realists because their activities are supported by the Vedic authorities who have given aural reception to the facts mentioned in the Vedic literatures.

The word *parayā* is very significant. *Parā bhakti*, or spontaneous love of God, is the basis of an intimate relationship with the Lord. This highest stage of relationship with the Lord can be attained simply by hearing about Him (His name, form, quality, etc.) from authentic sources like *Bhagavad-gītā* and *Śrīmad-Bhāgavatam*, recited by pure, unalloyed devotees of the Lord.

TEXT 6

तावद्भयं द्रविणदेहसुहृन्निमित्तं
शोकः स्पृहा परिभवो विपुलश्च लोभः ।
तावन्ममेत्यसदवग्रह आर्तिमूलं
यावन्न तेऽङ्घ्रिमभयं प्रवृणीत लोकः ॥६॥

tāvad bhayaṁ draviṇa-deha-suhṛn-nimittaṁ
śokaḥ spṛhā paribhavo vipulaś ca lobhaḥ
tāvan mamety asad-avagraha ārti-mūlaṁ
yāvan na te 'ṅghrim abhayaṁ pravṛṇīta lokaḥ

tāvat—until then; *bhayam*—fear; *draviṇa*—wealth; *deha*—body; *suhṛt*—relatives; *nimittam*—for the matter of; *śokaḥ*—lamentation; *spṛhā*—desire; *paribhavaḥ*—paraphernalia; *vipulaḥ*—very great; *ca*—also; *lobhaḥ*—avarice; *tāvat*—up to that time; *mama*—mine; *iti*—thus; *asat*—perishable; *avagrahaḥ*—undertaking; *ārti-mūlam*—full of anxieties; *yāvat*—as long as; *na*—do not; *te*—Your; *aṅghrim abhayam*—safe lotus feet; *pravṛṇīta*—take shelter; *lokaḥ*—the people of the world.

TRANSLATION

O my Lord, the people of the world are embarrassed by all material anxieties—they are always afraid. They always try to protect wealth, body and friends, they are filled with lamentation and

unlawful desires and paraphernalia, and they avariciously base their undertakings on the perishable conceptions of "my" and "mine." As long as they do not take shelter of Your safe lotus feet, they are full of such anxieties.

PURPORT

One may question how one can always think of the Lord in regard to His name, fame, quality, etc., if one is embarrassed by thoughts of family affairs. Everyone in the material world is full of thoughts about how to maintain his family, how to protect his wealth, how to keep pace with friends and relatives, etc. Thus he is always in fear and lamentation, trying to keep up with the status quo. In answer to this question, this verse spoken by Brahmā is very appropriate.

A pure devotee of the Lord never thinks of himself as the proprietor of his home. He surrenders everything unto the supreme control of the Lord, and thus he has no fear for maintaining his family or protecting the interests of his family. Because of this surrender, he no longer has any attraction for wealth. Even if there is attraction for wealth, it is not for sense enjoyment, but for the service of the Lord. A pure devotee may be attracted to accumulating wealth just like an ordinary man, but the difference is that a devotee acquires money for the service of the Lord, whereas the ordinary man acquires money for his sense enjoyment. Thus the acquisition of wealth by a devotee is not a source of anxieties, as is the case for a worldly man. And because a pure devotee accepts everything in the sense of serving the Lord, the poisonous teeth of accumulation of wealth are extracted. If a snake has its poison removed and bites a man, there is no fatal effect. Similarly, wealth accumulated in the cause of the Lord has no poisonous teeth, and the effect is not fatal. A pure devotee is never entangled in material worldly affairs even though he may remain in the world like an ordinary man.

TEXT 7

दैवेन ते हतधियो भवतः प्रसङ्गा-
त्सर्वाशुभोपशमनाद्विमुखेन्द्रिया ये ।
कुर्वन्ति कामसुखलेशलवाय दीना
लोभाभिभूतमनसोऽकुशलानि शश्वत् ॥७॥

daivena te hata-dhiyo bhavataḥ prasaṅgāt
sarvāśubhopaśamanād vimukhendriyā ye
kurvanti kāma-sukha-leśa-lavāya dīnā
lobhābhibhūta-manaso 'kuśalāni śaśvat

daivena—by fate of misfortune; *te*—they; *hata-dhiyaḥ*—bereft of memory; *bhavataḥ*—of You; *prasaṅgāt*—from the topics; *sarva*—all; *aśubha*—inauspiciousness; *upaśamanāt*—curbing down; *vimukha*—turned against; *indriyāḥ*—senses; *ye*—those; *kurvanti*—act; *kāma*—sense gratification; *sukha*—happiness; *leśa*—brief; *lavāya*—for a moment only; *dīnāḥ*—poor fellows; *lobha-abhibhūta*—overwhelmed by greed; *manasaḥ*—of one whose mind; *akuśalāni*—inauspicious activities; *śaśvat*—always.

TRANSLATION

O my Lord, persons who are bereft of the all-auspicious performance of chanting and hearing about Your transcendental activities are certainly unfortunate and are also bereft of good sense. They engage in inauspicious activities, enjoying sense gratification for a very little while.

PURPORT

The next question is why people are against such auspicious activities as chanting and hearing the glories and pastimes of the Lord, which can bring total freedom from the cares and anxieties of material existence. The only answer to this question is that they are unfortunate because of supernatural control due to their offensive activities performed simply for the sake of sense gratification. The Lord's pure devotees, however, take compassion upon such unfortunate persons and, in a missionary spirit, try to persuade them into the line of devotional service. Only by the grace of pure devotees can such unfortunate men be elevated to the position of transcendental service.

TEXT 8

क्षुत्तृट्त्रिधातुभिरिमा मुहुरर्द्यमानाः
शीतोष्णवातवरषैरितरेतराच्च ।

कामाग्निनाच्युत रुषा च सुदुर्भरेण
सम्पश्यतो मन उरुक्रम सीदते मे ॥ ८ ॥

kṣut-tṛṭ-tridhātubhir imā muhur ardyamānāḥ
śītoṣṇa-vāta-varaṣair itaretarāc ca
kāmāgninācyuta-ruṣā ca sudurbhareṇa
sampaśyato mana urukrama sīdate me

kṣut—hunger; *tṛṭ*—thirst; *tri-dhātubhiḥ*—three humors, namely mucus, bile and wind; *imāḥ*—all of them; *muhuḥ*—always; *ardyamānāḥ*—perplexed; *śīta*—winter; *uṣṇa*—summer; *vāta*—wind; *varaṣaiḥ*—by rains; *itara-itarāt*—and many other disturbances; *ca*—also; *kāma-agninā*—by strong sex urges; *acyuta-ruṣā*—indefatigable anger; *ca*—also; *sudurbhareṇa*—most unbearable; *sampaśyataḥ*—so observing; *manaḥ*—mind; *urukrama*—O great actor; *sīdate*—becomes despondent; *me*—my.

TRANSLATION

O great actor, my Lord, all these poor creatures are constantly perplexed by hunger, thirst, severe cold, secretion and bile, attacked by coughing winter, blasting summer, rains and many other disturbing elements, and overwhelmed by strong sex urges and indefatigable anger. I take pity on them, and I am very much aggrieved for them.

PURPORT

A pure devotee of the Lord like Brahmā and persons in his disciplic succession are always unhappy to see the perplexities of the conditioned souls, who are suffering the onslaughts of the threefold miseries which pertain to the body and mind, to the disturbances of material nature, and to many other such material disadvantages. Not knowing adequate measures for relieving such difficulties, suffering persons sometimes pose themselves as leaders of the people, and the unfortunate followers are put into further disadvantages under such so-called leadership. This is like a blind man's leading another blind man to fall into a ditch. Therefore, unless the devotees of the Lord take pity on them and teach them the right path, their lives are hopeless failures. The devotees of the

Lord who voluntarily take the responsibility of raising the foolish materialistic sense enjoyers are as confidential to the Lord as Lord Brahmā.

TEXT 9

यावत्पृथक्त्वमिदमात्मन इन्द्रियार्थ-
मायाबलं भगवतो जन ईश पश्येत् ।
तावन्न संसृतिरसौ प्रतिसंक्रमेत
व्यर्थापि दुःखनिवहं वहती क्रियार्था ॥९॥

yāvat pṛthaktvam idam ātmana indriyārtha-
māyā-balaṁ bhagavato jana īśa paśyet
tāvan na saṁsṛtir asau pratisaṅkrameta
vyarthāpi duḥkha-nivahaṁ vahatī kriyārthā

yāvat—as long as; *pṛthaktvam*—separatism; *idam*—this; *ātmanaḥ*—of the body; *indriya-artha*—for sense gratification; *māyā-balam*—influence of external energy; *bhagavataḥ*—of the Personality of Godhead; *janaḥ*—a person; *īśa*—O my Lord; *paśyet*—sees; *tāvat*—so long; *na*—not; *saṁsṛtiḥ*—the influence of material existence; *asau*—that man; *pratisaṅkrameta*—can overcome; *vyarthā api*—although without meaning; *duḥkha-nivaham*—multiple miseries; *vahatī*—bringing; *kriyā-arthā*—for fruitive activities.

TRANSLATION

O my Lord, the material miseries are without factual existence for the soul. Yet as long as the conditioned soul sees the body as meant for sense enjoyment, he cannot get out of the entanglement of material miseries, being influenced by Your external energy.

PURPORT

The whole trouble of the living entity in material existence is that he has an independent conception of life. He is always dependent on the rules of the Supreme Lord, in both the conditioned and liberated states, but by the influence of the external energy the conditioned soul thinks himself independent of the supremacy of the Personality of Godhead.

His constitutional position is to dovetail himself with the desire of the supreme will, but as long as he does not do so, he is sure to drag on in the shackles of material bondage. As stated in *Bhagavad-gītā* (2.55), *prajahāti yadā kāmān sarvān pārtha mano-gatān:* he has to give up all sorts of plans manufactured by mental concoction. The living entity has to dovetail himself with the supreme will. That will help him to get out of the entanglement of material existence.

TEXT 10

अह्न्याप्ृतार्तकरणा निशि निःशयाना
नानामनोरथधिया क्षणभग्ननिद्राः ।
दैवाहतार्थरचना ऋषयोऽपि देव
युष्मत्प्रसङ्गविमुखा इह संसरन्ति ॥१०॥

ahny āpṛtārta-karaṇā niśi niḥśayānā
nānā-manoratha-dhiyā kṣaṇa-bhagna-nidrāḥ
daivāhatārtha-racanā ṛṣayo 'pi deva
yuṣmat-prasaṅga-vimukhā iha saṁsaranti

ahni—during the daytime; *āpṛta*—engaged; *ārta*—distressing engagement; *karaṇāḥ*—senses; *niśi*—at night; *niḥśayānāḥ*—insomnia; *nānā*—various; *manoratha*—mental speculations; *dhiyā*—by intelligence; *kṣaṇa*—constantly; *bhagna*—broken; *nidrāḥ*—sleep; *daiva*—superhuman; *āhata-artha*—frustrated; *racanāḥ*—plans; *ṛṣayaḥ*—great sages; *api*—also; *deva*—O my Lord; *yuṣmat*—Your Lordship's; *prasaṅga*—topic; *vimukhāḥ*—turned against; *iha*—in this (material world); *saṁsaranti*—do rotate.

TRANSLATION

Such nondevotees engage their senses in very troublesome and extensive work, and they suffer insomnia at night because their intelligence constantly breaks their sleep with various mental speculations. They are frustrated in all their various plans by supernatural power. Even great sages, if they are against Your transcendental topics, must rotate in this material world.

PURPORT

As described in the previous verse, people who have no taste for the devotional service of the Lord are occupied in material engagements. Most of them engage during the daytime in hard physical labor; their senses are engaged very extensively in troublesome duties in the gigantic plants of heavy industrial enterprise. The owners of such factories are engaged in finding a market for their industrial products, and the laborers are engaged in extensive production involving huge mechanical arrangements. "Factory" is another name for hell. At night, hellishly engaged persons take advantage of wine and women to satisfy their tired senses, but they are not even able to have sound sleep because their various mental speculative plans constantly interrupt their sleep. Because they suffer from insomnia sometimes they feel sleepy in the morning for lack of sufficient rest. By the arrangement of supernatural power, even the great scientists and thinkers of the world suffer frustration of their various plans and thus rot in the material world birth after birth. A great scientist may make discoveries in atomic energy for the quick destruction of the world and may be awarded the best prize in recognition of his service (or disservice), but he also has to undergo the reactions of his work by rotating in the cycle of repeated births and deaths under the superhuman law of material nature. All these people who are against the principle of devotional service are destined to rotate in this material world without fail.

This verse particularly mentions that even sages who are averse to the principles of devotional service to the Lord are also condemned to undergo the terms of material existence. Not only in this age, but formerly also, there were many sages who tried to invent their own systems of religion without reference to devotional service to the Supreme Lord, but there cannot be any religious principle without devotional service to the Lord. The Supreme Lord is the leader of the entire range of living entities, and no one can be equal to or greater than Him. Even the Lord's impersonal feature and all-pervading localized feature cannot be on an equal level with the Supreme Personality of Godhead. Therefore, there cannot be any religion or system of genuine philosophy for the advancement of the living entities without the principle of devotional service.

The impersonalists, who take much trouble in penance and austerity for self-liberation, may approach the impersonal *brahmajyoti*, but ultimately, because of not being situated in devotional service, they glide down again to the material world to undergo another term of material existence. This is confirmed as follows:

ye 'nye 'ravindākṣa vimukta-māninas
tvayy asta-bhāvād aviśuddha-buddhayaḥ
āruhya kṛcchreṇa paraṁ padaṁ tataḥ
patanty adho 'nādṛta-yuṣmad-aṅghrayaḥ

"Persons who are falsely under the impression of being liberated, without devotional service to the Lord, may reach the goal of the *brahmajyoti*, but because of their impure consciousness and for want of shelter in the Vaikuṇṭhalokas, such so-called liberated persons again fall down into material existence." (*Bhāg.* 10.2.32)

Therefore, no one can manufacture any system of religion without the principle of devotional service to the Lord. As we find in the Sixth Canto of *Śrīmad-Bhāgavatam*, the initiator of religious principles is the Lord Himself. In *Bhagavad-gītā* also we find that the Lord condemns all forms of religion other than that which entails the process of surrendering unto the Supreme. Any system which leads one to the devotional service of the Lord, and nothing else, is actually religion or philosophy. In the Sixth Canto we find the following statements of Yamarāja, the controller of all unfaithful living entities:

dharmaṁ tu sākṣād bhagavat-praṇītaṁ
na vai vidur ṛṣayo nāpi devāḥ
na siddha-mukhyā asurā manuṣyāḥ
kuto nu vidyādhara-cāraṇādayaḥ

svayambhūr nāradaḥ śambhuḥ
kumāraḥ kapilo manuḥ
prahlādo janako bhīṣmo
balir vaiyāsakir vayam

dvādaśaite vijānīmo
dharmaṁ bhāgavataṁ bhaṭāḥ

guhyaṁ viśuddhaṁ durbodhaṁ
yaṁ jñātvāmṛtam aśnute

"The principles of religion are initiated by the Supreme Personality of Godhead, and no one else, including the sages and demigods, can manufacture any such principles. Since even great sages and demigods are unauthorized to inaugurate such principles of religion, what to speak of others—the so-called mystics, demons, human beings, Vidyādharas and Cāraṇas living in the lower planets? Twelve personalities—Brahmā, Nārada, Lord Śiva, Kumāra, Kapila, Manu, Prahlāda Mahārāja, Janaka Mahārāja, Bhīṣma, Bali, Śukadeva Gosvāmī and Yamarāja—are agents of the Lord authorized to speak and propagate the principles of religion." (*Bhāg.* 6.3.19–21)

The principles of religion are not open to any ordinary living entity. They are just to bring the human being onto the platform of morality. Nonviolence, etc., are necessary for misguided persons because unless one is moral and nonviolent one cannot understand the principles of religion. To understand what is actually religion is very difficult even if one is situated in the principles of morality and nonviolence. It is very confidential because as soon as one is conversant with the real principles of religion, he is at once liberated to the eternal life of bliss and knowledge. Therefore, one who is not situated in the principles of devotional service to the Lord should not pose himself as a religious leader of the innocent public. The *Īśopaniṣad* emphatically forbids this nonsense in the following *mantra:*

andhaṁ tamaḥ praviśanti
ye 'sambhūtim upāsate
tato bhūya iva te tamo
ya u sambhūtyāṁ ratāḥ
(*Īśopaniṣad* 12)

A person in ignorance of the principles of religion who therefore does nothing in the matter of religion is far better than a person who misguides others in the name of religion without reference to the factual religious principles of devotional service. Such so-called leaders of religion are sure to be condemned by Brahmā and other great authorities.

TEXT 11

त्वं भक्तियोगपरिभावितहृत्सरोज
आस्से श्रुतेक्षितपथो ननु नाथ पुंसाम् ।
यद्यद्धिया त उरुगाय विभावयन्ति
तत्तद्वपुः प्रणयसे सदनुग्रहाय ॥११॥

tvaṁ bhakti-yoga-paribhāvita-hṛt-saroja
āsse śruteksịta-patho nanu nātha puṁsām
yad-yad-dhiyā ta urugāya vibhāvayanti
tat-tad-vapuḥ praṇayase sad-anugrahāya

tvam—unto You; *bhakti-yoga*—in devotional service; *paribhāvita*—being one hundred percent engaged; *hṛt*—of the heart; *saroje*—on the lotus; *āsse*—You reside; *śruta-īkṣita*—seen through the ear; *pathaḥ*—the path; *nanu*—now; *nātha*—O my Lord; *puṁsām*—of the devotees; *yat-yat*—whichever; *dhiyā*—by meditating; *te*—Your; *urugāya*—O multiglorious; *vibhāvayanti*—they specifically think of; *tat-tat*—the very same; *vapuḥ*—transcendental form; *praṇayase*—do You manifest; *sat-anugrahāya*—to show Your causeless mercy.

TRANSLATION

O my Lord, Your devotees can see You through the ears by the process of bona fide hearing, and thus their hearts become cleansed, and You take Your seat there. You are so merciful to Your devotees that You manifest Yourself in the particular eternal form of transcendence in which they always think of You.

PURPORT

The statement here that the Lord manifests Himself before the devotee in the form in which the devotee likes to worship Him indicates that the Lord becomes subordinate to the desire of the devotee—so much so that He manifests His particular form as the devotee demands. This demand of the devotee is satisfied by the Lord because He is pliable in terms of the transcendental loving service of the devotee. This is also confirmed in *Bhagavad-gītā* (4.11): *ye yathā māṁ prapadyante tāṁs tathaiva bhajāmy aham.* We should note, however, that the Lord is never the order supplier of the devotee. Here in this verse it is particularly mentioned: *tvaṁ bhakti-yoga-paribhāvita.* This indicates the efficiency achieved through execution of matured devotional service, or *premā*, love of Godhead. This state of *premā* is achieved by the gradual process of development from faith to love. On faith one associates with bona fide devotees, and by such association one can become engaged in bona fide devotional service, which includes proper initiation and the execution of the primary devotional duties prescribed in the revealed scriptures. This is clearly indicated herein by the word *śrutekṣita.* The *śrutekṣita* path is to hear from bona fide devotees who are conversant with Vedic wisdom, free from mundane sentiment. By this bona fide hearing process, the neophyte devotee becomes cleansed of all material rubbish, and thus he becomes attached to one of the many transcendental forms of the Lord, as described in the *Vedas.*

This attachment of the devotee to a particular form of the Lord is due to natural inclination. Each and every living entity is originally attached to a particular type of transcendental service because he is eternally the servitor of the Lord. Lord Caitanya says that the living entity is eternally a servitor of the Supreme Personality of Godhead, Śrī Kṛṣṇa. Therefore, every living entity has a particular type of service relationship with the Lord, eternally. This particular attachment is invoked by practice of regulative devotional service to the Lord, and thus the devotee becomes attached to the eternal form of the Lord, exactly like one who is already eternally attached. This attachment for a particular form of the Lord is called *svarūpa-siddhi.* The Lord sits on the lotus heart of the devotee in the eternal form the pure devotee desires, and thus the Lord does not part from the devotee, as confirmed in the previous verse. The Lord, however, does not disclose Himself to a casual or inauthentic worshiper to be exploited. This is confirmed in *Bhagavad-gītā* (7.25): *nāhaṁ prakāśaḥ sarvasya yoga-māyā-samāvṛtaḥ.* Rather, by *yoga-māyā*, the Lord remains concealed to the nondevotees or casual devotees who are serving their sense gratification. The Lord is never visible to the pseudodevotees who worship the demigods in charge of universal affairs. The conclusion is that the Lord cannot become the order supplier of a pseudodevotee, but He is always prepared to respond to the desires of a pure, unconditional devotee, who is free from all tinges of material infection.

TEXT 12

नातिप्रसीदति तथोपचितोपचारै-
राराधितः सुरगणैर्हृदिबद्धकामैः ।
यत्सर्वभूतदययासदलभ्ययैको
नानाजनेष्ववहितः सुहृदन्तरात्मा ॥१२॥

nātiprasīdati tathopacitopacārair
ārādhitaḥ sura-gaṇair hṛdi baddha-kāmaiḥ
yat sarva-bhūta-dayayāsad-alabhyayaiko
nānā-janeṣv avahitaḥ suhṛd antar-ātmā

na—never; *ati*—very much; *prasīdati*—become satisfied; *tathā*—as much as; *upacita*—by pompous arrangement; *upacāraiḥ*—with much worshipable paraphernalia; *ārādhitaḥ*—being worshiped; *sura-gaṇaiḥ*—by the celestial demigods; *hṛdi baddha-kāmaiḥ*—with hearts full of all sorts of material desires; *yat*—that which; *sarva*—all; *bhūta*—living entities; *dayayā*—to show them causeless mercy; *asat*—nondevotee; *alabhyayā*—not being achieved; *ekaḥ*—one without a second; *nānā*—various; *janeṣu*—in living entities; *avahitaḥ*—perceived; *suhṛt*—well-wishing friend; *antaḥ*—within; *ātmā*—Supersoul.

TRANSLATION

My Lord, You are not very much satisfied by the worship of the demigods, who arrange for Your worship very pompously, with various paraphernalia, but who are full of material hankerings. You are situated in everyone's heart as the Supersoul just to show Your causeless mercy, and You are the eternal well-wisher, but You are unavailable for the nondevotee.

PURPORT

The demigods in the celestial heavenly planets, who are appointed administrators of the material affairs, are also devotees of the Lord. But, at the same time, they have desires for material opulence and sense gratification. The Lord is so kind that He awards them all sorts of material happiness, more than they can desire, but He is not satisfied with them because they are not pure devotees. The Lord does not want any one of His innumerable sons (the living entities) to remain in the material world of threefold miseries to perpetually suffer the material pangs of birth, death, old age and disease. The demigods in the heavenly planets, and many devotees on this planet also, want to remain in the material world as devotees of the Lord and take advantage of material happiness. They do so at a risk of falling down to the lower status of existence, and this makes the Lord dissatisfied with them.

Pure devotees are not desirous of any material enjoyment, nor are they averse to it. They completely dovetail their desires with the desires of the Lord and perform nothing on their personal account. Arjuna is a good example. On his own sentiment, due to family affection, Arjuna did not want to fight, but finally, after hearing *Śrīmad Bhagavad-gītā,* he agreed to fight in the interests of the Lord. Therefore, the Lord is very much satisfied with pure devotees because they do not act for sense gratification but only in terms of the Lord's desire. As Paramātmā, or Supersoul, He is situated in everyone's heart, always giving everyone the chance of good counsel. Thus everyone should take the opportunity and render transcendental loving service to Him wholly and solely.

The nondevotees, however, are neither like the demigods nor like the pure devotees, but are averse to the transcendental relationship with the Lord. They have revolted against the Lord and must perpetually undergo the reactions of their own activities.

Bhagavad-gītā (4.11) states: *ye yathā māṁ prapadyante tāṁs tathaiva bhajāmy aham.* "Although the Lord is equally kind to every living being, the living beings, for their own part, are able to please the Lord to either a greater or lesser extent." The demigods are called *sakāma* devotees, or devotees with material desires in mind, while the pure devotees are called *niṣkāma* devotees because they have no desires for their personal interests. The *sakāma* devotees are self-interested because they do not think of others, and therefore they are not able to satisfy the Lord perfectly, whereas the pure devotees take the missionary responsibility of turning nondevotees into devotees, and they are therefore able to satisfy the Lord more than the demigods. The Lord is unmindful of the nondevotees, although He is sitting within everyone's heart as well-wisher and Supersoul. However, He also gives them the chance to receive His mercy through His pure devotees who are engaged in missionary activities. Sometimes the Lord Himself descends for missionary activities, as He did in the form of Lord Caitanya, but mostly He sends His bona fide representatives, and thus He shows His causeless mercy towards the nondevotees. The Lord is so satisfied with His pure devotees that He wants to give them the credit for missionary success, although He could do the work personally. This is the sign of His satisfaction with His pure, *niṣkāma* devotees, compared to the *sakāma* devotees. By such transcendental activities the Lord simultaneously becomes free from the charge of partiality and exhibits His pleasure with the devotees.

Now a question arises: If the Lord is sitting in the hearts of nondevotees, why are they not moved to become devotees? It may be answered that the stubborn nondevotees are like the barren land or alkaline field, where no agricultural activities can be successful. As part and parcel of the Lord, every individual living entity has a minute quantity of independence, and by misuse of this minute independence, the nondevotees commit offense after offense, to both the Lord and His pure devotees engaged in missionary work. As a result of such acts, they become as barren as an alkaline field, where there is no strength to produce.

TEXT 13

पुंसामतो विविधकर्मभिरध्वराद्यै-
दानेन चोग्रतपसा परिचर्यया च ।
आराधनं भगवतस्तव सत्क्रियार्थो
धर्मोऽर्पितः कर्हिचिद्म्रियते न यत्र ॥१३॥

puṁsām ato vividha-karmabhir adhvarādyair
dānena cogra-tapasā paricaryayā ca
ārādhanaṁ bhagavatas tava sat-kriyārtho
dharmo 'rpitaḥ karhicid mriyate na yatra

puṁsām—of the people; *ataḥ*—therefore; *vividha-karmabhiḥ*—by various fruitive activities; *adhvara-ādyaiḥ*—by performance of Vedic rituals; *dānena*—by charities; *ca*—and; *ugra*—very hard; *tapasā*—austerity; *paricaryayā*—by transcendental service; *ca*—also; *ārādhanam*—worship; *bhagavataḥ*—of the Personality of Godhead; *tava*—

Your; *sat-kriyā-arthaḥ*—simply for pleasing Your Lordship; *dharmaḥ*—religion; *arpitaḥ*—so offered; *karhicit*—at any time; *mriyate*—vanquishes; *na*—never; *yatra*—there.

TRANSLATION

But the pious activities of the people, such as performance of Vedic rituals, charity, austere penances, and transcendental service, performed with a view to worship You and satisfy You by offering You the fruitive results, are also beneficial. Such acts of religion never go in vain.

PURPORT

Absolute devotional service, conducted in nine different spiritual activities—hearing, chanting, remembering, worshiping, praying, etc.—does not always appeal to people with a pompous nature; they are more attracted by the Vedic superficial rituals and other costly performances of social religious shows. But the process according to the Vedic injunctions is that the fruits of all pious activities should be offered to the Supreme Lord. In *Bhagavad-gītā* (9.27), the Lord demands that whatever one may do in one's daily activities, such as worship, sacrifice, and offering charity, all the results should be offered to Him only. This offering of the results of pious acts unto the Supreme Lord is a sign of devotional service to the Lord and is of permanent value, whereas enjoying the same results for oneself is only temporary. Anything done on account of the Lord is a permanent asset and accumulates in the form of unseen piety for gradual promotion to the unalloyed devotional service of the Lord. These undetected pious activities will one day result in full-fledged devotional service by the grace of the Supreme Lord. Therefore, any pious act done on account of the Supreme Lord is also recommended here for those who are not pure devotees.

TEXT 14

शश्वत्स्वरूपमहसैव निपीतभेद-
मोहाय बोधधिषणाय नमः परस्मै ।
विश्वोद्भवस्थितिलयेषु निमित्तलीला-
रासाय ते नम इदं चकृमेश्वराय ॥१४॥

śaśvat svarūpa-mahasaiva nipīta-bheda-
mohāya bodha-dhiṣaṇāya namaḥ parasmai
viśvodbhava-sthiti-layeṣu nimitta-līlā-
rāsāya te nama idaṁ cakṛmeśvarāya

śaśvat—eternally; *svarūpa*—transcendental form; *mahasā*—by the glories; *eva*—certainly; *nipīta*—distinguished; *bheda*—differentiation; *mohāya*—unto the illusory conception; *bodha*—self-knowledge; *dhiṣaṇāya*—intelligence; *namaḥ*—obeisances; *parasmai*—unto the Transcendence; *viśva-udbhava*—creation of the cosmic manifestation; *sthiti*—maintenance; *layeṣu*—also destruction; *nimitta*—for the matter of; *līlā*—by such pastimes; *rāsāya*—for enjoyment; *te*—unto You; *namaḥ*—obeisances; *idam*—this; *cakṛma*—do I perform; *īśvarāya*—unto the Supreme.

TRANSLATION

Let me offer my obeisances unto the Supreme Transcendence, who is eternally distinguished by His internal potency. His indistinguishable impersonal feature is realized by intelligence for self-realization. I offer my obeisances unto Him who by His pastimes enjoys the creation, maintenance and dissolution of the cosmic manifestation.

PURPORT

The Supreme Lord is eternally distinguished from the living entities by His internal potency, although He is also understood in His impersonal feature by self-realized intelligence. Devotees of the Lord, therefore, offer all respectful obeisances unto the impersonal feature of the Lord. The word *rāsa* is significant herein. The *rāsa* dance is performed by Lord Kṛṣṇa in the company of the cowherd damsels at Vṛndāvana, and the Personality of Godhead Garbhodakaśāyī Viṣṇu is also engaged in *rāsa* enjoyment with His external potency, by which He creates, maintains and dissolves the entire material manifestation. Indirectly, Lord Brahmā offers his respectful obeisances unto Lord Śrī Kṛṣṇa, who is factually ever engaged in *rāsa* enjoyment with the *gopīs*, as confirmed in the *Gopāla-tāpanī Upaniṣad* in the following words: *parārdhānte so 'budhyata gopa-veśo me puruṣaḥ purastād āvirbabhūva.*

The distinction between the Lord and the living entity is definitely experienced when there is sufficient intelligence to understand His internal potency, as distinguished from the external potency by which He makes possible the material manifestation.

TEXT 15

यस्यावतारगुणकर्मविडम्बनानि
नामानि येऽसुविगमे विवशा गृणन्ति ।
तेऽनैकजन्मशमलं सहसैव हित्वा
संयान्त्यपावृतामृतं तमजं प्रपद्ये ॥१५॥

yasyāvatāra-guṇa-karma-viḍambanāni
nāmāni ye 'su-vigame vivaśā gṛṇanti
te 'naika-janma-śamalaṁ sahasaiva hitvā
saṁyānty apāvṛtāmṛtaṁ tam ajaṁ prapadye

yasya—whose; *avatāra*—incarnations; *guṇa*—transcendental qualities; *karma*—activities; *viḍambanāni*—all mysterious; *nāmāni*—transcendental names; *ye*—those; *asu-vigame*—while quitting this life; *vivaśāḥ*—automatically; *gṛṇanti*—invoke; *te*—they; *anaika*—many; *janma*—births; *śamalam*—accumulated sins; *sahasā*—immediately; *eva*—certainly; *hitvā*—giving up; *saṁyānti*—obtain; *apāvṛta*—open; *amṛtam*—immortality; *tam*—Him; *ajam*—the unborn; *prapadye*—I take shelter.

TRANSLATION

Let me take shelter of the lotus feet of Him whose incarnations, qualities and activities are mysterious imitations of worldly affairs. One who invokes His transcendental names, even unconsciously, at the time he quits this life, is certainly washed immediately of the sins of many, many births and attains Him without fail.

PURPORT

The activities of the incarnations of the Supreme Personality of Godhead are a kind of imitation of the activities going on in the material world. He is just like an actor on a stage. An actor imitates the activities of a king on stage, although actually he is not the king. Similarly, when the Lord incarnates, He imitates parts with which He has nothing to do. In *Bhagavad-gītā* (4.14), it is said that the Lord has nothing to do with the activities in which He is supposedly engaged: *na māṁ karmāṇi limpanti na me karma-phale spṛhā.* The Lord is omnipotent; simply by His will He can perform anything and everything. When the Lord appeared as Lord Kṛṣṇa, He played the part of the son of Yaśodā and Nanda, and He lifted the Govardhana Hill, although lifting a hill is not His concern. He can lift millions of Govardhana Hills by His simple desire; He does not need to lift it with His hand. But He imitates the ordinary living entity by this lifting, and at the same time He exhibits His supernatural power. Thus His name is chanted as the lifter of Govardhana Hill, or Śrī Govardhanadhārī. Therefore, His acts in His incarnations and His partiality to the devotees are all imitations only, just like the stage makeup of an expert dramatical player. His acts in that capacity, however, are all omnipotent, and the remembrance of such activities of the incarnations of the Supreme Personality of Godhead is as powerful as the Lord Himself. Ajāmila remembered the holy name of the Lord, Nārāyaṇa, by merely calling the name of his son Nārāyaṇa, and that gave him a complete opportunity to achieve the highest perfection of life.

TEXT 16

यो वा अहं च गिरिशश्च विभुः स्वयं च
स्थित्युद्भवप्रलयहेतव आत्ममूलम् ।
भित्त्वा त्रिपाद्ववृध एक उरुप्ररोह-
स्तस्मै नमो भगवते भुवनद्रुमाय ॥१६॥

yo vā ahaṁ ca giriśaś ca vibhuḥ svayaṁ ca
sthity-udbhava-pralaya-hetava ātma-mūlam
bhittvā tri-pād vavṛdha eka uru-prarohas
tasmai namo bhagavate bhuvana-drumāya

yaḥ—one who; *vai*—certainly; *aham ca*—also I; *giriśaḥ ca*—also Śiva; *vibhuḥ*—the Almighty; *svayam*—personality (as Viṣṇu); *ca*—

and; *sthiti*—maintenance; *udbhava*—creation; *pralaya*—dissolution; *hetavaḥ*—the causes; *ātma-mūlam*—self-rooted; *bhittvā*—having penetrated; *tri-pāt*—three trunks; *vavṛdhe*—grew; *ekaḥ*—one without a second; *uru*—many; *prarohaḥ*—branches; *tasmai*—unto Him; *namaḥ*—obeisances; *bhagavate*—unto the Personality of Godhead; *bhuvana-drumāya*—unto the tree of the planetary system.

TRANSLATION

Your Lordship is the prime root of the tree of the planetary systems. This tree has grown by first penetrating the material nature in three trunks—as me, Śiva and You, the Almighty—for creation, maintenance and dissolution, and we three have grown with many branches. Therefore I offer my obeisances unto You, the tree of the cosmic manifestation.

PURPORT

The cosmic manifestation is grossly divided into three worlds, the upper, lower and middle planetary systems, and then it broadens into the cosmos of fourteen planetary systems, with the manifestation of the Supreme Personality of Godhead as the supreme root. Material nature, which appears to be the cause of the cosmic manifestation, is only the agency or energy of the Lord. This is confirmed in *Bhagavad-gītā* (9.10): *mayādhyakṣeṇa prakṛtiḥ sūyate sa-carācaram.* "Only under the superintendence of the Supreme Lord does material nature appear to be the cause of all creation, maintenance and dissolution." The Lord expands Himself into three—Viṣṇu, Brahmā and Śiva—for maintenance, creation and destruction respectively. Of the three principal agents controlling the three modes of material nature, Viṣṇu is the Almighty; even though He is within material nature for the purpose of maintenance, He is not controlled by the laws of material nature. The other two, Brahmā and Śiva, although almost as greatly powerful as Viṣṇu, are within the control of the material energy of the Supreme Lord. The conception of many gods controlling the many departments of material nature is ill conceived of by the foolish pantheist. God is one without a second, and He is the primal cause of all causes. As there are many departmental heads of governmental affairs, so there are many heads of management of the universal affairs.

Due to a poor fund of knowledge, the impersonalist does not believe in the personal management of things as they are. But in this verse it is clearly explained that everything is personal and nothing is impersonal. We have already discussed this point in the Introduction, and it is confirmed here in this verse. The tree of the material manifestation is described in the Fifteenth Chapter of *Bhagavad-gītā* as an *aśvattha* tree whose root is upward. We have actual experience of such a tree when we see the shadow of a tree on the bank of a reservoir of water. The reflection of the tree on the water appears to hang down from its upward roots. The tree of creation described here is only a shadow of the reality which is Parabrahman, Viṣṇu. In the internal potential manifestation of the Vaikuṇṭhalokas, the actual tree exists, and the tree reflected in the material nature is only the shadow of this actual tree. The impersonalists' theory that Brahman is void of all variegatedness is false because the shadow-tree described in *Bhagavad-gītā* cannot exist without being the reflection of a real tree. The real tree is situated in the eternal existence of spiritual nature, full of transcendental varieties, and Lord Viṣṇu is the root of that tree also. The root is the same—the Lord—both for the real tree and the false, but the false tree is only the perverted reflection of the real tree. The Lord, being the real tree, is here offered obeisances by Brahmā on his own behalf and also on behalf of Lord Śiva.

TEXT 17

लोको विकर्मनिरतः कुशले प्रमत्तः
कर्मण्ययं त्वदुदिते भवदर्चने स्वे ।
यस्तावदस्य बलवानिह जीविताशां
सद्यश्छिनत्त्यनिमिषाय नमोऽस्तु तस्मै ॥१७॥

loko vikarma-arataḥ kuśale pramattaḥ
karmaṇy ayaṁ tvad-udite bhavad-arcane sve
yas tāvad asya balavān iha jīvitāśāṁ
sadyaś chinatty animiṣāya namo 'stu tasmai

lokaḥ—people in general; *vikarma*—work without sense; *nirataḥ*—engaged in; *kuśale*—in beneficial activity; *pramattaḥ*—negligent; *karmaṇi*—in activity; *ayam*—this; *tvat*—by You; *udite*—enunciated;

bhavat—of You; *arcane*—in worship; *sve*—their own; *yaḥ*—who; *tāvat*—as long as; *asya*—of the people in general; *balavān*—very strong; *iha*—this; *jīvita-āśām*—struggle for existence; *sadyaḥ*—directly; *chinatti*—is cut to pieces; *animiṣāya*—by the eternal time; *namaḥ*—my obeisances; *astu*—let there be; *tasmai*—unto Him.

TRANSLATION

People in general all engage in foolish acts, not in the really beneficial activities enunciated directly by You for their guidance. As long as their tendency for foolish work remains powerful, all their plans in the struggle for existence will be cut to pieces. I therefore offer my obeisances unto Him who acts as eternal time.

PURPORT

People in general are all engaged in senseless work. They are systematically unmindful of the real beneficial work, which is the devotional service of the Lord, technically called the *arcanā* regulations. The *arcanā* regulations are directly instructed by the Lord in the *Nārada-pañcarātra* and are strictly followed by the intelligent men, who know well that the highest perfectional goal of life is to reach Lord Viṣṇu, who is the root of the tree called the cosmic manifestation. Also, in the *Bhāgavatam* and in *Bhagavad-gītā* such regulative activities are clearly mentioned. Foolish people do not know that their self-interest is in realization of Viṣṇu. The *Bhāgavatam* (7.5.30–32) says:

matir na kṛṣṇe parataḥ svato vā
mitho 'bhipadyeta gṛha-vratānām
adānta-gobhir viśatāṁ tamisraṁ
punaḥ punaś carvita-carvaṇānām

na te viduḥ svārtha-gatiṁ hi viṣṇuṁ
durāśayā ye bahir-artha-māninaḥ
andhā yathāndhair upanīyamānās
te 'pīśa-tantryām uru-dāmni baddhāḥ

naiṣāṁ matis tāvad urukramāṅghriṁ
spṛśaty anarthāpagamo yad-arthaḥ

mahīyasāṁ pāda-rajo-'bhiṣekaṁ
niṣkiñcanānāṁ na vṛṇīta yāvat

"Persons who are determined to totally rot in false, material happiness cannot become Kṛṣṇa-minded either by instructions from teachers, by self-realization or by parliamentary discussions. They are dragged by the unbridled senses into the darkest region of ignorance, and thus they madly engage in what is called 'chewing the chewed.'

"Because of their foolish activities, they are unaware that the ultimate goal of human life is to achieve Viṣṇu, the Lord of the cosmic manifestation, and so their struggle for existence is in the wrong direction of material civilization, which is under the external energy. They are led by similar foolish persons, just as one blind man is led by another blind man and both fall in the ditch.

"Such foolish men cannot be attracted towards the activities of the Supreme Powerful, who is actually the neutralizing measure for their foolish activities, unless and until they have the good sense to be guided by the great souls who are completely freed from material attachment."

In *Bhagavad-gītā* the Lord asks everyone to give up all other occupational duties and absolutely engage in *arcanā* activities, or in pleasing the Lord. But almost no one is attracted to such *arcanā* activity. Everyone is more or less attracted by activities which are conditions of rebellion against the Supreme Lord. The systems of *jñāna* and *yoga* are also indirectly rebellious acts against the Lord. There is no auspicious activity except *arcanā* of the Lord. *Jñāna* and *yoga* are sometimes accepted within the purview of *arcanā* when the ultimate aim is Viṣṇu, and not otherwise. The conclusion is that only the devotees of the Lord are bona fide human beings eligible for salvation. Others are vainly struggling for existence without any actual benefit.

TEXT 18

यस्माद्बिभेम्यहमपि द्विपरार्धधिष्ण्य-
मध्यासितः सकललोकनमस्कृतं यत् ।
तेपे तपो बहुसवोऽवरुरुत्समान-
स्तस्मै नमो भगवतेऽधिमखाय तुभ्यम् ॥१८॥

yasmād bibhemy aham api dviparārdha-dhiṣṇyam
adhyāsitaḥ sakala-loka-namaskṛtaṁ yat
tepe tapo bahu-savo 'varurutsamānas
tasmai namo bhagavate 'dhimakhāya tubhyam

yasmāt—from whom; *bibhemi*—fear; *aham*—I; *api*—also; *dvi-para-ardha*—up to the limit of 4,300,000,000 X 2 X 30 X 12 X 100 solar years; *dhiṣṇyam*—place; *adhyāsitaḥ*—situated in; *sakala-loka*—all other planets; *namaskṛtam*—honored by; *yat*—that; *tepe*—underwent; *tapaḥ*—penances; *bahu-savaḥ*—many, many years; *avarurut-samānaḥ*—desiring to obtain You; *tasmai*—unto Him; *namaḥ*—I do offer my obeisances; *bhagavate*—unto the Supreme Personality of Godhead; *adhimakhāya*—unto Him who is the enjoyer of all sacrifices; *tubhyam*—unto Your Lordship.

TRANSLATION

Your Lordship, I offer my respectful obeisances unto You who are indefatigable time and the enjoyer of all sacrifices. Although I am situated in an abode which will continue to exist for a time duration of two parārdhas, although I am the leader of all other planets in the universe, and although I have undergone many, many years of penance for self-realization, still I offer my respects unto You.

PURPORT

Brahmā is the greatest personality in the universe because he has the longest duration of life. He is the most respectable personality because of his penance, influence, prestige, etc., and still he has to offer his respectful obeisances unto the Lord. Therefore, it is incumbent upon all others, who are far, far below the standard of Brahmā, to do as he did and offer respects as a matter of duty.

TEXT 19

तिर्यङ्मनुष्यविबुधादिषु जीवयोनि-
ष्वात्मेच्छयात्मकृतसेतुपरीप्सया यः ।

रेमे निरस्तविषयोऽप्यवरुद्धदेह-
स्तस्मै नमो भगवते पुरुषोत्तमाय ॥१९॥

tiryaṅ-manuṣya-vibudhādiṣu jīva-yoniṣv
ātmecchayātma-kṛta-setu-parīpsayā yaḥ
reme nirasta-viṣayo 'py avaruddha-dehas
tasmai namo bhagavate puruṣottamāya

tiryak—animals lower than human beings; *manuṣya*—human beings, etc.; *vibudha-ādiṣu*—amongst the demigods; *jīva-yoniṣu*—in different species of life; *ātma*—self; *icchayā*—by the will; *ātma-kṛta*—self-created; *setu*—obligations; *parīpsayā*—desiring to preserve; *yaḥ*—who; *reme*—performing transcendental pastimes; *nirasta*—not being affected; *viṣayaḥ*—material contamination; *api*—certainly; *avaruddha*—manifested; *dehaḥ*—transcendental body; *tasmai*—unto Him; *namaḥ*—my obeisances; *bhagavate*—unto the Personality of Godhead; *puruṣottamāya*—the primeval Lord.

TRANSLATION

O my Lord, by Your own will You appear in the various species of living entities, among animals lower than human beings as well as among the demigods, to perform Your transcendental pastimes. You are not affected by material contamination. You come just to fulfill the obligations of Your own principles of religion, and therefore, O Supreme Personality, I offer my obeisances unto You for manifesting such different forms.

PURPORT

The Lord's incarnations in different species of life are all transcendental. He appears as a human being in His incarnations of Kṛṣṇa, Rāma, etc., but He is not a human being. Anyone who mistakes Him for an ordinary human being is certainly not very intelligent, as confirmed in *Bhagavad-gītā* (9.11): *avajānanti māṁ mūḍhā mānuṣīṁ tanum āśritam.* The same principle is applicable when He appears as the hog or fish incarnations. They are transcendental forms of the Lord and are manifested under certain necessities of His own pleasure and pastimes.

Such manifestations of the transcendental forms of the Lord are accepted by Him mostly to enliven His devotees. All His incarnations are manifested whenever there is a need to deliver His devotees and maintain His own principles.

TEXT 20

योऽविद्ययानुपहतोऽपि दशार्धवृत्त्या
निद्रामुवाह जठरीकृतलोकयात्रः ।
अन्तर्जलेऽहिकशिपुस्पर्शानुकूलां
भीमोर्मिमालिनि जनस्य सुखं विवृण्वन् ॥२०॥

yo 'vidyayānupahato 'pi daśārdha-vṛttyā
nidrām uvāha jaṭharī-kṛta-loka-yātraḥ
antar-jale 'hi-kaśipu-sparśānukūlāṁ
bhīmormi-mālini janasya sukhaṁ vivṛṇvan

yaḥ—one; *avidyayā*—influenced by nescience; *anupahataḥ*—without being affected; *api*—in spite of; *daśa-ardha*—five; *vṛttyā*—interaction; *nidrām*—sleep; *uvāha*—accepted; *jaṭharī*—within the abdomen; *kṛta*—doing so; *loka-yātraḥ*—maintenance of the different entities; *antaḥ-jale*—within the water of devastation; *ahi-kaśipu*—on the snake bed; *sparśa-anukūlām*—happy for the touch; *bhīma-ūrmi*—violent waves; *mālini*—chain of; *janasya*—of the intelligent person; *sukham*—happiness; *vivṛṇvan*—showing.

TRANSLATION

My Lord, You accept the pleasure of sleeping in the water of devastation, where there are violent waves, and You enjoy pleasure on the bed of snakes, showing the happiness of Your sleep to intelligent persons. At that time, all the universal planets are stationed within Your abdomen.

PURPORT

Persons who cannot think of anything beyond the limit of their own power are like frogs in a well who cannot imagine the length and breadth of the great Pacific Ocean. Such people take it as legendary when they hear that the Supreme Lord is lying on His bed within the great ocean of the universe. They are surprised that one can lie down within water and sleep very happily. But a little intelligence can mitigate this foolish astonishment. There are many living entities within the bed of the ocean who also enjoy the material bodily activities of eating, sleeping, defending and mating. If such insignificant living entities can enjoy life within the water, why can't the Supreme Lord, who is all-powerful, sleep on the cool body of a serpent and enjoy in the turmoil of violent ocean waves? The distinction of the Lord is that His activities are all transcendental, and He is able to do anything and everything without being deterred by limitations of time and space. He can enjoy His transcendental happiness regardless of material considerations.

TEXT 21

यन्नाभिपद्मभवनादहमासमीड्य
लोकत्रयोपकरणो यदनुग्रहेण ।
तस्मै नमस्त उदरस्थभवाय योग-
निद्रावसानविकसन्नलिनेक्षणाय ॥२१॥

yan-nābhi-padma-bhavanād aham āsam īḍya
loka-trayopakaraṇo yad-anugraheṇa
tasmai namas ta udara-stha-bhavāya yoga-
nidrāvasāna-vikasan-nalinekṣaṇāya

yat—whose; *nābhi*—navel; *padma*—lotus; *bhavanāt*—from the house of; *aham*—I; *āsam*—became manifested; *īḍya*—O worshipable one; *loka-traya*—the three worlds; *upakaraṇaḥ*—helping in the creation of; *yat*—whose; *anugraheṇa*—by the mercy; *tasmai*—unto Him; *namaḥ*—my obeisances; *te*—unto You; *udara-stha*—situated within the abdomen; *bhavāya*—having the universe; *yoga-nidrā-avasāna*—after the end of that transcendental sleep; *vikasat*—blossoming; *nalina-īkṣaṇāya*—unto Him whose opening eyes are like lotuses.

TRANSLATION

O object of my worship, I am born from the house of Your lotus navel for the purpose of creating the universe by Your mercy. All

these planets of the universe were stationed within Your transcendental abdomen while You were enjoying sleep. Now, Your sleep having ended, Your eyes are open like blossoming lotuses in the morning.

PURPORT

Brahmā is teaching us the beginning of *arcanā* regulations from morning (four o'clock) to night (ten o'clock). Early in the morning, the devotee has to rise from his bed and pray to the Lord, and there are other regulative principles for offering *maṅgala-ārati* early in the morning. Foolish nondevotees, not understanding the importance of *arcanā*, criticize the regulative principles, but they have no eyes to see that the Lord also sleeps, by His own will. The impersonal conception of the Supreme is so detrimental to the path of devotional service that it is very difficult to associate with the stubborn nondevotees, who always think in terms of material conceptions.

Impersonalists always think backwards. They think that because there is form in matter, spirit should be formless; because in matter there is sleep, in spirit there cannot be sleep; and because the sleeping of the Deity is accepted in *arcanā* worship, the *arcanā* is *māyā*. All these thoughts are basically material. To think either positively or negatively is still thinking materially. Knowledge accepted from the superior source of the *Vedas* is standard. Here in these verses of the *Śrīmad-Bhāgavatam*, we find that *arcanā* is recommended. Before Brahmā took up the task of creation, he found the Lord sleeping on the serpent bed in the waves of the water of devastation. Therefore, sleeping exists in the internal potency of the Lord, and this is not denied by pure devotees of the Lord like Brahmā and his disciplic succession. It is clearly said here that the Lord slept very happily within the violent waves of the water, manifesting thereby that He is able to do anything and everything by His transcendental will and not be hampered by any circumstances. The Māyāvādī cannot think beyond this material experience, and thus he denies the Lord's ability to sleep within the water. His mistake is that he compares the Lord to himself—and that comparison is also a material thought. The whole philosophy of the Māyāvāda school, based on "not this, not that" (*neti, neti*), is basically material. Such thought cannot give one the chance to know the Supreme Personality of Godhead as He is.

TEXT 22

सोऽयं समस्तजगतां सुहृदेक आत्मा
सत्त्वेन यन्मृडयते भगवान् भगेन ।
तेनैव मे दृशमनुस्पृशताद्यथाहं
स्रक्ष्यामि पूर्ववदिदं प्रणतप्रियोऽसौ ॥२२॥

so 'yaṁ samasta-jagatāṁ suhṛd eka ātmā
sattvena yan mṛḍayate bhagavān bhagena
tenaiva me dṛśam anuspṛśatād yathāhaṁ
srakṣyāmi pūrvavad idaṁ praṇata-priyo 'sau

saḥ—He; *ayam*—the Lord; *samasta-jagatām*—of all the universes; *suhṛt ekaḥ*—the one friend and philosopher; *ātmā*—the Supersoul; *sattvena*—by the mode of goodness; *yat*—one who; *mṛḍayate*—causes happiness; *bhagavān*—the Personality of Godhead; *bhagena*—with six opulences; *tena*—by Him; *eva*—certainly; *me*—to me; *dṛśam*—power of introspection; *anuspṛśatāt*—let Him give; *yathā*—as; *aham*—I; *srakṣyāmi*—will be able to create; *pūrva-vat*—as before; *idam*—this universe; *praṇata*—surrendered; *priyaḥ*—dear; *asau*—He (the Lord).

TRANSLATION

Let the Supreme Lord be merciful towards me. He is the one friend and soul of all living entities in the world, and He maintains all, for their ultimate happiness, by His six transcendental opulences. May He be merciful towards me so that I, as before, may be empowered with the introspection to create, for I am also one of the surrendered souls who are dear to the Lord.

PURPORT

The Supreme Lord, Puruṣottama, or Śrī Kṛṣṇa, is the maintainer of all, in both the transcendental and material worlds. He is the life and friend of all because there is eternally natural affection and love between the living entities and the Lord. He is the one friend and well-wisher for all, and He is one without a second. The Lord maintains all the living entities everywhere by His six transcendental opulences, for which He is known as *bhagavān*, or the Supreme Personality of Godhead. Lord Brahmā prayed for His mercy so that he might be able to create the universal affairs as he did before; only by the Lord's causeless mercy could he create both material and spiritual personalities like Marīci and Nārada respectively. Brahmā prayed to the Lord because He is very much dear to the surrendered soul. The surrendered soul knows nothing but the Lord, and therefore the Lord is very affectionate towards him.

TEXT 23

एष प्रपन्नवरदो रमयात्मशक्त्या
यद्यत्करिष्यति गृहीतगुणावतारः ।
तस्मिन् स्वविक्रममिदं सृजतोऽपि चेतो
युञ्जीत कर्मशमलं च यथा विजह्याम् ॥२३॥

eṣa prapanna-varado ramayātma-śaktyā
yad yat kariṣyati gṛhīta-guṇāvatāraḥ
tasmin sva-vikramam idaṁ sṛjato 'pi ceto
yuñjīta karma-śamalaṁ ca yathā vijahyām

eṣaḥ—this; *prapanna*—one who is surrendered; *vara-daḥ*—benefactor; *ramayā*—enjoying always with the goddess of fortune (Lakṣmī); *ātma-śaktyā*—with His internal potency; *yat yat*—whatever; *kariṣyati*—He may act; *gṛhīta*—accepting; *guṇa-avatāraḥ*—incarnation of the mode of goodness; *tasmin*—unto Him; *sva-vikramam*—with omnipotency; *idam*—this cosmic manifestation; *sṛjataḥ*—creating; *api*—in spite of; *cetaḥ*—heart; *yuñjīta*—be engaged; *karma*—work; *śamalam*—material affection; *ca*—also; *yathā*—as much as; *vijahyām*—I can give up.

TRANSLATION

The Supreme Lord, the Personality of Godhead, is always the benefactor of the surrendered souls. His activities are always enacted through His internal potency, Ramā, or the goddess of fortune. I pray only to engage in His service in the creation of the material world, and I pray that I not be materially affected by my

works, for thus I may be able to give up the false prestige of being the creator.

PURPORT

In the matter of material creation, maintenance and destruction, there are three incarnations of the material modes of nature—Brahmā, Viṣṇu and Maheśvara. But the Lord's incarnation as Viṣṇu, in His internal potency, is the supreme energy for the total activities. Brahmā, who is only an assistant in the modes of creation, wanted to remain in his actual position as an instrument of the Lord instead of becoming puffed up by the false prestige of thinking himself the creator. That is the way of becoming dear to the Supreme Lord and receiving His benediction. Foolish men want to take credit for all creations made by them, but intelligent persons know very well that not a blade of grass can move without the will of the Lord; thus all the credit for wonderful creations must go to Him. By spiritual consciousness only can one be free from the contamination of material affection and receive the benedictions offered by the Lord.

TEXT 24

नाभिह्रदादिह सतोऽम्भसि यस्य पुंसो
विज्ञानशक्तिरहमासमनन्तशक्तेः ।
रूपं विचित्रमिदमस्य विवृण्वतो मे
मा रीरिषीष्ट निगमस्य गिरां विसर्गः ॥२४॥

nābhi-hradād iha sato 'mbhasi yasya puṁso
vijñāna-śaktir aham āsam ananta-śakteḥ
rūpaṁ vicitram idam asya vivṛṇvato me
mā rīriṣīṣṭa nigamasya girāṁ visargaḥ

nābhi-hradāt—from the navel lake; *iha*—in this millennium; *sataḥ*—lying; *ambhasi*—in the water; *yasya*—one whose; *puṁsaḥ*—of the Personality of Godhead; *vijñāna*—of the total universe; *śaktiḥ*—energy; *aham*—I; *āsam*—was born; *ananta*—unlimited; *śakteḥ*—of the powerful; *rūpam*—form; *vicitram*—variegated; *idam*—this; *asya*—His; *vivṛṇvataḥ*—manifesting; *me*—unto me; *mā*—may not; *rīriṣīṣṭa*—vanish; *nigamasya*—of the *Vedas;* *girām*—of the sounds; *visargaḥ*—vibration.

TRANSLATION

The Lord's potencies are innumerable. As He lies down in the water of devastation, I am born as the total universal energy from the navel lake in which the lotus sprouts. I am now engaged in manifesting His diverse energies in the form of the cosmic manifestation. I therefore pray that in the course of my material activities I may not be deviated from the vibration of the Vedic hymns.

PURPORT

Every person engaged in the transcendental loving service of the Lord in this material world is prone to so many material activities, and if one is not strong enough to protect himself against the onslaught of material affection, he may be diverted from the spiritual energy. In the material creation Brahmā has to create all kinds of living entities with bodies suitable to their material conditions. Brahmā wants to be protected by the Lord because he has to contact many, many vicious living entities. An ordinary *brāhmaṇa* may fall from the *brahma-tejas*, or the power of brahminical excellence, due to his association with many fallen, conditioned souls. Brahmā, as the supermost *brāhmaṇa*, is afraid of such a falldown, and therefore he prays to the Lord for protection. This is a warning for one and all in the spiritual advancement of life. Unless one is sufficiently protected by the Lord, he may fall down from his spiritual position; therefore one has to pray constantly to the Lord for protection and the blessing to carry out one's duty. Lord Caitanya also entrusted His missionary work to His devotees and assured them of His protection against the onslaught of material affection. The path of spiritual life is stated in the *Vedas* to be like the edge of a sharpened razor. A little inattentiveness may at once create havoc and bloodshed, but one who is a completely surrendered soul, always seeking protection from the Lord in the discharge of his entrusted duties, has no fear of falling into material contamination.

TEXT 25

सोऽसावदभ्रकरुणो भगवान् विवृद्ध-
प्रेमस्मितेन नयनाम्बुरुहं विजृम्भन् ।
उत्थाय विश्वविजयाय च नो विषादं
माध्व्या गिरापनयतात्पुरुषः पुराणः ॥२५॥

so 'sāv adabhra-karuṇo bhagavān vivṛddha-
prema-smitena nayanāmburuhaṁ vijṛmbhan
utthāya viśva-vijayāya ca no viṣādaṁ
mādhvyā girāpanayatāt puruṣaḥ purāṇaḥ

saḥ—He (the Lord); *asau*—that; *adabhra*—unlimited; *karuṇaḥ*—merciful; *bhagavān*—the Personality of Godhead; *vivṛddha*—excessive; *prema*—love; *smitena*—by smiling; *nayana-amburuham*—the lotus eyes; *vijṛmbhan*—by opening; *utthāya*—for flourishing; *viśva-vijayāya*—for glorifying the cosmic creation; *ca*—as also; *naḥ*—our; *viṣādam*—dejection; *mādhvyā*—by sweet; *girā*—words; *apanayatāt*—let Him kindly remove; *puruṣaḥ*—the Supreme; *purāṇaḥ*—oldest.

TRANSLATION

The Lord, who is supreme and is the oldest of all, is unlimitedly merciful. I wish that He may smilingly bestow His benediction upon me by opening His lotus eyes. He can uplift the entire cosmic creation and remove our dejection by kindly speaking His directions.

PURPORT

The Lord is ever increasingly merciful upon the fallen souls of this material world. The whole cosmic manifestation is a chance for all to improve themselves in devotional service to the Lord, and everyone is meant for that purpose. The Lord expands Himself into many personalities who are either self-expansions or separated expansions. The personalities of the individual souls are His separated expansions, whereas the self-expansions are the Lord Himself. The self-expansions are predominators, and the separated expansions are predominated for reciprocation of transcendental bliss with the supreme form of bliss and knowledge. The liberated souls can join in this blissful reciprocation of predominator and predominated without materially concocted ideas. The typical example of such a transcendental exchange between the predominator and the predominated is the Lord's *rāsa-līlā* with the *gopīs.* The *gopīs* are predominated expansions of the internal potency, and therefore the Lord's participation in the *rāsa-līlā* dance is never to be considered like the mundane relationship of man and woman. It is, rather, the highest perfectional stage of the exchange of feelings between the Lord and the living entities. The Lord gives the fallen souls the chance for this highest perfection of life. Lord Brahmā is entrusted with the management of the complete cosmic show, and therefore he prays that the Lord bestow His blessings upon him so that he may execute its purpose.

TEXT 26

मैत्रेय उवाच

स्वसम्भवं निशाम्यैवं तपोविद्यासमाधिभिः ।
यावन्मनोवचः स्तुत्वा विरराम स खिन्नवत् ॥२६॥

maitreya uvāca
sva-sambhavaṁ niśāmyaivaṁ
tapo-vidyā-samādhibhiḥ
yāvan mano-vacaḥ stutvā
virarāma sa khinnavat

maitreyaḥ uvāca—the great sage Maitreya said; *sva-sambhavam*—the source of his appearance; *niśāmya*—by seeing; *evam*—thus; *tapaḥ*—penance; *vidyā*—knowledge; *samādhibhiḥ*—as also by concentration of the mind; *yāvat*—as far as possible; *manaḥ*—mind; *vacaḥ*—words; *stutvā*—having prayed; *virarāma*—became silent; *saḥ*—he (Brahmā); *khinna-vat*—as if tired.

TRANSLATION

The sage Maitreya said: O Vidura, after observing the source of his appearance, namely the Personality of Godhead, Brahmā prayed for His mercy as far as his mind and words would permit him. Thus having prayed, he became silent, as if tired from his activities of penance, knowledge and mental concentration.

PURPORT

Brahmā's enlightenment in knowledge was due to the Lord sitting within his heart. After being created, Brahmā could not ascertain the source of his appearance, but after penance and mental concentration he could see the source of his birth, and thus he became enlightened through his heart. The spiritual master outside and the spiritual master within are both representations of the Lord. Unless one has contact with such bona fide representations, one cannot claim to be a spiritual master. Lord Brahmā had no opportunity to take the help of a spiritual master from outside because at that time Brahmā himself was the only creature in the universe. Therefore, on becoming satisfied by the prayers of Brahmā, the Lord enlightened him about everything from within.

TEXTS 27–28

अथाभिप्रेतमन्वीक्ष्य ब्रह्मणो मधुसूदनः ।
विषण्णचेतसं तेन कल्पव्यतिकराम्भसा ॥२७॥
लोकसंस्थानविज्ञान आत्मनः परिखिद्यतः ।
तमाहागाधया वाचा कश्मलं शमयन्निव ॥२८॥

athābhipretam anvīkṣya
brahmaṇo madhusūdanaḥ
viṣaṇṇa-cetasaṁ tena
kalpa-vyatikarāmbhasā

loka-saṁsthāna-vijñāna
ātmanaḥ parikhidyataḥ
tam āhāgādhayā vācā
kaśmalaṁ śamayann iva

atha—thereupon; *abhipretam*—intention; *anvīkṣya*—observing; *brahmaṇaḥ*—of Brahmā; *madhusūdanaḥ*—the killer of the Madhu demon; *viṣaṇṇa*—depressed; *cetasam*—of the heart; *tena*—by him; *kalpa*—millennium; *vyatikara-ambhasā*—devastating water; *loka-saṁsthāna*—situation of the planetary system; *vijñāne*—in the science; *ātmanaḥ*—of himself; *parikhidyataḥ*—sufficiently anxious; *tam*—unto him; *āha*—said; *agādhayā*—deeply thoughtful; *vācā*—by words; *kaśmalam*—impurities; *śamayan*—removing; *iva*—like that.

TRANSLATION

The Lord saw that Brahmā was very anxious about the planning and construction of the different planetary systems and was

depressed upon seeing the devastating water. He could understand the intention of Brahmā, and thus He spoke in deep, thoughtful words, removing all the illusion that had arisen.

PURPORT

The devastating water was so fearful that even Brahmā was perturbed at its appearance and became very anxious about how to situate the different planetary systems in outer space to accommodate the different kinds of living entities, such as the human beings, those lower than the human beings, and the superhuman beings. All the planets in the universe are situated according to the different grades of living entities under the influence of the modes of material nature. There are three modes of material nature, and when they are mixed with one another they become nine. When the nine are mixed they become eighty-one, and the eighty-one also become mixed, and thus we ultimately do not know how the delusion increases and increases. Lord Brahmā had to accommodate different places and situations for the requisite bodies of the conditioned souls. The task was meant only for Brahmā, and no one in the universe can even understand how difficult it was. But by the grace of the Lord, Brahmā was able to execute the tremendous task so perfectly that everyone is amazed to see the workmanship of the *vidhātā*, or the regulator.

TEXT 29

श्रीभगवानुवाच
मा वेदगर्भ गास्तन्द्रीं सर्ग उद्यममावह ।
तन्मयापादितं ह्यग्रे यन्मां प्रार्थयते भवान् ॥२९॥

śrī-bhagavān uvāca
mā veda-garbha gās tandrīṁ
sarga udyamam āvaha
tan mayāpāditaṁ hy agre
yan māṁ prārthayate bhavān

śrī-bhagavān uvāca—the Lord, the Personality of Godhead, said; *mā*—do not; *veda-garbha*—O You who have the depth of all Vedic wisdom; *gāḥ tandrīm*—become dejected; *sarge*—for creation;

udyamam—enterprises; *āvaha*—you just undertake; *tat*—that (which you want); *mayā*—by Me; *āpāditam*—executed; *hi*—certainly; *agre*—previously; *yat*—which; *mām*—from Me; *prārthayate*—begging; *bhavān*—you.

TRANSLATION

The Supreme Personality of Godhead then said: O Brahmā, O depth of Vedic wisdom, be neither depressed nor anxious about the execution of creation. What you are begging from Me has already been granted before.

PURPORT

Any person authorized by either the Lord or by His bona fide representative is already blessed, as is the work entrusted to him. Of course, the person entrusted with such a responsibility should always be aware of his incapability and must always look for the mercy of the Lord for the successful execution of his duty. One should not be puffed up because he is entrusted with certain executive work. Fortunate is he who is so entrusted, and if he is always fixed in the sense of being subordinate to the will of the Supreme, he is sure to come out successful in the discharge of his work. Arjuna was entrusted with the work of fighting on the Battlefield of Kurukṣetra, and before he was so entrusted, the Lord had already arranged for his victory. But Arjuna was always conscious of his position as subordinate to the Lord, and thus he accepted Him as the supreme guide in his responsibility. Anyone who takes pride in doing responsible work but does not give credit to the Supreme Lord is certainly falsely proud and cannot execute anything nicely. Brahmā and persons in the line of his disciplic succession who follow in his footsteps are always successful in the discharge of loving transcendental service to the Supreme Lord.

TEXT 30

भूयस्त्वं तप आतिष्ठ विद्यां चैव मदाश्रयाम् ।
ताभ्यामन्तर्हृदि ब्रह्मन् लोकान्द्रक्ष्यस्यपावृतान् ॥३०॥

bhūyas tvaṁ tapa ātiṣṭha
vidyāṁ caiva mad-āśrayām

tābhyām antar-hṛdi brahman
lokān drakṣyasy apāvṛtān

bhūyaḥ—again; *tvam*—yourself; *tapaḥ*—penance; *ātiṣṭha*—be situated; *vidyām*—in the knowledge; *ca*—also; *eva*—certainly; *mat*—My; *āśrayām*—under the protection; *tābhyām*—by those qualifications; *antaḥ*—within; *hṛdi*—in the heart; *brahman*—O *brāhmaṇa; lokān*—all the worlds; *drakṣyasi*—you will see; *apāvṛtān*—all disclosed.

TRANSLATION

O Brahmā, situate yourself in penance and meditation and follow the principles of knowledge to receive My favor. By these actions you will be able to understand everything from within your heart.

PURPORT

The mercy the Lord bestows upon a particular person engaged in executing the responsible work entrusted unto him is beyond imagination. But His mercy is received due to our penance and perseverance in executing devotional service. Brahmā was entrusted with the work of creating the planetary systems. The Lord instructed him that when he meditated he would very easily know where and how the planetary systems must be arranged. The directions were to come from within, and there was no necessity for anxiety in that task. Such instructions of *buddhi-yoga* are directly imparted by the Lord from within, as confirmed in *Bhagavad-gītā* (10.10).

TEXT 31

तत आत्मनि लोके च भक्तियुक्तः समाहितः ।
द्रष्टासि मां ततं ब्रह्मन्मयि लोकांस्त्वमात्मनः ॥३१॥

tata ātmani loke ca
bhakti-yuktaḥ samāhitaḥ
draṣṭāsi māṁ tataṁ brahman
mayi lokāṁs tvam ātmanaḥ

tataḥ—thereafter; *ātmani*—in yourself; *loke*—in the universe; *ca*—also; *bhakti-yuktaḥ*—being situated in devotional service; *samāhitaḥ*—being completely absorbed; *draṣṭā asi*—you shall see; *mām*—Me; *tatam*—spread throughout; *brahman*—O Brahmā; *mayi*—in Me; *lokān*—all the universe; *tvam*—you; *ātmanaḥ*—the living entities.

TRANSLATION

O Brahmā, when you are absorbed in devotional service, in the course of your creative activities, you will see Me in you and throughout the universe, and you will see that you yourself, the universe and the living entities are all in Me.

PURPORT

It is cited herein by the Lord that during his daytime Brahmā would see Him as Lord Śrī Kṛṣṇa. He would appreciate how the Lord expanded Himself into all the calves during His childhood at Vṛndāvana, he would know how Yaśodāmayī saw all the universes and planetary systems within the mouth of Kṛṣṇa during His playful childhood pastimes, and he would also see that there are many millions of Brahmās during the appearance of Lord Kṛṣṇa in Brahmā's daytime. But all these manifestations of the Lord, appearing everywhere in His eternal, transcendental forms, cannot be understood by anyone but the pure devotees, who are always engaged in devotional service to the Lord and are fully absorbed in the Lord. The high qualifications of Brahmā are also indicated herein.

TEXT 32

यदा तु सर्वभूतेषु दारुष्वग्निमिव स्थितम् ।
प्रतिचक्षीत मां लोको जह्यात्तर्ह्येव कश्मलम् ॥३२॥

yadā tu sarva-bhūteṣu
dāruṣv agnim iva sthitam
praticakṣīta māṁ loko
jahyāt tarhy eva kaśmalam

yadā—when; *tu*—but; *sarva*—all; *bhūteṣu*—in the living entities; *dāruṣu*—in wood; *agnim*—fire; *iva*—like; *sthitam*—situated; *pra-*

ticakṣīta—you shall see; *mām*—Me; *lokaḥ*—and the universe; *jahyāt*—can give up; *tarhi*—then at once; *eva*—certainly; *kaśmalam*—illusion.

TRANSLATION

You will see Me in all living entities as well as all over the universe, just as fire is situated in wood. Only in that state of transcendental vision will you be able to be free from all kinds of illusion.

PURPORT

Brahmā prayed that he might not forget his eternal relationship with the Lord during the course of his material activities. In answer to that prayer, the Lord said that he should not think of existing without a relationship with His omnipotency. The example is given of the fire in wood. The fire kindled in wood is always the same, although the wood may be of different types. Similarly, the bodies within the material creation may be specifically different according to shape and quality, but the spirit souls within them are not different from one another. The quality of fire, warmth, is the same everywhere, and the spiritual spark, or part and parcel of the Supreme Spirit, is the same in every living being; thus the potency of the Lord is distributed all over His creation. This transcendental knowledge alone can save one from the contamination of material illusion. Since the Lord's potency is distributed everywhere, a pure soul, or devotee of the Lord, can see everything in relationship with the Lord, and therefore he has no affection for the outer coverings. That pure spiritual conception makes him immune to all contamination of material association. The pure devotee never forgets the touch of the Lord in all circumstances.

TEXT 33

यदा रहितमात्मानं भूतेन्द्रियगुणाशयैः ।
स्वरूपेण मयोपेतं पश्यन् स्वाराज्यमृच्छति ॥३३॥

yadā rahitam ātmānaṁ
bhūtendriya-guṇāśayaiḥ
svarūpeṇa mayopetaṁ
paśyan svārājyam ṛcchati

yadā—when; *rahitam*—freed from; *ātmānam*—self; *bhūta*—material elements; *indriya*—material senses; *guṇa-āśayaiḥ*—under the influence of the material modes of nature; *svarūpeṇa*—in pure existence; *mayā*—by Me; *upetam*—approaching; *paśyan*—by seeing; *svārājyam*—spiritual kingdom; *ṛcchati*—enjoy.

TRANSLATION

When you are free from the conception of gross and subtle bodies and when your senses are free from all influences of the modes of material nature, you will realize your pure form in My association. At that time you will be situated in pure consciousness.

PURPORT

In the *Bhakti-rasāmṛta-sindhu* it is said that a person whose only desire is to render transcendental loving service to the Lord is a free person in any condition of material existence. That service attitude is the *svarūpa*, or real form, of the living entity. Lord Śrī Caitanya Mahāprabhu, in the *Caitanya-caritāmṛta*, also confirms this statement by declaring that the real, spiritual form of the living entity is eternal servitorship to the Supreme Lord. The Māyāvāda school shudders at the thought of a service attitude in the living entity, not knowing that in the transcendental world the service of the Lord is based on transcendental love. Transcendental loving service is never to be compared to the forced service of the material world. In the material world, even if one is under the conception that he is no one's servant, he is still the servant of his senses, under the dictation of the material modes. Factually no one is master here in the material world, and therefore the servants of the senses have a very bad experience of servitude. They shudder at the thought of service because they have no knowledge of the transcendental position. In transcendental loving service, the servitor is as free as the Lord. The Lord is *svarāṭ*, or fully independent, and the servant is also fully independent, or *svarāṭ*, in the spiritual atmosphere because there is no forced service. There the transcendental loving service is due to spontaneous love. A reflected glimpse of such service is experienced in the service of the mother unto the son, the friend's service unto the friend, or the wife's service unto the husband. These reflections of service by friends, parents or wives are not forced, but are due only to love. Here in this material world, however, the loving service is only a reflection. The real service, or service in *svarūpa*, is present in the transcendental world, in association with the Lord. The very same service in transcendental love can be practiced in devotion here.

This verse is also applicable to the *jñānī* school. The enlightened *jñānī*, when free from all material contaminations, namely the gross and subtle bodies together with the senses of the material modes of nature, is placed in the Supreme and is thus liberated from material bondage. The *jñānīs* and the devotees are actually in agreement up to the point of liberation from material contamination. But whereas the *jñānīs* remain pacified on the platform of simple understanding, the devotees develop further spiritual advancement in loving service. The devotees develop a spiritual individuality in their spontaneous service attitude, which is enhanced on and on, up to the point of *mādhurya-rasa*, or transcendental loving service reciprocated between the lover and the beloved.

TEXT 34

नानाकर्मवितानेन प्रजा बह्वीः सिसृक्षतः ।
नात्मावसीदत्यस्मिंस्ते वर्षीयान्मदनुग्रहः ॥३४॥

nānā-karma-vitānena
prajā bahvīḥ sisṛkṣataḥ
nātmāvasīdaty asmiṁs te
varṣīyān mad-anugrahaḥ

nānā-karma—varieties of service; *vitānena*—by expansion of; *prajāḥ*—population; *bahvīḥ*—innumerable; *sisṛkṣataḥ*—desiring to increase; *na*—never; *ātmā*—self; *avasīdati*—will be bereaved; *asmin*—in the matter; *te*—of you; *varṣīyān*—always increasing; *mat*—My; *anugrahaḥ*—causeless mercy.

TRANSLATION

Since you have desired to increase the population innumerably and expand your varieties of service, you shall never be deprived in this matter because My causeless mercy upon you will always increase for all time.

PURPORT

A pure devotee of the Lord, being cognizant of the facts of the particular time, object and circumstances, always desires to expand the number of devotees of the Lord in various ways. Such expansions of transcendental service may appear to be material to the materialist, but factually they are expansions of the causeless mercy of the Lord towards the devotee. Plans for such activities may appear to be material activities, but they are different in potency, being engaged in the satisfaction of the transcendental senses of the Supreme.

TEXT 35

ऋषिमाद्यं न बध्नाति पापीयांस्त्वां रजोगुणः ।
यन्मनो मयि निर्बद्धं प्रजाः संसृजतोऽपि ते ॥३५॥

ṛṣim ādyaṁ na badhnāti
pāpīyāṁs tvāṁ rajo-guṇaḥ
yan mano mayi nirbaddhaṁ
prajāḥ saṁsṛjato 'pi te

ṛṣim—unto the great sage; *ādyam*—the first of the kind; *na*—never; *badhnāti*—encroaches; *pāpīyān*—vicious; *tvām*—you; *rajaḥ-guṇaḥ*—the material mode of passion; *yat*—because; *manaḥ*—mind; *mayi*—in Me; *nirbaddham*—compact in; *prajāḥ*—progeny; *saṁsṛjataḥ*—generating; *api*—in spite of; *te*—your.

TRANSLATION

You are the original ṛṣi, and because your mind is always fixed on Me, even though you will be engaged in generating various progeny, the vicious mode of passion will never encroach upon you.

PURPORT

The same assurance is given to Brahmā in the Second Canto, Chapter Nine, verse 36. Being so favored by the Lord, Brahmā's schemes and plans are all infallible. If sometimes Brahmā is seen to be bewildered, as, in the Tenth Canto, he is bewildered by seeing the action of the internal potency, that is also for his further advancement in transcendental service. Arjuna is found to be similarly bewildered. All such bewilderment of the pure devotees of the Lord is specifically meant for their further advancement in knowledge of the Lord.

TEXT 36

ज्ञातोऽहं भवता त्वद्य दुर्विज्ञेयोऽपि देहिनाम् ।
यन्मां त्वं मन्यसेऽयुक्तं भूतेन्द्रियगुणात्मभिः॥३६॥

jñāto 'haṁ bhavatā tv adya
durvijñeyo 'pi dehinām
yan māṁ tvaṁ manyase 'yuktaṁ
bhūtendriya-guṇātmabhiḥ

jñātaḥ—known; *aham*—Myself; *bhavatā*—by you; *tu*—but; *adya*—today; *duḥ*—difficult; *vijñeyaḥ*—to be known; *api*—in spite of; *dehinām*—for the conditioned soul; *yat*—because; *mām*—Me; *tvam*—you; *manyase*—understand; *ayuktam*—without being made of; *bhūta*—material elements; *indriya*—material senses; *guṇa*—material modes; *ātmabhiḥ*—and false ego like the conditioned soul.

TRANSLATION

Although I am not easily knowable by the conditioned soul, you have known Me today because you know that My personality is not constituted of anything material, and specifically not of the five gross and three subtle elements.

PURPORT

Knowledge of the Supreme Absolute Truth does not necessitate negation of the material manifestation but understanding of spiritual existence as it is. To think that because material existence is realized in forms therefore spiritual existence must be formless is only a negative material conception of spirit. The real spiritual conception is that spiritual form is not material form. Brahmā appreciated the eternal form of the Lord in that way, and the Personality of Godhead approved of Brahmā's spiritual conception. In *Bhagavad-gītā* the Lord condemned the material conception of Kṛṣṇa's body which arises because He is apparently present like a man. The Lord may appear in any of His many, many spiritual forms, but He is not materially composed, nor has He any difference between body and self. That is the way of conceiving the spiritual form of the Lord.

TEXT 37

तुभ्यं मद्विचिकित्सायामात्मा मे दर्शितोऽबहिः ।
नालेन सलिले मूलं पुष्करस्य विचिन्वतः ॥३७॥

tubhyaṁ mad-vicikitsāyām
ātmā me darśito 'bahiḥ
nālena salile mūlaṁ
puṣkarasya vicinvataḥ

tubhyam—unto you; *mat*—Me; *vicikitsāyām*—on your trying to know; *ātmā*—self; *me*—of Myself; *darśitaḥ*—exhibited; *abahiḥ*—from within; *nālena*—through the stem; *salile*—in the water; *mūlam*—root; *puṣkarasya*—of the lotus, the primeval source; *vicinvataḥ*—contemplating.

TRANSLATION

When you were contemplating whether there was a source to the stem of the lotus of your birth and you even entered into that stem, you could not trace out anything. But at that time I manifested My form from within.

PURPORT

The Personality of Godhead can be experienced only by His causeless mercy, not by mental speculation or with the help of the material senses. Material senses cannot approach the transcendental understanding of the Supreme Personality of Godhead. He can be appreciated only by submissive devotional service when He reveals Himself before the devotee. Only by love of Godhead can one know God, and not otherwise. The Personality of Godhead cannot be seen with the material eyes, but He can be seen from within by spiritual eyes opened by the ointment of love of

Godhead. As long as one's spiritual eyes are closed due to the dirty covering of matter, one cannot see the Lord. But when the dirt is removed by the process of devotional service, one can see the Lord, without a doubt. Brahmā's personal endeavor to see the root of the lotus pipe failed, but when the Lord was satisfied by his penance and devotion, He revealed Himself from within with no external endeavor.

TEXT 38

यच्चकर्थाङ्ग मत्स्तोत्रं मत्कथाभ्युदयाङ्कितम् ।
यद्वा तपसि ते निष्ठा स एष मदनुग्रहः ॥३८॥

yac cakarthāṅga mat-stotraṁ
mat-kathābhyudayāṅkitam
yad vā tapasi te niṣṭhā
sa eṣa mad-anugrahaḥ

yat—that which; *cakartha*—performed; *aṅga*—O Brahmā; *mat-stotram*—prayers for Me; *mat-kathā*—words regarding My activities; *abhyudaya-aṅkitam*—enumerating My transcendental glories; *yat*—or that; *vā*—either; *tapasi*—in penance; *te*—your; *niṣṭhā*—faith; *saḥ*—that; *eṣaḥ*—all these; *mat*—My; *anugrahaḥ*—causeless mercy.

TRANSLATION

O Brahmā, the prayers that you have chanted praising the glories of My transcendental activities, the penances you have undertaken to understand Me, and your firm faith in Me—all these are to be considered My causeless mercy.

PURPORT

When a living entity desires to serve the Lord in transcendental loving service, the Lord helps the devotee in so many ways as the *caitya-guru*, or the spiritual master within, and thus the devotee can perform many wonderful activities beyond material estimation. By the mercy of the Lord even a layman can compose prayers of the highest spiritual perfection. Such spiritual perfection is not limited by material qualifications but is developed by dint of one's sincere endeavor to render transcendental service. Voluntary endeavor is the only qualification for spiritual perfection. Material acquisitions of wealth or education are not considered.

TEXT 39

प्रीतोऽहमस्तु भद्रं ते लोकानां विजयेच्छया ।
यदस्तौषीर्गुणमयं निर्गुणं मानुवर्णयन् ॥३९॥

prīto 'ham astu bhadraṁ te
lokānāṁ vijayecchayā
yad astauṣīr guṇamayaṁ
nirguṇaṁ mānuvarṇayan

prītaḥ—pleased; *aham*—Myself; *astu*—let it be so; *bhadram*—all benediction; *te*—unto you; *lokānām*—of the planets; *vijaya*—for glorification; *icchayā*—by your desire; *yat*—that which; *astauṣīḥ*—you prayed for; *guṇa-mayam*—describing all transcendental qualities; *nirguṇam*—although I am free from all material qualities; *mā*—Me; *anuvarṇayan*—nicely describing.

TRANSLATION

I am very much pleased by your description of Me in terms of My transcendental qualities, which appear mundane to the mundaners. I grant you all benedictions in your desire to glorify all the planets by your activities.

PURPORT

A pure devotee of the Lord like Brahmā and those in his line of disciplic succession always desire that the Lord be known all over the universe by each and every one of the living entities. That desire of the devotee is always blessed by the Lord. The impersonalist sometimes prays for the mercy of the Personality of Godhead Nārāyaṇa as the embodiment of material goodness, but such prayers do not satisfy the Lord because He is not thereby glorified in terms of His actual transcendental qualities. The pure devotees of the Lord are always most dear to Him, although He is always kind and merciful to all living entities. Here the word *guṇamayam* is significant because it indicates the Lord's possessing transcendental qualities.

TEXT 40

य एतेन पुमान्नित्यं स्तुत्वा स्तोत्रेण मां भजेत् ।
तस्याशु सम्प्रसीदेयं सर्वकामवरेश्वरः ॥४०॥

ya etena pumān nityaṁ
stutvā stotreṇa māṁ bhajet
tasyāśu samprasīdeyaṁ
sarva-kāma-vareśvaraḥ

yaḥ—anyone who; *etena*—by this; *pumān*—human being; *nityam*—regularly; *stutvā*—praying; *stotreṇa*—by the verses; *mām*—Me; *bhajet*—may worship; *tasya*—his; *āśu*—very soon; *samprasīdeyam*—I shall fulfill; *sarva*—all; *kāma*—desires; *vara-īśvaraḥ*—the Lord of all benediction.

TRANSLATION

Any human being who prays like Brahmā, and who thus worships Me, shall very soon be blessed with the fulfillment of all his desires, for I am the Lord of all benediction.

PURPORT

The prayers offered by Brahmā cannot be chanted by anyone who desires to fulfill his own sense gratification. Such prayers can be selected only by a person who wants to satisfy the Lord in His service. The Lord certainly fulfills all desires in regard to transcendental loving service, but He cannot fulfill the whims of nondevotees, even when such casual devotees offer Him the best of prayers.

TEXT 41

पूर्तेन तपसा यज्ञैर्दानैर्योगसमाधिना ।
राद्धं निःश्रेयसं पुंसां मत्प्रीतिस्तत्त्वविन्मतम् ॥४१॥

pūrtena tapasā yajñair
dānair yoga-samādhinā
rāddhaṁ niḥśreyasaṁ puṁsāṁ
mat-prītis tattvavin-matam

pūrtena—by traditional good work; *tapasā*—by penances; *yajñaiḥ*—by sacrifices; *dānaiḥ*—by charities; *yoga*—by mysticism; *samādhinā*—by trance; *rāddham*—success; *niḥśreyasam*—ultimately beneficial; *puṁsām*—of the human being; *mat*—of Me; *prītiḥ*—satisfaction; *tattva-vit*—expert transcendentalist; *matam*—opinion.

TRANSLATION

It is the opinion of expert transcendentalists that the ultimate goal of performing all traditional good works, penances, sacrifices, charities, mystic activities, trances, etc., is to invoke My satisfaction.

PURPORT

There are many traditionally pious activities in human society, such as altruism, philanthropy, nationalism, internationalism, charity, sacrifice, penance, and even meditation in trance, and all of them can be fully beneficial only when they lead to the satisfaction of the Supreme Personality of Godhead. The perfection of any activity—social, political, religious or philanthropic—is to satisfy the Supreme Lord. This secret of success is known to the devotee of the Lord, as exemplified by Arjuna on the Battlefield of Kurukṣetra. As a good, nonviolent man, Arjuna did not want to fight with his kinsmen, but when he understood that Kṛṣṇa wanted the fight and had arranged it at Kurukṣetra, he gave up his own satisfaction and fought for the satisfaction of the Lord. That is the right decision for all intelligent men. One's only concern should be to satisfy the Lord by one's activities. If the Lord is satisfied by an action, whatever it may be, then it is successful. Otherwise, it is simply a waste of time. That is the standard of all sacrifice, penance, austerity, mystic trance and other good and pious work.

TEXT 42

अहमात्मात्मनां धातः प्रेष्ठः सन् प्रेयसामपि ।
अतो मयि रतिं कुर्याद्देहादिर्यत्कृते प्रियः ॥४२॥

aham ātmātmanāṁ dhātaḥ
preṣṭhaḥ san preyasām api
ato mayi ratiṁ kuryād
dehādir yat-kṛte priyaḥ

aham—I am; *ātmā*—the Supersoul; *ātmanām*—of all other souls; *dhātaḥ*—director; *preṣṭhaḥ*—the dearest; *san*—being; *preyasām*—of all dear things; *api*—certainly; *ataḥ*—therefore; *mayi*—unto Me; *ratim*—attachment; *kuryāt*—one should do; *deha-ādiḥ*—the body and mind; *yat-kṛte*—on whose account; *priyaḥ*—very dear.

TRANSLATION

I am the Supersoul of every individual. I am the supreme director and the dearest. People are wrongly attached to the gross and subtle bodies, but they should be attached to Me only.

PURPORT

The Supreme Lord, the Personality of Godhead, is the dearest in both the conditioned and liberated states. When a person does not know that the Lord is the only dearmost object, then he is in the conditioned state of life, and when one knows perfectly well that the Lord is the only dearmost object, he is considered to be liberated. There are degrees of knowing one's relationship with the Lord, depending on the degree of realization as to why the Supreme Lord is the dearmost object of every living being. The real reason is clearly stated in *Bhagavad-gītā* (15.7). *Mamaivāṁśo jīva-loke jīva-bhūtaḥ sanātanaḥ:* the living entities are eternally parts and parcels of the Supreme Lord. The living entity is called the *ātmā*, and the Lord is called the Paramātmā. The living entity is called Brahman, and the Lord is called the Parabrahman, or the Parameśvara. *Īśvaraḥ paramaḥ kṛṣṇaḥ.* The conditioned souls, who do not have self-realization, accept the material body as the dearmost. The idea of the dearmost is then spread all over the body, both concentrated and extended. The attachment for one's own body and its extensions like children and relatives is actually developed on the basis of the real living entity. As soon as the real living entity is out of the body, even the body of the most dear son is no longer attractive. Therefore the living spark, or eternal part of the Supreme, is the real basis of affection, and not the body. Because the living entities are also parts of the whole living entity, that supreme living entity is the factual basis of affection for all. One who has forgotten the basic principle of his love for everything has only flickering love because he is in *māyā*. The more one is affected by the principle of *māyā*, the more he is detached from the basic principle of love. One cannot factually love anything unless he is fully developed in the loving service of the Lord.

In the present verse, stress is given to focusing love upon the Supreme Personality of Godhead. The word *kuryāt* is significant here. This means "one must have it." It is just to stress that we must have more and more attachment to the principle of love. The influence of *māyā* is experienced by the part and parcel spiritual entity, but it cannot influence the Supersoul, the Paramātmā. The Māyāvādī philosophers, accepting the influence of *māyā* on the living entity, want to become one with the Paramātmā. But because they have no actual love for Paramātmā, they remain ever entrapped by the influence of *māyā* and are unable to approach the vicinity of Paramātmā. This inability is due to their lack of affection for the Paramātmā. A rich miser does not know how to utilize his wealth, and therefore, in spite of his being very rich, his miserly behavior keeps him everlastingly a poor man. On the other hand, a person who knows how to utilize wealth can quickly become a rich man, even with a small credit balance.

The eyes and the sun are very intimately related because without sunlight the eyes are unable to see. But the other parts of the body, being attached to the sun as a source of warmth, take more advantage of the sun than do the eyes. Without possessing affection for the sun, the eyes cannot bear the rays of the sun; or, in other words, such eyes have no capacity to understand the utility of the sun's rays. Similarly, the empiric philosophers, despite their theoretical knowledge of Brahman, cannot utilize the mercy of the Supreme Brahman because they lack affection. So many impersonal philosophers remain everlastingly under the influence of *māyā* Lecause, although they indulge in theoretical knowledge of Brahman, they do not develop affection for Brahman nor do they have any scope for development of affection because of their defective method. A devotee of the sun-god, even though devoid of eyesight, can see the sun-god as he is even from this planet, whereas one who is not a devotee of the sun cannot even bear the glaring sunlight. Similarly, by devotional service, even though one is not on the level of a *jñānī*, one can see the Personality of Godhead within himself due to his development of pure love. In all circumstances one should try to develop love of Godhead, and that will solve all contending problems.

TEXT 43

सर्ववेदमयेनेदमात्मनात्मात्मयोनिना ।
प्रजाः सृज यथापूर्वं याश्च मय्यनुशेरते ॥४३॥

sarva-veda-mayenedam
ātmanātmātma-yoninā
prajāḥ sṛja yathā-pūrvaṁ
yāś ca mayy anuśerate

sarva—all; *veda-mayena*—under complete Vedic wisdom; *idam*—this; *ātmanā*—by the body; *ātmā*—you; *ātma-yoninā*—directly born of the Lord; *prajāḥ*—living entities; *sṛja*—generate; *yathā-pūrvam*—as it was hereinbefore; *yāḥ*—which; *ca*—also; *mayi*—in Me; *anuśerate*—lie.

TRANSLATION

By following My instructions you can now generate the living entities as before, by dint of your complete Vedic wisdom and the body you have directly received from Me, the supreme cause of everything.

TEXT 44

मैत्रेय उवाच
तस्मा एवं जगत्स्रष्ट्रे प्रधानपुरुषेश्वरः ।
व्यज्येदं स्वेन रूपेण कञ्जनाभस्तिरोदधे ॥४४॥

maitreya uvāca
tasmā evaṁ jagat-sraṣṭre
pradhāna-puruṣeśvaraḥ
vyajyedaṁ svena rūpeṇa
kañja-nābhas tirodadhe

maitreyaḥ uvāca—the sage Maitreya said; *tasmai*—unto him; *evam*—thus; *jagat-sraṣṭre*—unto the creator of the universe; *pradhāna-puruṣa-īśvaraḥ*—the primeval Lord, the Personality of Godhead; *vyajya idam*—after instructing this; *svena*—in His person; *rūpeṇa*—by the form; *kañja-nābhaḥ*—the Personality of Godhead Nārāyaṇa; *tirodadhe*—disappeared.

TRANSLATION

The sage Maitreya said: After instructing Brahmā, the creator of the universe, to expand, the primeval Lord, the Personality of Godhead in His personal form as Nārāyaṇa, disappeared.

PURPORT

Before his activity in creating the universe, Brahmā saw the Lord. That is the explanation of the *catuḥ-ślokī Bhāgavatam.* When the creation awaited Brahmā's activity, Brahmā saw the Lord, and therefore the Lord existed in His personal form before the creation. His eternal form is not created by the attempt of Brahmā, as imagined by less intelligent men. The Personality of Godhead appeared as He is before Brahmā, and He disappeared from him in the same form, which is not materially tinged.

Thus end the Bhaktivedanta purports of the Third Canto, Ninth Chapter, of the Śrīmad-Bhāgavatam, *entitled "Brahmā's Prayers for Creative Energy."*

CHAPTER TEN

Divisions of the Creation

TEXT 1

विदुर उवाच
अन्तर्हिते भगवति ब्रह्मा लोकपितामहः ।
प्रजाः ससर्ज कतिधा दैहिकीर्मानसीर्विभुः ॥ १ ॥

vidura uvāca
antarhite bhagavati
brahmā loka-pitāmahaḥ
prajāḥ sasarja katidhā
daihikīr mānasīr vibhuḥ

viduraḥ uvāca—Śrī Vidura said; *antarhite*—after the disappearance; *bhagavati*—of the Personality of Godhead; *brahmā*—the first created living being; *loka-pitāmahaḥ*—the grandfather of all planetary inhabitants; *prajāḥ*—generations; *sasarja*—created; *katidhāḥ*—how many; *daihikīḥ*—from his body; *mānasīḥ*—from his mind; *vibhuḥ*—the great.

TRANSLATION

Śrī Vidura said: O great sage, please let me know how Brahmā, the grandfather of the planetary inhabitants, created the bodies of the living entities from his own body and mind after the disappearance of the Supreme Personality of Godhead.

TEXT 2

ये च मे भगवन् पृष्टास्त्वय्यर्था बहुवित्तम ।
तान् वदस्वानुपूर्व्येण छिन्धि नः सर्वसंशयान् ॥२॥

ye ca me bhagavan pṛṣṭās
tvayy arthā bahuvittama

tān vadasvānupūrvyeṇa
chindhi naḥ sarva-saṁśayān

ye—all those; *ca*—also; *me*—by me; *bhagavan*—O powerful one; *pṛṣṭāḥ*—inquired; *tvayi*—unto you; *arthāḥ*—purpose; *bahu-vit-tama*—O greatly learned one; *tān*—all of them; *vadasva*—kindly describe; *ānupūrvyeṇa*—from beginning to end; *chindhi*—kindly eradicate; *naḥ*—my; *sarva*—all; *saṁśayān*—doubts.

TRANSLATION

O greatly learned one, kindly eradicate all my doubts, and let me know of all that I have inquired from you from the beginning to the end.

PURPORT

Vidura asked all relevant questions of Maitreya because he knew well that Maitreya was the right person to reply to all the points of his inquiries. One must be confident about the qualifications of his teacher; one should not approach a layman for replies to specific spiritual inquiries. Such inquiries, when replied to with imaginative answers by the teacher, are a program for wasting time.

TEXT 3

सूत उवाच
एवं सञ्चोदितस्तेन क्षत्त्रा कौषारविर्मुनिः ।
प्रीतः प्रत्याह तान् प्रश्नान् हृदिस्थानथ भार्गव ॥३॥

sūta uvāca
evaṁ sañcoditas tena
kṣattrā kauṣāravir muniḥ
prītaḥ pratyāha tān praśnān
hṛdi-sthān atha bhārgava

sūtaḥ uvāca—Śrī Sūta Gosvāmī said; *evam*—thus; *sañcoditaḥ*—being enlivened; *tena*—by him; *kṣattrā*—by Vidura; *kauṣāraviḥ*—the son of Kuṣāra; *muniḥ*—great sage; *prītaḥ*—being pleased; *pratyāha*—replied;

tān—those; *praśnān*—questions; *hṛdi-sthān*—from the core of his heart; *atha*—thus; *bhārgava*—O son of Bhṛgu.

TRANSLATION

Sūta Gosvāmī said: O son of Bhṛgu, the great sage Maitreya Muni, thus hearing from Vidura, felt very much enlivened. Everything was in his heart, and thus he began to reply to the questions one after another.

PURPORT

The phrase *sūta uvāca* ("Sūta Gosvāmī said") appears to indicate a break in the discourse between Mahārāja Parīkṣit and Śukadeva Gosvāmī. While Śukadeva Gosvāmī was speaking to Mahārāja Parīkṣit, Sūta Gosvāmī was only one member of a large audience. But Sūta Gosvāmī was speaking to the sages of Naimiṣāraṇya, headed by the sage Śaunaka, a descendant of Śukadeva Gosvāmī. This, however, does not make any substantial difference in the topics under discussion.

TEXT 4

मैत्रेय उवाच
विरिञ्चोऽपि तथा चक्रे दिव्यं वर्षशतं तपः ।
आत्मन्यात्मानमावेश्य यथाह भगवानजः ॥ ४ ॥

maitreya uvāca
viriñco 'pi tathā cakre
divyaṁ varṣa-śataṁ tapaḥ
ātmany ātmānam āveśya
yathāha bhagavān ajaḥ

maitreyaḥ uvāca—the great sage Maitreya said; *viriñcaḥ*—Brahmā; *api*—also; *tathā*—in that manner; *cakre*—performed; *divyam*—celestial; *varṣa-śatam*—one hundred years; *tapaḥ*—penances; *ātmani*—unto the Lord; *ātmānam*—his own self; *āveśya*—engaging; *yathā āha*—as it was spoken; *bhagavān*—the Personality of Godhead; *ajaḥ*—the unborn.

TRANSLATION

The greatly learned sage Maitreya said: O Vidura, Brahmā thus engaged himself in penances for one hundred celestial years, as advised by the Personality of Godhead, and applied himself in devotional service to the Lord.

PURPORT

That Brahmā engaged himself for the Personality of Godhead, Nārāyaṇa, means that he engaged himself in the service of the Lord; that is the highest penance one can perform for any number of years. There is no retirement from such service, which is eternal and ever encouraging.

TEXT 5

तद्विलोक्याब्जसम्भूतो वायुना यदधिष्ठितः ।
पद्ममम्भश्च तत्कालकृतवीर्येण कम्पितम् ॥ ५ ॥

tad vilokyābja-sambhūto
vāyunā yad-adhiṣṭhitaḥ
padmam ambhaś ca tat-kāla-
kṛta-vīryeṇa kampitam

tat vilokya—looking into that; *abja-sambhūtaḥ*—whose source of birth was a lotus; *vāyunā*—by the air; *yat*—that; *adhiṣṭhitaḥ*—on which he was situated; *padmam*—lotus; *ambhaḥ*—water; *ca*—also; *tat-kāla-kṛta*—which was effected by eternal time; *vīryeṇa*—by its inherent force; *kampitam*—trembling.

TRANSLATION

Thereafter Brahmā saw that both the lotus on which he was situated and the water on which the lotus was growing were trembling due to a strong, violent wind.

PURPORT

The material world is called illusory because it is a place of forgetfulness of the transcendental service of the Lord. Thus one engaged in the

the Lord's devotional service in the material world may sometimes be very much disturbed by awkward circumstances. There is a declaration of war between the two parties, the illusory energy and the devotee, and sometimes the weak devotees fall victim to the onslaught of the powerful illusory energy. Lord Brahmā, however, was sufficiently strong, by the causeless mercy of the Lord, and he could not be victimized by the material energy, although it gave him cause for anxiety when it managed to totter the existence of his position.

TEXT 6

तपसा ह्येधमानेन विद्यया चात्मसंस्थया ।
विवृद्धविज्ञानबलो न्यपाद् वायुं सहाम्भसा ॥ ६ ॥

tapasā hy edhamānena
vidyayā cātma-saṁsthayā
vivṛddha-vijñāna-balo
nyapād vāyuṁ sahāmbhasā

tapasā—by penance; *hi*—certainly; *edhamānena*—increasing; *vidyayā*—by transcendental knowledge; *ca*—also; *ātma*—self; *saṁsthayā*—situated in the self; *vivṛddha*—matured; *vijñāna*—practical knowledge; *balaḥ*—power; *nyapāt*—drank; *vāyum*—the wind; *saha ambhasā*—along with the water.

TRANSLATION

Long penance and transcendental knowledge of self-realization had matured Brahmā in practical knowledge, and thus he drank the wind completely, along with the water.

PURPORT

Lord Brahmā's struggle for existence is a personal example of the continued fight between the living entities in the material world and the illusory energy called *māyā*. Beginning from Brahmā down to this age, the living entities are struggling with the forces of material nature. By advanced knowledge in science and transcendental realization, one can try to control the material energy, which works against our endeavors, and in the modern age advanced material scientific knowledge and penance have played very wonderful roles in controlling the powers of the material energy. Such control of the material energy, however, can be most successfully carried out if one is a soul surrendered unto the Supreme Personality of Godhead and carries out His order in the spirit of loving transcendental service.

TEXT 7

तद्विलोक्य वियद्व्यापि पुष्करं यदधिष्ठितम् ।
अनेन लोकान् प्राग्लीनान् कल्पितास्मीत्यचिन्तयत् ॥ ७ ॥

tad vilokya viyad-vyāpi
puṣkaraṁ yad-adhiṣṭhitam
anena lokān prāg-līnān
kalpitāsmīty acintayat

tat vilokya—looking into that; *viyat-vyāpi*—extensively widespread; *puṣkaram*—the lotus; *yat*—that which; *adhiṣṭhitam*—he was situated; *anena*—by this; *lokān*—all the planets; *prāk-līnān*—previously merged in dissolution; *kalpitā asmi*—I shall create; *iti*—thus; *acintayat*—he thought.

TRANSLATION

Thereafter he saw that the lotus on which he was situated was spread throughout the universe, and he contemplated how to create all the planets, which were previously merged in that very same lotus.

PURPORT

The seeds of all the planets in the universe were impregnated in the lotus on which Brahmā was situated. All the planets were already generated by the Lord, and all the living entities were also born in Brahmā. The material world and the living entities were all already generated in seedling forms by the Supreme Personality of Godhead, and Brahmā was to disseminate the same seedlings all over the universe. The real creation is therefore called *sarga*, and, later on, the manifestation by Brahmā is called *visarga*.

TEXT 8

पद्मकोशं तदाविश्य भगवत्कर्मचोदितः ।
एकं व्यभाङ्क्षीदुरुधा त्रिधा भाव्यं द्विसप्तधा ॥ ८ ॥

padma-kośaṁ tadāviśya
bhagavat-karma-coditaḥ
ekaṁ vyabhāṅkṣīd urudhā
tridhā bhāvyaṁ dvi-saptadhā

padma-kośam—the whorl of the lotus; *tadā*—then; *āviśya*—entering into; *bhagavat*—by the Supreme Personality of Godhead; *karma*—in activities; *coditaḥ*—being encouraged by; *ekam*—one; *vyabhāṅkṣīt*—divided into; *urudhā*—great division; *tridhā*—three divisions; *bhāvyam*—capable of further creation; *dvi-saptadhā*—fourteen divisions.

TRANSLATION

Thus engaged in the service of the Supreme Personality of Godhead, Lord Brahmā entered into the whorl of the lotus, and as it spread all over the universe he divided it into three divisions of worlds and later into fourteen divisions.

TEXT 9

एतावाञ्जीवलोकस्य संस्थाभेदः समाहृतः ।
धर्मस्य ह्यनिमित्तस्य विपाकः परमेष्ठ्यसौ ॥ ९ ॥

etāvāñ jīva-lokasya
saṁsthā-bhedaḥ samāhṛtaḥ
dharmasya hy animittasya
vipākaḥ parameṣṭhy asau

etāvān—up to this; *jīva-lokasya*—of the planets inhabited by the living entities; *saṁsthā-bhedaḥ*—different situations of habitation; *samāhṛtaḥ*—performed completely; *dharmasya*—of religion; *hi*—certainly; *animittasya*—of causelessness; *vipākaḥ*—mature stage; *parameṣṭhī*—the highest personality in the universe; *asau*—that.

TRANSLATION

Lord Brahmā is the most exalted personality in the universe because of his causeless devotional service unto the Lord in mature transcendental knowledge. He therefore created all the fourteen planetary divisions for inhabitation by the different types of living entities.

PURPORT

The Supreme Lord is the reservoir of all the qualities of the living entities. The conditioned souls in the material world reflect only part of those qualities, and therefore they are sometimes called *pratibimbas.* These *pratibimba* living entities, as parts and parcels of the Supreme Lord, have inherited different proportions of His original qualities, and in terms of their inheritance of these qualities, they appear as different species of life and are accommodated in different planets according to the plan of Brahmā. Brahmā is the creator of the three worlds, namely the lower planets, called the Pātālalokas, the middle planets, called the Bhūrlokas, and the upper planets, called the Svarlokas. Still higher planets, such as Maharloka, Tapoloka, Satyaloka and Brahmaloka, do not dissolve in the devastating water. This is because of the causeless devotional service rendered unto the Lord by their inhabitants, whose existence continues up to the end of *dvi-parārdha* time, when they are generally liberated from the chain of birth and death in the material world.

TEXT 10

विदुर उवाच

यथात्थ बहुरूपस्य हरेरद्भुतकर्मणः ।
कालाख्यं लक्षणं ब्रह्मन् यथा वर्णय नः प्रभो ॥१०॥

vidura uvāca
yathāttha bahu-rūpasya
harer adbhuta-karmaṇaḥ
kālākhyaṁ lakṣaṇaṁ brahman
yathā varṇaya naḥ prabho

viduraḥ uvāca—Vidura said; *yathā*—as; *āttha*—you have said; *bahu-rūpasya*—having varieties of forms; *hareḥ*—of the Lord;

adbhuta—wonderful; *karmaṇaḥ*—of the actor; *kāla*—time; *ākhyam*—of the name; *lakṣaṇam*—symptoms; *brahman*—O learned *brāhmaṇa;* *yathā*—as it is; *varṇaya*—please describe; *naḥ*—unto us; *prabho*—O lord.

TRANSLATION

Vidura inquired from Maitreya: O my lord, O greatly learned sage, kindly describe eternal time, which is another form of the Supreme Lord, the wonderful actor. What are the symptoms of that eternal time? Please describe them to us in detail.

PURPORT

The complete universe is a manifestation of varieties of entities, beginning from the atoms up to the gigantic universe itself, and all is under the control of the Supreme Lord in His form of *kāla*, or eternal time. The controlling time has different dimensions in relation to particular physical embodiments. There is a time for atomic dissolution and a time for the universal dissolution. There is a time for the annihilation of the body of the human being, and there is a time for the annihilation of the universal body. Also, growth, development and resultant actions all depend on the time factor. Vidura wanted to know in detail the different physical manifestations and their times of annihilation.

TEXT 11

मैत्रेय उवाच
गुणव्यतिकराकारो निर्विशेषोऽप्रतिष्ठितः ।
पुरुषस्तदुपादानमात्मानं लीलयासृजत् ॥११॥

maitreya uvāca
guṇa-vyatikarākāro
nirviśeṣo 'pratiṣṭhitaḥ
puruṣas tad-upādānam
ātmānaṁ līlayāsṛjat

maitreyaḥ uvāca—Maitreya said; *guṇa-vyatikara*—of the interactions of the modes of material nature; *ākāraḥ*—source; *nirviśeṣaḥ*—

without diversity; *apratiṣṭhitaḥ*—unlimited; *puruṣaḥ*—of the Supreme Person; *tat*—that; *upādānam*—instrument; *ātmānam*—the material creation; *līlayā*—by pastimes; *asṛjat*—created.

TRANSLATION

Maitreya said: Eternal time is the primeval source of the interactions of the three modes of material nature. It is unchangeable and limitless, and it works as the instrument of the Supreme Personality of Godhead for His pastimes in the material creation.

PURPORT

The impersonal time factor is the background of the material manifestation as the instrument of the Supreme Lord. It is the ingredient of assistance offered to material nature. No one knows where time began and where it ends, and it is time only which can keep a record of the creation, maintenance and destruction of the material manifestation. This time factor is the material cause of creation and is therefore a self-expansion of the Personality of Godhead. Time is considered the impersonal feature of the Lord.

The time factor is also explained by modern men in various ways. Some accept it almost as it is explained in the *Śrīmad-Bhāgavatam*. For example, in Hebrew literature time is accepted, in the same spirit, as a representation of God. It is stated therein: "God, who at sundry times and in diverse manners spake in time past unto the fathers by the prophets. . . ." Metaphysically, time is distinguished as absolute and real. Absolute time is continuous and is unaffected by the speed or slowness of material things. Time is astronomically and mathematically calculated in relation to the speed, change and life of a particular object. Factually, however, time has nothing to do with the relativities of things; rather, everything is shaped and calculated in terms of the facility offered by time. Time is the basic measurement of the activity of our senses, by which we calculate past, present and future; but in factual calculation, time has no beginning and no end. Paṇḍita Cāṇakya says that even a slight fraction of time cannot be purchased with millions of dollars, and therefore even a moment of time lost without profit must be calculated as the greatest loss in life. Time is not subject to any form of psychology, nor are the moments objective realities in themselves, but they are dependent on particular experiences.

Therefore, Śrīla Jīva Gosvāmī concludes that the time factor is intermixed with the activities—actions and reactions—of the external energy of the Lord. The external energy, or material nature, works under the superintendence of the time factor as the Lord Himself, and that is why material nature appears to have produced so many wonderful things in the cosmic manifestation. *Bhagavad-gītā* (9.10) confirms this conclusion as follows:

mayādhyakṣeṇa prakṛtiḥ
sūyate sa-carācaram
hetunānena kaunteya
jagad viparivartate

TEXT 12

विश्वं वै ब्रह्मतन्मात्रं संस्थितं विष्णुमायया ।
ईश्वरेण परिच्छिन्नं कालेनाव्यक्तमूर्तिना ॥१२॥

viśvaṁ vai brahma-tan-mātraṁ
saṁsthitaṁ viṣṇu-māyayā
īśvareṇa paricchinnaṁ
kālenāvyakta-mūrtinā

viśvam—the material phenomenon; *vai*—certainly; *brahma*—the Supreme; *tat-mātram*—the same as; *saṁsthitam*—situated; *viṣṇu-māyayā*—by the energy of Viṣṇu; *īśvareṇa*—by the Personality of Godhead; *paricchinnam*—separated; *kālena*—by the eternal time; *avyakta*—unmanifested; *mūrtinā*—by such a feature.

TRANSLATION

This cosmic manifestation is separated from the Supreme Lord as material energy by means of kāla, which is the unmanifested, impersonal feature of the Lord. It is situated as the objective manifestation of the Lord under the influence of the same material energy of Viṣṇu.

PURPORT

As stated previously by Nārada before Vyāsadeva (*Bhāg.* 1.5.20), *idaṁ hi viśvaṁ bhagavān ivetaraḥ:* this unmanifested world is the selfsame Personality of Godhead, but it appears to be something else beyond or besides the Lord. It appears so because of its being separated from the Lord by means of *kāla.* It is something like the tape-recorded voice of a person who is now separated from the voice. As the tape recording is situated on the tape, so the whole cosmic manifestation is situated on the material energy and appears separate by means of *kāla.* The material manifestation is therefore the objective manifestation of the Supreme Lord and exhibits His impersonal feature so much adored by impersonalist philosophers.

TEXT 13

यथेदानीं तथाग्रे च पश्चादप्येतदीदृशम् ॥१३॥

yathedānīṁ tathāgre ca
paścād apy etad īdṛśam

yathā—as it is; *idānīm*—at present; *tathā*—so it was; *agre*—in the beginning; *ca*—and; *paścāt*—at the end; *api*—also; *etat īdṛśam*—it continues to be the same.

TRANSLATION

This cosmic manifestation is as it is now, it was the same in the past, and it will continue in the same way in the future.

PURPORT

There is a systematic schedule for the perpetual manifestation, maintenance and annihilation of the material world, as stated in *Bhagavad-gītā* (9.8): *bhūta-grāmam imaṁ kṛtsnam avaśaṁ prakṛter vaśāt.* As it is created now and as it will be destroyed later on, so also it existed in the past and again will be created, maintained and destroyed in due course of time. Therefore, the systematic activities of the time factor are perpetual and eternal and cannot be stated to be false. The manifestation is temporary and occasional, but it is not false as claimed by the Māyāvādī philosophers.

TEXT 14

सर्गो नवविधस्तस्य प्राकृतो वैकृतस्तु यः ।
कालद्रव्यगुणैरस्य त्रिविधः प्रतिसंक्रमः ॥१४॥

sargo nava-vidhas tasya
prākṛto vaikṛtas tu yaḥ
kāla-dravya-guṇair asya
tri-vidhaḥ pratisaṅkramaḥ

sargaḥ—creation; *nava-vidhaḥ*—of nine different kinds; *tasya*—its; *prākṛtaḥ*—material; *vaikṛtaḥ*—by the modes of material nature; *tu*—but; *yaḥ*—that which; *kāla*—eternal time; *dravya*—matter; *guṇaiḥ*—qualities; *asya*—its; *tri-vidhaḥ*—three kinds; *pratisaṅkramaḥ*—annihilation.

TRANSLATION

There are nine different kinds of creations besides the one which naturally occurs due to the interactions of the modes. There are three kinds of annihilations due to eternal time, the material elements and the quality of one's work.

PURPORT

The scheduled creations and annihilations take place in terms of the supreme will. There are other creations due to interactions of material elements which take place by the intelligence of Brahmā. Later these will be more explicitly explained. At present, only preliminary information is given. The three kinds of annihilations are (1) due to the scheduled time of the annihilation of the entire universe, (2) due to a fire which emanates from the mouth of Ananta, and (3) due to one's qualitative actions and reactions.

TEXT 15

आद्यस्तु महतः सर्गो गुणवैषम्यमात्मनः ।
द्वितीयस्त्वहमो यत्र द्रव्यज्ञानक्रियोदयः ॥१५॥

ādyas tu mahataḥ sargo
guṇa-vaiṣamyam ātmanaḥ

dvitīyas tv ahamo yatra
dravya-jñāna-kriyodayaḥ

ādyaḥ—the first; *tu*—but; *mahataḥ*—of the total emanation from the Lord; *sargaḥ*—creation; *guṇa-vaiṣamyam*—interaction of the material modes; *ātmanaḥ*—of the Supreme; *dvitīyaḥ*—the second; *tu*—but; *ahamaḥ*—false ego; *yatra*—wherein; *dravya*—material ingredients; *jñāna*—material knowledge; *kriyā-udayaḥ*—awakening of activities (work).

TRANSLATION

Of the nine creations, the first one is the creation of the mahat-tattva, or the sum total of the material ingredients, wherein the modes interact due to the presence of the Supreme Lord. In the second, the false ego is generated in which the material ingredients, material knowledge and material activities arise.

PURPORT

The first emanation from the Supreme Lord for material creation is called the *mahat-tattva.* The interaction of the material modes is the cause of false identification, or the sense that a living being is made of material elements. This false ego is the cause of identifying the body and mind with the soul proper. Material resources and the capacity and knowledge to work are all generated in the second term of creation, after the *mahat-tattva. Jñāna* indicates the senses which are sources of knowledge, and their controlling deities. Work entails the working organs and their controlling deities. All these are generated in the second creation.

TEXT 16

भूतसर्गस्तृतीयस्तु तन्मात्रो द्रव्यशक्तिमान् ।
चतुर्थ ऐन्द्रियः सर्गो यस्तु ज्ञानक्रियात्मकः ॥ १६ ॥

bhūta-sargas tṛtīyas tu
tan-mātro dravya-śaktimān

caturtha aindriyaḥ sargo
yas tu jñāna-kriyātmakaḥ

bhūta-sargaḥ—creation of matter; *tṛtīyaḥ*—is the third; *tu*—but; *tat-mātraḥ*—sense perception; *dravya*—of the elements; *śaktimān*—generator; *caturthaḥ*—the fourth; *aindriyaḥ*—in the matter of the senses; *sargaḥ*—creation; *yaḥ*—that which; *tu*—but; *jñāna*—knowledge-acquiring; *kriyā*—working; *ātmakaḥ*—basically.

TRANSLATION

The sense perceptions are created in the third creation, and from these the elements are generated. The fourth creation is the creation of knowledge and of working capacity.

TEXT 17

वैकारिको देवसर्गः पञ्चमो यन्मयं मनः ।
षष्ठस्तु तमसः सर्गो यस्त्वबुद्धिकृतः प्रभोः॥१७॥

vaikāriko deva-sargaḥ
pañcamo yan-mayaṁ manaḥ
ṣaṣṭhas tu tamasaḥ sargo
yas tv abuddhi-kṛtaḥ prabhoḥ

vaikārikaḥ—interaction of the mode of goodness; *deva*—the demigods, or controlling deities; *sargaḥ*—creation; *pañcamaḥ*—fifth; *yat*—that which; *mayam*—sum total; *manaḥ*—mind; *ṣaṣṭhaḥ*—sixth; *tu*—but; *tamasaḥ*—of darkness; *sargaḥ*—creation; *yaḥ*—that which; *tu*—expletive; *abuddhi-kṛtaḥ*—made foolish; *prabhoḥ*—of the master.

TRANSLATION

The fifth creation is that of the controlling deities by the interaction of the mode of goodness, of which the mind is the sum total. The sixth creation is the ignorant darkness of the living entity, by which the master acts as a fool.

PURPORT

The demigods in the higher planets are called *devas* because they are all devotees of Lord Viṣṇu. *Viṣṇu-bhaktaḥ smṛto daiva āsuras tad-viparyayaḥ:* all the devotees of Lord Viṣṇu are *devas*, or demigods, whereas all others are *asuras*. That is the division of the *devas* and the *asuras*. *Devas* are situated in the mode of goodness of material nature, whereas the *asuras* are situated in the modes of passion or ignorance. The demigods, or controlling deities, are entrusted with departmental management of all the different functions of the material world. For example, one of our sense organs, the eye, is controlled by light, light is distributed by the sun rays, and their controlling deity is the sun. Similarly, mind is controlled by the moon. All other senses, both for working and for acquiring knowledge, are controlled by the different demigods. The demigods are assistants of the Lord in the management of material affairs.

After the creation of the demigods, all entities are covered by the darkness of ignorance. Each and every living being in the material world is conditioned by his mentality of lording it over the resources of material nature. Although a living entity is the master of the material world, he is conditioned by ignorance, by the false impression of being the proprietor of material things.

The energy of the Lord called *avidyā* is the bewildering factor of the conditioned souls. The material nature is called *avidyā*, or ignorance, but to the devotees of the Lord engaged in pure devotional service, this energy becomes *vidyā*, or pure knowledge. This is confirmed in *Bhagavad-gītā.* The energy of the Lord transforms from *mahāmāyā* to *yogamāyā* and appears to pure devotees in her real feature. The material nature therefore appears to function in three phases: as the creative principle of the material world, as ignorance and as knowledge. As disclosed in the previous verse, in the fourth creation the power of knowledge is also created. The conditioned souls are not originally fools, but by the influence of the *avidyā* function of material nature they are made fools, and thus they are unable to utilize knowledge in the proper channel.

By the influence of darkness, the conditioned soul forgets his relationship with the Supreme Lord and is overwhelmed by attachment, hatred, pride, ignorance and false identification, the five kinds of illusion that cause material bondage.

TEXT 18

षडिमे प्राकृताः सर्गा वैकृतानपि मे शृणु ।
रजोभाजो भगवतो लीलेयं हरिमेधसः ॥१८॥

ṣaḍ ime prākṛtāḥ sargā
vaikṛtān api me śṛṇu
rajo-bhājo bhagavato
līleyaṁ hari-medhasaḥ

ṣaṭ—six; *ime*—all these; *prākṛtāḥ*—of the material energy; *sargāḥ*—creations; *vaikṛtān*—secondary creations by Brahmā; *api*—also; *me*—from me; *śṛṇu*—just hear; *rajaḥ-bhājaḥ*—of the incarnation of the mode of passion (Brahmā); *bhagavataḥ*—of the greatly powerful; *līlā*—pastime; *iyam*—this; *hari*—the Supreme Personality of Godhead; *medhasaḥ*—of one who has such a brain.

TRANSLATION

All the above are natural creations by the external energy of the Lord. Now hear from me about the creations by Brahmā, who is an incarnation of the mode of passion and who, in the matter of creation, has a brain like that of the Personality of Godhead.

TEXT 19

सप्तमो मुख्यसर्गस्तु षड्विधस्तस्थुषां च यः ।
वनस्पत्योषधिलतात्वक्सारा वीरुधो द्रुमाः ॥१९॥

saptamo mukhya-sargas tu
ṣaḍ-vidhas tasthuṣāṁ ca yaḥ
vanaspaty-oṣadhi-latā-
tvaksārā vīrudho drumāḥ

saptamaḥ—the seventh; *mukhya*—principle; *sargaḥ*—creation; *tu*—indeed; *ṣaṭ-vidhaḥ*—six kinds of; *tasthuṣām*—of those who do not move; *ca*—also; *yaḥ*—those; *vanaspati*—fruit trees without flowers; *oṣadhi*—trees and plants existing until the fruit is ripe; *latā*—creepers;

tvaksārāḥ—pipe plants; *vīrudhaḥ*—creepers without support; *drumāḥ*—trees with flowers and fruits.

TRANSLATION

The seventh creation is that of the immovable entities, which are of six kinds: the fruit trees without flowers, trees and plants which exist until the fruit is ripe, creepers, pipe plants, creepers which have no support, and trees with flowers and fruits.

TEXT 20

उत्स्रोतसस्तमःप्राया अन्तःस्पर्शा विशेषिणः ॥२०॥

utsrotasas tamaḥ-prāyā
antaḥ-sparśā viśeṣiṇaḥ

utsrotasaḥ—they seek their subsistence upwards; *tamaḥ-prāyāḥ*—almost unconscious; *antaḥ-sparśāḥ*—slightly feeling within; *viśeṣiṇaḥ*—with varieties of manifestation.

TRANSLATION

All the immovable trees and plants seek their subsistence upwards. They are almost unconscious but have feelings of pain within. They are manifested in variegatedness.

TEXT 21

तिरश्चामष्टमः सर्गः सोऽष्टाविंशद्विधो मतः ।
अविदो भूरितमसो घ्राणज्ञा हृद्यवेदिनः ॥२१॥

tiraścām aṣṭamaḥ sargaḥ
so 'ṣṭāviṁśad-vidho mataḥ
avido bhūri-tamaso
ghrāṇa-jñā hṛdy avedinaḥ

tiraścām—species of lower animals; *aṣṭamaḥ*—the eighth; *sargaḥ*—creation; *saḥ*—they are; *aṣṭāviṁśat*—twenty-eight; *vidhaḥ*—varieties; *mataḥ*—considered; *avidaḥ*—without knowledge of tomorrow; *bhūri*—

extensively; *tamasaḥ*—ignorant; *ghrāṇa-jñāḥ*—can know desirables by smell; *hṛdi avedinaḥ*—can remember very little in the heart.

TRANSLATION

The eighth creation is that of the lower species of life, and they are of different varieties, numbering twenty-eight. They are all extensively foolish and ignorant. They know their desirables by smell, but are unable to remember anything within the heart.

PURPORT

In the *Vedas* the symptoms of the lower animals are described as follows: *athetareṣāṁ paśūnāḥ aśanāpipāse evābhivijñānaṁ na vijñātaṁ vadanti na vijñātaṁ paśyanti na viduḥ śvastanaṁ na lokālokāv iti; yad vā, bhūri-tamaso bahu-ruṣaḥ ghrāṇenaiva jānanti hṛdyaṁ prati svapriyaṁ vastv eva vindanti bhojana-śayanādy-arthaṁ gṛhṇanti.* "Lower animals have knowledge only of their hunger and thirst. They have no acquired knowledge, no vision. Their behavior exhibits no dependence on formalities. Extensively ignorant, they can know their desirables only by smell, and by such intelligence only can they understand what is favorable and unfavorable. Their knowledge is concerned only with eating and sleeping." Therefore, even the most ferocious lower animals, such as tigers, can be tamed simply by regularly supplying meals and accommodations for sleeping. Only snakes cannot be tamed by such an arrangement.

TEXT 22

गौरजो महिषः कृष्णः सूकरो गवयो रुरुः ।
द्विशफाः पशवश्चेमे अविरुष्ट्रश्च सत्तम ॥२२॥

gaur ajo mahiṣaḥ kṛṣṇaḥ
sūkaro gavayo ruruḥ
dvi-śaphāḥ paśavaś ceme
avir uṣṭraś ca sattama

gauḥ—the cow; *ajaḥ*—the goat; *mahiṣaḥ*—the buffalo; *kṛṣṇaḥ*—a kind of stag; *sūkaraḥ*—hog; *gavayaḥ*—a species of animal; *ruruḥ*—

deer; *dvi-śaphāḥ*—having two hooves; *paśavaḥ*—animals; *ca*—also; *ime*—all these; *aviḥ*—lamb; *uṣṭraḥ*—camel; *ca*—and; *sattama*—O purest.

TRANSLATION

O purest Vidura, of the lower animals the cow, goat, buffalo, kṛṣṇa-stag, hog, gavaya animal, deer, lamb and camel all have two hooves.

TEXT 23

खरोऽश्वोऽश्वतरो गौरः शरभश्चमरी तथा ।
एते चैकशफाः क्षत्तः शृणु पञ्चनखान् पशून् ॥२३॥

kharo 'śvo 'śvataro gauraḥ
śarabhaś camarī tathā
ete caika-śaphāḥ kṣattaḥ
śṛṇu pañca-nakhān paśūn

kharaḥ—ass; *aśvaḥ*—horse; *aśvataraḥ*—mule; *gauraḥ*—white deer; *śarabhaḥ*—bison; *camarī*—wild cow; *tathā*—thus; *ete*—all these; *ca*—and; *eka*—only one; *śaphāḥ*—hoof; *kṣattaḥ*—O Vidura; *śṛṇu*—just hear now; *pañca*—five; *nakhān*—nails; *paśūn*—animals.

TRANSLATION

The horse, mule, ass, gaura, śarabha bison and wild cow all have only one hoof. Now you may hear from me about the animals who have five nails.

TEXT 24

श्वा सृगालो वृको व्याघ्रो मार्जारः शशशल्लकौ ।
सिंहः कपिर्गजः कूर्मो गोधा च मकरादयः ॥२४॥

śvā sṛgālo vṛko vyāghro
mārjāraḥ śaśa-śallakau
siṁhaḥ kapir gajaḥ kūrmo
godhā ca makarādayaḥ

śvā—dog; *sṛgālaḥ*—jackal; *vṛkaḥ*—fox; *vyāghraḥ*—tiger; *mārjāraḥ*—cat; *śaśa*—rabbit; *śallakau*—*sajāru* (with thorns on the body); *siṁhaḥ*—lion; *kapiḥ*—monkey; *gajaḥ*—elephant; *kūrmaḥ*—tortoise; *godhā*—*gosāpa* (snake with four legs); *ca*—also; *makara-ādayaḥ*—the alligator and others.

TRANSLATION

The dog, jackal, tiger, fox, cat, rabbit, sajāru, lion, monkey, elephant, tortoise, alligator, gosāpa, etc., all have five nails in their claws. They are known as pañca-nakhas, or animals having five nails.

TEXT 25

कङ्कगृध्रबककश्येनभासभल्लूकबर्हिणः ।
हंससारसचक्राह्वकाकोलूकादयः खगाः ॥२५॥

kaṅka-gṛdhra-baka-śyena-
bhāsa-bhallūka-barhiṇaḥ
haṁsa-sārasa-cakrāhva-
kākolūkādayaḥ khagāḥ

kaṅka—heron; *gṛdhra*—vulture; *baka*—crane; *śyena*—hawk; *bhāsa*—the *bhāsa; bhallūka*—the *bhallūka; barhiṇaḥ*—the peacock; *haṁsa*—swan; *sārasa*—the *sārasa; cakrāhva*—the *cakravāka; kāka*—crow; *ulūka*—owl; *ādayaḥ*—and others; *khagāḥ*—the birds.

TRANSLATION

The heron, vulture, crane, hawk, bhāsa, bhallūka, peacock, swan, sārasa, cakravāka, crow, owl and others are the birds.

TEXT 26

अर्वाक्स्रोतस्तु नवमः क्षत्तरेकविधो नृणाम् ।
रजोऽधिकाः कर्मपरा दुःखे च सुखमानिनः ॥२६॥

arvāk-srotas tu navamaḥ
kṣattar eka-vidho nṛṇām

rajo 'dhikāḥ karma-parā
duḥkhe ca sukha-māninaḥ

arvāk—downwards; *srotaḥ*—passage of food; *tu*—but; *navamaḥ*—the ninth; *kṣattaḥ*—O Vidura; *eka-vidhaḥ*—one species; *nṛṇām*—of human beings; *rajaḥ*—the mode of passion; *adhikāḥ*—very prominent; *karma-parāḥ*—interested in working; *duḥkhe*—in misery; *ca*—but; *sukha*—happiness; *māninaḥ*—thinking.

TRANSLATION

The creation of the human beings, who are of one species only and who stock their eatables in the belly, is the ninth in the rotation. In the human race, the mode of passion is very prominent. Humans are always busy in the midst of miserable life, but they think themselves happy in all respects.

PURPORT

The human being is more passionate than the animals, and thus the sex life of the human being is more irregular. The animals have their due time for sexual intercourse, but the human being has no regular time for such activities. The human being is endowed with a higher, advanced stage of consciousness for getting relief from the existence of material miseries, but due to his ignorance he thinks that his higher consciousness is meant for advancing in the material comforts of life. Thus his intelligence is misused in the animal propensities—eating, sleeping, defending and mating—instead of spiritual realization. By advancing in material comforts the human being puts himself into a more miserable condition, but, illusioned by the material energy, he always thinks himself happy, even while in the midst of misery. Such misery of human life is distinct from the natural comfortable life enjoyed even by the animals.

TEXT 27

वैकृतास्त्रय एवैते देवसर्गश्च सत्तम ।
वैकारिकस्तु यः प्रोक्तः कौमारस्तूभयात्मकः ॥२७॥

vaikṛtās traya evaite
deva-sargaś ca sattama
vaikārikas tu yaḥ proktaḥ
kaumāras tūbhayātmakaḥ

vaikṛtāḥ—creations of Brahmā; *trayaḥ*—three kinds; *eva*—certainly; *ete*—all these; *deva-sargaḥ*—appearance of the demigods; *ca*—also; *sattama*—O good Vidura; *vaikārikaḥ*—creation of demigods by nature; *tu*—but; *yaḥ*—which; *proktaḥ*—described before; *kaumāraḥ*—the four Kumāras; *tu*—but; *ubhaya-ātmakaḥ*—both ways (namely *vaikṛta* and *prākṛta*).

TRANSLATION

O good Vidura, these last three creations and the creation of demigods (the tenth creation) are vaikṛta creations, which are different from the previously described prākṛta (natural) creations. The appearance of the Kumāras is both.

TEXTS 28–29

देवसर्गश्चाष्टविधो विबुधाः पितरोऽसुराः ।
गन्धर्वाप्सरसः सिद्धा यक्षरक्षांसि चारणाः ॥२८॥
भूतप्रेतपिशाचाश्च विद्याध्राः किन्नरादयः ।
दशैते विदुराख्याताः सर्गास्ते विश्वसृक्कृताः ॥२९॥

deva-sargaś cāṣṭa-vidho
vibudhāḥ pitaro 'surāḥ
gandharvāpsarasaḥ siddhā
yakṣa-rakṣāṁsi cāraṇāḥ

bhūta-preta-piśācāś ca
vidyādhrāḥ kinnarādayaḥ
daśaite vidurākhyātāḥ
sargās te viśva-sṛk-kṛtāḥ

deva-sargaḥ—creation of the demigods; *ca*—also; *aṣṭa-vidhaḥ*—eight kinds; *vibudhāḥ*—the demigods; *pitaraḥ*—the forefathers; *asurāḥ*—the demons; *gandharva*—the expert artisans in the higher planets; *apsarasaḥ*—the angels; *siddhāḥ*—persons who are perfect in mystic powers; *yakṣa*—the superprotectors; *rakṣāṁsi*—giants; *cāraṇāḥ*—the celestial singers; *bhūta*—jinn; *preta*—evil spirits; *piśācāḥ*—attendant spirits; *ca*—also; *vidyādhrāḥ*—the celestial denizens named Vidyādharas; *kinnara*—superhuman beings; *ādayaḥ*—and others; *daśa ete*—all these ten (creations); *vidura*—O Vidura; *ākhyātāḥ*—described; *sargāḥ*—creations; *te*—unto you; *viśva-sṛk*—the creator of the universe (Brahmā); *kṛtāḥ*—done by him.

TRANSLATION

The creation of the demigods is of eight varieties: (1) the demigods, (2) the forefathers, (3) the asuras, or demons, (4) the Gandharvas and Apsarās, or angels, (5) the Yakṣas and Rākṣasas, (6) the Siddhas, Cāraṇas and Vidyādharas, (7) the Bhūtas, Pretas and Piśācas, and (8) the superhuman beings, celestial singers, etc. All are created by Brahmā, the creator of the universe.

PURPORT

As explained in the Second Canto of *Śrīmad-Bhāgavatam*, the Siddhas are inhabitants of Siddhaloka, where the residents travel in space without vehicles. At their mere will they can pass from one planet to another without difficulty. Therefore, in the upper planets the inhabitants are far superior to the inhabitants of this planet in all matters of art, culture and science, since they possess brains superior to those of human beings. The spirits and jinn mentioned in this connection are also counted among the demigods because they are able to perform uncommon functions not possible for men.

TEXT 30

अतः परं प्रवक्ष्यामि वंशान्मन्वन्तराणि च ।
एवं रजःप्लुतः स्रष्टा कल्पादिष्वात्मभूर्हरिः ।
सृजत्यमोघसङ्कल्प आत्मैवात्मानमात्मना ॥३०॥

ataḥ paraṁ pravakṣyāmi
vaṁśān manvantarāṇi ca

evaṁ rajaḥ-plutaḥ sraṣṭā
kalpādiṣv ātmabhūr hariḥ
sṛjaty amogha-saṅkalpa
ātmaivātmānam ātmanā

ataḥ—here; *param*—after; *pravakṣyāmi*—I shall explain; *vaṁśān*—descendants; *manvantarāṇi*—different advents of Manus; *ca*—and; *evam*—thus; *rajaḥ-plutaḥ*—infused with the mode of passion; *sraṣṭā*—the creator; *kalpa-ādiṣu*—in different millenniums; *ātma-bhūḥ*—self-advent; *hariḥ*—the Personality of Godhead; *sṛjati*—creates; *amogha*—unfailing; *saṅkalpaḥ*—determination; *ātmā eva*—He Himself; *ātmānam*—Himself; *ātmanā*—by His own energy.

TRANSLATION

Now I shall describe the descendants of the Manus. The creator, Brahmā, as the incarnation of the passion mode of the Personality of Godhead, creates the universal affairs with unfailing desires in every millennium by the force of the Lord's energy.

PURPORT

The cosmic manifestation is an expansion of one of the many energies of the Supreme Personality of Godhead; the creator and the created are both emanations of the same Supreme Truth, as stated in the beginning of the *Bhāgavatam: janmādy asya yataḥ.*

Thus end the Bhaktivedanta purports of the Third Canto, Tenth Chapter, of the Śrīmad-Bhāgavatam, *entitled "Divisions of the Creation."*

CHAPTER ELEVEN

Calculation of Time, From the Atom

TEXT 1

मैत्रेय उवाच
चरमः सद्विशेषाणामनेकोऽसंयुतः सदा ।
परमाणुः स विज्ञेयो नृणामैक्यभ्रमो यतः

maitreya uvāca
caramaḥ sad-viśeṣāṇām
aneko 'saṁyutaḥ sadā
paramāṇuḥ sa vijñeyo
nṛṇām aikya-bhramo yataḥ

maitreyaḥ uvāca—Maitreya said; *caramaḥ*—ultimate; *sat*—effect; *viśeṣāṇām*—symptoms; *anekaḥ*—innumerable; *asaṁyutaḥ*—unmixed; *sadā*—always; *parama-aṇuḥ*—atoms; *saḥ*—that; *vijñeyaḥ*—should be understood; *nṛṇām*—of men; *aikya*—oneness; *bhramaḥ*—mistaken; *yataḥ*—from which.

TRANSLATION

The material manifestation's ultimate particle, which is indivisible and not formed into a body, is called the atom. It exists always as an invisible identity, even after the dissolution of all forms. The material body is but a combination of such atoms, but it is misunderstood by the common man.

PURPORT

The atomic description of the *Śrīmad-Bhāgavatam* is almost the same as the modern science of atomism, and this is further described in the Paramāṇu-vāda of Kaṇāda. In modern science also, the atom is accepted as the ultimate indivisible particle of which the universe is composed.

Śrīmad-Bhāgavatam is the full text of all descriptions of knowledge, including the theory of atomism. The atom is the minute subtle form of eternal time.

TEXT 2

सत एव पदार्थस्य स्वरूपावस्थितस्य यत् ।
कैवल्यं परममहानविशेषो निरन्तरः ॥ २ ॥

sata eva padārthasya
svarūpāvasthitasya yat
kaivalyaṁ parama-mahān
aviśeṣo nirantaraḥ

sataḥ—of the effective manifestation; *eva*—certainly; *pada-arthasya*—of physical bodies; *svarūpa-avasthitasya*—staying in the same form even to the time of dissolution; *yat*—that which; *kaivalyam*—oneness; *parama*—the supreme; *mahān*—unlimited; *aviśeṣaḥ*—forms; *nirantaraḥ*—eternally.

TRANSLATION

Atoms are the ultimate state of the manifest universe. When they stay in their own forms without forming different bodies, they are called the unlimited oneness. There are certainly different bodies in physical forms, but the atoms themselves form the complete manifestation.

TEXT 3

एवं कालोऽप्यनुमितः सौक्ष्म्ये स्थौल्ये च सत्तम ।
संस्थानभुक्त्या भगवानव्यक्तो व्यक्तभुग्विभुः ॥ ३ ॥

evaṁ kālo 'py anumitaḥ
saukṣmye sthaulye ca sattama
saṁsthāna-bhuktyā bhagavān
avyakto vyakta-bhug vibhuḥ

evam—thus; *kālaḥ*—time; *api*—also; *anumitaḥ*—measured; *saukṣmye*—in the subtle; *sthaulye*—in the gross forms; *ca*—also; *sat-*

tama—O best; *saṁsthāna*—combinations of the atoms; *bhuktyā*—by the motion; *bhagavān*—the Supreme Personality of Godhead; *avyaktaḥ*—unmanifested; *vyakta-bhuk*—controlling all physical movement; *vibhuḥ*—the great potential.

TRANSLATION

One can estimate time by measuring the movement of the atomic combination of bodies. Time is the potency of the almighty Personality of Godhead, Hari, who controls all physical movement although He is not visible in the physical world.

TEXT 4

स कालः परमाणुर्वै यो भुङ्क्ते परमाणुताम् ।
सतोऽविशेषभुग्यस्तु स कालः परमो महान् ॥ ४ ॥

sa kālaḥ paramāṇur vai
yo bhuṅkte paramāṇutām
sato 'viśeṣa-bhug yas tu
sa kālaḥ paramo mahān

saḥ—that; *kālaḥ*—eternal time; *parama-aṇuḥ*—atomic; *vai*—certainly; *yaḥ*—which; *bhuṅkte*—passes through; *parama-aṇutām*—the space of an atom; *sataḥ*—of the entire aggregate; *aviśeṣa-bhuk*—passing through the nondual exhibition; *yaḥ tu*—which; *saḥ*—that; *kālaḥ*—time; *paramaḥ*—the supreme; *mahān*—the great.

TRANSLATION

Atomic time is measured according to its covering a particular atomic space. That time which covers the unmanifest aggregate of atoms is called the great time.

PURPORT

Time and space are two correlative terms. Time is measured in terms of its covering a certain space of atoms. Standard time is calculated in terms of the movement of the sun. The time covered by the sun in passing over an atom is calculated as atomic time. The greatest time of all covers the entire existence of the nondual manifestation. All the planets rotate and cover space, and space is calculated in terms of atoms. Each planet has its particular orbit for rotating, in which it moves without deviation, and similarly the sun has its orbit. The complete calculation of the time of creation, maintenance and dissolution, measured in terms of the circulation of the total planetary systems until the end of creation, is known as the supreme *kāla.*

TEXT 5

अणुर्द्वौ परमाणू स्यात्त्रसरेणुस्त्रयः स्मृतः ।
जालार्करश्म्यवगतः खमेवानुपतन्नगात् ॥ ५ ॥

aṇur dvau paramāṇū syāt
trasareṇus trayaḥ smṛtaḥ
jālārka-raśmy-avagataḥ
kham evānupatann agāt

aṇuḥ—double atom; *dvau*—two; *parama-aṇu*—atoms; *syāt*—become; *trasareṇuḥ*—hexatom; *trayaḥ*—three; *smṛtaḥ*—considered; *jāla-arka*—of sunshine through the holes of a window screen; *raśmi*—by the rays; *avagataḥ*—can be known; *kham eva*—towards the sky; *anupatan agāt*—going up.

TRANSLATION

The division of gross time is calculated as follows: two atoms make one double atom, and three double atoms make one hexatom. This hexatom is visible in the sunshine which enters through the holes of a window screen. One can clearly see that the hexatom goes up towards the sky.

PURPORT

The atom is described as an invisible particle, but when six such atoms combine together, they are called a *trasareṇu,* and this is visible in the sunshine pouring through the holes of a window screen.

TEXT 6

**त्रसरेणुत्रिकं भुङ्क्ते यः कालः स त्रुटिः स्मृतः।
शतभागस्तु वेधः स्यात्तैस्त्रिभिस्तु लवः स्मृतः ॥ ६ ॥**

*trasareṇu-trikaṁ bhuṅkte
yaḥ kālaḥ sa truṭiḥ smṛtaḥ
śata-bhāgas tu vedhaḥ syāt
tais tribhis tu lavaḥ smṛtaḥ*

trasareṇu-trikam—combination of three hexatoms; *bhuṅkte*—as they take time to integrate; *yaḥ*—that which; *kālaḥ*—duration of time; *saḥ*—that; *truṭiḥ*—by the name *truṭi; smṛtaḥ*—is called; *śata-bhāgaḥ*—one hundred *truṭis; tu*—but; *vedhaḥ*—called a *vedha; syāt*—it so happens; *taiḥ*—by them; *tribhiḥ*—three times; *tu*—but; *lavaḥ*—*lava; smṛtaḥ*—so called.

TRANSLATION

The time duration needed for the integration of three trasareṇus is called a truṭi, and one hundred truṭis make one vedha. Three vedhas make one lava.

PURPORT

It is calculated that if a second is divided into 1687.5 parts, each part is the duration of a *truṭi*, which is the time occupied in the integration of eighteen atomic particles. Such a combination of atoms into different bodies creates the calculation of material time. The sun is the central point for calculating all different durations.

TEXT 7

**निमेषस्त्रिलवो ज्ञेय आम्नातस्ते त्रयः क्षणः।
क्षणान् पञ्च विदुः काष्ठां लघु ता दश पञ्च च ॥ ७ ॥**

*nimeṣas tri-lavo jñeya
āmnātas te trayaḥ kṣaṇaḥ
kṣaṇān pañca viduḥ kāṣṭhāṁ
laghu tā daśa pañca ca*

nimeṣaḥ—the duration of time called a *nimeṣa; tri-lavaḥ*—the duration of three *lavas; jñeyaḥ*—is to be known; *āmnātaḥ*—it is so called; *te*—they; *trayaḥ*—three; *kṣaṇaḥ*—the duration of time called a *kṣaṇa; kṣaṇān*—such *kṣaṇas; pañca*—five; *viduḥ*—one should understand; *kāṣṭhām*—the duration of time called a *kāṣṭhā; laghu*—the duration of time called a *laghu; tāḥ*—those; *daśa pañca*—fifteen; *ca*—also.

TRANSLATION

The duration of time of three lavas is equal to one nimeṣa, the combination of three nimeṣas makes one kṣaṇa, five kṣaṇas combined together make one kāṣṭhā, and fifteen kāṣṭhās make one laghu.

PURPORT

By calculation it is found that one *laghu* is equal to two minutes. The atomic calculation of time in terms of Vedic wisdom may be converted into present time with this understanding.

TEXT 8

लघूनि वै समाम्नाता दश पञ्च च नाडिका ।
ते द्वे मुहूर्तः प्रहरः षड्यामः सप्त वा नृणाम् ॥ ८ ॥

laghūni vai samāmnātā
daśa pañca ca nāḍikā
te dve muhūrtaḥ praharaḥ
ṣaḍ yāmaḥ sapta vā nṛṇām

laghūni—such *laghus* (each of two minutes); *vai*—exactly; *samāmnātā*—is called; *daśa pañca*—fifteen; *ca*—also; *nāḍikā*—a *nāḍikā; te*—of them; *dve*—two; *muhūrtaḥ*—a moment; *praharaḥ*—three hours; *ṣaṭ*—six; *yāmaḥ*—one fourth of a day or night; *sapta*—seven; *vā*—or; *nṛṇām*—of human calculation.

TRANSLATION

Fifteen laghus make one nāḍikā, which is also called a daṇḍa. Two daṇḍas make one muhūrta, and six or seven daṇḍas make one fourth of a day or night, according to human calculation.

TEXT 9

द्वादशार्धपलोन्मानं चतुर्भिश्चतुरङ्गुलैः ।
स्वर्णमाषैः कृतच्छिद्रं यावत्प्रस्थजलप्लुतम् ॥ ९ ॥

dvādaśārdha-palonmānaṁ
caturbhiś catur-aṅgulaiḥ
svarṇa-māṣaiḥ kṛta-cchidraṁ
yāvat prastha-jala-plutam

dvādaśa-ardha—six; *pala*—of the scale of weight; *unmānam*—measuring pot; *caturbhiḥ*—by weight of four; *catuḥ-aṅgulaiḥ*—four fingers by measure; *svarṇa*—of gold; *māṣaiḥ*—of the weight; *kṛta-chidram*—making a hole; *yāvat*—as long as; *prastha*—measuring one *prastha*; *jala-plutam*—filled by water.

TRANSLATION

The measuring pot for one nāḍikā, or daṇḍa, can be prepared with a six-pala-weight [fourteen ounce] pot of copper, in which a hole is bored with a gold probe weighing four māṣa and measuring four fingers long. When the pot is placed on water, the time before the water overflows in the pot is called one daṇḍa.

PURPORT

It is advised herein that the bore in the copper measuring pot must be made with a probe weighing not more than four *māṣa* and measuring not longer than four fingers. This regulates the diameter of the hole. The pot is submerged in water, and the overflooding time is called a *daṇḍa*. This is another way of measuring the duration of a *daṇḍa*, just as time is measured by sand in a glass. It appears that in the days of Vedic civilization there was no dearth of knowledge in physics, chemistry or higher mathematics. Measurements were calculated in different ways, as simply as could be done.

TEXT 10

यामाश्चत्वारश्चत्वारो मर्त्यानामहनी उभे ।
पक्षः पञ्चदशाहानि शुक्लः कृष्णश्च मानद ॥१०॥

yāmāś catvāraś catvāro
martyānām ahanī ubhe
pakṣaḥ pañca-daśāhāni
śuklaḥ kṛṣṇaś ca mānada

yāmāḥ—three hours; *catvāraḥ*—four; *catvāraḥ*—and four; *martyānām*—of the human beings; *ahanī*—duration of day; *ubhe*—both day and night; *pakṣaḥ*—fortnight; *pañca-daśa*—fifteen; *ahāni*—days; *śuklaḥ*—white; *kṛṣṇaḥ*—black; *ca*—also; *mānada*—measured.

TRANSLATION

It is calculated that there are four praharas, which are also called yāmas, in the day and four in the night of the human being. Similarly, fifteen days and nights are a fortnight, and there are two fortnights, white and black, in a month.

TEXT 11

तयोः समुच्चयो मासः पितॄणां तदहर्निशम् ।
द्वौ तावृतुः षडयनं दक्षिणं चोत्तरं दिवि ॥११॥

tayoḥ samuccayo māsaḥ
pitṝṇāṁ tad ahar-niśam
dvau tāv ṛtuḥ ṣaḍ ayanaṁ
dakṣiṇaṁ cottaraṁ divi

tayoḥ—of them; *samuccayaḥ*—aggregate; *māsaḥ*—month; *pitṝṇām*—of the Pitā planets; *tat*—that (month); *ahaḥ-niśam*—day and night; *dvau*—two; *tau*—months; *ṛtuḥ*—a season; *ṣaṭ*—six; *ayanam*—the movement of the sun in six months; *dakṣiṇam*—southern; *ca*—also; *uttaram*—northern; *divi*—in the heavens.

TRANSLATION

The aggregate of two fortnights is one month, and that period is one complete day and night for the Pitā planets. Two of such months comprise one season, and six months comprise one complete movement of the sun from south to north.

TEXT 12

अयने चाहनी प्राहुर्वत्सरो द्वादश स्मृतः ।
संवत्सरशतं नृणां परमायुर्निरूपितम् ॥१२॥

ayane cāhanī prāhur
vatsaro dvādaśa smṛtaḥ
saṁvatsara-śataṁ nṝṇāṁ
paramāyur nirūpitam

ayane—in the solar movement (of six months); *ca*—and; *ahanī*—a day of the demigods; *prāhuḥ*—it is said; *vatsaraḥ*—one calendar year; *dvādaśa*—twelve months; *smṛtaḥ*—is so called; *saṁvatsara-śatam*—one hundred years; *nṝṇām*—of human beings; *parama-āyuḥ*—duration of life; *nirūpitam*—is estimated.

TRANSLATION

Two solar movements make one day and night of the demigods, and that combination of day and night is one complete calendar year for the human being. The human being has a duration of life of one hundred years.

TEXT 13

ग्रहर्क्षताराचक्रस्थः परमाण्वादिना जगत् ।
संवत्सरावसानेन पर्येत्यनिमिषो विभुः ॥१३॥

graharkṣa-tārā-cakra-sthaḥ
paramāṇv-ādinā jagat
saṁvatsarāvasānena
paryety animiṣo vibhuḥ

graha—influential planets like the moon; *ṛkṣa*—luminaries like Aśvinī; *tārā*—stars; *cakra-sthaḥ*—in the orbit; *parama-aṇu-ādinā*—along with the atoms; *jagat*—the entire universe; *saṁvatsara-avasānena*—by the end of one year; *paryeti*—completes its orbit; *animiṣaḥ*—the eternal time; *vibhuḥ*—the Almighty.

TRANSLATION

Influential stars, planets, luminaries and atoms all over the universe are rotating in their respective orbits under the direction of the Supreme, represented by eternal kāla.

PURPORT

In the *Brahma-saṁhitā* it is stated that the sun is the eye of the Supreme and it rotates in its particular orbit of time. Similarly, beginning from the sun down to the atom, all bodies are under the influence of the *kāla-cakra,* or the orbit of eternal time, and each of them has a scheduled orbital time of one *saṁvatsara.*

TEXT 14

संवत्सरः परिवत्सर इडावत्सर एव च ।
अनुवत्सरो वत्सरश्च विदुरैवं प्रभाष्यते ॥१४॥

saṁvatsaraḥ parivatsara
iḍā-vatsara eva ca
anuvatsaro vatsaraś ca
viduraivaṁ prabhāṣyate

saṁvatsaraḥ—orbit of the sun; *parivatsaraḥ*—circumambulation of Bṛhaspati; *iḍā-vatsaraḥ*—orbit of the stars; *eva*—as they are; *ca*—also; *anuvatsaraḥ*—orbit of the moon; *vatsaraḥ*—one calendar year; *ca*—also; *vidura*—O Vidura; *evam*—thus; *prabhāṣyate*—they are so told.

TRANSLATION

There are five different names for the orbits of the sun, moon, stars and luminaries in the firmament, and they each have their own saṁvatsara.

PURPORT

The subject matters of physics, chemistry, mathematics, astronomy, time and space dealt with in the above verses of *Śrīmad-Bhāgavatam* are certainly very interesting to students of the particular subject, but as far as we are concerned, we cannot explain them very thoroughly in terms of technical knowledge. The subject is summarized by the statement that above all the different branches of knowledge is the supreme control of *kāla*, the plenary representation of the Supreme Personality of Godhead. Nothing exists without Him, and therefore everything, however wonderful it may appear to our meager knowledge, is but the work of the magical wand of the Supreme Lord. As far as time is concerned, we beg to subjoin herewith a table of timings in terms of the modern clock.

One *truṭi*	-	8/13,500	second	One *laghu*	-	2	minutes
One *vedha*	-	8/135	second	One *daṇḍa*	-	30	minutes
One *lava*	-	8/45	second	One *prahara*	-	3	hours
One *nimeṣa*	-	8/15	second	One day	-	12	hours
One *kṣaṇa*	-	8/5	second	One night	-	12	hours
One *kāṣṭhā*	-	8	seconds	One *pakṣa*	-	15	days

Two *pakṣas* comprise one month, and twelve months comprise one calendar year, or one full orbit of the sun. A human being is expected to live up to one hundred years. That is the way of the controlling measure of eternal time.

The *Brahma-saṁhitā* (5.52) affirms this control in this way:

yac-cakṣur eṣa savitā sakala-grahāṇāṁ
rājā samasta-sura-mūrtir aśeṣa-tejāḥ
yasyājñayā bhramati saṁbhṛta-kāla-cakro
govindam ādi-puruṣaṁ tam ahaṁ bhajāmi

"I worship Govinda, the primeval Lord, the Supreme Personality of Godhead, under whose control even the sun, which is considered to be the eye of the Lord, rotates within the fixed orbit of eternal time. The sun is the king of all planetary systems and has unlimited potency in heat and light."

TEXT 15

यः सृज्यशक्तिमुरुधोच्छ्वसयन् स्वशक्त्या
पुंसोऽभ्रमाय दिवि धावति भूतभेदः ।

कालाख्यया गुणमयं क्रतुभिर्वितन्वं-
स्तस्मै बलिं हरत वत्सरपञ्चकाय ॥१५॥

yaḥ sṛjya-śaktim urudhocchvasayan sva-śaktyā
puṁso 'bhramāya divi dhāvati bhūta-bhedaḥ
kālākhyayā guṇamayaṁ kratubhir vitanvaṁs
tasmai baliṁ harata vatsara-pañcakāya

yaḥ—one who; _sṛjya_—of creation; _śaktim_—the seeds; _urudhā_—in various ways; _ucchvasayan_—invigorating; _sva-śaktyā_—by his own energy; _puṁsaḥ_—of the living entity; _abhramāya_—to dissipate darkness; _divi_—during the daytime; _dhāvati_—moves; _bhūta-bhedaḥ_—distinct from all other material form; _kāla-ākhyayā_—by the name eternal time; _guṇa-mayam_—the material results; _kratubhiḥ_—by offerings; _vitanvan_—enlarging; _tasmai_—unto him; _balim_—ingredients of offerings; _harata_—one should offer; _vatsara-pañcakāya_—offerings every five years.

TRANSLATION

O Vidura, the sun enlivens all living entities with his unlimited heat and light. He diminishes the duration of life of all living entities in order to release them from their illusion of material attachment, and he enlarges the path of elevation to the heavenly kingdom. He thus moves in the firmament with great velocity, and therefore everyone should offer him respects once every five years with all ingredients of worship.

TEXT 16

विदुर उवाच

पितृदेवमनुष्याणामायुः परमिदं स्मृतम् ।
परेषां गतिमाचक्ष्व ये स्युःकल्पाद् बहिर्विदः ॥१६॥

vidura uvāca
pitṛ-deva-manuṣyāṇām
āyuḥ param idaṁ smṛtam

pareṣāṁ gatim ācakṣva
ye syuḥ kalpād bahir vidaḥ

viduraḥ uvāca—Vidura said; *pitṛ*—the Pitā planets; *deva*—the heavenly planets; *manuṣyāṇām*—and that of the human beings; *āyuḥ*—duration of life; *param*—final; *idam*—in their own measurement; *smṛtam*—calculated; *pareṣām*—of the superior living entities; *gatim*—duration of life; *ācakṣva*—kindly calculate; *ye*—all those who; *syuḥ*—are; *kalpāt*—from the millennium; *bahiḥ*—outside; *vidaḥ*—greatly learned.

TRANSLATION

Vidura said: I now understand the life durations of the residents of the Pitā planets and heavenly planets as well as that of the human beings. Now kindly inform me of the durations of life of those greatly learned living entities who are beyond the range of a kalpa.

PURPORT

The partial dissolution of the universe that takes place at the end of Brahmā's day does not affect all the planetary systems. The planets of highly learned living entities like the sages Sanaka and Bhṛgu are not affected by the dissolutions of the millenniums. All the planets are of different types, and each is controlled by a different *kāla-cakra*, or schedule of eternal time. The time of the earth planet is not applicable to other, more elevated planets. Therefore, Vidura herein inquires about the duration of life on other planets.

TEXT 17

भगवान् वेद कालस्य गतिं भगवतो ननु ।
विश्वं विचक्षते धीरा योगराद्धेन चक्षुषा ॥१७॥

bhagavān veda kālasya
gatiṁ bhagavato nanu
viśvaṁ vicakṣate dhīrā
yoga-rāddhena cakṣuṣā

bhagavān—O spiritually powerful one; *veda*—you know; *kālasya*—of the eternal time; *gatim*—movements; *bhagavataḥ*—of the Supreme Personality of Godhead; *nanu*—as a matter of course; *viśvam*—the whole universe; *vicakṣate*—see; *dhīrāḥ*—those who are self-realized; *yoga-rāddhena*—by dint of mystic vision; *cakṣuṣā*—by the eyes.

TRANSLATION

O spiritually powerful one, you can understand the movements of eternal time, which is the controlling form of the Supreme Personality of Godhead. Because you are a self-realized person, you can see everything by the power of mystic vision.

PURPORT

Those who have reached the highest perfectional stage of mystic power and can see everything in the past, present and future are called *tri-kāla-jñas.* Similarly, the devotees of the Lord can see everything clearly that is in the revealed scriptures. The devotees of Lord Śrī Kṛṣṇa can very easily understand the science of Kṛṣṇa, as well as the situation of the material and spiritual creations, without difficulty. Devotees do not have to endeavor for any *yoga-siddhi,* or perfection in mystic powers. They are competent to understand everything by the grace of the Lord, who is sitting in everyone's heart.

TEXT 18

मैत्रेय उवाच
कृतं त्रेता द्वापरं च कलिश्चेति चतुर्युगम् ।
दिव्यैर्द्वादशभिर्वर्षैः सावधानं निरूपितम् ॥१८॥

maitreya uvāca
kṛtaṁ tretā dvāparaṁ ca
kaliś ceti catur-yugam
divyair dvādaśabhir varṣaiḥ
sāvadhānaṁ nirūpitam

maitreyaḥ uvāca—Maitreya said; *kṛtam*—the age of Satya; *tretā*—the age of Tretā; *dvāparam*—the age of Dvāpara; *ca*—also; *kaliḥ*—the age of Kali; *ca*—and; *iti*—thus; *catuḥ-yugam*—four millenniums; *divyaiḥ*—of the demigods; *dvādaśabhiḥ*—twelve; *varṣaiḥ*—thousands of years; *sa-avadhānam*—approximately; *nirūpitam*—ascertained.

TRANSLATION

Maitreya said: O Vidura, the four millenniums are called the Satya, Tretā, Dvāpara and Kali yugas. The aggregate number of years of all of these combined is equal to twelve thousand years of the demigods.

PURPORT

The years of the demigods are equal to 360 years of humankind. As will be clarified in the subsequent verses, 12,000 of the demigods' years, including the transitional periods which are called *yuga-sandhyās*, comprise the total of the aforementioned four millenniums. Thus the aggregate of the above-mentioned four millenniums is 4,320,000 years.

TEXT 19

चत्वारि त्रीणि द्वे चैकं कृतादिषु यथाक्रमम् ।
संख्यातानि सहस्राणि द्विगुणानि शतानि च ॥१९॥

catvāri trīṇi dve caikaṁ
kṛtādiṣu yathā-kramam
saṅkhyātāni sahasrāṇi
dvi-guṇāni śatāni ca

catvāri—four; *trīṇi*—three; *dve*—two; *ca*—also; *ekam*—one; *kṛta-ādiṣu*—in the Satya-yuga; *yathā-kramam*—and subsequently others; *saṅkhyātāni*—numbering; *sahasrāṇi*—thousands; *dvi-guṇāni*—twice; *śatāni*—hundreds; *ca*—also.

TRANSLATION

The duration of the Satya millennium equals 4,800 years of the demigods; the duration of the Tretā millennium equals 3,600 years of the demigods; the duration of the Dvāpara millennium

equals 2,400 years; and that of the Kali millennium is 1,200 years of the demigods.

PURPORT

As aforementioned, one year of the demigods is equal to 360 years of the human beings. The duration of the Satya-yuga is therefore 4,800 X 360, or 1,728,000 years. The duration of the Tretā-yuga is 3,600 X 360, or 1,296,000 years. The duration of the Dvāpara-yuga is 2,400 X 360, or 864,000 years. And the last, the Kali-yuga, is 1,200 X 360, or 432,000 years.

TEXT 20

संध्यासंध्यांशयोरन्तर्यः कालः शतसंख्ययोः ।
तमेवाहुर्युगं तज्ज्ञा यत्र धर्मो विधीयते ॥२०॥

sandhyā-sandhyāṁśayor antar
yaḥ kālaḥ śata-saṅkhyayoḥ
tam evāhur yugaṁ taj-jñā
yatra dharmo vidhīyate

sandhyā—transitional period before; *sandhyā-aṁśayoḥ*—and transitional period after; *antaḥ*—within; *yaḥ*—that which; *kālaḥ*—duration of time; *śata-saṅkhyayoḥ*—hundreds of years; *tam eva*—that period; *āhuḥ*—they call; *yugam*—millennium; *tat-jñāḥ*—the expert astronomers; *yatra*—wherein; *dharmaḥ*—religion; *vidhīyate*—is performed.

TRANSLATION

The transitional periods before and after every millennium, which are a few hundred years as aforementioned, are known as yuga-sandhyās, or the conjunctions of two millenniums, according to the expert astronomers. In those periods all kinds of religious activities are performed.

TEXT 21

धर्मश्चतुष्पान्मनुजान् कृते समनुवर्तते ।
स एवान्येष्वधर्मेण व्येति पादेन वर्धता ॥२१॥

dharmaś catuṣ-pān manujān
kṛte samanuvartate
sa evānyeṣv adharmeṇa
vyeti pādena vardhatā

dharmaḥ—religion; *catuḥ-pāt*—complete four dimensions; *manujān*—mankind; *kṛte*—in the Satya-yuga; *samanuvartate*—properly maintained; *saḥ*—that; *eva*—certainly; *anyeṣu*—in other; *adharmeṇa*—by the influence of irreligion; *vyeti*—declined; *pādena*—by one part; *vardhatā*—gradually increasing proportionately.

TRANSLATION

O Vidura, in the Satya millennium mankind properly and completely maintained the principles of religion, but in other millenniums religion gradually decreased by one part as irreligion was proportionately admitted.

PURPORT

In the Satya millennium, complete execution of religious principles prevailed. Gradually, the principles of religion decreased by one part in each of the subsequent millenniums. In other words, at present there is one part religion and three parts irreligion. Therefore people in this age are not very happy.

TEXT 22

त्रिलोक्या युगसाहस्रं बहिराब्रह्मणो दिनम् ।
तावत्येव निशा तात यन्निमीलति विश्वसृक् ॥२२॥

tri-lokyā yuga-sāhasraṁ
bahir ābrahmaṇo dinam
tāvaty eva niśā tāta
yan nimīlati viśva-sṛk

tri-lokyāḥ—of the three worlds; *yuga*—the four *yugas; sāhasram*—one thousand; *bahiḥ*—outside of; *ābrahmaṇaḥ*—up to Brahmaloka; *dinam*—is a day; *tāvatī*—a similar (period); *eva*—certainly; *niśā*—is night; *tāta*—O dear one; *yat*—because; *nimīlati*—goes to sleep; *viśva-sṛk*—Brahmā.

TRANSLATION

Outside of the three planetary systems [Svarga, Martya and Pātāla], the four yugas multiplied by one thousand comprise one day on the planet of Brahmā. A similar period comprises a night of Brahmā, in which the creator of the universe goes to sleep.

PURPORT

When Brahmā goes to sleep in his nighttime, the three planetary systems below Brahmaloka are all submerged in the water of devastation. In his sleeping condition, Brahmā dreams about the Garbhodakaśāyī Viṣṇu and takes instruction from the Lord for the rehabilitation of the devastated area of space.

TEXT 23

निशावसान आरब्धो लोककल्पोऽनुवर्तते ।
यावद्दिनं भगवतो मनून् भुञ्जंश्चतुर्दश ॥२३॥

niśāvasāna ārabdho
loka-kalpo 'nuvartate
yāvad dinaṁ bhagavato
manūn bhuñjaṁś catur-daśa

niśā—night; *avasāne*—termination; *ārabdhaḥ*—beginning from; *loka-kalpaḥ*—further creation of the three worlds; *anuvartate*—follows; *yāvat*—until; *dinam*—the daytime; *bhagavataḥ*—of the lord (Brahmā); *manūn*—the Manus; *bhuñjan*—existing through; *catuḥ-daśa*—fourteen.

TRANSLATION

After the end of Brahmā's night, the creation of the three worlds begins again in the daytime of Brahmā, and they continue to exist through the life durations of fourteen consecutive Manus, or fathers of mankind.

PURPORT

At the end of the life of each Manu there are shorter dissolutions also.

TEXT 24

स्वं स्वं कालं मनुर्भुङ्क्ते साधिकां ह्येकसप्ततिम् ॥२४॥

svaṁ svaṁ kālaṁ manur bhuṅkte
sādhikāṁ hy eka-saptatim

svam—own; *svam*—accordingly; *kālam*—duration of life; *manuḥ*—Manu; *bhuṅkte*—enjoys; *sa-adhikām*—a little more than; *hi*—certainly; *eka-saptatim*—seventy-one.

TRANSLATION

Each and every Manu enjoys a life of a little more than seventy-one sets of four millenniums.

PURPORT

The duration of life of a Manu comprises seventy-one sets of four millenniums, as described in the *Viṣṇu Purāṇa.* The duration of life of one Manu is about 852,000 years in the calculation of the demigods, or, in the calculation of human beings, 306,720,000 years.

TEXT 25

मन्वन्तरेषु मनवस्तद्वंश्या ऋषयः सुराः ।
भवन्ति चैव युगपत्सुरेशाश्चानु ये च तान् ॥२५॥

manvantareṣu manavas
tad-vaṁśyā ṛṣayaḥ surāḥ
bhavanti caiva yugapat
sureśāś cānu ye ca tān

manu-antareṣu—after the dissolution of each and every Manu; *manavaḥ*—other Manus; *tat-vaṁśyāḥ*—and their descendants; *ṛṣayaḥ*—the seven famous sages; *surāḥ*—devotees of the Lord;

bhavanti—flourish; *ca eva*—also all of them; *yugapat*—simultaneously; *sura-īśāḥ*—demigods like Indra; *ca*—and; *anu*—followers; *ye*—all; *ca*—also; *tān*—them.

TRANSLATION

After the dissolution of each and every Manu, the next Manu comes in order, along with his descendants, who rule over the different planets; but the seven famous sages, and demigods like Indra and their followers, such as the Gandharvas, all appear simultaneously with Manu.

PURPORT

There are fourteen Manus in one day of Brahmā, and each of them has different descendants.

TEXT 26

एष दैनन्दिनः सर्गो ब्राह्मस्त्रैलोक्यवर्तनः ।
तिर्यङ्नृपितृदेवानां सम्भवो यत्र कर्मभिः ॥२६॥

eṣa dainan-dinaḥ sargo
brāhmas trailokya-vartanaḥ
tiryaṅ-nṛ-pitṛ-devānāṁ
sambhavo yatra karmabhiḥ

eṣaḥ—all these creations; *dainam-dinaḥ*—daily; *sargaḥ*—creation; *brāhmaḥ*—in terms of the days of Brahmā; *trailokya-vartanaḥ*—revolution of the three worlds; *tiryak*—animals lower than the human beings; *nṛ*—human beings; *pitṛ*—of the Pitā planets; *devānām*—of the demigods; *sambhavaḥ*—appearance; *yatra*—wherein; *karmabhiḥ*—in the cycle of fruitive activities.

TRANSLATION

In the creation, during Brahmā's day, the three planetary systems—Svarga, Martya and Pātāla—revolve, and the inhabitants, including the lower animals, human beings, demigods and Pitās, appear and disappear in terms of their fruitive activities.

TEXT 27

मन्वन्तरेषु भगवान् बिभ्रत्सत्त्वं स्वमूर्तिभिः ।
मन्वादिभिरिदं विश्वमवत्युदितपौरुषः ॥२७॥

manvantareṣu bhagavān
bibhrat sattvaṁ sva-mūrtibhiḥ
manv-ādibhir idaṁ viśvam
avaty udita-pauruṣaḥ

manu-antareṣu—in each change of Manu; *bhagavān*—the Personality of Godhead; *bibhrat*—manifesting; *sattvam*—His internal potency; *sva-mūrtibhiḥ*—by His different incarnations; *manu-ādibhiḥ*—as Manus; *idam*—this; *viśvam*—the universe; *avati*—maintains; *udita*—discovering; *pauruṣaḥ*—divine potencies.

TRANSLATION

In each and every change of Manu, the Supreme Personality of Godhead appears by manifesting His internal potency in different incarnations, as Manu and others. Thus He maintains the universe by discovered power.

TEXT 28

तमोमात्रामुपादाय प्रतिसंरुद्धविक्रमः ।
कालेनानुगताशेष आस्ते तूष्णीं दिनात्यये ॥२८॥

tamo-mātrām upādāya
pratisaṁruddha-vikramaḥ
kālenānugatāśeṣa
āste tūṣṇīṁ dinātyaye

tamaḥ—the mode of ignorance, or the darkness of night; *mātrām*—an insignificant portion only; *upādāya*—accepting; *pratisaṁruddha-vikramaḥ*—suspending all power of manifestation; *kālena*—by means of the eternal *kāla; anugata*—merged in; *aśeṣaḥ*—innumerable living entities; *āste*—remains; *tūṣṇīm*—silent; *dina-atyaye*—at the end of the day.

TRANSLATION

At the end of the day, under the insignificant portion of the mode of darkness, the powerful manifestation of the universe merges in the darkness of night. By the influence of eternal time, the innumerable living entities remain merged in that dissolution, and everything is silent.

PURPORT

This verse is an explanation of the night of Brahmā, which is the effect of the influence of time in touch with an insignificant portion of the modes of material nature in darkness. The dissolution of the three worlds is effected by the incarnation of darkness, Rudra, represented by the fire of eternal time which blazes over the three worlds. These three worlds are known as Bhūḥ, Bhuvaḥ and Svaḥ (Pātāla, Martya and Svarga). The innumerable living entities merge into that dissolution, which appears to be the dropping of the curtain of the scene of the Supreme Lord's energy, and so everything becomes silent.

TEXT 29

तमेवान्वपिधीयन्ते लोका भूरादयस्त्रयः ।
निशायामनुवृत्तायां निर्मुक्तशशिभास्करम् ॥२९॥

tam evānv api dhīyante
lokā bhūr-ādayas trayaḥ
niśāyām anuvṛttāyāṁ
nirmukta-śaśi-bhāskaram

tam—that; *eva*—certainly; *anu*—after; *api dhīyante*—are out of sight; *lokāḥ*—the planets; *bhūḥ-ādayaḥ*—the three worlds, Bhūḥ, Bhuvaḥ and Svaḥ; *trayaḥ*—three; *niśāyām*—in the night; *anuvṛttāyām*—ordinary; *nirmukta*—without glare; *śaśi*—the moon; *bhāskaram*—the sun.

TRANSLATION

When the night of Brahmā ensues, all the three worlds are out of sight, and the sun and the moon are without glare, just as in the due course of an ordinary night.

PURPORT

It is understood that the glare of the sun and moon disappear from the sphere of the three worlds, but the sun and the moon themselves do not vanish. They appear in the remaining portion of the universe, which is beyond the sphere of the three worlds. The portion in dissolution remains without sunrays or moonglow. It all remains dark and full of water, and there are indefatigable winds, as explained in the following verses.

TEXT 30

त्रिलोक्यां दह्यमानायां शक्त्या सङ्कर्षणाग्निना ।
यान्त्यूष्मणा महर्लोकाज्जनं भृग्वादयोऽर्दिताः ॥३०॥

tri-lokyāṁ dahyamānāyāṁ
śaktyā saṅkarṣaṇāgninā
yānty ūṣmaṇā maharlokāj
janaṁ bhṛgv-ādayo 'rditāḥ

tri-lokyām—when the spheres of the three worlds; *dahyamānāyām*—being set ablaze; *śaktyā*—by the potency; *saṅkarṣaṇa*—from the mouth of Saṅkarṣaṇa; *agninā*—by the fire; *yānti*—they go; *ūṣmaṇā*—heated by the warmth; *mahaḥ-lokāt*—from Maharloka; *janam*—to Janaloka; *bhṛgu*—the sage Bhṛgu; *ādayaḥ*—and others; *arditāḥ*—being so distressed.

TRANSLATION

The devastation takes place due to the fire emanating from the mouth of Saṅkarṣaṇa, and thus great sages like Bhṛgu and other inhabitants of Maharloka transport themselves to Janaloka, being distressed by the warmth of the blazing fire which rages through the three worlds below.

TEXT 31

तावत्त्रिभुवनं सद्यः कल्पान्तैधितसिन्धवः ।
प्लावयन्त्युत्कटाटोपचण्डवातेरितोर्मयः ॥३१॥

tāvat tri-bhuvanaṁ sadyaḥ
kalpāntaidhita-sindhavaḥ
plāvayanty utkaṭāṭopa-
caṇḍa-vāteritormayaḥ

tāvat—then; *tri-bhuvanam*—all the three worlds; *sadyaḥ*—immediately after; *kalpa-anta*—in the beginning of the devastation; *edhita*—inflated; *sindhavaḥ*—all the oceans; *plāvayanti*—inundate; *utkaṭa*—violent; *āṭopa*—agitation; *caṇḍa*—hurricane; *vāta*—by winds; *īrita*—blown; *ūrmayaḥ*—waves.

TRANSLATION

At the beginning of the devastation all the seas overflow, and hurricane winds blow very violently. Thus the waves of the seas become ferocious, and in no time at all the three worlds are full of water.

PURPORT

It is said that the blazing fire from the mouth of Saṅkarṣaṇa rages for one hundred years of the demigods, or 36,000 human years. Then for another 36,000 years there are torrents of rain, accompanied by violent winds and waves, and the seas and oceans overflow. These reactions of 72,000 years are the beginning of the partial devastation of the three worlds. People forget all these devastations of the worlds and think themselves happy in the material progress of civilization. This is called *māyā*, or "that which is not."

TEXT 32

अन्तः स तस्मिन् सलिल आस्तेऽनन्तासनो हरिः ।
योगनिद्रानिमीलाक्षः स्तूयमानो जनालयैः ॥३२॥

antaḥ sa tasmin salila
āste 'nantāsano hariḥ
yoga-nidrā-nimīlākṣaḥ
stūyamāno janālayaiḥ

antaḥ—within; *saḥ*—that; *tasmin*—in that; *salile*—water; *āste*—there is; *ananta*—Ananta; *āsanaḥ*—on the seat of; *hariḥ*—the Lord;

yoga—mystic; *nidrā*—sleep; *nimīla-akṣaḥ*—eyes closed; *stūya-mānaḥ*—being glorified; *jana-ālayaiḥ*—by the inhabitants of the Janaloka planets.

TRANSLATION

The Supreme Lord, the Personality of Godhead, lies down in the water on the seat of Ananta, with His eyes closed, and the inhabitants of the Janaloka planets offer their glorious prayers unto the Lord with folded hands.

PURPORT

We should not understand the sleeping condition of the Lord to be the same as our sleep. Here the word *yoga-nidrā* is specifically mentioned, which indicates that the Lord's sleeping condition is also a manifestation of His internal potency. Whenever the word *yoga* is used it should be understood to refer to that which is transcendental. In the transcendental stage all activities are always present, and they are glorified by prayers of great sages like Bhṛgu.

TEXT 33

एवंविधैरहोरात्रैः कालगत्योपलक्षितैः ।
अपक्षितमिवास्यापि परमायुर्वयःशतम् ॥३३॥

evaṁ-vidhair aho-rātraiḥ
kāla-gatyopalakṣitaiḥ
apakṣitam ivāsyāpi
paramāyur vayaḥ-śatam

evam—thus; *vidhaiḥ*—by the process of; *ahaḥ*—days; *rātraiḥ*—by nights; *kāla-gatyā*—advancement of time; *upalakṣitaiḥ*—by such symptoms; *apakṣitam*—declined; *iva*—just like; *asya*—his; *api*—although; *parama-āyuḥ*—duration of life; *vayaḥ*—years; *śatam*—one hundred.

TRANSLATION

Thus the process of the exhaustion of the duration of life exists for every one of the living beings, including Lord Brahmā. One's

life endures for only one hundred years, in terms of the times in the different planets.

PURPORT

Every living being lives for one hundred years in terms of the times in different planets for different entities. These one hundred years of life are not equal in every case. The longest duration of one hundred years belongs to Brahmā, but although the life of Brahmā is very long, it expires in the course of time. Brahmā is also afraid of his death, and thus he performs devotional service to the Lord, just to release himself from the clutches of illusory energy. Animals, of course, have no sense of responsibility, but even humans, who have developed a sense of responsibility, while away their valuable time without engaging in devotional service to the Lord; they live merrily, unafraid of impending death. This is the madness of human society. The madman has no responsibility in life. Similarly, a human being who does not develop a sense of responsibility before he dies is no better than the madman who tries to enjoy material life very happily without concern for the future. It is necessary that every human being be responsible in preparing himself for the next life, even if he has a duration of life like that of Brahmā, the greatest of all living creatures within the universe.

TEXT 34

यदर्धमायुषस्तस्य परार्धमभिधीयते ।
पूर्वः परार्धोऽपक्रान्तो ह्यपरोऽद्य प्रवर्तते ॥३४॥

yad ardham āyuṣas tasya
parārdham abhidhīyate
pūrvaḥ parārdho 'pakrānto
hy aparo 'dya pravartate

yat—that which; *ardham*—half; *āyuṣaḥ*—of the duration of life; *tasya*—his; *parārdham*—a *parārdha; abhidhīyate*—is called; *pūrvaḥ*—the former; *para-ardhaḥ*—half of the duration of life; *apakrāntaḥ*—having passed; *hi*—certainly; *aparaḥ*—the latter; *adya*—in this millennium; *pravartate*—shall begin.

TRANSLATION

The one hundred years of Brahmā's life are divided into two parts, the first half and the second half. The first half of the duration of Brahmā's life is already over, and the second half is now current.

PURPORT

The duration of one hundred years in the life of Brahmā has already been discussed in many places in this work, and it is described in *Bhagavad-gītā* (8.17) also. Fifty years of the life of Brahmā are already over, and fifty years are yet to be completed; then, for Brahmā also, death is inevitable.

TEXT 35

पूर्वस्यादौ परार्धस्य ब्राह्मो नाम महानभूत् ।
कल्पो यत्राभवद्ब्रह्मा शब्दब्रह्मेति यं विदुः ॥३५॥

pūrvasyādau parārdhasya
brāhmo nāma mahān abhūt
kalpo yatrābhavad brahmā
śabda-brahmeti yaṁ viduḥ

pūrvasya—of the first half; *ādau*—in the beginning; *para-ardhasya*—of the superior half; *brāhmaḥ*—Brāhma-kalpa; *nāma*—of the name; *mahān*—very great; *abhūt*—was manifest; *kalpaḥ*—millennium; *yatra*—whereupon; *abhavat*—appeared; *brahmā*—Lord Brahmā; *śabda-brahma iti*—the sounds of the *Vedas; yam*—which; *viduḥ*—they know.

TRANSLATION

In the beginning of the first half of Brahmā's life, there was a millennium called Brāhma-kalpa, wherein Lord Brahmā appeared. The birth of the Vedas was simultaneous with Brahmā's birth.

PURPORT

According to *Padma Purāṇa* (*Prabhāsa-khaṇḍa*), in thirty days of Brahmā many *kalpas* take place, such as the Varāha-kalpa and Pitṛ-kalpa. Thirty days make one month of Brahmā, beginning from the full moon to the disappearance of the moon. Twelve such months complete one year, and fifty years complete one *parārdha*, or one half the duration of the life of Brahmā. The Śveta-varāha appearance of the Lord is the first birthday of Brahmā. The birth date of Brahmā is in the month of March, according to Hindu astronomical calculation. This statement is reproduced from the explanation of Śrīla Viśvanātha Cakravartī Ṭhākura.

TEXT 36

तस्यैव चान्ते कल्पोऽभूद् यं पाद्ममभिचक्षते ।
यद्धरेर्नाभिसरस आसील्लोकसरोरुहम् ॥३६॥

tasyaiva cānte kalpo 'bhūd
yaṁ pādmam abhicakṣate
yad dharer nābhi-sarasa
āsīl loka-saroruham

tasya—of the Brāhma-kalpa; *eva*—certainly; *ca*—also; *ante*—at the end of; *kalpaḥ*—millennium; *abhūt*—came into existence; *yam*—which; *pādmam*—Pādma; *abhicakṣate*—is called; *yat*—in which; *hareḥ*—of the Personality of Godhead; *nābhi*—in the navel; *sarasaḥ*—from the reservoir of water; *āsīt*—there was; *loka*—of the universe; *saroruham*—lotus.

TRANSLATION

The millennium which followed the first Brāhma millennium is known as the Pādma-kalpa because in that millennium the universal lotus flower grew out of the navel reservoir of water of the Personality of Godhead, Hari.

PURPORT

The millennium following the Brāhma-kalpa is known as the Pādma-kalpa because the universal lotus grows in that millennium. The Pādma-kalpa is also called the Pitṛ-kalpa in certain *Purāṇas*.

TEXT 37

अयं तु कथितः कल्पो द्वितीयस्यापि भारत ।
वाराह इति विख्यातो यत्रासीच्छूकरो हरिः ॥३७॥

ayaṁ tu kathitaḥ kalpo
dvitīyasyāpi bhārata
vārāha iti vikhyāto
yatrāsīc chūkaro hariḥ

ayam—this; *tu*—but; *kathitaḥ*—known as; *kalpaḥ*—the current millennium; *dvitīyasya*—of the second half; *api*—certainly; *bhārata*—O descendant of Bharata; *vārāhaḥ*—Vārāha; *iti*—thus; *vikhyātaḥ*—is celebrated; *yatra*—in which; *āsīt*—appeared; *śūkaraḥ*—hog shape; *hariḥ*—the Personality of Godhead.

TRANSLATION

O descendant of Bharata, the first millennium in the second half of the life of Brahmā is also known as the Vārāha millennium because the Personality of Godhead appeared in that millennium as the hog incarnation.

PURPORT

The different millenniums known as the Brāhma, Pādma and Vārāha *kalpas* appear a little puzzling for the layman. There are some scholars who think these *kalpas* to be one and the same. According to Śrīla Viśvanātha Cakravartī, the Brāhma-kalpa in the beginning of the first half appears to be the Pādma-kalpa. We can, however, simply abide by the text and understand that the present millennium is in the second half of the duration of the life of Brahmā.

TEXT 38

कालोऽयं द्विपरार्धाख्यो निमेष उपचर्यते ।
अव्याकृतस्यानन्तस्य ह्यनादेर्जगदात्मनः ॥३८॥

kālo 'yaṁ dvi-parārdhākhyo
nimeṣa upacaryate
avyākṛtasyānantasya
hy anāder jagad-ātmanaḥ

kālaḥ—eternal time; *ayam*—this (as measured by Brahmā's duration of life); *dvi-parārdha-ākhyaḥ*—measured by the two halves of Brahmā's life; *nimeṣaḥ*—less than a second; *upacaryate*—is so measured; *avyākṛtasya*—of one who is unchanged; *anantasya*—of the unlimited; *hi*—certainly; *anādeḥ*—of the beginningless; *jagat-ātmanaḥ*—of the soul of the universe.

TRANSLATION

The duration of the two parts of Brahmā's life, as above mentioned, is calculated to be equal to one nimeṣa [less than a second] for the Supreme Personality of Godhead, who is unchanging and unlimited and is the cause of all causes of the universe.

PURPORT

The great sage Maitreya has given a considerable description of the time of different dimensions, beginning from the atom up to the duration of the life of Brahmā. Now he attempts to give some idea of the time of the unlimited Personality of Godhead. He just gives a hint of His unlimited time by the standard of the life of Brahmā. The entire duration of the life of Brahmā is calculated to be less than a second of the Lord's time, and it is explained in the *Brahma-saṁhitā* (5.48) as follows:

yasyaika-niśvasita-kālam athāvalambya
jīvanti loma-vilajā jagad-aṇḍa-nāthāḥ
viṣṇur mahān sa iha yasya kalā-viśeṣo
govindam ādi-puruṣaṁ tam ahaṁ bhajāmi

"I worship Govinda, the Supreme Personality of Godhead, the cause of all causes, whose plenary portion is Mahā-Viṣṇu. All the heads of the innumerable universes [the Brahmās] live only by taking shelter of the time occupied by one of His breaths." The impersonalists do not believe in the form of the Lord, and thus they would hardly believe in the Lord's sleeping. Their idea is obtained by a poor fund of knowledge; they calculate everything in terms of man's capacity. They think that the existence of the Supreme is just the opposite of active human existence; because the human being has senses, the Supreme must be without sense perception; because the human being has a form, the Supreme must be formless; and because the human being sleeps, the Supreme must not sleep. *Śrīmad-Bhāgavatam*, however, does not agree with such impersonalists. It is clearly stated herein that the Supreme Lord rests in *yoga-*

nidrā, as previously discussed. And because He sleeps, naturally He must breathe, and the *Brahma-saṁhitā* confirms that within His breathing period innumerable Brahmās take birth and die.

There is complete agreement between *Śrīmad-Bhāgavatam* and the *Brahma-saṁhitā*. Eternal time is never lost along with the life of Brahmā. It continues, but it has no ability to control the Supreme Personality of Godhead because the Lord is the controller of time. In the spiritual world there is undoubtedly time, but it has no control over activities. Time is unlimited, and the spiritual world is also unlimited, since everything there exists on the absolute plane.

TEXT 39

कालोऽयं परमाण्वादिर्द्विपरार्धान्त ईश्वरः ।
नैवेशितुं प्रभुर्भूम्न ईश्वरो धाममानिनाम् ॥३९॥

kālo 'yaṁ paramāṇv-ādir
dvi-parārdhānta īśvaraḥ
naiveśituṁ prabhur bhūmna
īśvaro dhāma-māninām

kālaḥ—the eternal time; *ayam*—this; *parama-aṇu*—atom; *ādiḥ*—beginning from; *dvi-parārdha*—two superdurations of time; *antaḥ*—to the end; *īśvaraḥ*—controller; *na*—never; *eva*—certainly; *īśitum*—to control; *prabhuḥ*—capable; *bhūmnaḥ*—of the Supreme; *īśvaraḥ*—controller; *dhāma-māninām*—of those who are body conscious.

TRANSLATION

Eternal time is certainly the controller of different dimensions, from that of the atom up to the superdivisions of the duration of Brahmā's life; but, nevertheless, it is controlled by the Supreme. Time can control only those who are body conscious, even up to the Satyaloka or the other higher planets of the universe.

TEXT 40

विकारैः सहितो युक्तैर्विशेषादिभिरावृतः ।
आण्डकोशो बहिरयं पञ्चाशत्कोटिविस्तृतः ॥४०॥

vikāraiḥ sahito yuktair
viśeṣādibhir āvṛtaḥ
āṇḍakośo bahir ayaṁ
pañcāśat-koṭi-vistṛtaḥ

vikāraiḥ—by the transformation of the elements; *sahitaḥ*—along with; *yuktaiḥ*—being so amalgamated; *viśeṣa*—manifestations; *ādibhiḥ*—by them; *āvṛtaḥ*—covered; *āṇḍa-kośaḥ*—the universe; *bahiḥ*—outside; *ayam*—this; *pañcāśat*—fifty; *koṭi*—ten million; *vistṛtaḥ*—widespread.

TRANSLATION

This phenomenal material world is expanded to a diameter of four billion miles, as a combination of eight material elements transformed into sixteen further categories, within and without, as follows.

PURPORT

As explained before, the entire material world is a display of sixteen diversities and eight material elements. The analytical studies of the material world are the subject matter of Sāṅkhya philosophy. The first sixteen diversities are the eleven senses and five sense objects, and the eight elements are the gross and subtle matter, namely earth, water, fire, air, sky, mind, intelligence and ego. All these combined together are distributed throughout the entire universe, which extends diametrically to four billion miles. Besides this universe of our experience, there are innumerable other universes. Some of them are bigger than the present one, and all of them are clustered together under similar material elements as described below.

TEXT 41

दशोत्तराधिकैर्यत्र प्रविष्टः परमाणुवत् ।
लक्ष्यतेऽन्तर्गताश्चान्ये कोटिशो ह्यण्डराशयः ॥४१॥

daśottarādhikair yatra
praviṣṭaḥ paramāṇuvat
lakṣyate 'ntar-gatāś cānye
koṭiśo hy aṇḍa-rāśayaḥ

daśa-uttara-adhikaiḥ—with ten times greater thickness; *yatra*—in which; *praviṣṭaḥ*—entered; *parama-aṇu-vat*—like atoms; *lakṣyate*—it (the mass of universes) appears; *antaḥ-gatāḥ*—come together; *ca*—and; *anye*—in the other; *koṭiśaḥ*—clustered; *hi*—for; *aṇḍa-rāśayaḥ*—huge combination of universes.

TRANSLATION

The layers of elements covering the universes are each ten times thicker than the one before, and all the universes clustered together appear like atoms in a huge combination.

PURPORT

The coverings of the universes are also constituted of the elements of earth, water, fire, air and ether, and each is ten times thicker than the one before. The first covering of the universe is earth, and it is ten times thicker than the universe itself. If the universe is four billion miles in size, then the size of the earthly covering of the universe is four billion times ten. The covering of water is ten times greater than the earthly covering, the covering of fire is ten times greater than the watery covering, the covering of air is ten times greater than that of the fire, the covering of ether is ten times greater still than that of air, and so on. The universe within the coverings of matter appears to be like an atom in comparison to the coverings, and the number of universes is unknown even to those who can estimate the coverings of the universes.

TEXT 42

तदाहुरक्षरं ब्रह्म सर्वकारणकारणम् ।
विष्णोर्धाम परं साक्षात्पुरुषस्य महात्मनः ॥४२॥

tad āhur akṣaraṁ brahma
sarva-kāraṇa-kāraṇam
viṣṇor dhāma paraṁ sākṣāt
puruṣasya mahātmanaḥ

tat—that; *āhuḥ*—is said; *akṣaram*—infallible; *brahma*—the supreme; *sarva-kāraṇa*—all causes; *kāraṇam*—the supreme cause;

viṣṇoḥ dhāma—the spiritual abode of Viṣṇu; *param*—the supreme; *sākṣāt*—without doubt; *puruṣasya*—of the *puruṣa* incarnation; *mahātmanaḥ*—of the Mahā-Viṣṇu.

TRANSLATION

The Supreme Personality of Godhead, Śrī Kṛṣṇa, is therefore said to be the original cause of all causes. Thus the spiritual abode of Viṣṇu is eternal without a doubt, and it is also the abode of Mahā-Viṣṇu, the origin of all manifestations.

PURPORT

Lord Mahā-Viṣṇu, who is resting in *yoga-nidrā* on the Causal Ocean and creating innumerable universes by His breathing process, only temporarily appears in the *mahat-tattva* for the temporary manifestation of the material worlds. He is a plenary portion of Lord Śrī Kṛṣṇa, and thus although He is nondifferent from Lord Kṛṣṇa, His formal appearance in the material world as an incarnation is temporary. The original form of the Personality of Godhead is actually the *svarūpa*, or real form, and He eternally resides in the Vaikuṇṭha world (Viṣṇuloka). The word *mahātmanaḥ* is used here to indicate Mahā-Viṣṇu, and His real manifestation is Lord Kṛṣṇa, who is called *parama*, as confirmed in the *Brahma-saṁhitā:*

īśvaraḥ paramaḥ kṛṣṇaḥ
sac-cid-ānanda-vigrahaḥ
anādir ādir govindaḥ
sarva-kāraṇa-kāraṇam

"The Supreme Lord is Kṛṣṇa, the original Personality of Godhead known as Govinda. His form is eternal, full of bliss and knowledge, and He is the original cause of all causes."

Thus end the Bhaktivedanta purports of the Third Canto, Eleventh Chapter, of the Śrīmad-Bhāgavatam, *entitled "Calculation of Time, From the Atom."*

CHAPTER TWELVE

Creation of the Kumāras and Others

TEXT 1

मैत्रेय उवाच

इति ते वर्णितः क्षत्तः कालाख्यः परमात्मनः ।
महिमा वेदगर्भोऽथ यथास्राक्षीन्निबोध मे ॥ १ ॥

maitreya uvāca
iti te varṇitaḥ kṣattaḥ
kālākhyaḥ paramātmanaḥ
mahimā veda-garbho 'tha
yathāsrākṣīn nibodha me

maitreyaḥ uvāca—Śrī Maitreya said; *iti*—thus; *te*—unto you; *varṇitaḥ*—described; *kṣattaḥ*—O Vidura; *kāla-ākhyaḥ*—by the name eternal time; *paramātmanaḥ*—of the Supersoul; *mahimā*—glories; *veda-garbhaḥ*—Lord Brahmā, the reservoir of the *Vedas; atha*—hereafter; *yathā*—as it is; *asrākṣīt*—did create; *nibodha*—just try to understand; *me*—from me.

TRANSLATION

Śrī Maitreya said: O learned Vidura, so far I have explained to you the glories of the form of the Supreme Personality of Godhead in His feature of kāla. Now you can hear from me about the creation of Brahmā, the reservoir of all Vedic knowledge.

TEXT 2

ससर्जाग्रेऽन्धतामिस्रमथ तामिस्रमादिकृत् ।
महामोहं च मोहं च तमश्चाज्ञानवृत्तयः ॥ २ ॥

sasarjāgre 'ndha-tāmisram
atha tāmisram ādi-kṛt

mahāmohaṁ ca mohaṁ ca
tamaś cājñāna-vṛttayaḥ

sasarja—created; *agre*—at first; *andha-tāmisram*—the sense of death; *atha*—then; *tāmisram*—anger upon frustration; *ādi-kṛt*—all these; *mahā-moham*—ownership of enjoyable objects; *ca*—also; *moham*—illusory conception; *ca*—also; *tamaḥ*—darkness in self-knowledge; *ca*—as well as; *ajñāna*—nescience; *vṛttayaḥ*—engagements.

TRANSLATION

Brahmā first created the nescient engagements like self-deception, the sense of death, anger after frustration, the sense of false ownership, and the illusory bodily conception, or forgetfulness of one's real identity.

PURPORT

Before the factual creation of the living entities in different varieties of species, the conditions under which a living being in the material world has to live were created by Brahmā. Unless a living entity forgets his real identity, it is impossible for him to live in the material conditions of life. Therefore the first condition of material existence is forgetfulness of one's real identity. And by forgetting one's real identity, one is sure to be afraid of death, although a pure living soul is deathless and birthless. This false identification with material nature is the cause of false ownership of things which are offered by the arrangement of superior control. All material resources are offered to the living entity for his peaceful living and for the discharge of the duties of self-realization in conditioned life. But due to false identification, the conditioned soul becomes entrapped by the sense of false ownership of the property of the Supreme Lord. It is evident from this verse that Brahmā himself is a creation of the Supreme Lord, and the five kinds of nescience which condition the living entities in material existence are creations of Brahmā. It is simply ludicrous to think the living entity to be equal with the Supreme Being when one can understand that the conditioned souls are under the influence of Brahmā's magic wand. Patañjali also accepts that there are five kinds of nescience, as mentioned herein.

TEXT 3

दृष्ट्वा पापीयसीं सृष्टिं नात्मानं बह्वमन्यत ।
भगवद्ध्यानपूतेन मनसान्यां ततोऽसृजत ॥ ३ ॥

dṛṣṭvā pāpīyasīṁ sṛṣṭiṁ
nātmānaṁ bahv amanyata
bhagavad-dhyāna-pūtena
manasānyāṁ tato 'sṛjat

dṛṣṭvā—by seeing; *pāpīyasīm*—sinful; *sṛṣṭim*—creation; *na*—did not; *ātmānam*—unto himself; *bahu*—much pleasure; *amanyata*—felt; *bhagavat*—on the Personality of Godhead; *dhyāna*—meditation; *pūtena*—purified by that; *manasā*—by such a mentality; *anyām*—another; *tataḥ*—thereafter; *asṛjat*—created.

TRANSLATION

Seeing such a misleading creation as a sinful task, Brahmā did not feel much pleasure in his activity, and therefore he purified himself by meditation on the Personality of Godhead. Then he began another term of creation.

PURPORT

Although he created the different influences of nescience, Lord Brahmā was not satisfied in performing such a thankless task, but he had to do it because most of the conditioned souls wanted it to be so. Lord Kṛṣṇa says in *Bhagavad-gītā* (15.15) that He is present in everyone's heart and is helping everyone to either remember or forget. The question may be raised why the Lord, who is all-merciful, helps one to remember and another to forget. Actually, His mercy is not exhibited in partiality towards one and enmity towards another. The living entity, as part and parcel of the Lord, is partially independent because he partially possesses all the qualities of the Lord. Anyone who has some independence may sometimes misuse it due to ignorance. When the living entity prefers to misuse his independence and glide down towards nescience, the all-merciful Lord first of all tries to protect him from the trap, but when the living entity persists in gliding down to hell, the Lord helps him to forget his real position. The Lord helps the falling living entity glide down to the lowest point, just to give him the chance to see if he is happy by misusing his independence.

Almost all the conditioned souls who are rotting in the material world are misusing their independence, and therefore five kinds of nescience are imposed upon them. As an obedient servitor of the Lord, Brahmā creates all these as a matter of necessity, but he is not happy in doing so because a devotee of the Lord naturally does not like to see anyone falling down from his real position. Persons who do not care for the path of realization get full facilities from the Lord for executing their proclivities to the fullest extent, and Brahmā helps in that procedure without fail.

TEXT 4

सनकं च सनन्दं च सनातनमथात्मभूः ।
सनत्कुमारं च मुनीन्निष्क्रियानूर्ध्वरेतसः ॥ ४ ॥

sanakaṁ ca sanandaṁ ca
sanātanam athātmabhūḥ
sanat-kumāraṁ ca munīn
niṣkriyān ūrdhva-retasaḥ

sanakam—Sanaka; *ca*—also; *sanandam*—Sananda; *ca*—and; *sanātanam*—Sanātana; *atha*—thereafter; *ātma-bhūḥ*—Brahmā, who is self-born; *sanat-kumāram*—Sanat-kumāra; *ca*—also; *munīn*—the great sages; *niṣkriyān*—free from all fruitive action; *ūrdhva-retasaḥ*—those whose semen flows upwards.

TRANSLATION

In the beginning, Brahmā created four great sages named Sanaka, Sananda, Sanātana and Sanat-kumāra. All of them were unwilling to adopt materialistic activities because they were highly elevated due to their semen's flowing upwards.

PURPORT

Although Brahmā created the principles of nescience as a matter of necessity for those living entities who were destined to ignorance by the will of the Lord, he was not satisfied in performing such a thankless task. He therefore created four principles of knowledge: *sāṅkhya*, or empirical philosophy for the analytical study of material conditions; *yoga*, or mysticism for liberation of the pure soul from material bondage; *vairāgya*, the acceptance of complete detachment from material enjoyment in life to elevate oneself to the highest spiritual understanding; and *tapas*, or the various kinds of voluntary austerities performed for spiritual perfection. Brahmā created the four great sages Sanaka, Sananda, Sanātana and Sanat to entrust them with these four principles of spiritual advancement, and they inaugurated their own spiritual party, or *sampradāya*, known as the Kumāra-sampradāya, or later on as the Nimbārka-sampradāya, for the advancement of *bhakti*. All of these great sages became great devotees, for without devotional service to the Personality of Godhead one cannot achieve success in any activity of spiritual value.

TEXT 5

तान् बभाषे स्वभूः पुत्रान् प्रजाः सृजत पुत्रकाः ।
तन्नैच्छन्मोक्षधर्माणो वासुदेवपरायणाः ॥ ५ ॥

tān babhāṣe svabhūḥ putrān
prajāḥ sṛjata putrakāḥ
tan naicchan mokṣa-dharmāṇo
vāsudeva-parāyaṇāḥ

tān—unto the Kumāras, as above mentioned; *babhāṣe*—addressed; *svabhūḥ*—Brahmā; *putrān*—unto the sons; *prajāḥ*—generations; *sṛjata*—to create; *putrakāḥ*—O my sons; *tat*—that; *na*—not; *aicchan*—desired; *mokṣa-dharmāṇaḥ*—pledged to the principles of liberation; *vāsudeva*—the Personality of Godhead; *parāyaṇāḥ*—who are so devoted.

TRANSLATION

Brahmā spoke to his sons after generating them. "My dear sons," he said, "now generate progeny." But due to their being attached to Vāsudeva, the Supreme Personality of Godhead, they aimed at liberation, and therefore they expressed their unwillingness.

PURPORT

The four sons of Brahmā, the Kumāras, declined to become family men even on the request of their great father, Brahmā. Those who are serious about gaining release from material bondage should not be entangled in the false relationship of family bondage. People may ask how the Kumāras could refuse the orders of Brahmā, who was their father and above all the creator of the universe. The reply is that one who is *vāsudeva-parāyaṇa,* or seriously engaged in the devotional service of the Personality of Godhead, Vāsudeva, need not care for any other obligation. It is enjoined in the *Bhāgavatam* (11.5.41):

devarṣi-bhūtāpta-nṛṇāṁ pitṝṇāṁ
na kiṅkaro nāyam ṛṇī ca rājan
sarvātmanā yaḥ śaraṇaṁ śaraṇyaṁ
gato mukundaṁ parihṛtya kartam

"Anyone who has completely given up all worldly relationships and has taken absolute shelter of the lotus feet of the Lord, who gives us salvation and who alone is fit to be taken shelter of, is no longer a debtor or servant of anyone, including the demigods, forefathers, sages, other living entities, relatives and members of human society." Thus there was nothing wrong in the acts of the Kumāras when they refused their great father's request that they become family men.

TEXT 6

सोऽवध्यातः सुतैरेवं प्रत्याख्यातानुशासनैः ।
क्रोधं दुर्विषहं जातं नियन्तुमुपचक्रमे ॥ ६ ॥

so 'vadhyātaḥ sutair evaṁ
pratyākhyātānuśāsanaiḥ
krodhaṁ durviṣahaṁ jātaṁ
niyantum upacakrame

saḥ—he (Brahmā); *avadhyātaḥ*—thus being disrespected; *sutaiḥ*—by the sons; *evam*—thus; *pratyākhyāta*—refusing to obey; *anuśāsanaiḥ*—the order of their father; *krodham*—anger; *durviṣaham*—too much to be tolerated; *jātam*—thus generated; *niyantum*—to control; *upacakrame*—tried his best.

TRANSLATION

On the refusal of the sons to obey the order of their father, there was much anger generated in the mind of Brahmā, which he tried to control and not express.

PURPORT

Brahmā is the director in charge of the mode of passion of material nature. Therefore it was natural for him to become angry on the refusal of his sons to obey his order. Although the Kumāras were right in such acts of refusal, Brahmā, being absorbed in the mode of passion, could not check his passionate anger. He did not express it, however, because he knew that his sons were far enlightened in spiritual advancement and thus he should not express his anger before them.

TEXT 7

धिया निगृह्यमाणोऽपि भ्रुवोर्मध्यात्प्रजापतेः ।
सद्योऽजायत तन्मन्युः कुमारो नीललोहितः ॥ ७ ॥

dhiyā nigṛhyamāṇo 'pi
bhruvor madhyāt prajāpateḥ
sadyo 'jāyata tan-manyuḥ
kumāro nīla-lohitaḥ

dhiyā—by intelligence; *nigṛhyamāṇaḥ*—being controlled; *api*—in spite of; *bhruvoḥ*—of the eyebrows; *madhyāt*—from between; *prajāpateḥ*—of Brahmā; *sadyaḥ*—at once; *ajāyata*—generated; *tat*—his; *manyuḥ*—anger; *kumāraḥ*—a child; *nīla-lohitaḥ*—mixture of blue and red.

TRANSLATION

Although he tried to curb his anger, it came out from between his eyebrows, and a child of mixed blue and red was immediately generated.

PURPORT

The face of anger is the same whether exhibited due to ignorance or knowledge. Although Brahmā tried to curb his anger, he could not do so, even though he is the supreme being. Such anger in its true color came from between the eyebrows of Brahmā as Rudra, in a mixed color of blue (ignorance) and red (passion), because anger is the product of passion and ignorance.

TEXT 8

स वै रुरोद देवानां पूर्वजो भगवान् भवः ।
नामानि कुरु मे धातः स्थानानि च जगद्गुरो ॥ ८ ॥

sa vai ruroda devānāṁ
pūrvajo bhagavān bhavaḥ
nāmāni kuru me dhātaḥ
sthānāni ca jagad-guro

saḥ—he; *vai*—certainly; *ruroda*—cried loudly; *devānām pūrvajaḥ*—the eldest of all demigods; *bhagavān*—the most powerful; *bhavaḥ*—Lord Śiva; *nāmāni*—different names; *kuru*—designate; *me*—my; *dhātaḥ*—O destiny maker; *sthānāni*—places; *ca*—also; *jagat-guro*—O teacher of the universe.

TRANSLATION

After his birth he began to cry: O destiny maker, teacher of the universe, kindly designate my name and place.

TEXT 9

इति तस्य वचः पाद्मो भगवान् परिपालयन् ।
अभ्यधाद्भद्रया वाचा मा रोदीस्तत्करोमि ते ॥ ९ ॥

iti tasya vacaḥ pādmo
bhagavān paripālayan
abhyadhād bhadrayā vācā
mā rodīs tat karomi te

iti—thus; *tasya*—his; *vacaḥ*—request; *pādmaḥ*—one who is born from the lotus flower; *bhagavān*—the powerful; *paripālayan*—accepting the request; *abhyadhāt*—pacified; *bhadrayā*—by gentle; *vācā*—words; *mā*—do not; *rodīḥ*—cry; *tat*—that; *karomi*—I shall do it; *te*—as desired by you.

TRANSLATION

The all-powerful Brahmā, who was born from the lotus flower, pacified the boy with gentle words, accepting his request, and said: Do not cry. I shall certainly do as you desire.

TEXT 10

यदरोदीः सुरश्रेष्ठ सोद्वेग इव बालकः ।
ततस्त्वामभिधास्यन्ति नाम्ना रुद्र इति प्रजाः ॥१०॥

yad arodīḥ sura-śreṣṭha
sodvega iva bālakaḥ
tatas tvām abhidhāsyanti
nāmnā rudra iti prajāḥ

yat—as much as; *arodīḥ*—cried loudly; *sura-śreṣṭha*—O chief of the demigods; *sa-udvegaḥ*—with great anxiety; *iva*—like; *bālakaḥ*—a boy; *tataḥ*—therefore; *tvām*—you; *abhidhāsyanti*—will call; *nāmnā*—by the name; *rudraḥ*—Rudra; *iti*—thus; *prajāḥ*—people.

TRANSLATION

Thereafter Brahmā said: O chief of the demigods, you shall be called by the name Rudra by all people because you have so anxiously cried.

TEXT 11

हृदिन्द्रियाण्यसुर्व्योम वायुरग्निर्जलं मही ।
सूर्यश्चन्द्रस्तपश्चैव स्थानान्यग्रे कृतानि ते ॥११॥

hṛd indriyāṇy asur vyoma
vāyur agnir jalaṁ mahī

sūryaś candras tapaś caiva
sthānāny agre kṛtāni te

hṛt—the heart; *indriyāṇi*—the senses; *asuḥ*—life air; *vyoma*—the sky; *vāyuḥ*—the air; *agniḥ*—fire; *jalam*—water; *mahī*—the earth; *sūryaḥ*—the sun; *candraḥ*—the moon; *tapaḥ*—austerity; *ca*—as well as; *eva*—certainly; *sthānāni*—all these places; *agre*—hereinbefore; *kṛtāni*—already made; *te*—for you.

TRANSLATION

My dear boy, I have already selected the following places for your residence: the heart, the senses, the air of life, the sky, the air, the fire, the water, the earth, the sun, the moon and austerity.

PURPORT

The creation of Rudra from between the eyebrows of Brahmā as the result of his anger, generated from the mode of passion partly touched by ignorance, is very significant. In *Bhagavad-gītā* (3.37) the principle of Rudra is described. *Krodha* (anger) is the product of *kāma* (lust), which is the result of the mode of passion. When lust and hankering are unsatisfied, the element of *krodha* appears, which is the formidable enemy of the conditioned soul. This most sinful and inimical passion is represented as *ahaṅkāra*, or the false egocentric attitude of thinking oneself to be all in all. Such an egocentric attitude on the part of the conditioned soul, who is completely under the control of material nature, is described in *Bhagavad-gītā* as foolish. The egocentric attitude is a manifestation of the Rudra principle in the heart, wherein *krodha* (anger) is generated. This anger develops in the heart and is further manifested through various senses, like the eyes, hands and legs. When a man is angry he expresses such anger with red-hot eyes and sometimes makes a display of clenching his fists or kicking his legs. This exhibition of the Rudra principle is the proof of Rudra's presence in such places. When a man is angry he breathes very rapidly, and thus Rudra is represented in the air of life, or in the activities of breathing. When the sky is overcast with dense clouds and roars in anger, and when the wind blows very fiercely, the Rudra principle is manifested, and so also when the seawater is infuriated by the wind it appears in a gloomy feature of Rudra, which is very fearful to the common man. When fire is ablaze we can also experience the presence of Rudra, and when there is an inundation over the earth we can understand that this is also the representation of Rudra.

There are many earthly creatures who constantly represent the Rudra element. The snake, tiger and lion are always representations of Rudra. Sometimes, because of the extreme heat of the sun, there are cases of heatstroke, and due to the extreme coldness created by the moon there are cases of collapse. There are many sages empowered with the influence of austerity and many *yogīs*, philosophers and renouncers who sometimes exhibit their acquired power under the influence of the Rudra principles of anger and passion. The great *yogī* Durvāsā, under the influence of this Rudra principle, picked a quarrel with Mahārāja Ambarīṣa, and a *brāhmaṇa* boy exhibited the Rudra principle by cursing the great King Parīkṣit. When the Rudra principle is exhibited by persons who are not engaged in the devotional service of the Supreme Personality of Godhead, the angry person falls down from the peak of his improved position. This is confirmed as follows:

ye 'nye 'ravindākṣa vimukta-māninas
tvayy asta-bhāvād aviśuddha-buddhayaḥ
āruhya kṛcchreṇa paraṁ padaṁ tataḥ
patanty adho 'nādṛta-yuṣmad-aṅghrayaḥ
(*Bhāg.* 10.2.32)

The most lamentable falldown of the impersonalist is due to his false and unreasonable claim of being one with the Supreme.

TEXT 12

मन्युर्मनुर्महिनसो महाञ्छिव ऋतध्वजः ।
उग्ररेता भवः कालो वामदेवो धृतव्रतः ॥१२॥

manyur manur mahinaso
mahāñ chiva ṛtadhvajaḥ
ugraretā bhavaḥ kālo
vāmadevo dhṛtavrataḥ

manyuḥ, manuḥ, mahinasaḥ, mahān, śivaḥ, ṛtadhvajaḥ, ugraretāḥ, bhavaḥ, kālaḥ, vāmadevaḥ, dhṛtavrataḥ—all names of Rudra.

TRANSLATION

Lord Brahmā said: My dear boy Rudra, you have eleven other names: Manyu, Manu, Mahinasa, Mahān, Śiva, Ṛtadhvaja, Ugraretā, Bhava, Kāla, Vāmadeva and Dhṛtavrata.

TEXT 13

धीर्धृतिरसलोमा च नियुत्सर्पिरिलाम्बिका ।
इरावती स्वधा दीक्षा रुद्राण्यो रुद्र ते स्त्रियः ॥१३॥

dhīr dhṛti-rasalomā ca
niyut sarpir ilāmbikā
irāvatī svadhā dīkṣā
rudrāṇyo rudra te striyaḥ

dhīḥ, dhṛti, rasalā, umā, niyut, sarpiḥ, ilā, ambikā, irāvatī, svadhā, dīkṣā rudrāṇyaḥ—the eleven Rudrāṇīs; *rudra*—O Rudra; *te*—unto you; *striyaḥ*—wives.

TRANSLATION

O Rudra, you also have eleven wives, called the Rudrāṇīs, and they are as follows: Dhī, Dhṛti, Rasalā, Umā, Niyut, Sarpi, Ilā, Ambikā, Irāvatī, Svadhā and Dīkṣā.

TEXT 14

गृहाणैतानि नामानि स्थानानि च सयोषणः ।
एभिः सृज प्रजा बह्वीः प्रजानामसि यत्पतिः ॥१४॥

gṛhāṇaitāni nāmāni
sthānāni ca sa-yoṣaṇaḥ
ebhiḥ sṛja prajā bahvīḥ
prajānām asi yat patiḥ

gṛhāṇa—just accept; *etāni*—all these; *nāmāni*—different names; *sthānāni*—as well as places; *ca*—also; *sa-yoṣaṇaḥ*—along with wives;

ebhiḥ—with them; *sṛja*—just generate; *prajāḥ*—progeny; *bahvīḥ*—on a large scale; *prajānām*—of the living entities; *asi*—you are; *yat*—since; *patiḥ*—the master.

TRANSLATION

My dear boy, you may now accept all the names and places designated for you and your different wives, and since you are now one of the masters of the living entities, you may increase the population on a large scale.

PURPORT

Brahmā, as the father of Rudra, selected the wives of his son, his living places, and his names as well. It is natural that one should accept the wife selected by one's father, just as a son accepts the name given by the father or as he accepts the property offered by the father. That is the general course in increasing the population of the world. On the other hand, the Kumāras did not accept the offering of their father because they were elevated far beyond the business of generating a great number of sons. As the son can refuse the order of the father for higher purposes, so the father can refuse to maintain his sons in increasing population because of higher purposes.

TEXT 15

इत्यादिष्टः स्वगुरुणा भगवान्नीललोहितः ।
सत्त्वाकृतिस्वभावेन ससर्जात्मसमाः प्रजाः ॥१५॥

ity ādiṣṭaḥ sva-guruṇā
bhagavān nīla-lohitaḥ
sattvākṛti-svabhāvena
sasarjātma-samāḥ prajāḥ

iti—thus; *ādiṣṭaḥ*—being ordered; *sva-guruṇā* -by his own spiritual master; *bhagavān*—the most powerful; *nīla-lohitaḥ*—Rudra, whose color is mixed blue and red; *sattva*—power; *ākṛti*—bodily features; *svabhāvena*—and with a very furious mode of nature; *sasarja*—created; *ātma-samāḥ*—like his own prototype; *prajāḥ*—generations.

TRANSLATION

The most powerful Rudra, whose bodily color was blue mixed with red, created many offspring exactly resembling him in features, strength and furious nature.

TEXT 16

रुद्राणां रुद्रसृष्टानां समन्ताद् ग्रसतां जगत् ।
निशाम्यासंख्यशो यूथान् प्रजापतिरशङ्कत ॥१६॥

rudrāṇāṁ rudra-sṛṣṭānāṁ
samantād grasatāṁ jagat
niśāmyāsaṅkhyaśo yūthān
prajāpatir aśaṅkata

rudrāṇām—of the sons of Rudra; *rudra-sṛṣṭānām*—who were generated by Rudra; *samantāt*—being assembled together; *grasatām*—while devouring; *jagat*—the universe; *niśāmya*—by observing their activities; *asaṅkhyaśaḥ*—unlimited; *yūthān*—assembly; *prajā-patiḥ*—the father of the living entities; *aśaṅkata*—became afraid of.

TRANSLATION

The sons and grandsons generated by Rudra were unlimited in number, and when they assembled together they attempted to devour the entire universe. When Brahmā, the father of the living entities, saw this, he became afraid of the situation.

PURPORT

The generations of Rudra, the incarnation of anger, were so dangerous to the maintenance of universal affairs that even Brahmā, the father of the living entities, became afraid of them. The so-called devotees or followers of Rudra are also a menace. They are sometimes dangerous even to Rudra himself. Descendants of Rudra sometimes make plans to kill Rudra—by the grace of Rudra. That is the nature of his devotees.

TEXT 17

अलं प्रजाभिः सृष्टाभिरीदृशीभिः सुरोत्तम ।
मया सह दहन्तीभिर्दिशश्चक्षुर्भिरुल्बणैः ॥१७॥

alaṁ prajābhiḥ sṛṣṭābhir
īdṛśībhiḥ surottama
mayā saha dahantībhir
diśaś cakṣurbhir ulbaṇaiḥ

alam—unnecessary; *prajābhiḥ*—by such living entities; *sṛṣṭābhiḥ*—generated; *īdṛśībhiḥ*—of this type; *sura-uttama*—O best among the demigods; *mayā*—me; *saha*—along with; *dahantībhiḥ*—who are burning; *diśaḥ*—all sides; *cakṣurbhiḥ*—by the eyes; *ulbaṇaiḥ*—fiery flames.

TRANSLATION

Brahmā told Rudra: O best among the demigods, there is no need for you to generate living entities of this nature. They have begun to devastate everything on all sides with the fiery flames from their eyes, and they have even attacked me.

TEXT 18

तप आतिष्ठ भद्रं ते सर्वभूतसुखावहम् ।
तपसैव यथापूर्वं स्रष्टा विश्वमिदं भवान् ॥१८॥

tapa ātiṣṭha bhadraṁ te
sarva-bhūta-sukhāvaham
tapasaiva yathā pūrvaṁ
sraṣṭā viśvam idaṁ bhavān

tapaḥ—penance; *ātiṣṭha*—be situated; *bhadram*—auspicious; *te*—unto you; *sarva*—all; *bhūta*—living entities; *sukha-āvaham*—bringing happiness; *tapasā*—by penance; *eva*—only; *yathā*—as much as; *pūrvam*—before; *sraṣṭā*—will create; *viśvam*—the universe; *idam*—this; *bhavān*—yourself.

TRANSLATION

My dear son, you had better situate yourself in penance, which is auspicious for all living entities and which will bring all benediction upon you. By penance only shall you be able to create the universe as it was before.

PURPORT

In the creation, maintenance and dissolution of the cosmic manifestation, the three deities Brahmā, Viṣṇu and Maheśvara, or Śiva, are respectively in charge. Rudra was advised not to destroy while the period of creation and maintenance was going on, but to situate himself in penance and wait for the time of dissolution, when his services would be called for.

TEXT 19

तपसैव परं ज्योतिर्भगवन्तमधोक्षजम् ।
सर्वभूतगुहावासमञ्जसा विन्दते पुमान् ॥१९॥

tapasaiva paraṁ jyotir
bhagavantam adhokṣajam
sarva-bhūta-guhāvāsam
añjasā vindate pumān

tapasā—by penance; *eva*—only; *param*—the supreme; *jyotiḥ*—light; *bhagavantam*—unto the Personality of Godhead; *adhokṣajam*—He who is beyond the approach of the senses; *sarva-bhūta-guhā-āvāsam*—residing in the heart of all living entities; *añjasā*—completely; *vindate*—can know; *pumān*—a person.

TRANSLATION

By penance only can one even approach the Personality of Godhead, who is within the heart of every living entity and at the same time beyond the reach of all senses.

PURPORT

Rudra was advised by Brahmā to perform penance as an example to his sons and followers that penance is necessary for attaining the favor of the Supreme Personality of Godhead. In *Bhagavad-gītā* it is said that the common mass of people follow the path shown by an authority. Thus Brahmā, disgusted with the Rudra generations and afraid of being devoured by the increase of population, asked Rudra to stop producing such an unwanted generation and take to penance for attaining the favor of the Supreme Lord. We find, therefore, in pictures, that Rudra is always sitting in meditation for the attainment of the favor of the Lord. Indirectly, the sons and followers of Rudra are advised to stop the business of annihilation, following the Rudra principle while the peaceful creation of Brahmā is going on.

TEXT 20

मैत्रेय उवाच
एवमात्मभुवादिष्टः परिक्रम्य गिरां पतिम् ।
बाढमित्यमुमामन्त्र्य विवेश तपसे वनम् ॥२०॥

maitreya uvāca
evam ātmabhuvādiṣṭaḥ
parikramya girāṁ patim
bāḍham ity amum āmantrya
viveśa tapase vanam

maitreyaḥ uvāca—Śrī Maitreya said; *evam*—thus; *ātma-bhuvā*—by Brahmā; *ādiṣṭaḥ*—being so requested; *parikramya*—by circumambulating; *girām*—of the *Vedas; patim*—unto the master; *bāḍham*—that is right; *iti*—thus; *amum*—unto Brahmā; *āmantrya*—thus addressing; *viveśa*—entered into; *tapase*—for the matter of penance; *vanam*—into the forest.

TRANSLATION

Śrī Maitreya said: Thus Rudra, having been ordered by Brahmā, circumambulated his father, the master of the Vedas. Addressing him with words of assent, he entered the forest to perform austere penances.

TEXT 21

अथाभिध्यायतः सर्गं दश पुत्राः प्रजज्ञिरे ।
भगवच्छक्तियुक्तस्य लोकसन्तानहेतवः ॥२१॥

athābhidhyāyataḥ sargaṁ
daśa putrāḥ prajajñire
bhagavac-chakti-yuktasya
loka-santāna-hetavaḥ

atha—thus; *abhidhyāyataḥ*—while thinking of; *sargam*—creation; *daśa*—ten; *putrāḥ*—sons; *prajajñire*—were begotten; *bhagavat*—regarding the Personality of Godhead; *śakti*—potency; *yuktasya*—empowered with; *loka*—the world; *santāna*—generation; *hetavaḥ*—the causes.

TRANSLATION

Brahmā, who was empowered by the Supreme Personality of Godhead, thought of generating living entities and begot ten sons for the extension of the generations.

TEXT 22

मरीचिरत्र्यङ्गिरसौ पुलस्त्यः पुलहः क्रतुः ।
भृगुर्वसिष्ठो दक्षश्च दशमस्तत्र नारदः ॥२२॥

marīcir atry-aṅgirasau
pulastyaḥ pulahaḥ kratuḥ
bhṛgur vasiṣṭho dakṣaś ca
daśamas tatra nāradaḥ

marīciḥ, atri, aṅgirasau, pulastyaḥ, pulahaḥ, kratuḥ, bhṛguḥ, vasiṣṭhaḥ, dakṣaḥ—names of sons of Brahmā; *ca*—and; *daśamaḥ*—the tenth; *tatra*—there; *nāradaḥ*—Nārada.

TRANSLATION

Marīci, Atri, Aṅgirā, Pulastya, Pulaha, Kratu, Bhṛgu, Vasiṣṭha, Dakṣa, and the tenth son, Nārada, were thus born.

PURPORT

The whole process of the creation, maintenance and dissolution of the cosmic manifestation is meant to give the conditioned souls a chance to go back home, back to Godhead. Brahmā created Rudra to help him in his creative endeavor, but from the very beginning Rudra began to devour the whole creation, and thus he had to be stopped from such devastating activities. Brahmā therefore created another set of good children, who were mostly in favor of worldly fruitive activities. He knew very well, however, that without devotional service to the Lord there is hardly any benefit for the conditioned souls, and therefore he at last created his worthy son Nārada, who is the supreme spiritual master of all transcendentalists. Without devotional service to the Lord one cannot make progress in any department of activity, although the path of devotional service is always independent of anything material. Only the transcendental loving service of the Lord can deliver the real goal of life, and thus the service rendered by Śrīman Nārada Muni is the highest among all the sons of Brahmā.

TEXT 23

उत्सङ्गान्नारदो जज्ञे दक्षोऽङ्गुष्ठात्स्वयम्भुवः ।
प्राणाद्वसिष्ठः सञ्जातो भृगुस्त्वचि करात्क्रतुः ॥२३॥

utsaṅgān nārado jajñe
dakṣo 'ṅguṣṭhāt svayambhuvaḥ
prāṇād vasiṣṭhaḥ sañjāto
bhṛgus tvaci karāt kratuḥ

utsaṅgāt—by transcendental deliberation; *nāradaḥ*—Mahāmuni Nārada; *jajñe*—was generated; *dakṣaḥ*—Dakṣa; *aṅguṣṭhāt*—from the thumb; *svayambhuvaḥ*—of Brahmā; *prāṇāt*—from the life air, or breathing; *vasiṣṭhaḥ*—Vasiṣṭha; *sañjātaḥ*—was born; *bhṛguḥ*—the sage Bhṛgu; *tvaci*—from the touch; *karāt*—from the hand; *kratuḥ*—the sage Kratu.

TRANSLATION

Nārada was born from the deliberation of Brahmā, which is the best part of his body. Vasiṣṭha was born from his breathing, Dakṣa from a thumb, Bhṛgu from his touch, and Kratu from his hand.

PURPORT

Nārada was born from the best deliberation of Brahmā because Nārada was able to deliver the Supreme Lord to anyone he liked. The Supreme Personality of Godhead cannot be realized by any amount of Vedic knowledge or by any number of penances. But a pure devotee of the Lord like Nārada can deliver the Supreme Lord by his good will. The very name Nārada suggests that he can deliver the Supreme Lord. *Nāra* means the "Supreme Lord," and *da* means "one who can deliver." That he can deliver the Supreme Lord does not mean that the Lord is like a commodity that can be delivered to any person. But Nārada can deliver to anyone the transcendental loving service of the Lord as a servitor, friend, parent or lover, as one may desire out of one's own transcendental love for the Lord. In other words, it is Nārada only who can deliver the path of *bhakti-yoga*, the highest mystic means for attainment of the Supreme Lord.

TEXT 24

पुलहो नाभितो जज्ञे पुलस्त्यः कर्णयोर्ऋषिः ।
अङ्गिरा मुखतोऽक्ष्णोऽत्रिर्मरीचिर्मनसोऽभवत् ॥२४॥

pulaho nābhito jajñe
pulastyaḥ karṇayor ṛṣiḥ
aṅgirā mukhato 'kṣṇo 'trir
marīcir manaso 'bhavat

pulahaḥ—the sage Pulaha; *nābhitaḥ*—from the navel; *jajñe*—generated; *pulastyaḥ*—the sage Pulastya; *karṇayoḥ*—from the ears; *ṛṣiḥ*—the great sage; *aṅgirāḥ*—the sage Aṅgirā; *mukhataḥ*—from the mouth; *akṣṇaḥ*—from the eyes; *atriḥ*—the sage Atri; *marīciḥ*—the sage Marīci; *manasaḥ*—from the mind; *abhavat*—appeared.

TRANSLATION

Pulastya was generated from the ears, Aṅgirā from the mouth, Atri from the eyes, Marīci from the mind and Pulaha from the navel of Brahmā.

TEXT 25

धर्मः स्तनाद्दक्षिणतो यत्र नारायणः स्वयम् ।
अधर्मः पृष्ठतो यस्मान्मृत्युर्लोकभयङ्करः ॥२५॥

dharmaḥ stanād dakṣiṇato
yatra nārāyaṇaḥ svayam

adharmaḥ pṛṣṭhato yasmān
mṛtyur loka-bhayaṅkaraḥ

dharmaḥ—religion; *stanāt*—from the breast; *dakṣiṇataḥ*—on the right side; *yatra*—wherein; *nārāyaṇaḥ*—the Supreme Lord; *svayam*—personally; *adharmaḥ*—irreligion; *pṛṣṭhataḥ*—from the back; *yasmāt*—from which; *mṛtyuḥ*—death; *loka*—to the living entity; *bhayam-karaḥ*—horrible.

TRANSLATION

Religion was manifested from the breast of Brahmā, wherein is seated the Supreme Personality of Godhead Nārāyaṇa, and irreligion appeared from his back, where horrible death takes place for the living entity.

PURPORT

That religion was manifested from the place where the Personality of Godhead is personally situated is very significant because religion means devotional service to the Personality of Godhead, as confirmed in *Bhagavad-gītā* as well as the *Bhāgavatam.* In *Bhagavad-gītā* the last instruction is to give up all other engagements in the name of religion and take shelter of the Personality of Godhead. *Śrīmad-Bhāgavatam* also confirms that the highest perfection of religion is that which leads to the devotional service of the Lord, unmotivated and unhampered by material impediments. Religion in its perfect form is the devotional service of the Lord, and irreligion is just the opposite. The heart is the most important part of the body, whereas the back is the most neglected part. When one is attacked by an enemy one is apt to endure attacks from the back and protect himself carefully from all attacks on the chest. All types of irreligion spring from the back of Brahmā, whereas real religion, the devotional service of the Lord, is generated from the chest, the seat of Nārāyaṇa. Anything which does not lead to the devotional service of the Lord is irreligion, and anything which leads to the devotional service of the Lord is called religion.

TEXT 26

हृदि कामो भ्रुवः क्रोधो लोभश्चाधरदच्छदात् ।
आस्याद्वाक्सिन्धवो मेढ्रान्निर्ऋतिः पायोरघाश्रयः ॥२६॥

hṛdi kāmo bhruvaḥ krodho
lobhaś cādhara-dacchadāt
āsyād vāk sindhavo meḍhrān
nirṛtiḥ pāyor aghāśrayaḥ

hṛdi—from the heart; *kāmaḥ*—lust; *bhruvaḥ*—from the eyebrows; *krodhaḥ*—anger; *lobhaḥ*—greed; *ca*—also; *adhara-dacchadāt*—from between the lips; *āsyāt*—from the mouth; *vāk*—speaking; *sindhavaḥ*—the seas; *meḍhrāt*—from the penis; *nirṛtiḥ*—low activities; *pāyoḥ*—from the anus; *agha-āśrayaḥ*—reservoir of all vices.

TRANSLATION

Lust and desire became manifested from the heart of Brahmā, anger from between his eyebrows, greed from between his lips, the power of speaking from his mouth, the ocean from his penis, and low and abominable activities from his anus, the source of all sins.

PURPORT

A conditioned soul is under the influence of mental speculation. However great one may be in the estimation of mundane education and learning, he cannot be free from the influence of psychic activities. Therefore it is very difficult to give up lust and the desires for low activities until one is in the line of devotional service to the Lord. When one is frustrated in lust and low desires, anger is generated from the mind and expressed from between the eyebrows. Ordinary men are therefore advised to concentrate the mind by focusing on the place between the eyebrows, whereas the devotees of the Lord are already practiced to place the Supreme Personality of Godhead on the seat of their minds. The theory of becoming desireless is untenable because the mind cannot be made desireless. When it is recommended that one be desireless, it is understood that one should not desire things which are destructive to spiritual values. A devotee of the Lord always has the Lord in his mind, and thus he does not need to be desireless because all his desires are in relationship with the service of the Lord. The power of speaking is called Sarasvatī, or the goddess of learning, and the birthplace of the goddess of learning is the mouth of Brahmā. Even if a man is endowed with the favor of the goddess of learning, it is quite possible for his heart to be full of lust and material desire and his eyebrows to display symptoms of anger. One may be very learned in the mundane estimation, but that does not mean that he is free from all low activities of lust and anger. Good qualifications can be expected only from a pure devotee, who is always engaged in the thought of the Lord, or in *samādhi*, with faith.

TEXT 27

छायायाः कर्दमो जज्ञे देवहूत्याः पतिः प्रभुः ।
मनसो देहतश्चेदं जज्ञे विश्वकृतो जगत् ॥२७॥

chāyāyāḥ kardamo jajñe
devahūtyāḥ patiḥ prabhuḥ
manaso dehataś cedaṁ
jajñe viśva-kṛto jagat

chāyāyāḥ—by the shadow; *kardamaḥ*—Kardama Muni; *jajñe*—became manifested; *devahūtyāḥ*—of Devahūti; *patiḥ*—husband; *prabhuḥ*—the master; *manasaḥ*—from the mind; *dehataḥ*—from the body; *ca*—also; *idam*—this; *jajñe*—developed; *viśva*—the universe; *kṛtaḥ*—of the creator; *jagat*—cosmic manifestation.

TRANSLATION

Sage Kardama, husband of the great Devahūti, was manifested from the shadow of Brahmā. Thus all became manifested from either the body or the mind of Brahmā.

PURPORT

Although one of the three modes of material nature is always prominent, they are never represented unalloyed by one another. Even in the most prominent existence of the two lower qualities, the modes of passion and ignorance, there is sometimes a tinge of the mode of goodness. Therefore all the sons generated from the body or the mind of Brahmā were in the modes of passion and ignorance, but some of them, like

Kardama, were born in the mode of goodness. Nārada was born in the transcendental state of Brahmā.

TEXT 28

वाचं दुहितरं तन्वीं स्वयम्भूर्हरतीं मनः ।
अकामां चकमे क्षत्तः सकाम इति नः श्रुतम् ॥२८॥

vācaṁ duhitaraṁ tanvīṁ
svayambhūr haratīṁ manaḥ
akāmāṁ cakame kṣattaḥ
sa-kāma iti naḥ śrutam

vācam—Vāk; *duhitaram*—unto the daughter; *tanvīm*—born of his body; *svayambhūḥ*—Brahmā; *haratīm*—attracting; *manaḥ*—his mind; *akāmām*—without being sexually inclined; *cakame*—desired; *kṣattaḥ*—O Vidura; *sa-kāmaḥ*—being sexually inclined; *iti*—thus; *naḥ*—we; *śrutam*—have heard.

TRANSLATION

O Vidura, we have heard that Brahmā had a daughter named Vāk who was born from his body and who attracted his mind toward sex, although she was not sexually inclined towards him.

PURPORT

Balavān indriya-grāmo vidvāṁsam api karṣati (*Bhāg.* 9.19.17). It is said that the senses are so mad and strong that they can bewilder even the most sensible and learned man. Therefore it is advised that one should not indulge in living alone even with one's mother, sister or daughter. *Vidvāṁsam api karṣati* means that even the most learned also become victims of the sensuous urge. Maitreya hesitated to state this anomaly on the part of Brahmā, who was sexually inclined to his own daughter, but still he mentioned it because sometimes it so happens, and the living example is Brahmā himself, although he is the primeval living being and the most learned within the whole universe. If Brahmā could be a victim of the sexual urge, then what of others, who are prone to so many mundane frailties? This extraordinary immorality on the part of

Brahmā was heard to have occurred in some particular *kalpa*, but it could not have happened in the *kalpa* in which Brahmā heard directly from the Lord the four essential verses of *Śrīmad-Bhāgavatam* because the Lord benedicted Brahmā, after giving him lessons on the *Bhāgavatam*, that he would never be bewildered in any *kalpa* whatsoever. This indicates that before the hearing of *Śrīmad-Bhāgavatam* he might have fallen a victim to such sensuality, but after hearing *Śrīmad-Bhāgavatam* directly from the Lord, there was no possibility of such failures.

One should, however, take serious note of this incident. The human being is a social animal, and his unrestricted mixing with the fair sex leads to downfall. Such social freedom of man and woman, especially among the younger section, is certainly a great stumbling block on the path of spiritual progress. Material bondage is due only to sexual bondage, and therefore unrestricted association of man and woman is surely a great impediment. Maitreya cited this example on the part of Brahmā just to bring to our notice this great danger.

TEXT 29

तमधर्मे कृतमतिं विलोक्य पितरं सुताः ।
मरीचिमुख्या मुनयो विश्रम्भात्प्रत्यबोधयन् ॥२९॥

tam adharme kṛta-matiṁ
vilokya pitaraṁ sutāḥ
marīci-mukhyā munayo
viśrambhāt pratyabodhayan

tam—unto him; *adharme*—in the matter of immorality; *kṛta-matim*—the mind being so given; *vilokya*—seeing thus; *pitaram*—unto the father; *sutāḥ*—sons; *marīci-mukhyāḥ*—headed by Marīci; *munayaḥ*—sages; *viśrambhāt*—with due respect; *pratyabodhayan*—submitted as follows.

TRANSLATION

Thus, finding their father so deluded in an act of immorality, the sages headed by Marīci, all sons of Brahmā, spoke as follows with great respect.

PURPORT

The sages like Marīci were not in the wrong in submitting their protests against the acts of their great father. They knew very well that even though their father committed a mistake, there must have been some great purpose behind the show, otherwise such a great personality could not have committed such a mistake. It might be that Brahmā wanted to warn his subordinates about human frailties in their dealings with women. This is always very dangerous for persons who are on the path of self-realization. Therefore, great personalities like Brahmā, even when in the wrong, should not be neglected, nor could the great sages headed by Marīci show any disrespect because of his extraordinary behavior.

TEXT 30

नैतत्पूर्वैः कृतं त्वद्ये न करिष्यन्ति चापरे ।
यस्त्वं दुहितरं गच्छेरनिगृह्याङ्गजं प्रभुः ॥३०॥

naitat pūrvaiḥ kṛtaṁ tvad ye
na kariṣyanti cāpare
yas tvaṁ duhitaraṁ gaccher
anigṛhyāṅgajaṁ prabhuḥ

na—never; *etat*—such a thing; *pūrvaiḥ*—by any other Brahmā, or yourself in any previous *kalpa; kṛtam*—performed; *tvat*—by you; *ye*—that which; *na*—nor; *kariṣyanti*—will do; *ca*—also; *apare*—anyone else; *yaḥ*—that which; *tvam*—you; *duhitaram*—unto the daughter; *gaccheḥ*—would go; *anigṛhya*—without controlling; *aṅgajam*—sex desire; *prabhuḥ*—O father.

TRANSLATION

O father, this performance in which you are endeavoring to complicate yourself was never attempted by any other Brahmā, nor by anyone else, nor by you in previous kalpas, nor will anyone dare to attempt it in the future. You are the supreme being in the universe, so how is it that you want to have sex with your daughter and cannot control your desire?

PURPORT

The post of Brahmā is the supermost post in the universe, and it appears that there are many Brahmās and many universes besides the one in which we are situated. One who fills this post must be ideal in behavior, for Brahmā sets the example for all living entities. Brahmā, the living entity who is the most pious and spiritually elevated, is entrusted with a post next to that of the Personality of Godhead.

TEXT 31

तेजीयसामपि ह्येतन्न सुश्लोक्यं जगद्गुरो ।
यद्वृत्तमनुतिष्ठन् वै लोकः क्षेमाय कल्पते ॥३१॥

tejīyasām api hy etan
na suślokyaṁ jagad-guro
yad-vṛttam anutiṣṭhan vai
lokaḥ kṣemāya kalpate

tejīyasām—of the most powerful; *api*—also; *hi*—certainly; *etat*—such an act; *na*—not suitable; *su-ślokyam*—good behavior; *jagat-guro*—O spiritual master of the universe; *yat*—whose; *vṛttam*—character; *anutiṣṭhan*—following; *vai*—certainly; *lokaḥ*—the world; *kṣemāya*—for prosperity; *kalpate*—becomes eligible.

TRANSLATION

Even though you are the most powerful being, this act does not suit you because your character is followed for spiritual improvement by people in general.

PURPORT

It is said that a supremely powerful living entity can do anything and everything he likes and such acts do not affect him in any way. For example, the sun, the most powerful fiery planet in the universe, can evaporate water from anywhere and still remain as powerful. The sun evaporates water from filthy places and yet is not infected with the quality of the filth. Similarly, Brahmā remains unimpeachable in all conditions. But still, since he is the spiritual master of all living entities, his behavior and character should be so ideal that people will follow such sublime behavior and derive the highest spiritual benefit. Therefore, he should not have acted as he did.

TEXT 32

तस्मै नमो भगवते य इदं स्वेन रोचिषा ।
आत्मस्थं व्यञ्जयामास स धर्मं पातुमर्हति ॥३२॥

tasmai namo bhagavate
ya idaṁ svena rociṣā
ātma-sthaṁ vyañjayām āsa
sa dharmaṁ pātum arhati

tasmai—unto Him; *namaḥ*—obeisances; *bhagavate*—unto the Personality of Godhead; *yaḥ*—who; *idam*—this; *svena*—by His own; *rociṣā*—effulgence; *ātma-stham*—situated in Himself; *vyañjayām āsa*—has manifested; *saḥ*—He; *dharmam*—religion; *pātum*—for protection; *arhati*—may kindly do so.

TRANSLATION

Let us offer our respectful obeisances unto the Personality of Godhead, who, by His own effulgence, while situated in Himself, has manifested this cosmos. May He also protect religion for all goodness.

PURPORT

Lust for sexual intercourse is so strong that it appears herein that Brahmā could not be dissuaded from his determination in spite of the appeal by his great sons like Marīci. Therefore, the great sons began to pray to the Supreme Lord for the good sense of Brahmā. It is only by the grace of the Supreme Lord that one can be protected from the allurement of lusty material desires. The Lord gives protection to devotees who are always engaged in His transcendental loving service, and by His causeless mercy He forgives the accidental fall of a devotee. Therefore, sages like Marīci prayed for the mercy of the Lord, and their prayer was fruitful.

TEXT 33

स इत्थं गृणतः पुत्रान् पुरो दृष्ट्वा प्रजापतीन् ।
प्रजापतिपतिस्तन्वं तत्याज व्रीडितस्तदा ।
तां दिशो जगृहुर्घोरां नीहारं यद्विदुस्तमः ॥३३॥

sa ittham gṛṇataḥ putrān
puro dṛṣṭvā prajāpatīn
prajāpati-patis tanvaṁ
tatyāja vrīḍitas tadā
tāṁ diśo jagṛhur ghorāṁ
nīhāraṁ yad vidus tamaḥ

saḥ—he (Brahmā); *ittham*—thus; *gṛṇataḥ*—speaking; *putrān*—sons; *puraḥ*—before; *dṛṣṭvā*—seeing; *prajā-patīn*—all the progenitors of living entities; *prajāpati-patiḥ*—the father of all of them (Brahmā); *tanvam*—body; *tatyāja*—quit; *vrīḍitaḥ*—ashamed; *tadā*—at that time; *tām*—that body; *diśaḥ*—all directions; *jagṛhuḥ*—accepted; *ghorām*—blamable; *nīhāram*—fog; *yat*—which; *viduḥ*—they know as; *tamaḥ*—darkness.

TRANSLATION

The father of all Prajāpatis, Brahmā, thus seeing all his Prajāpati sons speaking in that way, became very much ashamed and at once gave up the body he had accepted. Later that body appeared in all directions as the dangerous fog in darkness.

PURPORT

The best way to compensate for one's sinful acts is to give up one's body at once, and Brahmā, the leader of the living entities, showed this by his personal example. Brahmā has a fabulous duration of life, but he was obliged to give up his body due to his grievous sin, even though he had merely contemplated it in his mind without having actually done it.

This is a lesson for the living entities, showing how sinful an act it is to indulge in unrestricted sex life. Even to think of abominable sex life is sinful, and to compensate for such sinful acts, one has to give up his body. In other words, one's duration of life, blessings, opulence, etc., are decreased by sinful acts, and the most dangerous type of sinful act is unrestricted sex.

Ignorance is the cause of sinful life, or sinful life is the cause of gross ignorance. The feature of ignorance is darkness or fog. Darkness or fog still covers the whole universe, and the sun is the only counteracting principle. One who takes shelter of the Lord, the perpetual light, has no fear of being annihilated in the darkness of fog or ignorance.

TEXT 34

कदाचिद् ध्यायतः स्रष्टुर्वेदा आसंश्चतुर्मुखात् ।
कथं स्रक्ष्याम्यहं लोकान् समवेतान् यथा पुरा ॥३४॥

kadācid dhyāyataḥ sraṣṭur
vedā āsaṁś catur-mukhāt
kathaṁ srakṣyāmy ahaṁ lokān
samavetān yathā purā

kadācit—once upon a time; *dhyāyataḥ*—while contemplating; *sraṣṭuḥ*—of Brahmā; *vedāḥ*—the Vedic literature; *āsan*—became manifested; *catuḥ-mukhāt*—from the four mouths; *katham srakṣyāmi*—how shall I create; *aham*—myself; *lokān*—all these worlds; *samavetān*—assembled; *yathā*—as they were; *purā*—in the past.

TRANSLATION

Once upon a time, when Brahmā was thinking of how to create the worlds as in the past millennium, the four Vedas, which contain all varieties of knowledge, became manifested from his four mouths.

PURPORT

As a fire can consume anything and everything without being contaminated, so, by the grace of the Lord, the fire of Brahmā's greatness consumed his desire for the sinful act of sex with his daughter. The *Vedas* are the source of all knowledge, and they were first revealed to Brahmā by the mercy of the Supreme Personality of Godhead while

Brahmā was thinking of re-creating the material world. Brahmā is powerful by dint of his devotional service unto the Lord, and the Lord is always ready to forgive His devotee if by chance he falls down from the noble path of devotional service. The *Śrīmad-Bhāgavatam* (11.5.42) confirms this as follows:

sva-pāda-mūlaṁ bhajataḥ priyasya
tyaktvānya-bhāvasya hariḥ pareśaḥ
vikarma yac cotpatitaṁ kathañ-cid
dhunoti sarvaṁ hṛdi sanniviṣṭaḥ

"Any person who is engaged one hundred percent in the transcendental loving service of the Lord, at His lotus feet, is very dear to the Personality of Godhead Hari, and the Lord, being situated in the heart of the devotee, excuses all kinds of sins committed by chance." It was never expected that a great personality like Brahmā would ever think of sex indulgence with his daughter. The example shown by Brahmā only suggests that the power of material nature is so strong that it can act upon everyone, even Brahmā. Brahmā was saved by the mercy of the Lord with a little punishment, but by the grace of the Lord he did not lose his prestige as the great Brahmā.

TEXT 35

चातुर्होत्रं कर्मतन्त्रमुपवेदनयैः सह ।
धर्मस्य पादाश्चत्वारस्तथैवाश्रमवृत्तयः ॥३५॥

cātur-hotraṁ karma-tantram
upaveda-nayaiḥ saha
dharmasya pādāś catvāras
tathaivāśrama-vṛttayaḥ

cātuḥ—four; *hotram*—paraphernalia for sacrifice; *karma*—action; *tantram*—expansions of such activities; *upaveda*—supplementary to the *Vedas;* *nayaiḥ*—by logical conclusions; *saha*—along with; *dharmasya*—of religiosity; *pādāḥ*—principles; *catvāraḥ*—four; *tathā eva*—in the same way; *āśrama*—social orders; *vṛttayaḥ*—occupations.

TRANSLATION

The four kinds of paraphernalia for conducting the fire sacrifice became manifest: the performer [the chanter], the offerer, the fire, and the action performed in terms of the supplementary Vedas. Also the four principles of religiosity [truth, austerity, mercy and cleanliness] and the duties in the four social orders all became manifest.

PURPORT

Eating, sleeping, defending and mating are the four principles of material bodily demands which are common to both the animals and human society. To distinguish human society from the animals there is the performance of religious activities in terms of the social statuses and orders of life. They are all clearly mentioned in the Vedic literatures and were manifested by Brahmā when the four *Vedas* were generated from his four mouths. Thus the duties of humankind in terms of the statuses and social orders were established to be observed by the civilized man. Those who traditionally follow these principles are called Āryans, or progressive human beings.

TEXT 36

विदुर उवाच

स वै विश्वसृजामीशो वेदादीन् मुखतोऽसृजत् ।
यद् यद् येनासृजद् देवस्तन्मे ब्रूहि तपोधन ॥३६॥

vidura uvāca
sa vai viśva-sṛjām īśo
vedādīn mukhato 'sṛjat
yad yad yenāsṛjad devas
tan me brūhi tapo-dhana

viduraḥ uvāca—Vidura said; *saḥ*—he (Brahmā); *vai*—certainly; *viśva*—the universe; *sṛjām*—of those who created; *īśaḥ*—the controller; *veda-ādīn*—the *Vedas*, etc.; *mukhataḥ*—from the mouth; *asṛjat*—established; *yat*—that; *yat*—which; *yena*—by which; *asṛjat*—created; *devaḥ*—the god; *tat*—that; *me*—unto me; *brūhi*—please explain; *tapaḥ-dhana*—O sage whose only wealth is penance.

TRANSLATION

Vidura said: O great sage whose only wealth is penance, kindly explain to me how and with whose help Brahmā established the Vedic knowledge which emanated from his mouth.

TEXT 37

मैत्रेय उवाच
ऋग्यजुःसामाथर्वाख्यान् वेदान् पूर्वादिभिर्मुखैः ।
शास्त्रमिज्यां स्तुतिस्तोमं प्रायश्चित्तं व्यधात्क्रमात् ॥३७॥

maitreya uvāca
ṛg-yajuḥ-sāmātharvākhyān
vedān pūrvādibhir mukhaiḥ
śāstram ijyāṁ stuti-stomaṁ
prāyaścittaṁ vyadhāt kramāt

maitreyaḥ uvāca—Maitreya said; *ṛk-yajuḥ-sāma-atharva*—the four *Vedas; ākhyān*—of the name; *vedān*—Vedic literatures; *pūrva-ādibhiḥ*—beginning with the front; *mukhaiḥ*—by the mouths; *śāstram*—Vedic hymns not pronounced before; *ijyām*—priestly rituals; *stuti-stomam*—the subject matter of the reciters; *prāyaścittam*—transcendental activities; *vyadhāt*—established; *kramāt*—one after another.

TRANSLATION

Maitreya said: Beginning from the front face of Brahmā, gradually the four Vedas—Ṛk, Yajur, Sāma and Atharva—became manifest. Thereafter, Vedic hymns which had not been pronounced before, priestly rituals, the subject matters of the recitation, and transcendental activities were all established, one after another.

TEXT 38

आयुर्वेदं धनुर्वेदं गान्धर्वं वेदमात्मनः ।
स्थापत्यं चासृजद् वेदं क्रमात्पूर्वादिभिर्मुखैः ॥३८॥

āyur-vedaṁ dhanur-vedaṁ
gāndharvaṁ vedam ātmanaḥ

sthāpatyaṁ cāsṛjad vedaṁ
kramāt pūrvādibhir mukhaiḥ

āyuḥ-vedam—medical science; *dhanuḥ-vedam*—military science; *gāndharvam*—musical art; *vedam*—they are all Vedic knowledge; *ātmanaḥ*—of his own; *sthāpatyam*—architectural; *ca*—also; *asṛjat*—created; *vedam*—knowledge; *kramāt*—respectively; *pūrva-ādibhiḥ*—beginning from the front face; *mukhaiḥ*—by the mouths.

TRANSLATION

He also created the medical science, military art, musical art and architectural science, all from the Vedas. They all emanated one after another, beginning from the front face.

PURPORT

The *Vedas* contain perfect knowledge, which includes all kinds of knowledge necessary for the human society, not only on this particular planet but on other planets as well. It is understood that military art is also necessary knowledge for the upkeep of social order, as is the art of music. All these groups of knowledge are called the *Upapurāṇa*, or supplements of the *Vedas*. Spiritual knowledge is the main topic of the *Vedas*, but to help the human being's spiritual pursuit of knowledge, the other information, as above mentioned, forms necessary branches of the Vedic knowledge.

TEXT 39

इतिहासपुराणानि पञ्चमं वेदमीश्वरः ।
सर्वेभ्य एव वक्त्रेभ्यः ससृजे सर्वदर्शनः ॥३९॥

itihāsa-purāṇāni
pañcamaṁ vedam īśvaraḥ
sarvebhya eva vaktrebhyaḥ
sasṛje sarva-darśanaḥ

itihāsa—histories; *purāṇāni*—the *Purāṇas* (supplementary *Vedas*); *pañcamam*—the fifth; *vedam*—the Vedic literature; *īśvaraḥ*—the Lord;

sarvebhyaḥ—all together; *eva*—certainly; *vaktrebhyaḥ*—from his mouths; *sasṛje*—created; *sarva*—all around; *darśanaḥ*—one who can see all time.

TRANSLATION

Then he created the fifth Veda—the Purāṇas and the histories—from all his mouths, since he could see all the past, present and future.

PURPORT

There are histories of particular countries and nations and of the world, but the *Purāṇas* are the histories of the universe, not only in one millennium, but in many *kalpas*. Brahmā has knowledge of those historical facts, and therefore all the *Purāṇas* are histories. As originally composed by Brahmā, they are part of the *Vedas* and are called the fifth *Veda*.

TEXT 40

षोडश्युक्थौ पूर्ववक्त्रात्पुरीष्यग्निष्टुतावथ ।
आप्तोर्यामातिरात्रौ च वाजपेयं सगोसवम् ॥४०॥

ṣoḍaśy-ukthau pūrva-vaktrāt
purīṣy-agniṣṭutāv atha
āptoryāmātirātrau ca
vājapeyaṁ sagosavam

ṣoḍaśī-ukthau—types of sacrifice; *pūrva-vaktrāt*—from the eastern mouth; *purīṣi-agniṣṭutau*—types of sacrifice; *atha*—then; *āptoryāma-atirātrau*—types of sacrifice; *ca*—and; *vājapeyam*—type of sacrifice; *sa-gosavam*—type of sacrifice.

TRANSLATION

All the different varieties of fire sacrifices [ṣoḍaśī, uktha, purīṣi, agniṣṭoma, āptoryāma, atirātra, vājapeya and gosava] became manifested from the eastern mouth of Brahmā.

TEXT 41

विद्या दानं तपः सत्यं धर्मस्येति पदानि च ।
आश्रमांश्च यथासंख्यमसृजत्सह वृत्तिभिः ॥४१॥

vidyā dānaṁ tapaḥ satyaṁ
dharmasyeti padāni ca
āśramāṁś ca yathā-saṅkhyam
asṛjat saha vṛttibhiḥ

vidyā—education; *dānam*—charity; *tapaḥ*—penance; *satyam*—truth; *dharmasya*—of religion; *iti*—thus; *padāni*—four legs; *ca*—also; *āśramān*—orders of life; *ca*—also; *yathā*—as they are; *saṅkhyam*—in number; *asṛjat*—created; *saha*—along with; *vṛttibhiḥ*—by vocations.

TRANSLATION

Education, charity, penance and truth are said to be the four legs of religion, and to learn this there are four orders of life with different classifications of castes according to vocation. Brahmā created all these in systematic order.

PURPORT

The nucleus of the four social orders—*brahmacarya*, or student life, *gṛhastha*, or household family life, *vānaprastha*, or retired life for practicing penance, and *sannyāsa*, or renounced life for preaching the truth—is the four legs of religion. The vocational divisions are the *brāhmaṇas*, or the intelligent class, the *kṣatriyas*, or administrative class, the *vaiśyas*, or mercantile productive class, and the *śūdras*, or general laborer class who have no specific qualifications. All were systematically planned and created by Brahmā for the regular promotion of self-realization. Student life is meant for acquiring the best education; household family life is meant for gratifying the senses, provided it is performed with a charitable disposition of mind, retirement from household life is meant for penance, for advancement in spiritual life, and renounced life is meant for preaching the Absolute Truth to the people in general. The combined actions of all members of society make the whole situation favorable for the upliftment of the mission of human life. The beginning of this social institution is based on education meant for purifying the animal propensities of the human being. The highest purificatory process is knowledge of the Supreme Personality of Godhead, the purest of the pure.

TEXT 42

सावित्रं प्राजापत्यं च ब्राह्मं चाथ बृहत्तथा ।
वार्तासञ्चयशालीनशिलोञ्छ इति वै गृहे ॥४२॥

sāvitraṁ prājāpatyaṁ ca
brāhmaṁ cātha bṛhat tathā
vārtā sañcaya-śālīna-
śiloñcha iti vai gṛhe

sāvitram—the thread ceremony of the twice-born; *prājāpatyam*—to execute the vow for one year; *ca*—and; *brāhmam*—acceptance of the *Vedas; ca*—and; *atha*—also; *bṛhat*—complete abstinence from sex life; *tathā*—then; *vārtā*—vocation in terms of Vedic sanction; *sañcaya*—professional duty; *śālīna*—livelihood without asking anyone for cooperation; *śila-uñchaḥ*—picking up rejected grains; *iti*—thus; *vai*—even though; *gṛhe*—in household life.

TRANSLATION

Then the thread ceremony for the twice-born was inaugurated, as were the rules to be followed for at least one year after acceptance of the Vedas, rules for observing complete abstinence from sex life, vocations in terms of Vedic injunctions, various professional duties in household life, and the method of maintaining a livelihood without anyone's cooperation by picking up rejected grains.

PURPORT

During student life the *brahmacārīs* were given full instructions about the importance of the human form of life. Thus the basic education was designed to encourage the student in becoming free from family encumbrances. Only students unable to accept such a vow in life were allowed to go home and marry a suitable wife. Otherwise, the student would remain a permanent *brahmacārī*, observing complete abstinence from sex life for his whole life. It all depended on the quality of the student's training. We had the opportunity to meet an avowed *brahmacārī* in the personality of our spiritual master, Oṁ Viṣṇupāda Śrī Śrīmad Bhaktisiddhānta Gosvāmī Mahārāja. Such a great soul is called a *naiṣṭhika-brahmacārī.*

TEXT 43

वैखानसा वालखिल्यौदुम्बराः फेनपा वने ।
न्यासे कुटीचकः पूर्वं बह्वोदो हंसनिष्क्रियौ ॥४३॥

vaikhānasā vālakhilyau-
dumbarāḥ phenapā vane
nyāse kuṭīcakaḥ pūrvaṁ
bahvodo haṁsa-niṣkriyau

vaikhānasāḥ—the section of men who retire from active life and live on half-boiled meals; *vālakhilya*—one who quits his former stock of grains on receipt of more; *audumbarāḥ*—one who lives on what he gets from the direction towards which he starts after rising from bed; *phenapāḥ*—one who lives on the fruits which automatically fall from the tree; *vane*—in the forest; *nyāse*—in the order of renunciation; *kuṭīcakaḥ*—life in the family without attachment; *pūrvam*—in the beginning; *bahvodaḥ*—giving up all material activities and engaging fully in transcendental service; *haṁsa*—fully engaged in transcendental knowledge; *niṣkriyau*—stopping all kinds of activities.

TRANSLATION

The four divisions of retired life are the vaikhānasas, vālakhilyas, audumbaras and phenapas. The four divisions of the renounced order of life are the kuṭīcakas, bahvodas, haṁsas and niṣkriyas. All these were manifested from Brahmā.

PURPORT

The *varṇāśrama-dharma*, or the institution of the four divisions and orders of social and spiritual life, is not a new invention of the modern age, as proposed by the less intelligent. It is an institution established by Brahmā from the beginning of the creation. This is also confirmed in the *Bhagavad-gītā* (4.13): *cātur-varṇyaṁ mayā sṛṣṭam.*

TEXT 44

आन्वीक्षिकी त्रयी वार्ता दण्डनीतिस्तथैव च।
एवं व्याहृतयश्चासन् प्रणवो ह्यस्य दह्रतः ॥४४॥

ānvīkṣikī trayī vārtā
daṇḍa-nītis tathaiva ca
evaṁ vyāhṛtayaś cāsan
praṇavo hy asya dahrataḥ

ānvīkṣikī—logic; *trayī*—the three goals, namely religion, economy and salvation; *vārtā*—sense gratification; *daṇḍa*—law and order; *nītiḥ*—moral codes; *tathā*—as also; *eva ca*—respectively; *evam*—thus; *vyāhṛtayaḥ*—the celebrated hymns *bhūḥ, bhuvaḥ* and *svaḥ; ca*—also; *āsan*—came into existence; *praṇavaḥ*—the *oṁkāra; hi*—certainly; *asya*—of him (Brahmā); *dahrataḥ*—from the heart.

TRANSLATION

The science of logical argument, the Vedic goals of life, and also law and order, moral codes, and the celebrated hymns bhūḥ, bhuvaḥ and svaḥ all became manifested from the mouths of Brahmā, and the praṇava oṁkāra was manifested from his heart.

TEXT 45

तस्योष्णिगासील्लोमभ्यो गायत्री च त्वचो विभोः।
त्रिष्टुम्मांसात्स्नुतोऽनुष्टुब्जगत्यस्थ्नः प्रजापतेः ॥४५॥

tasyoṣṇig āsīl lomabhyo
gāyatrī ca tvaco vibhoḥ
triṣṭum māṁsāt snuto 'nuṣṭub
jagaty asthnaḥ prajāpateḥ

tasya—his; *uṣṇik*—one of the Vedic meters; *āsīt*—generated; *lomabhyaḥ*—from the hairs on the body; *gāyatrī*—the principal Vedic hymn; *ca*—also; *tvacaḥ*—from the skin; *vibhoḥ*—of the lord; *triṣṭup*—a particular type of poetic meter; *māṁsāt*—from the flesh; *snutaḥ*—from the sinews; *anuṣṭup*—another type of poetic meter; *jagatī*—another type of poetic meter; *asthnaḥ*—from the bones; *prajāpateḥ*—of the father of the living entities.

TRANSLATION

Thereafter the art of literary expression, uṣṇik, was generated from the hairs on the body of the almighty Prajāpati. The principal Vedic hymn, gāyatrī, was generated from the skin, triṣṭup from the flesh, anuṣṭup from the veins, and jagatī from the bones of the lord of the living entities.

TEXT 46

मज्जायाः पङ्क्तिरुत्पन्ना बृहती प्राणतोऽभवत् : ॥४६॥

majjāyāḥ paṅktir utpannā
bṛhatī prāṇato 'bhavat

majjāyāḥ—from the bone marrow; *paṅktiḥ*—a particular type of verse; *utpannā*—became manifested; *bṛhatī*—another type of verse; *prāṇataḥ*—out of the life-breathing; *abhavat*—generated.

TRANSLATION

The art of writing verse, paṅkti, became manifested from the bone marrow, and that of bṛhatī, another type of verse, was generated from the life-breath of the lord of the living entities.

TEXT 47

स्पर्शस्तस्याभवज्जीवः स्वरो देह उदाहृत ।
ऊष्माणमिन्द्रियाण्याहुरन्तःस्था बलमात्मनः ।
स्वराः सप्त विहारेण भवन्ति स्म प्रजापतेः ॥४७॥

sparśas tasyābhavaj jīvaḥ
svaro deha udāhṛta
ūṣmāṇam indriyāṇy āhur
antaḥ-sthā balam ātmanaḥ
svarāḥ sapta vihāreṇa
bhavanti sma prajāpateḥ

sparśaḥ—the set of letters from *ka* to *ma; tasya*—his; *abhavat*—became; *jīvaḥ*—the soul; *svaraḥ*—vowels; *dehaḥ*—his body; *udāhṛtaḥ*—are expressed; *ūṣmāṇam*—the letters *śa, ṣa, sa* and *ha; indriyāṇi*—the senses; *āhuḥ*—are called; *antaḥ-sthāḥ*—the set of letters so known (*ya, ra, la* and *va*); *balam*—energy; *ātmanaḥ*—of his self; *svarāḥ*—music; *sapta*—seven; *vihāreṇa*—by the sensual activities; *bhavanti sma*—became manifested; *prajāpateḥ*—of the lord of the living entities.

TRANSLATION

Brahmā's soul was manifested as the touch alphabets, his body as the vowels, his senses as the sibilant alphabets, his strength as the intermediate alphabets and his sensual activities as the seven notes of music.

PURPORT

In Sanskrit there are thirteen vowels and thirty-five consonants. The vowels are *a, ā, i, ī, u, ū, ṛ, ṝ, ḷ, e, ai, o, au*, and the consonants are *ka, kha, ga, gha*, etc. Amongst the consonants, the first twenty-five letters are called the *sparśas*. There are also four *antaḥ-sthas*. Of the *ūṣmas* there are three *s*'s, called *tālavya, mūrdhanya* and *dantya*. The musical notes are *ṣa, ṛ, gā, ma, pa, dha* and *ni*. All these sound vibrations are originally called *śabda-brahma*, or spiritual sound. It is said, therefore, that Brahmā was created in the Mahā-kalpa as the incarnation of spiritual sound. The *Vedas* are spiritual sound, and therefore there is no need of material interpretation for the sound vibration of the Vedic literature. The *Vedas* should be vibrated as they are, although they are symbolically represented with letters which are known to us materially. In the ultimate issue there is nothing material because everything has its origin in the spiritual world. The material manifestation is therefore called illusion in the proper sense of the term. For those who are realized souls there is nothing but spirit.

TEXT 48

शब्दब्रह्मात्मनस्तस्य व्यक्ताव्यक्तात्मनः परः ।
ब्रह्मावभाति विततो नानाशक्त्युपबृंहितः ॥४८॥

śabda-brahmātmanas tasya
vyaktāvyaktātmanaḥ paraḥ

brahmāvabhāti vitato
nānā-śakty-upabṛṁhitaḥ

śabda-brahma—transcendental sound; *ātmanaḥ*—of the Supreme Lord; *tasya*—His; *vyakta*—manifested; *avyakta-ātmanaḥ*—of the unmanifested; *paraḥ*—transcendental; *brahmā*—the Absolute; *avabhāti*—completely manifested; *vitataḥ*—distributing; *nānā*—multifarious; *śakti*—energies; *upabṛṁhitaḥ*—invested with.

TRANSLATION

Brahmā is the personal representation of the Supreme Personality of Godhead as the source of transcendental sound and is therefore above the conception of manifested and unmanifested. Brahmā is the complete form of the Absolute Truth and is invested with multifarious energies.

PURPORT

The post of Brahmā is the highest responsible post within the universe, and it is offered to the most perfect personality of the universe. Sometimes the Supreme Personality of Godhead has to become Brahmā when there is no suitable living being to occupy the post. In the material world, Brahmā is the complete representation of the Supreme Personality of Godhead, and transcendental sound, *praṇava*, comes from him. He is therefore invested with multifarious energies, from which all the demigods like Indra, Candra and Varuṇa are manifested. His transcendental value is not to be minimized, even though he exhibited a tendency to enjoy his own daughter. There is a purpose for the exhibition of such a tendency by Brahmā, and he is not to be condemned like an ordinary living entity.

TEXT 49

ततोऽपरामुपादाय स सर्गाय मनो दधे ॥४९॥

tato 'parām upādāya
sa sargāya mano dadhe

tataḥ—thereafter; *aparām*—another; *upādāya*—having accepted; *saḥ*—he; *sargāya*—in the matter of creation; *manaḥ*—mind; *dadhe*—gave attention.

TRANSLATION

Thereafter Brahmā accepted another body, in which sex life was not forbidden, and thus he engaged himself in the matter of further creation.

PURPORT

In his former body, which was transcendental, affection for sex life was forbidden, and Brahmā therefore had to accept another body to allow himself to be connected with sex. He thus engaged himself in the matter of creation. His former body transformed into fog, as previously described.

TEXT 50

ऋषीणां भूरिवीर्याणामपि सर्गमविस्तृतम् ।
ज्ञात्वा तद्धृदये भूयश्चिन्तयामास कौरव ॥५०॥

ṛṣīṇāṁ bhūri-vīryāṇām
api sargam avistṛtam
jñātvā tad dhṛdaye bhūyaś
cintayām āsa kaurava

ṛṣīṇām—of the great sages; *bhūri-vīryāṇām*—with great potential power; *api*—in spite of; *sargam*—the creation; *avistṛtam*—not extended; *jñātvā*—knowing; *tat*—that; *hṛdaye*—in his heart; *bhūyaḥ*—again; *cintayām āsa*—he began to consider; *kaurava*—O son of the Kurus.

TRANSLATION

O son of the Kurus, when Brahmā saw that in spite of the presence of sages of great potency there was no sufficient increase in population, he seriously began to consider how the population could be increased.

TEXT 51

अहो अद्भुतमेतन्मे व्यापृतस्यापि नित्यदा ।
न ह्येधन्ते प्रजा नूनं दैवमत्र विघातकम् ॥५१॥

aho adbhutam etan me
vyāpṛtasyāpi nityadā

na hy edhante prajā nūnaṁ
daivam atra vighātakam

aho—alas; *adbhutam*—it is wonderful; *etat*—this; *me*—for me; *vyāpṛtasya*—being busy; *api*—although; *nityadā*—always; *na*—does not; *hi*—certainly; *edhante*—generate; *prajāḥ*—living entities; *nūnam*—however; *daivam*—destiny; *atra*—herein; *vighātakam*—against.

TRANSLATION

Brahmā thought to himself: Alas, it is wonderful that in spite of my being scattered all over, there is still insufficient population throughout the universe. There is no other cause for this misfortune but destiny.

TEXT 52

एवं युक्तकृतस्तस्य दैवञ्चावेक्षतस्तदा ।
कस्य रूपमभूद् द्वेधा यत्कायमभिचक्षते ॥५२॥

evaṁ yukta-kṛtas tasya
daivaṁ cāvekṣatas tadā
kasya rūpam abhūd dvedhā
yat kāyam abhicakṣate

evam—thus; *yukta*—contemplating; *kṛtaḥ*—while doing so; *tasya*—his; *daivam*—supernatural power; *ca*—also; *avekṣataḥ*—observing; *tadā*—at that time; *kasya*—of Brahmā; *rūpam*—form; *abhūt*—became manifested; *dvedhā*—twofold; *yat*—which is; *kāyam*—his body; *abhicakṣate*—is said to be.

TRANSLATION

While he was thus absorbed in contemplation and was observing the supernatural power, two other forms were generated from his body. They are still celebrated as the body of Brahmā.

PURPORT

Two bodies came out from the body of Brahmā. One had a mustache, and the other had swollen breasts. No one can explain the source of their manifestation, and therefore until today they are known as the *kāyam*, or the body of Brahmā, with no indication of their relationship as his son or daughter.

TEXT 53

ताभ्यां रूपविभागाभ्यां मिथुनं समपद्यत ॥५३॥

tābhyāṁ rūpa-vibhāgābhyāṁ
mithunaṁ samapadyata

tābhyām—of them; *rūpa*—form; *vibhāgābhyām*—thus being divided; *mithunam*—sex relation; *samapadyata*—perfectly executed.

TRANSLATION

The two newly separated bodies united together in a sexual relationship.

TEXT 54

यस्तु तत्र पुमान् सोऽभून्मनुः स्वायम्भुवः स्वराट् ।
स्त्री यासीच्छतरूपाख्या महिष्यस्य महात्मनः ॥५४॥

yas tu tatra pumān so 'bhūn
manuḥ svāyambhuvaḥ svarāṭ
strī yāsīc chatarūpākhyā
mahiṣy asya mahātmanaḥ

yaḥ—one who; *tu*—but; *tatra*—there; *pumān*—the male; *saḥ*—he; *abhūt*—became; *manuḥ*—the father of mankind; *svāyambhuvaḥ*—of the name Svāyambhuva; *sva-rāṭ*—fully independent; *strī*—the woman; *yā*—one who; *āsīt*—there was; *śatarūpā*—of the name Śatarūpā; *ākhyā*—known as; *mahiṣī*—the queen; *asya*—of him; *mahātmanaḥ*—the great soul.

TRANSLATION

Out of them, the one who had the male form became known as the Manu named Svāyambhuva, and the woman became known as Śatarūpā, the queen of the great soul Manu.

TEXT 55

तदा मिथुनधर्मेण प्रजा ह्येधाम्बभूविरे ॥५५॥

tadā mithuna-dharmeṇa
prajā hy edhām babhūvire

tadā—at that time; *mithuna*—sex life; *dharmeṇa*—according to regulative principles; *prajāḥ*—generations; *hi*—certainly; *edhām*—increased; *babhūvire*—took place.

TRANSLATION

Thereafter, by sex indulgence, they gradually increased generations of population one after another.

TEXT 56

स चापि शतरूपायां पञ्चापत्यान्यजीजनत् ।
प्रियव्रतोत्तानपादौ तिस्रः कन्याश्च भारत ।
आकूतिर्देवहूतिश्च प्रसूतिरिति सत्तम ॥५६॥

sa cāpi śatarūpāyāṁ
pañcāpatyāny ajījanat
priyavratottānapādau
tisraḥ kanyāś ca bhārata
ākūtir devahūtiś ca
prasūtir iti sattama

saḥ—he (Manu); *ca*—also; *api*—in due course; *śatarūpāyām*—unto Śatarūpā; *pañca*—five; *apatyāni*—children; *ajījanat*—begot; *priyavrata*—Priyavrata; *uttānapādau*—Uttānapāda; *tisraḥ*—three in number; *kanyāḥ*—daughters; *ca*—also; *bhārata*—O son of Bharata; *ākūtiḥ*—Ākūti; *devahūtiḥ*—Devahūti; *ca*—and; *prasūtiḥ*—Prasūti; *iti*—thus; *sattama*—O best of all.

TRANSLATION

O son of Bharata, in due course of time he [Manu] begot in Śatarūpā five children—two sons, Priyavrata and Uttānapāda, and three daughters, Ākūti, Devahūti and Prasūti.

TEXT 57

आकूतिं रुचये प्रादात्कर्दमाय तु मध्यमाम् ।
दक्षायादात्प्रसूतिं च यत आपूरितं जगत् ॥५७॥

ākūtiṁ rucaye prādāt
kardamāya tu madhyamām
dakṣāyādāt prasūtiṁ ca
yata āpūritaṁ jagat

ākūtim—the daughter named Ākūti; *rucaye*—unto the sage Ruci; *prādāt*—handed over; *kardamāya*—unto the sage Kardama; *tu*—but; *madhyamām*—the middle one (Devahūti); *dakṣāya*—unto Dakṣa; *adāt*—handed over; *prasūtim*—the youngest daughter; *ca*—also; *yataḥ*—wherefrom; *āpūritam*—is fulfilled; *jagat*—the whole world.

TRANSLATION

The father, Manu, handed over his first daughter, Ākūti, to the sage Ruci, the middle daughter, Devahūti, to the sage Kardama, and the youngest, Prasūti, to Dakṣa. From them, all the world filled with population.

PURPORT

The history of the creation of the population of the universe is given herewith. Brahmā is the original living creature in the universe, from whom were generated the Manu Svāyambhuva and his wife Śatarūpā. From Manu, two sons and three daughters were born, and from them all the population in different planets has sprung up until now. Therefore, Brahmā is known as the grandfather of everyone, and the Personality of Godhead, being the father of Brahmā, is known as the great-grandfather of all living beings. This is confirmed in *Bhagavad-gītā* (11.39) as follows:

vāyur yamo 'gnir varuṇaḥ śaśāṅkaḥ
prajāpatis tvaṁ prapitāmahaś ca
namo namas te 'stu sahasra-kṛtvaḥ
punaś ca bhūyo 'pi namo namas te

"You are the Lord of air, the supreme justice Yama, the fire, and the Lord of rains. You are the moon, and You are the great-grandfather. Therefore I offer my respectful obeisances unto You again and again."

Thus end the Bhaktivedanta purports of the Third Canto, Twelfth Chapter, of the Śrīmad-Bhāgavatam, *entitled "Creation of the Kumāras and Others."*

CHAPTER THIRTEEN

The Appearance of Lord Varāha

TEXT 1

श्रीशुक उवाच
निशम्य वाचं वदतो मुनेः पुण्यतमां नृप ।
भूयः पप्रच्छ कौरव्यो वासुदेवकथादृतः ॥ १ ॥

śrī-śuka uvāca
niśamya vācaṁ vadato
muneḥ puṇyatamāṁ nṛpa
bhūyaḥ papraccha kauravyo
vāsudeva-kathādṛtaḥ

śrī-śukaḥ uvāca—Śrī Śukadeva Gosvāmī said; *niśamya*—after hearing; *vācam*—talks; *vadataḥ*—while speaking; *muneḥ*—of Maitreya Muni; *puṇya-tamām*—the most virtuous; *nṛpa*—O King; *bhūyaḥ*—then again; *papraccha*—inquired; *kauravyaḥ*—the best amongst the Kurus (Vidura); *vāsudeva-kathā*—topics on the subject of the Personality of Godhead, Vāsudeva; *ādṛtaḥ*—one who so adores.

TRANSLATION

Śrī Śukadeva Gosvāmī said: O King, after hearing all these most virtuous topics from the sage Maitreya, Vidura inquired further on the topics of the Supreme Personality of Godhead, which he adored to hear.

PURPORT

The word *ādṛtaḥ* is significant because it indicates that Vidura had a natural inclination for hearing the transcendental message of the Supreme Personality of Godhead, and he was never fully satisfied though continuing to hear those topics. He wanted to hear more and more so that he could be more and more blessed by the transcendental message.

TEXT 2

विदुर उवाच
स वै स्वायम्भुवः सम्राट् प्रियः पुत्रः स्वयम्भुवः ।
प्रतिलभ्य प्रियां पत्नीं किं चकार ततो मुने ॥ २ ॥

vidura uvāca
sa vai svāyambhuvaḥ samrāṭ
priyaḥ putraḥ svayambhuvaḥ
pratilabhya priyāṁ patnīṁ
kiṁ cakāra tato mune

viduraḥ uvāca—Vidura said; *saḥ*—he; *vai*—easily; *svāyambhuvaḥ*—Svāyambhuva Manu; *samrāṭ*—the king of all kings; *priyaḥ*—dear; *putraḥ*—son; *svayambhuvaḥ*—of Brahmā; *pratilabhya*—after obtaining; *priyām*—most loving; *patnīm*—wife; *kim*—what; *cakāra*—did; *tataḥ*—thereafter; *mune*—O great sage.

TRANSLATION

Vidura said: O great sage, what did Svāyambhuva, the dear son of Brahmā, do after obtaining his very loving wife?

TEXT 3

चरितं तस्य राजर्षेरादिराजस्य सत्तम ।
ब्रूहि मे श्रद्दधानाय विष्वक्सेनाश्रयो ह्यसौ ॥ ३ ॥

caritaṁ tasya rājarṣer
ādi-rājasya sattama
brūhi me śraddadhānāya
viṣvaksenāśrayo hy asau

caritam—character; *tasya*—his; *rājarṣeḥ*—of the saintly king; *ādi-rājasya*—of the original king; *sattama*—O most pious one; *brūhi*—kindly speak; *me*—unto me; *śraddadhānāya*—unto one eager to receive; *viṣvaksena*—of the Personality of Godhead; *āśrayaḥ*—one who has taken shelter; *hi*—certainly; *asau*—that king.

TRANSLATION

O best of the virtuous, the original king of kings [Manu] was a great devotee of the Personality of Godhead Hari, and thus it is worth hearing of his sublime character and activities. Please describe them. I am very eager to hear.

PURPORT

Śrīmad-Bhāgavatam is full of the transcendental topics of the Personality of Godhead and His pure devotees. In the absolute world there is no difference in quality between the Supreme Lord and His pure devotee. Therefore, hearing the topics of the Lord and hearing of the character and activities of the pure devotee have the same result, namely, the development of devotional service.

TEXT 4

श्रुतस्य पुंसां सुचिरश्रमस्य
नन्वञ्जसा सूरिभिरीडितोऽर्थः ।
तत्तद्गुणानुश्रवणं मुकुन्द-
पादारविन्दं हृदयेषु येषाम् ॥ ४ ॥

śrutasya puṁsāṁ sucira-śramasya
nanv añjasā sūribhir īḍito 'rthaḥ
tat-tad-guṇānuśravaṇaṁ mukunda-
pādāravindaṁ hṛdayeṣu yeṣām

śrutasya—of persons who are in the process of hearing; *puṁsām*—of such persons; *sucira*—for a long time; *śramasya*—laboring very hard; *nanu*—certainly *añjasā*—elaborately; *sūribhiḥ*—by pure devotees; *īḍitaḥ*—explained by; *arthaḥ*—statements; *tat*—that; *tat*—that; *guṇa*—transcendental qualities; *anuśravaṇam*—thinking; *mukunda*—the Personality of Godhead, who awards liberation; *pāda-aravindam*—the lotus feet; *hṛdayeṣu*—within the heart; *yeṣām*—of them.

TRANSLATION

Persons who hear from a spiritual master with great labor and for a long time must hear from the mouths of pure devotees about

the character and activities of pure devotees. Pure devotees always think within their hearts of the lotus feet of the Personality of Godhead, who awards His devotees liberation.

PURPORT

Transcendental students are those who undergo great penance in being trained by hearing the *Vedas* from a bona fide spiritual master. Not only must they hear about the activities of the Lord, but they must also hear about the transcendental qualities of the devotees who are constantly thinking of the lotus feet of the Lord within their hearts. A pure devotee of the Lord cannot be separated from the lotus feet of the Lord for even a moment. Undoubtedly the Lord is always within the hearts of all living creatures, but they hardly know about it because they are deluded by the illusory material energy. The devotees, however, realize the presence of the Lord, and therefore they can always see the lotus feet of the Lord within their hearts. Such pure devotees of the Lord are as glorious as the Lord; they are, in fact, recommended by the Lord as more worshipable then He Himself. Worship of the devotee is more potent than worship of the Lord. It is therefore the duty of the transcendental students to hear of pure devotees, as explained by similar devotees of the Lord, because one cannot explain about the Lord or His devotee unless one happens to be a pure devotee himself.

TEXT 5

श्रीशुक उवाच

इति ब्रुवाणं विदुरं विनीतं
सहस्रशीर्ष्णश्चरणोपधानम् ।
प्रहृष्टरोमा भगवत्कथायां
प्रणीयमानो मुनिरभ्यचष्ट ॥ ५ ॥

śrī-śuka uvāca

iti bruvāṇaṁ viduraṁ vinītaṁ
sahasra-śīrṣṇaś caraṇopadhānam
prahṛṣṭa-romā bhagavat-kathāyāṁ
praṇīyamāno munir abhyacaṣṭa

śrī-śukaḥ uvāca—Śrī Śukadeva Gosvāmī said; *iti*—thus; *bruvāṇam*—speaking; *viduram*—unto Vidura; *vinītam*—very gentle; *sahasra-śīrṣṇaḥ*—the Personality of Godhead Kṛṣṇa; *caraṇa*—lotus feet; *upadhānam*—pillow; *prahṛṣṭa-romā*—hairs standing in ecstasy; *bhagavat*—in relationship with the Personality of Godhead; *kathāyām*—in the words; *praṇīyamānaḥ*—being influenced by such spirit; *muniḥ*—the sage; *abhyacaṣṭa*—attempted to speak.

TRANSLATION

Śrī Śukadeva Gosvāmī said: The Personality of Godhead Śrī Kṛṣṇa was pleased to place His lotus feet on the lap of Vidura because Vidura was very meek and gentle. The sage Maitreya was very pleased with Vidura's words, and, being influenced by his spirit, he attempted to speak.

PURPORT

The word *sahasra-śīrṣṇaḥ* is very significant. One who has diverse energies and activities and a wonderful brain is known as the *sahasra-śīrṣṇaḥ.* This qualification is applicable only to the Personality of Godhead, Śrī Kṛṣṇa, and no one else. The Personality of Godhead was pleased to dine sometimes with Vidura at his home, and while resting He placed His lotus feet on the lap of Vidura. Maitreya was inspired by the thought of Vidura's wonderful fortune. The hairs of his body stood on end, and he was pleased to narrate the topics of the Personality of Godhead with great delight.

TEXT 6

मैत्रेय उवाच

यदा स्वभार्यया साधं जातः स्वायम्भुवो मनुः ।
प्राञ्जलिः प्रणतश्चेदं वेदगर्भमभाषत ॥ ६ ॥

maitreya uvāca
yadā sva-bhāryayā sārdhaṁ
jātaḥ svāyambhuvo manuḥ
prāñjaliḥ praṇataś cedaṁ
veda-garbham abhāṣata

maitreyaḥ uvāca—Maitreya said; *yadā*—when; *sva-bhāryayā*—along with his wife; *sārdham*—accompanied by; *jātaḥ*—appeared; *svāyambhuvaḥ*—Svāyambhuva Manu; *manuḥ*—the father of mankind; *prāñjaliḥ*—with folded hands; *praṇataḥ*—in obeisances; *ca*—also; *idam*—this; *veda-garbham*—unto the reservoir of Vedic wisdom; *abhāṣata*—addressed.

TRANSLATION

The sage Maitreya said to Vidura: After his appearance, Manu, the father of mankind, along with his wife, thus addressed the reservoir of Vedic wisdom, Brahmā, with obeisances and folded hands.

TEXT 7

त्वमेकः सर्वभूतानां जन्मकृद् वृत्तिदः पिता ।
तथापि नः प्रजानां ते शुश्रूषा केन वा भवेत् ॥ ७ ॥

tvam ekaḥ sarva-bhūtānāṁ
janma-kṛd vṛttidaḥ pitā
tathāpi naḥ prajānāṁ te
śuśrūṣā kena vā bhavet

tvam—you; *ekaḥ*—one; *sarva*—all; *bhūtānām*—living entities; *janma-kṛt*—progenitor; *vṛtti-daḥ*—source of subsistence; *pitā*—the father; *tathā api*—yet; *naḥ*—ourselves; *prajānām*—of all who are born; *te*—of you; *śuśrūṣā*—service; *kena*—how; *vā*—either; *bhavet*—may be possible.

TRANSLATION

You are the father of all living entities and the source of their subsistence because they are all born of you. Please order us how we may be able to render service unto you.

PURPORT

A son's duty is not only to make the father the source of supply for all his needs, but also, when he is grown up, to render service unto him. That is the law of creation beginning from the time of Brahmā. A father's duty is to bring up the son until he is grown, and when the son is grown up, it is his duty to render service unto the father.

TEXT 8

तद्विधेहि नमस्तुभ्यं कर्मस्वीड्यात्मशक्तिषु ।
यत्कृत्वेह यशो विष्वगमुत्र च भवेद्गतिः ॥ ८ ॥

tad vidhehi namas tubhyaṁ
karmasv īḍyātma-śaktiṣu
yat kṛtveha yaśo viṣvag
amutra ca bhaved gatiḥ

tat—that; *vidhehi*—give direction; *namaḥ*—my obeisances; *tubhyam*—unto you; *karmasu*—in duties; *īḍya*—O worshipful one; *ātma-śaktiṣu*—within our working capacity; *yat*—which; *kṛtvā*—doing; *iha*—in this world; *yaśaḥ*—fame; *viṣvak*—everywhere; *amutra*—in the next world; *ca*—and; *bhavet*—it should be; *gatiḥ*—progress.

TRANSLATION

O worshipful one, please give us your direction for the execution of duty within our working capacity so that we can follow it for fame in this life and progress in the next.

PURPORT

Brahmā is the direct recipient of Vedic knowledge from the Personality of Godhead, and anyone discharging his entrusted duties in disciplic succession from Brahmā is sure to gain fame in this life and salvation in the next. The disciplic succession from Brahmā is called the Brahma-sampradāya, and it descends as follows: Brahmā, Nārada, Vyāsa, Madhva Muni (Pūrṇaprajña), Padmanābha, Nṛhari, Mādhava, Akṣobhya, Jayatīrtha, Jñānasindhu, Dayānidhi, Vidyānidhi, Rājendra, Jayadharma, Puruṣottama, Brahmaṇyatīrtha, Vyāsatīrtha, Lakṣmīpati, Mādhavendra Purī, Īśvara Purī, Śrī Caitanya Mahāprabhu, Svarūpa Dāmodara and Śrī Rūpa Gosvāmī and others, Śrī Raghunātha dāsa Gosvāmī, Kṛṣṇadāsa Gosvāmī, Narottama dāsa Ṭhākura, Viśvanātha Cakravartī, Jagannātha dāsa Bābājī, Bhaktivinoda Ṭhākura, Gaurakiśora dāsa Bābājī, Śrīmad Bhaktisiddhānta Sarasvatī, A. C. Bhaktivedanta Swami.

This line of disciplic succession from Brahmā is spiritual, whereas the genealogical succession from Manu is material, but both are on the progressive march towards the same goal of Kṛṣṇa consciousness.

TEXT 9

ब्रह्मोवाच
प्रीतस्तुभ्यमहं तात स्वस्ति स्ताद्वां क्षितीश्वर ।
यन्निर्व्यलीकेन हृदा शाधि मेत्यात्मनार्पितम् ॥ ९ ॥

brahmovāca
prītas tubhyam ahaṁ tāta
svasti stād vāṁ kṣitīśvara
yan nirvyalīkena hṛdā
śādhi mety ātmanārpitam

brahmā uvāca—Brahmā said; *prītaḥ*—pleased; *tubhyam*—unto you; *aham*—I; *tāta*—my dear son; *svasti*—all blessings; *stāt*—let there be; *vām*—unto you both; *kṣiti-īśvara*—O lord of the world; *yat*—because; *nirvyalīkena*—without reservation; *hṛdā*—by the heart; *śādhi*—give instruction; *mā*—unto me; *iti*—thus; *ātmanā*—by self; *arpitam*—surrendered.

TRANSLATION

Lord Brahmā said: My dear son, O lord of the world, I am very pleased with you, and I desire all blessings for both you and your wife. You have without reservation surrendered yourself unto me with your heart for my instructions.

PURPORT

The relationship between the father and the son is always sublime. The father is naturally disposed with good will towards the son, and he is always ready to help the son in his progress in life. But in spite of the father's good will, the son is sometimes misguided because of his misuse of personal independence. Every living entity, however small or big he may be, has the choice of independence. If the son is unreservedly willing to be guided by the father, the father is ten times more eager to instruct and guide him by all means. The father and son relationship as exhibited here in the dealings of Brahmā and Manu is excellent. Both the father and the son are well qualified, and their example should be followed by all humankind. Manu, the son, unreservedly asked the father, Brahmā, to instruct him, and the father, who was full of Vedic wisdom, was very glad to instruct. The example of the father of mankind may be rigidly followed by mankind, and that will advance the cause of the relationship of fathers and sons.

TEXT 10

एतावत्यात्मजैर्वीर कार्या ह्यपचितिर्गुरौ ।
शक्त्याप्रमत्तैर्गृह्येत सादरं गतमत्सरैः ॥१०॥

etāvaty ātmajair vīra
kāryā hy apacitir gurau
śaktyāpramattair gṛhyeta
sādaraṁ gata-matsaraiḥ

etāvati—just exactly like this; *ātmajaiḥ*—by the offspring; *vīra*—O hero; *kāryā*—should be performed; *hi*—certainly; *apacitiḥ*—worship; *gurau*—unto the superior; *śaktyā*—with full capacity; *apramattaiḥ*—by the sane; *gṛhyeta*—should be accepted; *sa-ādaram*—with great delight; *gata-matsaraiḥ*—by those who are beyond the limit of envy.

TRANSLATION

O hero, your example is quite befitting a son in relationship with his father. This sort of adoration for the superior is required. One who is beyond the limit of envy and who is sane accepts the order of his father with great delight and executes it to his full capacity.

PURPORT

When the four previous sons of Brahmā, the sages Sanaka, Sanātana, Sanandana and Sanat-kumāra, refused to obey their father, Brahmā was mortified, and his anger was manifested in the shape of Rudra. That incident was not forgotten by Brahmā, and therefore the obedience of Manu Svāyambhuva was very encouraging. From the material point of view, the four sages' disobedience to the order of their father was certainly abominable, but because such disobedience was for a higher purpose, they were free from the reaction of disobedience. Those who disobey their fathers on material grounds, however, are surely subjected to disciplinary reaction for such disobedience. Manu's obedience to his father on material grounds was certainly free from envy, and in the material world it is imperative for ordinary men to follow the example of Manu.

TEXT 11

स त्वमस्यामपत्यानि सदृशान्यात्मनो गुणैः ।
उत्पाद्य शास धर्मेण गां यज्ञैः पुरुषं यज ॥११॥

sa tvam asyām apatyāni
sadṛśāny ātmano guṇaiḥ
utpādya śāsa dharmeṇa
gāṁ yajñaiḥ puruṣaṁ yaja

saḥ—therefore that obedient son; *tvam*—as you are; *asyām*—in her; *apatyāni*—children; *sadṛśāni*—equally qualified; *ātmanaḥ*—of yourself; *guṇaiḥ*—with the characteristics; *utpādya*—having begotten; *śāsa*—rule; *dharmeṇa*—on the principles of devotional service; *gām*—the world; *yajñaiḥ*—by sacrifices; *puruṣam*—the Supreme Personality of Godhead; *yaja*—worship.

TRANSLATION

Since you are my very obedient son, I ask you to beget children qualified like yourself in the womb of your wife. Rule the world in pursuance of the principles of devotional service unto the Supreme Personality of Godhead, and thus worship the Lord by performances of yajña.

PURPORT

The purpose of the material creation by Brahmā is clearly described herein. Every human being should beget nice children in the womb of his wife, as a sacrifice for the purpose of worshiping the Supreme Personality of Godhead in devotional service. In the *Viṣṇu Purāṇa* (3.8.9) it is stated:

varṇāśramācāravatā
puruṣeṇa paraḥ pumān
viṣṇur ārādhyate panthā
nānyat tat-toṣa-kāraṇam

"One can worship the Supreme Personality of Godhead, Viṣṇu, by proper discharge of the principles of *varṇa* and *āśrama.* There is no alternative to pacifying the Lord by execution of the principles of the *varṇāśrama* system."

Viṣṇu worship is the ultimate aim of human life. Those who take the license of married life for sense enjoyment must also take the responsibility to satisfy the Supreme Personality of Godhead, Viṣṇu, and the first stepping-stone is the *varṇāśrama-dharma* system. *Varṇāśrama-dharma* is the systematic institution for advancing in worship of Viṣṇu. However, if one directly engages in the process of devotional service to the Supreme Personality of Godhead, it may not be necessary to undergo the disciplinary system of *varṇāśrama-dharma.* The other sons of Brahmā, the Kumāras, directly engaged in devotional service, and thus they had no need to execute the principles of *varṇāśrama-dharma.*

TEXT 12

परं शुश्रूषणं मह्यं स्यात्प्रजारक्षया नृप ।
भगवांस्ते प्रजाभर्तुर्हृषीकेशोऽनुतुष्यति ॥१२॥

paraṁ śuśrūṣaṇaṁ mahyaṁ
syāt prajā-rakṣayā nṛpa
bhagavāṁs te prajā-bhartur
hṛṣīkeśo 'nutuṣyati

param—the greatest; *śuśrūṣaṇam*—devotional service; *mahyam*—unto me; *syāt*—should be; *prajā*—the living entities born in the material world; *rakṣayā*—by saving them from being spoiled; *nṛpa*—O King; *bhagavān*—the Personality of Godhead; *te*—with you; *prajā-bhartuḥ*—with the protector of the living beings; *hṛṣīkeśaḥ*—the Lord of the senses; *anutuṣyati*—is satisfied.

TRANSLATION

O King, if you can give proper protection to the living beings in the material world, that will be the best service for me. When the Supreme Lord sees you to be a good protector of the conditioned souls, certainly the master of the senses will be very pleased with you.

PURPORT

The whole administrative system is arranged for the purpose of going back home, back to Godhead. Brahmā is the representative of the Supreme Personality of Godhead, and Manu is the representative of Brahmā. Similarly, all other kings on different planets of the universe are representatives of Manu. The lawbook for the entire human society is the *Manu-saṁhitā*, which directs all activities towards the transcendental service of the Lord. Every king, therefore, must know that his responsibility in administration is not merely to exact taxes from the citizens but to see personally that the citizens under him are being trained in Viṣṇu worship. Everyone must be educated in Viṣṇu worship and engaged in the devotional service of Hṛṣīkeśa, the owner of the senses. The conditioned souls are meant not to satisfy their material senses but to satisfy the senses of Hṛṣīkeśa, the Supreme Personality of Godhead. That is the purpose of the complete administrative system. One who knows this secret, as disclosed here in the version of Brahmā, is the perfect administrative head. One who does not know this is a show-bottle administrator. By training the citizens in the devotional service of the Lord, the head of a state can be free in his responsibility, otherwise he will fail in the onerous duty entrusted to him and thus be punishable by the supreme authority. There is no other alternative in the discharge of administrative duty.

TEXT 13

येषां न तुष्टो भगवान् यज्ञलिङ्गो जनार्दनः ।
तेषां श्रमो ह्यपार्थाय यदात्मा नादृतः स्वयम् ॥१३॥

yeṣāṁ na tuṣṭo bhagavān
yajña-liṅgo janārdanaḥ
teṣāṁ śramo hy apārthāya
yad ātmā nādṛtaḥ svayam

yeṣām—of those with whom; *na*—never; *tuṣṭaḥ*—satisfied; *bhagavān*—the Personality of Godhead; *yajña-liṅgaḥ*—the form of sacrifice; *janārdanaḥ*—Lord Kṛṣṇa, or the *viṣṇu-tattva; teṣām*—of them; *śramaḥ*—labor; *hi*—certainly; *apārthāya*—without profit; *yat*—because; *ātmā*—the Supreme Soul; *na*—not; *ādṛtaḥ*—respected; *svayam*—his own self.

TRANSLATION

The Supreme Personality of Godhead, Janārdana [Lord Kṛṣṇa], is the form to accept all the results of sacrifice. If He is not satisfied, then one's labor for advancement is futile. He is the ultimate Self, and therefore one who does not satisfy Him certainly neglects his own interests.

PURPORT

Brahmā is deputed as the supreme head of universal affairs, and he in his turn deputes Manu and others as *chargés d'affaires* of the material manifestation, but the whole show is for the satisfaction of the Supreme Personality of Godhead. Brahmā knows how to satisfy the Lord, and similarly persons engaged in the line of Brahmā's plan of activities also know how to satisfy the Lord. The Lord is satisfied by the process of devotional service, consisting of the ninefold process of hearing, chanting, etc. It is in one's own self-interest to execute prescribed devotional service, and anyone who neglects this process neglects his own self-interest. Everyone wants to satisfy his senses, but above the senses is the mind, above the mind is the intelligence, above the intelligence is the individual self, and above the individual self is the Superself. Above even the Superself is the Supreme Personality of Godhead, *viṣṇu-tattva.* The primeval Lord and the cause of all causes is Śrī Kṛṣṇa. The complete process of perfectional service is to render service for the satisfaction of the transcendental senses of Lord Kṛṣṇa, who is known as Janārdana.

TEXT 14

मनुरुवाच

आदेशेऽहं भगवतो वर्तेयामीवसूदन ।
स्थानं त्विहानुजानीहि प्रजानां मम च प्रभो ॥१४॥

manur uvāca
ādeśe 'haṁ bhagavato
varteyāmīva-sūdana
sthānaṁ tv ihānujānīhi
prajānāṁ mama ca prabho

manuḥ uvāca—Śrī Manu said; *ādeśe*—under the order; *aham*—I; *bhagavataḥ*—of your powerful self; *varteya*—shall stay; *amīva-sūdana*—O killer of all sins; *sthānam*—the place; *tu*—but; *iha*—in this world; *anujānīhi*—please let me know; *prajānām*—of the living entities born from me; *mama*—my; *ca*—also; *prabho*—O lord.

TRANSLATION

Śrī Manu said: O all-powerful lord, O killer of all sins, I shall abide by your order. Now please let me know my place and that of the living entities born of me.

TEXT 15

यदोकः सर्वभूतानां मही मग्ना महाम्भसि ।
अस्या उद्धरणे यत्नो देव देव्या विधीयताम् ॥१५॥

yad okaḥ sarva-bhūtānāṁ
mahī magnā mahāmbhasi
asyā uddharaṇe yatno
deva devyā vidhīyatām

yat—because; *okaḥ*—the dwelling place; *sarva*—for all; *bhūtānām*—living entities; *mahī*—the earth; *magnā*—merged; *mahā-ambhasi*—in the great water; *asyāḥ*—of this; *uddharaṇe*—in the lifting; *yatnaḥ*—attempt; *deva*—O master of the demigods; *devyāḥ*—of this earth; *vidhīyatām*—let it be done.

TRANSLATION

O master of the demigods, please attempt to lift the earth, which is merged in the great water, because it is the dwelling place for all

the living entities. It can be done by your endeavor and by the mercy of the Lord.

PURPORT

The great water mentioned in this connection is the Garbhodaka Ocean, which fills half of the universe.

TEXT 16

मैत्रेय उवाच

परमेष्ठी त्वपां मध्ये तथा सन्नामवेक्ष्य गाम् ।
कथमेनां समुन्नेष्य इति दध्यौ धिया चिरम् ॥१६॥

maitreya uvāca
parameṣṭhī tv apāṁ madhye
tathā sannām avekṣya gām
katham enāṁ samunneṣya
iti dadhyau dhiyā ciram

maitreyaḥ uvāca—Śrī Maitreya Muni said; *parameṣṭhī*—Brahmā; *tu*—also; *apām*—the water; *madhye*—within; *tathā*—thus; *sannām*—situated; *avekṣya*—seeing; *gām*—the earth; *katham*—how; *enām*—this; *samunneṣye*—I shall lift; *iti*—thus; *dadhyau*—gave attention; *dhiyā*—by intelligence; *ciram*—for a long time.

TRANSLATION

Śrī Maitreya said: Thus, seeing the earth merged in the water, Brahmā gave his attention for a long time to how it could be lifted.

PURPORT

According to Jīva Gosvāmī, the topics delineated here are of different millenniums. The present topics are of the Śveta-varāha millennium, and topics regarding the Cākṣuṣa millennium will also be discussed in this chapter.

TEXT 17

सृजतो मे क्षितिर्वार्भिः प्लाव्यमाना रसां गता ।
अथात्र किमनुष्ठेयमस्माभिः सर्गयोजितैः ।
यस्याहं हृदयादासं स ईशो विदधातु मे ॥१७॥

sṛjato me kṣitir vārbhiḥ
plāvyamānā rasāṁ gatā
athātra kim anuṣṭheyam
asmābhiḥ sarga-yojitaiḥ
yasyāhaṁ hṛdayād āsaṁ
sa īśo vidadhātu me

sṛjataḥ—while engaged in creation; *me*—of me; *kṣitiḥ*—the earth; *vārbhiḥ*—by the water; *plāvyamānā*—being inundated; *rasām*—depth of water; *gatā*—gone down; *atha*—therefore; *atra*—in this matter; *kim*—what; *anuṣṭheyam*—is right to be attempted; *asmābhiḥ*—by us; *sarga*—creation; *yojitaiḥ*—engaged in; *yasya*—the one from whose; *aham*—I; *hṛdayāt*—from the heart; *āsam*—born; *saḥ*—He; *īśaḥ*—the Lord; *vidadhātu*—may direct; *me*—unto me.

TRANSLATION

Brahmā thought: While I have been engaged in the process of creation, the earth has been inundated by a deluge and has gone down into the depths of the ocean. What can we do who are engaged in this matter of creation? It is best to let the Almighty Lord direct us.

PURPORT

The devotees of the Lord, who are all confidential servitors, are sometimes perplexed in the discharge of their respective duties, but they are never discouraged. They have full faith in the Lord, and He paves the way for the smooth progress of the devotee's duty.

TEXT 18

इत्यभिध्यायतो नासाविवरात्सहसानघ ।
वराहतोको निरगादङ्गुष्ठपरिमाणकः ॥१८॥

ity abhidhyāyato nāsā-
vivarāt sahasānagha
varāha-toko niragād
aṅguṣṭha-parimāṇakaḥ

iti—thus; *abhidhyāyataḥ*—while thinking; *nāsā-vivarāt*—from the nostrils; *sahasā*—all of a sudden; *anagha*—O sinless one; *varāha-tokaḥ*—a minute form of Varāha (a boar); *niragāt*—came out; *aṅguṣṭha*—the upper portion of the thumb; *parimāṇakaḥ*—of the measurement.

TRANSLATION

O sinless Vidura, all of a sudden, while Brahmā was engaged in thinking, a small form of a boar came out of his nostril. The measurement of the creature was not more than the upper portion of a thumb.

TEXT 19

तस्याभिपश्यतः खस्थः क्षणेन किल भारत ।
गजमात्रः प्रववृधे तदद्भुतमभून्महत् ॥१९॥

tasyābhipaśyataḥ kha-sthaḥ
kṣaṇena kila bhārata
gaja-mātraḥ pravavṛdhe
tad adbhutam abhūn mahat

tasya—his; *abhipaśyataḥ*—while thus observing; *kha-sthaḥ*—situated in the sky; *kṣaṇena*—suddenly; *kila*—verily; *bhārata*—O descendant of Bharata; *gaja-mātraḥ*—just like an elephant; *pravavṛdhe*—thoroughly expanded; *tat*—that; *adbhutam*—extraordinary; *abhūt*—transformed; *mahat*—into a gigantic body.

TRANSLATION

O descendant of Bharata, while Brahmā was observing Him, that boar became situated in the sky in a wonderful manifestation as gigantic as a great elephant.

TEXT 20

मरीचिप्रमुखैर्विप्रैः कुमारैर्मनुना सह ।
दृष्ट्वा तत्सौकरं रूपं तर्कयामास चित्रधा ॥२०॥

marīci-pramukhair vipraiḥ
kumārair manunā saha
dṛṣṭvā tat saukaraṁ rūpaṁ
tarkayām āsa citradhā

marīci—the great sage Marīci; *pramukhaiḥ*—headed by; *vipraiḥ*—all *brāhmaṇas; kumāraiḥ*—with the four Kumāras; *manunā*—and with Manu; *saha*—with; *dṛṣṭvā*—seeing; *tat*—that; *saukaram*—appearance like a boar; *rūpam*—form; *tarkayām āsa*—argued among themselves; *citradhā*—in various ways.

TRANSLATION

Struck with wonder at observing the wonderful boarlike form in the sky, Brahmā, with great brāhmaṇas like Marīci, as well as the Kumāras and Manu, began to argue in various ways.

TEXT 21

किमेतत्सूकरव्याजं सत्त्वं दिव्यमवस्थितम् ।
अहो बताश्चर्यमिदं नासाया मे विनिःसृतम् ॥२१॥

kim etat sūkara-vyājaṁ
sattvaṁ divyam avasthitam
aho batāścaryam idaṁ
nāsāyā me viniḥsṛtam

kim—what; *etat*—this; *sūkara*—boar; *vyājam*—pretention; *sattvam*—entity; *divyam*—extraordinary; *avasthitam*—situated; *aho bata*—oh, it is; *āścaryam*—very wonderful; *idam*—this; *nāsāyāḥ*—from the nose; *me*—my; *viniḥsṛtam*—came out.

TRANSLATION

Is this some extraordinary entity come in the pretense of a boar? It is very wonderful that He has come from my nose.

TEXT 22

दृष्टोऽङ्गुष्ठशिरोमात्रः क्षणाद्गण्डशिलासमः ।
अपि स्विद्भगवानेष यज्ञो मे खेदयन्मनः ॥२२॥

dṛṣṭo 'ṅguṣṭha-śiro-mātraḥ
kṣaṇād gaṇḍa-śilā-samaḥ
api svid bhagavān eṣa
yajño me khedayan manaḥ

dṛṣṭaḥ—just seen; *aṅguṣṭha*—thumb; *śiraḥ*—tip; *mātraḥ*—only; *kṣaṇāt*—immediately; *gaṇḍa-śilā*—large stone; *samaḥ*—like; *api svit*—whether; *bhagavān*—the Personality of Godhead; *eṣaḥ*—this; *yajñaḥ*—Viṣṇu; *me*—my; *khedayan*—perturbing; *manaḥ*—mind.

TRANSLATION

First of all this boar was seen no bigger than the tip of a thumb, and within a moment He was as large as a stone. My mind is perturbed. Is He the Supreme Personality of Godhead, Viṣṇu?

PURPORT

Since Brahmā is the supermost person in the universe and he had never before experienced such a form, he could guess that the wonderful appearance of the boar was an incarnation of Viṣṇu. The uncommon features symptomatic of the incarnation of Godhead can bewilder even the mind of Brahmā.

TEXT 23

इति मीमांसतस्तस्य ब्रह्मणः सह सूनुभिः ।
भगवान् यज्ञपुरुषो जगर्जागेन्द्रसन्निभः ॥२३॥

iti mīmāṁsatas tasya
brahmaṇaḥ saha sūnubhiḥ
bhagavān yajña-puruṣo
jagarjāgendra-sannibhaḥ

iti—thus; *mīmāṁsataḥ*—while deliberating; *tasya*—his; *brahmaṇaḥ*—of Brahmā; *saha*—along with; *sūnubhiḥ*—his sons; *bhagavān*—the Personality of Godhead; *yajña*—Lord Viṣṇu; *puruṣaḥ*—the Supreme Person; *jagarja*—resounded; *aga-indra*—great mountain; *sannibhaḥ*—like.

TRANSLATION

While Brahmā was deliberating with his sons, the Supreme Personality of Godhead, Viṣṇu, roared tumultuously like a great mountain.

PURPORT

It appears that great hills and mountains also have their roaring power because they are also living entities. The volume of the sound vibrated is in proportion to the size of the material body. While Brahmā was guessing about the appearance of the Lord's incarnation as a boar, the Lord confirmed Brahmā's contemplation by roaring with His gorgeous voice.

TEXT 24

ब्रह्माणं हर्षयामास हरिस्तांश्च द्विजोत्तमान् ।
स्वगर्जितेन ककुभः प्रतिस्वनयता विभुः ॥२४॥

brahmāṇaṁ harṣayām āsa
haris tāṁś ca dvijottamān
sva-garjitena kakubhaḥ
pratisvanayatā vibhuḥ

brahmāṇam—unto Brahmā; *harṣayām āsa*—enlivened; *hariḥ*—the Personality of Godhead; *tān*—all of them; *ca*—also; *dvija-uttamān*—highly elevated *brāhmaṇas; sva-garjitena*—by His uncommon voice; *kakubhaḥ*—all directions; *pratisvanayatā*—which echoed; *vibhuḥ*—the omnipotent.

TRANSLATION

The omnipotent Supreme Personality of Godhead enlivened Brahmā and the other highly elevated brāhmaṇas by again roaring with His uncommon voice, which echoed in all directions.

PURPORT

Brahmā and other enlightened *brāhmaṇas* who know the Supreme Personality of Godhead are enlivened by the appearance of the Lord in any of His multi-incarnations. The appearance of the wonderful and gigantic incarnation of Viṣṇu as the mountainlike boar did not fill them with any kind of fear, although the Lord's resounding voice was tumultuous and echoed horribly in all directions as an open threat to all demons who might challenge His omnipotency.

TEXT 25

निशम्य ते घर्घरितं स्वखेद-
क्षयिष्णु मायामयसूकरस्य ।
जनस्तपःसत्यनिवासिनस्ते
त्रिभिः पवित्रैर्मुनयोऽगृणन् स्म ॥२५॥

niśamya te ghargharitaṁ sva-kheda-
kṣayiṣṇu māyāmaya-sūkarasya
janas-tapaḥ-satya-nivāsinas te
tribhiḥ pavitrair munayo 'gṛṇan sma

niśamya—just after hearing; *te*—those; *ghargharitam*—the tumultuous sound; *sva-kheda*—personal lamentation; *kṣayiṣṇu*—destroying; *māyā-maya*—all-merciful; *sūkarasya*—of Lord Boar; *janaḥ*—the Janaloka planet; *tapaḥ*—the Tapoloka planet; *satya*—the Satyaloka planet; *nivāsinaḥ*—residents; *te*—all of them; *tribhiḥ*—from the three *Vedas; pavitraiḥ*—by the all-auspicious *mantras; munayaḥ*—great thinkers and sages; *agṛṇan sma*—chanted.

TRANSLATION

When the great sages and thinkers who are residents of Janaloka, Tapoloka and Satyaloka heard the tumultuous voice of

Lord Boar, which was the all-auspicious sound of the all-merciful Lord, they chanted auspicious chants from the three Vedas.

PURPORT

The word *māyāmaya* is very significant in this verse. *Māyā* means "mercy," "specific knowledge" and also "illusion." Therefore Lord Boar is everything; He is merciful, He is all knowledge, and He is illusion also. The sound which He vibrated as the boar incarnation was answered by the Vedic hymns of the great sages in the planets Janaloka, Tapoloka and Satyaloka. The highest intellectual and pious living entities live in those planets, and when they heard the extraordinary voice of the boar, they could understand that the specific sound was vibrated by the Lord and no one else. Therefore they replied by praying to the Lord with Vedic hymns. The earth planet was submerged in the mire, but on hearing the sound of the Lord, the inhabitants of the higher planets were all jubilant because they knew that the Lord was there to deliver the earth. Therefore Brahmā and all the sages, such as Bhṛgu, Brahmā's other sons, and learned *brāhmaṇas*, were enlivened, and they concertedly joined in praising the Lord with the transcendental vibrations of the Vedic hymns. The most important is the *Bṛhan-nāradīya Purāṇa* verse Hare Kṛṣṇa, Hare Kṛṣṇa, Kṛṣṇa Kṛṣṇa, Hare Hare/ Hare Rāma, Hare Rāma, Rāma Rāma, Hare Hare.

TEXT 26

तेषां सतां वेदवितानमूर्ति-
ब्रह्मावधार्यात्मगुणानुवादम् ।
विनद्य भूयो विबुधोदयाय
गजेन्द्रलीलो जलमाविवेश ॥२६॥

teṣāṁ satāṁ veda-vitāna-mūrtir
brahmāvadhāryātma-guṇānuvādam
vinadya bhūyo vibudhodayāya
gajendra-līlo jalam āviveśa

teṣām—of them; *satām*—of the great devotees; *veda*—all knowledge; *vitāna-mūrtiḥ*—the form of expansion; *brahma*—Vedic sound;

avadhārya—knowing it well; *ātma*—of Himself; *guṇa-anuvādam*—transcendental glorification; *vinadya*—resounding; *bhūyaḥ*—again; *vibudha*—of the transcendentally learned; *udayāya*—for the elevation or benefit; *gajendra-līlaḥ*—playing like an elephant; *jalam*—the water; *āviveśa*—entered.

TRANSLATION

Playing like an elephant, He entered into the water after roaring again in reply to the Vedic prayers by the great devotees. The Lord is the object of the Vedic prayers, and thus He understood that the devotees' prayers were meant for Him.

PURPORT

The form of the Lord in any shape is always transcendental and full of knowledge and mercy. The Lord is the destroyer of all material contamination because His form is personified Vedic knowledge. All the *Vedas* worship the transcendental form of the Lord. In the Vedic *mantras* the devotees request the Lord to remove the glaring effulgence because it covers His real face. That is the version of the *Īśopaniṣad.* The Lord has no material form, but His form is always understood in terms of the *Vedas.* The *Vedas* are said to be the breath of the Lord, and that breath was inhaled by Brahmā, the original student of the *Vedas.* The breathing from the nostril of Brahmā caused the appearance of Lord Boar, and therefore the boar incarnation of the Lord is the personified *Vedas.* The glorification of the incarnation by the sages on the higher planets consisted of factual Vedic hymns. Whenever there is glorification of the Lord, it is to be understood that Vedic *mantras* are being rightly vibrated. The Lord was therefore pleased when such Vedic *mantras* were chanted, and to encourage His pure devotees, He roared once more and entered the water to rescue the submerged earth.

TEXT 27

उत्क्षिप्तवालः खचरः कठोरः
सटा विधुन्वन् खररोमशत्वक् ।
खुराहताभ्रः सितदंष्ट्र ईक्षा-
ज्योतिर्बभासे भगवान्महीध्रः ॥२७॥

utkṣipta-vālaḥ kha-caraḥ kaṭhoraḥ
saṭā vidhunvan khara-romaśa-tvak
khurāhatābhraḥ sita-daṁṣṭra īkṣā-
jyotir babhāse bhagavān mahīdhraḥ

utkṣipta-vālaḥ—slashing with the tail; *kha-caraḥ*—in the sky; *kaṭhoraḥ*—very hard; *saṭāḥ*—hairs on the shoulder; *vidhunvan*—quivering; *khara*—sharp; *romaśa-tvak*—skin full of hairs; *khura-āhata*—struck by the hooves; *abhraḥ*—the clouds; *sita-daṁṣṭraḥ*—white tusks; *īkṣā*—glance; *jyotiḥ*—luminous; *babhāse*—began to emit an effulgence; *bhagavān*—the Personality of Godhead; *mahī-dhraḥ*—the supporter of the world.

TRANSLATION

Before entering the water to rescue the earth, Lord Boar flew in the sky, slashing His tail, His hard hairs quivering. His very glance was luminous, and He scattered the clouds in the sky with His hooves and His glittering white tusks.

PURPORT

When the Lord is offered prayers by His devotees, His transcendental activities are described. Here are some of the transcendental features of Lord Boar. As the residents of the upper three planetary systems offered their prayers to the Lord, it is understood that His body expanded throughout the sky, beginning from the topmost planet, Brahmaloka, or Satyaloka. It is stated in the *Brahma-saṁhitā* that His eyes are the sun and the moon; therefore His very glance over the sky was as illuminating as the sun or the moon. The Lord is described herein as *mahīdhraḥ*, which means either a "big mountain" or the "sustainer of the earth." In other words, the Lord's body was as big and hard as the Himalayan Mountains; otherwise how was it possible that He kept the entire earth on the support of His white tusks? The poet Jayadeva, a great devotee of the Lord, has sung of the incident in his prayers for the incarnations:

vasati daśana-śikhare dharaṇī tava lagnā
śaśini kalaṅka-kaleva nimagnā
keśava dhṛta-śūkara-rūpa jaya jagadīśa hare

"All glories to Lord Keśava [Kṛṣṇa], who appeared as the boar. The earth was held between His tusks, which appeared like the scars on the moon."

TEXT 28

घ्राणेन पृथ्व्याः पदवीं विजिघ्रन्
क्रोडापदेशः स्वयमध्वराङ्गः ।
करालदंष्ट्रोऽप्यकरालदृग्भ्या-
मुद्वीक्ष्य विप्रान् गृणतोऽविशत्कम् ॥२८॥

ghrāṇena pṛthvyāḥ padavīṁ vijighran
kroḍāpadeśaḥ svayam adhvarāṅgaḥ
karāla-daṁṣṭro 'py akarāla-dṛgbhyām
udvīkṣya viprān gṛṇato 'viśat kam

ghrāṇena—by smelling; *pṛthvyāḥ*—of the earth; *padavīm*—situation; *vijighran*—searching after the earth; *kroḍa-apadeśaḥ*—assuming the body of a hog; *svayam*—personally; *adhvara*—transcendental; *aṅgaḥ*—body; *karāla*—fearful; *daṁṣṭraḥ*—teeth (tusks); *api*—in spite of; *akarāla*—not fearful; *dṛgbhyām*—by His glance; *udvīkṣya*—glancing over; *viprān*—all the *brāhmaṇa*-devotees; *gṛṇataḥ*—who were engaged in prayers; *aviśat*—entered; *kam*—the water.

TRANSLATION

He was personally the Supreme Lord Viṣṇu and was therefore transcendental, yet because He had the body of a hog, He searched after the earth by smell. His tusks were fearful, and He glanced over the devotee-brāhmaṇas engaged in offering prayers. Thus He entered the water.

PURPORT

We should always remember that although the body of a hog is material, the hog form of the Lord was not materially contaminated. It is not possible for an earthly hog to assume a gigantic form spreading throughout the sky, beginning from the Satyaloka. His body is always transcendental in all circumstances; therefore, the assumption of the form of a boar is only His pastime. His body is all *Vedas*, or transcendental. But since He had assumed the form of a boar, He began to search out the earth by smelling, just like a hog. The Lord can perfectly play the part of any living entity. The gigantic feature of the boar was certainly very fearful for all nondevotees, but to the pure devotees of the Lord He was not at all fearful; on the contrary, He was so pleasingly glancing upon His devotees that all of them felt transcendental happiness.

TEXT 29

स वज्रकूटाङ्गनिपातवेग-
विशीर्णकुक्षिः स्तनयन्नुदन्वान् ।
उत्सृष्टदीर्घोर्मिभुजैरिवार्त-
श्चुक्रोश यज्ञेश्वर पाहि मेति ॥२९॥

sa vajra-kūṭāṅga-nipāta-vega-
viśīrṇa-kukṣiḥ stanayann udanvān
utsṛṣṭa-dīrghormi-bhujair ivārtaś
cukrośa yajñeśvara pāhi meti

saḥ—that; *vajra-kūṭa-aṅga*—body like a great mountain; *nipāta-vega*—the force of diving; *viśīrṇa*—bifurcating; *kukṣiḥ*—the middle portion; *stanayan*—resounding like; *udanvān*—the ocean; *utsṛṣṭa*—creating; *dīrgha*—high; *ūrmi*—waves; *bhujaiḥ*—by the arms; *iva ārtaḥ*—like a distressed person; *cukrośa*—prayed loudly; *yajña-īśvara*—O master of all sacrifices; *pāhi*—please protect; *mā*—unto me; *iti*—thus.

TRANSLATION

Diving into the water like a giant mountain, Lord Boar divided the middle of the ocean, and two high waves appeared as the arms of the ocean, which cried loudly as if praying to the Lord, "O Lord of all sacrifices, please do not cut me in two! Kindly give me protection!"

PURPORT

Even the great ocean was perturbed by the falling of the mountainlike body of the transcendental boar, and it appeared to be frightened, as if death were imminent.

TEXT 30

खुरैः क्षुरप्रैर्दरयंस्तदाप
उत्पारपारं त्रिपरू रसायाम् ।
ददर्श गां तत्र सुषुप्सुरग्रे
यां जीवधानीं स्वयमभ्यधत्त ॥३०॥

khuraiḥ kṣuraprair darayaṁs tad āpa
utpāra-pāraṁ tri-parū rasāyām
dadarśa gāṁ tatra suṣupsur agre
yāṁ jīva-dhānīṁ svayam abhyadhatta

khuraiḥ—by the hooves; *kṣurapraiḥ*—compared to a sharp weapon; *darayan*—penetrating; *tat*—that; *āpaḥ*—water; *utpāra-pāram*—found the limitation of the unlimited; *tri-paruḥ*—the master of all sacrifices; *rasāyām*—within the water; *dadarśa*—found; *gām*—the earth; *tatra*—there; *suṣupsuḥ*—lying; *agre*—in the beginning; *yām*—whom; *jīva-dhānīm*—the resting place for all living entities; *svayam*—personally; *abhyadhatta*—uplifted.

TRANSLATION

Lord Boar penetrated the water with His hooves, which were like sharp arrows, and found the limits of the ocean, although it was unlimited. He saw the earth, the resting place for all living beings, lying as it was in the beginning of creation, and He personally lifted it.

PURPORT

The word *rasāyām* is sometimes interpreted to mean Rasātala, the lowest planetary system, but that is not applicable in this connection, according to Viśvanātha Cakravartī Ṭhākura. The earth is seven times superior to the other planetary systems, namely Tala, Atala, Talātala, Vitala, Rasātala, Pātāla, etc. Therefore the earth cannot be situated in the Rasātala planetary system. It is described in the *Viṣṇu-dharma:*

pātāla-mūleśvara-bhoga-saṁhatau
vinyasya pādau pṛthivīṁ ca bibhrataḥ
yasyopamāno na babhūva so 'cyuto
mamāstu māṅgalya-vivṛddhaye hariḥ

Therefore the Lord found the earth on the bottom of the Garbhodaka Ocean, where the planets rest during the devastation at the end of Brahmā's day.

TEXT 31

स्वदंष्ट्रयोद्धृत्य महीं निमग्नां
स उत्थितः संरुरुचे रसायाः ।
तत्रापि दैत्यं गदयापतन्तं
सुनाभसन्दीपिततीव्रमन्युः ॥३१॥

sva-daṁṣṭrayoddhṛtya mahīṁ nimagnāṁ
sa utthitaḥ saṁruruce rasāyāḥ
tatrāpi daityaṁ gadayāpatantaṁ
sunābha-sandīpita-tīvra-manyuḥ

sva-daṁṣṭrayā—by His own tusks; *uddhṛtya*—raising; *mahīm*—the earth; *nimagnām*—submerged; *saḥ*—He; *utthitaḥ*—getting up; *saṁruruce*—appeared very splendid; *rasāyāḥ*—from the water; *tatra*—there; *api*—also; *daityam*—unto the demon; *gadayā*—with the club; *āpatantam*—rushing towards Him; *sunābha*—the wheel of Kṛṣṇa; *sandīpita*—glowing; *tīvra*—fierce; *manyuḥ*—anger.

TRANSLATION

Lord Boar very easily took the earth on His tusks and got it out of the water. Thus He appeared very splendid. Then, His anger glowing like the Sudarśana wheel, He immediately killed the demon [Hiraṇyākṣa], although he tried to fight with the Lord.

PURPORT

According to Śrīla Jīva Gosvāmī, the Vedic literatures describe the incarnation of Lord Varāha (Boar) in two different devastations, namely the Cākṣuṣa devastation and the Svāyambhuva devastation. This particular appearance of the boar incarnation actually took place in the Svāyambhuva devastation, when all planets other than the higher ones—Jana, Mahar and Satya—merged in the water of devastation. This particular incarnation of the boar was seen by the inhabitants of the planets mentioned above. Śrīla Viśvanātha Cakravartī suggests that the sage Maitreya amalgamated both the boar incarnations in different devastations and summarized them in his description to Vidura.

TEXT 32

जघान रुन्धानमसह्यविक्रमं
स लीलयेभं मृगराडिवाम्भसि ।
तद्रक्तपङ्काङ्कितगण्डतुण्डो
यथा गजेन्द्रो जगतीं विभिन्दन् ॥३२॥

jaghāna rundhānam asahya-vikramaṁ
sa līlayebhaṁ mṛgarāḍ ivāmbhasi
tad-rakta-paṅkāṅkita-gaṇḍa-tuṇḍo
yathā gajendro jagatīṁ vibhindan

jaghāna—killed; *rundhānam*—the obstructive enemy; *asahya*—unbearable; *vikramam*—prowess; *saḥ*—He; *līlayā*—easily; *ibham*—the elephant; *mṛga-rāṭ*—the lion; *iva*—like; *ambhasi*—in the water; *tat-rakta*—of his blood; *paṅka-aṅkita*—smeared by the pool; *gaṇḍa*—cheeks; *tuṇḍaḥ*—tongue; *yathā*—as if; *gajendraḥ*—the elephant; *jagatīm*—earth; *vibhindan*—digging.

TRANSLATION

Thereupon Lord Boar killed the demon within the water, just as a lion kills an elephant. The cheeks and tongue of the Lord became smeared with the blood of the demon, just as an elephant becomes reddish from digging in the purple earth.

TEXT 33

तमालनीलं सितदन्तकोट्या
क्ष्मामुत्क्षिपन्तं गजलीलयाङ्ग ।
प्रज्ञाय बद्धाञ्जलयोऽनुवाकै-
र्विरिञ्चिमुख्या उपतस्थुरीशम् ॥३३॥

tamāla-nīlaṁ sita-danta-koṭyā
kṣmām utkṣipantaṁ gaja-līlayāṅga
prajñāya baddhāñjalayo 'nuvākair
viriñci-mukhyā upatasthur īśam

tamāla—a blue tree named the *tamāla; nīlam*—bluish; *sita*—white; *danta*—tusks; *koṭyā*—with the curved edge; *kṣmām*—the earth; *utkṣipantam*—while suspending; *gaja-līlayā*—playing like an elephant; *aṅga*—O Vidura; *prajñāya*—after knowing it well; *baddha*—folded; *añjalayaḥ*—hands; *anuvākaiḥ*—by Vedic hymns; *viriñci*—Brahmā; *mukhyāḥ*—headed by; *upatasthuḥ*—offered prayers; *īśam*—unto the Supreme Lord.

TRANSLATION

Then the Lord, playing like an elephant, suspended the earth on the edge of His curved white tusks. He assumed a bluish complexion like that of a tamāla tree, and thus the sages, headed by Brahmā, could understand Him to be the Supreme Personality of Godhead and offered respectful obeisances unto the Lord.

TEXT 34

ऋषय ऊचुः

जितं जितं तेऽजित यज्ञभावन
त्रयीं तनुं स्वां परिधुन्वते नमः ।
यद्रोमगर्तेषु निलिल्युरद्धय-
स्तस्मै नमः कारणसूकराय ते ॥३४॥

ṛṣaya ūcuḥ
jitaṁ jitaṁ te 'jita yajña-bhāvana
trayīṁ tanuṁ svāṁ paridhunvate namaḥ
yad-roma-garteṣu nililyur addhayas
tasmai namaḥ kāraṇa-sūkarāya te

ṛṣayaḥ ūcuḥ—the glorified sages uttered; *jitam*—all glories; *jitam*—all victories; *te*—unto You; *ajita*—O unconquerable one; *yajña-bhāvana*—one who is understood by performances of sacrifice; *trayīm*—personified *Vedas; tanum*—such a body; *svām*—own; *paridhunvate*—shaking; *namaḥ*—all obeisances; *yat*—whose; *roma*—hairs; *garteṣu*—in the holes; *nililyuḥ*—submerged; *addhayaḥ*—the oceans; *tasmai*—unto Him; *namaḥ*—offering obeisances; *kāraṇa-sūkarāya*—unto the hog form assumed for reasons; *te*—unto You.

TRANSLATION

All the sages uttered with great respect: O unconquerable enjoyer of all sacrifices, all glories and all victories unto You! You are moving in Your form of the personified Vedas, and in the hair holes of Your body the oceans are submerged. For certain reasons [to uplift the earth] You have now assumed the form of a boar.

PURPORT

The Lord can assume any form He likes, and in all circumstances He is the cause of all causes. Since His form is transcendental, He is always the Supreme Personality of Godhead, as He is in the Causal Ocean in the form of Mahā-Viṣṇu. Innumerable universes generate from the holes of His bodily hairs, and thus His transcendental body is the *Vedas* personified. He is the enjoyer of all sacrifices, and He is the unconquerable Supreme Personality of Godhead. He is never to be misunderstood to be other than the Supreme Lord because of His assuming the form of a boar to lift the earth. That is the clear understanding of sages and great personalities like Brahmā and other residents of the higher planetary systems.

TEXT 35

रूपं तवैतन्ननु दुष्कृतात्मनां
दुर्दर्शनं देव यदध्वरात्मकम् ।
छन्दांसि यस्य त्वचि बर्हिरोम-
स्वाज्यं दृशि त्वङ्घ्रिषु चातुर्होत्रम् ॥३५॥

rūpaṁ tavaitan nanu duṣkṛtātmanāṁ
durdarśanaṁ deva yad adhvarātmakam
chandāṁsi yasya tvaci barhi-romasv
ājyaṁ dṛśi tv aṅghriṣu cātur-hotram

rūpam—form; *tava*—Your; *etat*—this; *nanu*—but; *duṣkṛta-ātmanām*—of souls who are simply miscreants; *durdarśanam*—very difficult to see; *deva*—O Lord; *yat*—that; *adhvara-ātmakam*—worshipable by performances of sacrifice; *chandāṁsi*—the Gāyatrī *mantra* and others; *yasya*—whose; *tvaci*—touch of the skin; *barhiḥ*—sacred grass called *kuśa; romasu*—hairs on the body; *ājyam*—clarified butter; *dṛśi*—in the eyes; *tu*—also; *aṅghriṣu*—on the four legs; *cātuḥ-hotram*—four kinds of fruitive activities.

TRANSLATION

O Lord, Your form is worshipable by performances of sacrifice, but souls who are simply miscreants are unable to see it. All the Vedic hymns, Gāyatrī and others, are in the touch of Your skin. In Your bodily hairs is the kuśa grass, in Your eyes is the clarified butter, and in Your four legs are the four kinds of fruitive activities.

PURPORT

There is a class of miscreants who are known in the words of *Bhagavad-gītā* as *veda-vādī*, or so-called strict followers of the *Vedas*. They do not believe in the incarnation of the Lord, what to speak of the Lord's incarnation as the worshipable hog. They describe worship of the different forms or incarnations of the Lord as anthropomorphism. In the estimation of *Śrīmad-Bhāgavatam* these men are miscreants, and in

Bhagavad-gītā (7.15) they are called not only miscreants but also fools and the lowest of mankind, and it is said that their knowledge has been plundered by illusion due to their atheistic temperament. For such condemned persons, the Lord's incarnation as the gigantic hog is invisible. These strict followers of the *Vedas* who despise the eternal forms of the Lord may know from *Śrīmad-Bhāgavatam* that such incarnations are personified forms of the *Vedas.* Lord Boar's skin, His eyes and His bodily hair holes are all described here as different parts of the *Vedas.* He is therefore the personified form of the Vedic hymns, and specifically the Gāyatrī *mantra.*

TEXT 36

स्रक्तुण्ड आसीत्स्रुव ईश नासयो-
रिडोदरे चमसाः कर्णरन्ध्रे ।
प्राशित्रमास्ये ग्रसने ग्रहास्तु ते
यच्चर्वणं ते भगवन्नग्निहोत्रम् ॥३६॥

srak tuṇḍa āsīt sruva īśa nāsayor
iḍodare camasāḥ karṇa-randhre
prāśitram āsye grasane grahās tu te
yac carvaṇaṁ te bhagavann agni-hotram

srak—the plate for sacrifice; *tuṇḍe*—on the tongue; *āsīt*—there is; *sruvaḥ*—another plate for sacrifice; *īśa*—O Lord; *nāsayoḥ*—of the nostrils; *iḍā*—the plate for eating; *udare*—in the belly; *camasāḥ*—another plate for sacrifices; *karṇa-randhre*—in the holes of the ears; *prāśitram*—the plate called the Brahmā plate; *āsye*—in the mouth; *grasane*—in the throat; *grahāḥ*—the plates known as *soma* plates; *tu*—but; *te*—Your; *yat*—that which; *carvaṇam*—chewing; *te*—Your; *bhagavan*—O my Lord; *agni-hotram*—is Your eating through Your sacrificial fire.

TRANSLATION

O Lord, Your tongue is a plate of sacrifice, Your nostril is another plate of sacrifice, in Your belly is the eating plate of

sacrifice, and another plate of sacrifice is the holes of Your ears. In Your mouth is the Brahmā plate of sacrifice, Your throat is the plate of sacrifice known as soma, and whatever You chew is known as agni-hotra.

PURPORT

The *veda-vādīs* say that there is nothing more than the *Vedas* and the performances of sacrifice mentioned in the *Vedas.* They have recently made a rule in their group to formally observe daily sacrifice; they simply ignite a small fire and offer something whimsically, but they do not strictly follow the sacrificial rules and regulations mentioned in the *Vedas.* It is understood that by regulation there are different plates of sacrifice required, such as *srak, sruvā, barhis, cātur-hotra, iḍā, camasa, prāśitra, graha* and *agni-hotra.* One cannot achieve the results of sacrifice unless one observes the strict regulations. In this age there is practically no facility for performing sacrifices in strict discipline. Therefore, in this age of Kali there is a stricture regarding such sacrifices: it is explicitly directed that one should perform *saṅkīrtana-yajña* and nothing more. The incarnation of the Supreme Lord is Yajñeśvara, and unless one has respect for the incarnation of the Lord, he cannot perfectly perform sacrifice. In other words, taking shelter of the Lord and rendering service unto Him is the factual performance of all sacrifices, as explained herein. Different plates of sacrifice correspond to the different parts of the body of the Lord's incarnation. In the *Śrīmad-Bhāgavatam,* Eleventh Canto, it is explicitly directed that one should perform *saṅkīrtana-yajña* to please the Lord's incarnation as Śrī Caitanya Mahāprabhu. This should be rigidly followed in order to achieve the result of *yajña* performance.

TEXT 37

दीक्षानुजन्मोपसदः शिरोधरं
त्वं प्रायणीयोदयनीयदंष्ट्रः ।
जिह्वा प्रवर्ग्यस्तव शीर्षकं क्रतोः
सत्यावसथ्यं चितयोऽसवो हि ते ॥३७॥

dīkṣānujanmopasadaḥ śirodharaṁ
tvaṁ prāyaṇīyodayanīya-daṁṣṭraḥ
jihvā pravargyas tava śīrṣakaṁ kratoḥ
satyāvasathyaṁ citayo 'savo hi te

dīkṣā—initiation; *anujanma*—spiritual birth, or repeated incarnations; *upasadaḥ*—three kinds of desires (relationship, activities and ultimate goal); *śiraḥ-dharam*—the neck; *tvam*—You; *prāyaṇīya*—after the result of initiation; *udayanīya*—the last rites of desires; *daṁṣṭraḥ*—the tusks; *jihvā*—the tongue; *pravargyaḥ*—prior activities; *tava*—Your; *śīrṣakam*—head; *kratoḥ*—of the sacrifice; *satya*—fire without sacrifice; *āvasathyam*—fire of worship; *citayaḥ*—aggregate of all desires; *asavaḥ*—life breath; *hi*—certainly; *te*—Your.

TRANSLATION

Moreover, O Lord, the repetition of Your appearance is the desire for all kinds of initiation. Your neck is the place for three desires, and Your tusks are the result of initiation and the end of all desires. Your tongue is the prior activities of initiation, Your head is the fire without sacrifice as well as the fire of worship, and Your living forces are the aggregate of all desires.

TEXT 38

सोमस्तु रेतः सवनान्यवस्थितिः
संस्थाविभेदास्तव देव धातवः ।
सत्राणि सर्वाणि शरीरसन्धि-
स्त्वं सर्वयज्ञक्रतुरिष्टिबन्धनः ॥३८॥

somas tu retaḥ savanāny avasthitiḥ
saṁsthā-vibhedās tava deva dhātavaḥ
satrāṇi sarvāṇi śarīra-sandhis
tvaṁ sarva-yajña-kratur iṣṭi-bandhanaḥ

somaḥ tu retaḥ—Your semen is the sacrifice called *soma; savanāni*—ritualistic performances of the morning; *avasthitiḥ*—different statuses of bodily growth; *saṁsthā-vibhedāḥ*—seven varieties of sacrifices; *tava*—Your; *deva*—O Lord; *dhātavaḥ*—ingredients of the body such as skin and flesh; *satrāṇi*—sacrifices performed over twelve days; *sarvāṇi*—all of them; *śarīra*—the bodily; *sandhiḥ*—joints; *tvam*—Your Lordship; *sarva*—all; *yajña*—*asoma* sacrifices; *kratuḥ*—*soma* sacrifices; *iṣṭi*—the ultimate desire; *bandhanaḥ*—attachment.

TRANSLATION

O Lord, Your semen is the sacrifice called soma-yajña. Your growth is the ritualistic performances of the morning. Your skin and touch sensations are the seven elements of the agniṣṭoma sacrifice. Your bodily joints are symbols of various other sacrifices performed in twelve days. Therefore You are the object of all sacrifices called soma and asoma, and You are bound by yajñas only.

PURPORT

There are seven kinds of routine *yajñas* performed by all followers of the Vedic rituals, and they are called *agniṣṭoma, atyagniṣṭoma, uktha, ṣoḍaśī, vājapeya, atirātra* and *āptoryāma*. Anyone performing such *yajñas* regularly is supposed to be situated with the Lord. But anyone who is in contact with the Supreme Lord by discharging devotional service is understood to have performed all different varieties of *yajñas*.

TEXT 39

नमो नमस्तेऽखिलमन्त्रदेवता-
द्रव्याय सर्वक्रतवे क्रियात्मने ।
वैराग्यभक्त्यात्मजयानुभावित-
ज्ञानाय विद्यागुरवे नमो नमः ॥३९॥

namo namas te 'khila-mantra-devatā-
dravyāya sarva-kratave kriyātmane
vairāgya-bhaktyātmajayānubhāvita-
jñānāya vidyā-gurave namo namaḥ

namaḥ namaḥ—obeisances unto You; *te*—unto You, who are worshipable; *akhila*—all-inclusive; *mantra*—hymns; *devatā*—the Supreme Lord; *dravyāya*—unto all ingredients for performing sacrifices; *sarva-kratave*—unto all kinds of sacrifices; *kriyā-ātmane*—unto You, the supreme form of all sacrifices; *vairāgya*—renunciation; *bhaktyā*—by devotional service; *ātma-jaya-anubhāvita*—perceivable by conquering the mind; *jñānāya*—such knowledge; *vidyā-gurave*—the supreme spiritual master of all knowledge; *namaḥ namaḥ*—again I offer my respectful obeisances.

TRANSLATION

O Lord, You are the Supreme Personality of Godhead and are worshipable by universal prayers, Vedic hymns and sacrificial ingredients. We offer our obeisances unto You. You can be realized by the pure mind freed from all visible and invisible material contamination. We offer our respectful obeisances to You as the supreme spiritual master of knowledge in devotional service.

PURPORT

The qualification of *bhakti,* or devotional service to the Lord, is that the devotee should be free from all material contaminations and desires. This freedom is called *vairāgya,* or renouncement of material desires. One who engages in devotional service to the Lord according to regulative principles is automatically freed from material desires, and in that pure state of mind one can realize the Personality of Godhead. The Personality of Godhead, being situated in everyone's heart, instructs the devotee regarding pure devotional service so that he may ultimately achieve the association of the Lord. This is confirmed in *Bhagavad-gītā* (10.10) as follows:

teṣāṁ satata-yuktānāṁ
bhajatāṁ prīti-pūrvakam
dadāmi buddhi-yogaṁ taṁ
yena mām upayānti te

"To one who constantly engages in the devotional service of the Lord with faith and love, the Lord certainly gives the intelligence to achieve Him at the ultimate end."

One has to conquer the mind, and one may do it by following the Vedic rituals and by performing different types of sacrifice. The ultimate end of all those performances is to attain *bhakti*, or the devotional service of the Lord. Without *bhakti* one cannot understand the Supreme Personality of Godhead. The original Personality of Godhead or His innumerable expansions of Viṣṇu are the only objects of worship by all the Vedic rituals and sacrificial performances.

TEXT 40

दंष्ट्राग्रकोट्या भगवंस्त्वया धृता
विराजते भूधर भूः सभूधरा ।
यथा वनान्निःसरतो दता धृता
मतङ्गजेन्द्रस्य सपत्रपद्मिनी ॥४०॥

daṁṣṭrāgra-koṭyā bhagavaṁs tvayā dhṛtā
virājate bhūdhara bhūḥ sa-bhūdharā
yathā vanān niḥsarato datā dhṛtā
mataṅ-gajendrasya sa-patra-padminī

daṁṣṭra-agra—the tips of the tusks; *koṭyā*—by the edges; *bhagavan*—O Personality of Godhead; *tvayā*—by You; *dhṛtā*—sustained; *virājate*—is so beautifully situated; *bhū-dhara*—O lifter of the earth; *bhūḥ*—the earth; *sa-bhūdharā*—with mountains; *yathā*—as much as; *vanāt*—from the water; *niḥsarataḥ*—coming out; *datā*—by the tusk; *dhṛtā*—captured; *matam-gajendrasya*—infuriated elephant; *sa-patra*—with leaves; *padminī*—the lotus flower.

TRANSLATION

O lifter of the earth, the earth with its mountains, which You have lifted with Your tusks, is situated as beautifully as a lotus flower with leaves sustained by an infuriated elephant just coming out of the water.

PURPORT

The fortune of the earth planet is praised because of its being specifically sustained by the Lord; its beauty is appreciated and compared to that of a lotus flower situated on the trunk of an elephant. As a lotus flower with leaves is very beautifully situated, so the world, with its many beautiful mountains, appeared on the tusks of the Lord Boar.

TEXT 41

त्रयीमयं रूपमिदं च सौकरं
भूमण्डलेनाथ दता धृतेन ते ।
चकास्ति शृङ्गोढघनेन भूयसा
कुलाचलेन्द्रस्य यथैव विभ्रमः ॥४१॥

trayīmayaṁ rūpam idaṁ ca saukaraṁ
bhū-maṇḍalenātha datā dhṛtena te
cakāsti śṛṅgoḍha-ghanena bhūyasā
kulācalendrasya yathaiva vibhramaḥ

trayī-mayam—*Vedas* personified; *rūpam*—form; *idam*—this; *ca*—also; *saukaram*—the boar; *bhū-maṇḍalena*—by the earth planet; *atha*—now; *datā*—by the tusk; *dhṛtena*—sustained by; *te*—Your; *cakāsti*—is glowing; *śṛṅga-ūḍha*—sustained by the peaks; *ghanena*—by the clouds; *bhūyasā*—more glorified; *kula-acala-indrasya*—of the great mountains; *yathā*—as much as; *eva*—certainly; *vibhramaḥ*—decoration.

TRANSLATION

O Lord, as the peaks of great mountains become beautiful when decorated with clouds, Your transcendental body has become beautiful because of Your lifting the earth on the edge of Your tusks.

PURPORT

The word *vibhramaḥ* is significant. *Vibhramaḥ* means "illusion" as well as "beauty." When a cloud rests on the peak of a great mountain, it appears to be sustained by the mountain, and at the same time it looks very beautiful. Similarly, the Lord has no need to sustain the earth on His tusks, but when He does so the world becomes beautiful, just as the

Lord becomes more beautiful because of His pure devotees on the earth. Although the Lord is the transcendental personification of the Vedic hymns, He has become more beautiful because of His appearance to sustain the earth.

TEXT 42

संस्थापयैनां जगतां सतस्थुषां
लोकाय पत्नीमसि मातरं पिता ।
विधेम चास्यै नमसा सह त्वया
यस्यां स्वतेजोऽग्निमिवारणावधाः ॥४२॥

saṁsthāpayaināṁ jagatāṁ sa-tasthuṣāṁ
lokāya patnīm asi mātaraṁ pitā
vidhema cāsyai namasā saha tvayā
yasyāṁ sva-tejo 'gnim ivāraṇāv adhāḥ

saṁsthāpaya enām—raise this earth; *jagatām*—both the moving and; *sa-tasthuṣām*—nonmoving; *lokāya*—for their residence; *patnīm*—wife; *asi*—You are; *mātaram*—the mother; *pitā*—the father; *vidhema*—do we offer; *ca*—also; *asyai*—unto the mother; *namasā*—with all obeisances; *saha*—along with; *tvayā*—with You; *yasyām*—in whom; *sva-tejaḥ*—by Your own potency; *agnim*—fire; *iva*—likened; *araṇau*—in the *araṇi* wood; *adhāḥ*—invested.

TRANSLATION

O Lord, for the residential purposes of all inhabitants, both moving and nonmoving, this earth is Your wife, and You are the supreme father. We offer our respectful obeisances unto You, along with mother earth, in whom You have invested Your own potency, just as an expert sacrificer puts fire in the araṇi wood.

PURPORT

The so-called law of gravitation which sustains the planets is described herein as the potency of the Lord. This potency is invested by the Lord in the way that an expert sacrificial *brāhmaṇa* puts fire in the *araṇi* wood by the potency of Vedic *mantras.* By this arrangement the world becomes habitable for both the moving and nonmoving creatures. The conditioned souls, who are residents of the material world, are put in the womb of mother earth in the same way the seed of a child is put by the father in the womb of the mother. This conception of the Lord and the earth as father and mother is explained in *Bhagavad-gītā* (14.4). Conditioned souls are devoted to the motherland in which they take their birth, but they do not know their father. The mother is not independent in producing children. Similarly, material nature cannot produce living creatures unless in contact with the supreme father, the Supreme Personality of Godhead. *Śrīmad-Bhāgavatam* teaches us to offer obeisances unto the mother along with the Father, the Supreme Lord, because it is the Father only who impregnates the mother with all energies for the sustenance and maintenance of all living beings, both moving and nonmoving.

TEXT 43

कः श्रद्दधीतान्यतमस्तव प्रभो
रसां गताया भुव उद्विबर्हणम् ।
न विस्मयोऽसौ त्वयि विश्वविस्मये
यो माययेदं ससृजेऽतिविस्मयम् ॥४३॥

kaḥ śraddadhītānyatamas tava prabho
rasāṁ gatāyā bhuva udvibarhaṇam
na vismayo 'sau tvayi viśva-vismaye
yo māyayedaṁ sasṛje 'tivismayam

kaḥ—who else; *śraddadhīta*—can endeavor; *anyatamaḥ*—anyone besides Yourself; *tava*—Your; *prabho*—O Lord; *rasām*—in the water; *gatāyāḥ*—while lying in; *bhuvaḥ*—of the earth; *udvibarhaṇam*—deliverance; *na*—never; *vismayaḥ*—wonderful; *asau*—such an act; *tvayi*—unto You; *viśva*—universal; *vismaye*—full of wonders; *yaḥ*—one who; *māyayā*—by potencies; *idam*—this; *sasṛje*—created; *ati-vismayam*—surpassing all wonders.

TRANSLATION

Who else but You, the Supreme Personality of Godhead, could deliver the earth from within the water? It is not very wonderful for You, however, because You acted most wonderfully in the creation of the universe. By Your energy You have created this wonderful cosmic manifestation.

PURPORT

When a scientist discovers something impressive to the ignorant mass of people, the common man, without inquiry, accepts such a discovery as wonderful. But the intelligent man is not struck with wonder by such discoveries. He gives all credit to the person who created the wonderful brain of the scientist. A common man is also struck with wonder by the wonderful action of material nature, and he gives all credit to the cosmic manifestation. The learned Kṛṣṇa conscious person, however, knows well that behind the cosmic manifestation is the brain of Kṛṣṇa, as confirmed in *Bhagavad-gītā* (9.10): *mayādhyakṣeṇa prakṛtiḥ sūyate sa-carācaram.* Since Kṛṣṇa can direct the wonderful cosmic manifestation, it is not at all wonderful for Him to assume the gigantic form of a boar and thus deliver the earth from the mire of the water. A devotee is therefore not astonished to see the wonderful boar because he knows that the Lord is able to act far more wonderfully by His potencies, which are inconceivable to the brain of even the most erudite scientist.

TEXT 44

विधुन्वता वेदमयं निजं वपु-
जनस्तपःसत्यनिवासिनो वयम् ।
सटाशिखोद्धूतशिवाम्बुबिन्दुभि-
विंमृज्यमाना भृशमीश पाविताः ॥४४॥

vidhunvatā vedamayaṁ nijaṁ vapur
janas-tapaḥ-satya-nivāsino vayam
saṭā-śikhoddhūta-śivāmbu-bindubhir
vimṛjyamānā bhṛśam īśa pāvitāḥ

vidhunvatā—while shaking; *veda-mayam*—personified *Vedas; nijam*—own; *vapuḥ*—body; *janaḥ*—the Janaloka planetary system; *tapaḥ*—the Tapoloka planetary system; *satya*—the Satyaloka planetary system; *nivāsinaḥ*—the inhabitants; *vayam*—we; *saṭā*—hairs on the shoulder; *śikha-uddhūta*—sustained by the tip of the hair; *śiva*—auspicious; *ambu*—water; *bindubhiḥ*—by the particles; *vimṛjyamānāḥ*—we are thus sprinkled by; *bhṛśam*—highly; *īśa*—O Supreme Lord; *pāvitāḥ*—purified.

TRANSLATION

O Supreme Lord, undoubtedly we are inhabitants of the most pious planets—the Jana, Tapas and Satya lokas—but still we have been purified by the drops of water sprinkled from Your shoulder hairs by the shaking of Your body.

PURPORT

Ordinarily the body of a hog is considered impure, but one should not consider that the hog incarnation assumed by the Lord is also impure. That form of the Lord is the personified *Vedas* and is transcendental. The inhabitants of the Jana, Tapas and Satya *lokas* are the most pious persons in the material world, but because those planets are situated in the material world, there are so many material impurities there also. Therefore, when the drops of water from the tips of the Lord's shoulder hairs were sprinkled upon the bodies of the inhabitants of the higher planets, they felt purified. The Ganges water is pure because of its emanating from the toe of the Lord, and there is no difference between the water emanating from the toe and that from the tips of the hair on the shoulder of Lord Boar. They are both absolute and transcendental.

TEXT 45

स वै बत भ्रष्टमतिस्तवैषते
यः कर्मणां पारमपारकर्मणः ।
यद्योगमायागुणयोगमोहितं
विश्वं समस्तं भगवन् विधेहि शम् ॥४५॥

sa vai bata bhraṣṭa-matis tavaiṣate
yaḥ karmaṇāṁ pāram apāra-karmaṇaḥ
yad-yogamāyā-guṇa-yoga-mohitaṁ
viśvaṁ samastaṁ bhagavan vidhehi śam

saḥ—he; *vai*—certainly; *bata*—alas; *bhraṣṭa-matiḥ*—nonsense; *tava*—Your; *eṣate*—desires; *yaḥ*—one who; *karmaṇām*—of activities; *pāram*—limit; *apāra-karmaṇaḥ*—of one who has unlimited activities; *yat*—by whom; *yoga*—mystic power; *māyā*—potency; *guṇa*—modes of material nature; *yoga*—mystic power; *mohitam*—bewildered; *viśvam*—the universe; *samastam*—in total; *bhagavan*—O Supreme Personality of Godhead; *vidhehi*—just be pleased to bestow; *śam*—good fortune.

TRANSLATION

O Lord, there is no limit to Your wonderful activities. Anyone who desires to know the limit of Your activities is certainly nonsensical. Everyone in this world is conditioned by the powerful mystic potencies. Please bestow Your causeless mercy upon these conditioned souls.

PURPORT

Mental speculators who want to understand the limit of the Unlimited are certainly nonsensical. Every one of them is captivated by the external potencies of the Lord. The best thing for them is to surrender unto Him, knowing Him to be inconceivable, for thus they can receive His causeless mercy. This prayer was offered by the inhabitants of the higher planetary systems, namely the Jana, Tapas and Satya *lokas*, who are far more intelligent and powerful than humans.

Viśvaṁ samastam is very significant here. There are the material world and the spiritual world. The sages pray: "Both worlds are bewildered by Your different energies. Those who are in the spiritual world are absorbed in Your loving service, forgetting themselves and You also, and those in the material world are absorbed in material sense gratification and therefore also forget You. No one can know You, because You are unlimited. It is best not to try to know You by unnecessary mental speculation. Rather, kindly bless us so that we can worship You with causeless devotional service."

TEXT 46

मैत्रेय उवाच
इत्युपस्थीयमानोऽसौ मुनिभिर्ब्रह्मवादिभिः ।
सलिले स्वखुराक्रान्त उपाधत्तावितावनिम् ॥४६॥

maitreya uvāca
ity upasthīyamāno 'sau
munibhir brahma-vādibhiḥ
salile sva-khurākrānta
upādhattāvitāvanim

maitreyaḥ uvāca—the sage Maitreya said; *iti*—thus; *upasthīyamānaḥ*—being praised by; *asau*—Lord Boar; *munibhiḥ*—by the great sages; *brahma-vādibhiḥ*—by the transcendentalists; *salile*—on the water; *sva-khura-ākrānte*—touched by His own hooves; *upādhatta*—placed; *avitā*—the maintainer; *avanim*—the earth.

TRANSLATION

The sage Maitreya said: The Lord, being thus worshiped by all the great sages and transcendentalists, touched the earth with His hooves and placed it on the water.

PURPORT

The earth was placed on the water by His inconceivable potency. The Lord is all-powerful, and therefore He can sustain the huge planets either on the water or in the air, as He likes. The tiny human brain cannot conceive how these potencies of the Lord can act. Man can give some vague explanation of the laws by which such phenomena are made possible, but actually the tiny human brain is unable to conceive of the activities of the Lord, which are therefore called inconceivable. Yet the frog-philosophers still try to give some imaginary explanation.

TEXT 47

स इत्थं भगवानुर्वीं विष्वक्सेनः प्रजापतिः ।
रसाया लीलयोन्नीतामप्सु न्यस्य ययौ हरिः ॥४७॥

sa itthaṁ bhagavān urvīṁ
viṣvaksenaḥ prajāpatiḥ
rasāyā līlayonnītām
apsu nyasya yayau hariḥ

saḥ—He; *ittham*—in this manner; *bhagavān*—the Personality of Godhead; *urvīm*—the earth; *viṣvaksenaḥ*—another name of Viṣṇu; *prajā-patiḥ*—the Lord of the living entities; *rasāyāḥ*—from within the water; *līlayā*—very easily; *unnītām*—raised; *apsu*—on the water; *nyasya*—placing; *yayau*—returned to His own abode; *hariḥ*—the Personality of Godhead.

TRANSLATION

In this manner the Personality of Godhead, Lord Viṣṇu, the maintainer of all living entities, raised the earth from within the water, and having placed it afloat on the water, He returned to His own abode.

PURPORT

The Personality of Godhead Lord Viṣṇu descends by His will to the material planets in His innumerable incarnations for particular purposes, and again He goes back to His own abode. When He descends He is called an *avatāra* because *avatāra* means "one who descends." Neither the Lord Himself nor His specific devotees who come to this earth are ordinary living entities like us.

TEXT 48

य एवमेतां हरिमेधसो हरेः
कथां सुभद्रां कथनीयमायिनः ।
शृण्वीत भक्त्या श्रवयेत वोशतीं
जनार्दनोऽस्याशु हृदि प्रसीदति ॥४८॥

ya evam etāṁ hari-medhaso hareḥ
kathāṁ subhadrāṁ kathanīya-māyinaḥ
śṛṇvīta bhaktyā śravayeta vośatīṁ
janārdano 'syāśu hṛdi prasīdati

yaḥ—one who; *evam*—thus; *etām*—this; *hari-medhasaḥ*—who destroys the material existence of the devotee; *hareḥ*—of the Personality of Godhead; *kathām*—narration; *su-bhadrām*—auspicious; *katha-nīya*—worthy to narrate; *māyinaḥ*—of the merciful by His internal potency; *śṛṇvīta*—hears; *bhaktyā*—in devotion; *śravayeta*—also allows others to hear; *vā*—either; *uśatīm*—very pleasing; *janārdanaḥ*—the Lord; *asya*—his; *āśu*—very soon; *hṛdi*—within the heart; *prasīdati*—becomes very pleased.

TRANSLATION

If one hears and describes in a devotional service attitude this auspicious narration of Lord Boar, which is worthy of description, the Lord, who is within the heart of everyone, is very pleased.

PURPORT

In His various incarnations, the Lord appears, acts and leaves behind Him a narrative history which is as transcendental as He Himself. Every one of us is fond of hearing some wonderful narration, but most stories are neither auspicious nor worth hearing because they are of the inferior quality of material nature. Every living entity is of superior quality, spirit soul, and nothing material can be auspicious for him. Intelligent persons should therefore hear personally and cause others to hear the descriptive narrations of the Lord's activities, for that will destroy the pangs of material existence. Out of His causeless mercy only, the Lord comes to this earth and leaves behind His merciful activities so that the devotees may derive transcendental benefit.

TEXT 49

तस्मिन् प्रसन्ने सकलाशिषां प्रभौ
किं दुर्लभं ताभिरलं लवात्मभिः ।
अनन्यदृष्ट्या भजतां गुहाशयः
स्वयं विधत्ते स्वगतिं परः पराम् ॥४९॥

tasmin prasanne sakalāśiṣāṁ prabhau
kiṁ durlabhaṁ tābhir alaṁ lavātmabhiḥ
ananya-dṛṣṭyā bhajatāṁ guhāśayaḥ
svayaṁ vidhatte sva-gatiṁ paraḥ parām

tasmin—unto Him; *prasanne*—being pleased; *sakala-āśiṣām*—of all benediction; *prabhau*—unto the Lord; *kim*—what is that; *durlabham*—very difficult to obtain; *tābhiḥ*—with them; *alam*—away; *lava-ātmabhiḥ*—with insignificant gains; *ananya-dṛṣṭyā*—by nothing but devotional service; *bhajatām*—of those who are engaged in devotional service; *guhā-āśayaḥ*—residing within the heart; *svayam*—personally; *vidhatte*—executes; *sva-gatim*—in His own abode; *paraḥ*—the supreme; *parām*—transcendental.

TRANSLATION

Nothing remains unachieved when the Supreme Personality of Godhead is pleased with someone. By transcendental achievement one understands everything else to be insignificant. One who engages in transcendental loving service is elevated to the highest perfectional stage by the Lord Himself, who is seated in everyone's heart.

PURPORT

As stated in *Bhagavad-gītā* (10.10), the Lord gives intelligence to the pure devotees so that they may be elevated to the highest perfectional stage. It is confirmed herein that a pure devotee, who constantly engages in the loving service of the Lord, is awarded all knowledge necessary to reach the Supreme Personality of Godhead. For such a devotee there is nothing valuable to be achieved but the Lord's service. If one serves faithfully, there is no possibility of frustration because the Lord Himself takes charge of the devotee's advancement. The Lord is seated in everyone's heart, and He knows the devotee's motive and arranges everything achievable. In other words, the pseudo devotee, who is anxious to achieve material gains, cannot attain the highest perfectional stage because the Lord is in knowledge of his motive. One merely has to become sincere in his purpose, and then the Lord is there to help in every way.

TEXT 50

को नाम लोके पुरुषार्थसारवित्
पुराकथानां भगवत्कथासुधाम् ।
आपीय कर्णाञ्जलिभिर्भवापहा-
महो विरज्येत विना नरेतरम् ॥५०॥

ko nāma loke puruṣārtha-sāravit
purā-kathānāṁ bhagavat-kathā-sudhām
āpīya karṇāñjalibhir bhavāpahām
aho virajyeta vinā naretaram

kaḥ—who; *nāma*—indeed; *loke*—in the world; *puruṣa-artha*—goal of life; *sāra-vit*—one who knows the essence of; *purā-kathānām*—of all past histories; *bhagavat*—regarding the Personality of Godhead; *kathā-sudhām*—the nectar of the narrations about the Personality of Godhead; *āpīya*—by drinking; *karṇa-añjalibhiḥ*—by aural reception; *bhava-apahām*—that which kills all material pangs; *aho*—alas; *virajyeta*—could refuse; *vinā*—except; *nara-itaram*—other than the human being. being.

TRANSLATION

Who, other than one who is not a human being, can exist in this world and not be interested in the ultimate goal of life? Who can refuse the nectar of narrations about the Personality of Godhead's activities, which by itself can deliver one from all material pangs?

PURPORT

The narration of the activities of the Personality of Godhead is like a constant flow of nectar. No one can refuse to drink such nectar except one who is not a human being. Devotional service to the Lord is the highest goal of life for every human being, and such devotional service begins by hearing about the transcendental activities of the Personality of Godhead. Only an animal, or a man who is almost an animal in behavior, can refuse to take an interest in hearing the transcendental message of the Lord. There are many books of stories and histories in the world, but except for the histories or narrations on the topics of the Personality of Godhead, none are capable of diminishing the burden of material pangs. Therefore one who is serious about eliminating material existence must chant and hear of the transcendental activities of the Personality of Godhead. Otherwise one must be compared to the nonhumans.

Thus end the Bhaktivedanta purports of the Third Canto, Thirteenth Chapter, of the Śrīmad-Bhāgavatam, *entitled "The Appearance of Lord Varāha."*

CHAPTER FOURTEEN

Pregnancy of Diti in the Evening

TEXT 1

श्रीशुक उवाच
निशम्य कौषारविणोपवर्णितां
हरेः कथां कारणसूकरात्मनः ।
पुनः स पप्रच्छ तमुद्यताञ्जलि-
र्न चातितृप्तो विदुरो धृतव्रतः ॥ १ ॥

śrī-śuka uvāca
niśamya kauṣāraviṇopavarṇitāṁ
hareḥ kathāṁ kāraṇa-sūkarātmanaḥ
punaḥ sa papraccha tam udyatāñjalir
na cātitṛpto viduro dhṛta-vrataḥ

śrī-śukaḥ uvāca—Śrī Śukadeva Gosvāmī said; *niśamya*—after hearing; *kauṣāraviṇā*—by the sage Maitreya; *upavarṇitām*—described; *hareḥ*—of the Personality of Godhead; *kathām*—narrations; *kāraṇa*—for the reason of lifting the earth; *sūkara-ātmanaḥ*—of the boar incarnation; *punaḥ*—again; *saḥ*—he; *papraccha*—inquired; *tam*—from him (Maitreya); *udyata-añjaliḥ*—with folded hands; *na*—never; *ca*—also; *ati-tṛptaḥ*—very much satisfied; *viduraḥ*—Vidura; *dhṛta-vrataḥ*—taken to a vow.

TRANSLATION

Śukadeva Gosvāmī said: After hearing from the great sage Maitreya about the Lord's incarnation as Varāha, Vidura, who had taken a vow, begged him with folded hands to please narrate further transcendental activities of the Lord, since he [Vidura] did not yet feel satisfied.

TEXT 2

विदुर उवाच
तेनैव तु मुनिश्रेष्ठ हरिणा यज्ञमूर्तिना ।
आदिदैत्यो हिरण्याक्षो हत इत्यनुशुश्रुम ॥ २ ॥

vidura uvāca
tenaiva tu muni-śreṣṭha
hariṇā yajña-mūrtinā
ādi-daityo hiraṇyākṣo
hata ity anuśuśruma

viduraḥ uvāca—Śrī Vidura said; *tena*—by Him; *eva*—certainly; *tu*—but; *muni-śreṣṭha*—O chief among the sages; *hariṇā*—by the Personality of Godhead; *yajña-mūrtinā*—the form of sacrifices; *ādi*—original; *daityaḥ*—demon; *hiraṇyākṣaḥ*—by the name Hiraṇyākṣa; *hataḥ*—slain; *iti*—thus; *anuśuśruma*—heard in succession.

TRANSLATION

Śrī Vidura said: O chief amongst the great sages, I have heard by disciplic succession that Hiraṇyākṣa, the original demon, was slain by the same form of sacrifices, the Personality of Godhead [Lord Boar].

PURPORT

As referred to previously, the boar incarnation was manifested in two millenniums—namely Svāyambhuva and Cākṣuṣa. In both millenniums there was a boar incarnation of the Lord, but in the Svāyambhuva millennium He lifted the earth from within the water of the universe, whereas in the Cākṣuṣa millennium He killed the first demon, Hiraṇyākṣa. In the Svāyambhuva millennium He assumed the color white, and in the Cākṣuṣa millennium He assumed the color red. Vidura had already heard about one of them, and he proposed to hear about the other. The two different boar incarnations described are the one Supreme Personality of Godhead.

TEXT 3

तस्य चोद्धरतः क्षौणीं स्वदंष्ट्राग्रेण लीलया ।
दैत्यराजस्य च ब्रह्मन् कस्माद्धेतोरभून्मृधः ॥ ३ ॥

tasya coddharataḥ kṣauṇīṁ
sva-daṁṣṭrāgreṇa līlayā
daitya-rājasya ca brahman
kasmād dhetor abhūn mṛdhaḥ

tasya—His; *ca*—also; *uddharataḥ*—while lifting; *kṣauṇīm*—the earth planet; *sva-daṁṣṭra-agreṇa*—by the edge of His tusks; *līlayā*—in His pastimes; *daitya-rājasya*—of the king of demons; *ca*—and; *brahman*—O *brāhmaṇa; kasmāt*—from what; *hetoḥ*—reason; *abhūt*—there was; *mṛdhaḥ*—fight.

TRANSLATION

What was the reason, O brāhmaṇa, for the fight between the demon king and Lord Boar while the Lord was lifting the earth as His pastime?

TEXT 4

श्रद्दधानाय भक्ताय ब्रूहि तज्जन्मविस्तरम् ।
ऋषे न तृप्यति मनः परं कौतूहलं हि मे ॥ ४ ॥

śraddadhānāya bhaktāya
brūhi taj-janma-vistaram
ṛṣe na tṛpyati manaḥ
paraṁ kautūhalaṁ hi me

śraddadhānāya—unto a faithful person; *bhaktāya*—unto a devotee; *brūhi*—please narrate; *tat*—His; *janma*—appearance; *vistaram*—in detail; *ṛṣe*—O great sage; *na*—not; *tṛpyati*—become satisfied; *manaḥ*—mind; *param*—very much; *kautūhalam*—inquisitive; *hi*—certainly; *me*—my.

TRANSLATION

My mind has become very inquisitive, and therefore I am not satisfied with hearing the narration of the Lord's appearance. Please, therefore, speak more and more to a devotee who is faithful.

PURPORT

One who is actually faithful and inquisitive is qualified to hear the transcendental pastimes of the appearance and disappearance of the Supreme Personality of Godhead. Vidura was a suitable candidate to receive such transcendental messages.

TEXT 5

मैत्रेय उवाच

साधु वीर त्वया पृष्टमवतारकथां हरेः ।
यत्त्वं पृच्छसि मर्त्यानां मृत्युपाशविशातनीम् ॥ ५ ॥

maitreya uvāca
sādhu vīra tvayā pṛṣṭam
avatāra-kathāṁ hareḥ
yat tvaṁ pṛcchasi martyānāṁ
mṛtyu-pāśa-viśātanīm

maitreyaḥ uvāca—Maitreya said; *sādhu*—devotee; *vīra*—O warrior; *tvayā*—by you; *pṛṣṭam*—inquired; *avatāra-kathām*—topics on the incarnation of the Lord; *hareḥ*—of the Personality of Godhead; *yat*—that which; *tvam*—your good self; *pṛcchasi*—asking me; *martyānām*—of those who are destined for death; *mṛtyu-pāśa*—the chain of birth and death; *viśātanīm*—source of liberation.

TRANSLATION

The great sage Maitreya said: O warrior, the inquiry made by you is just befitting a devotee because it concerns the incarnation of the Personality of Godhead. He is the source of liberation from the chain of birth and death for all those who are otherwise destined to die.

PURPORT

The great sage Maitreya addressed Vidura as a warrior not only because Vidura belonged to the Kuru family but because he was anxious to hear about the chivalrous activities of the Lord in His incarnations of Varāha and Nṛsiṁha. Because the inquiries concerned the Lord, they were perfectly befitting a devotee. A devotee has no taste for hearing anything mundane. There are many topics of mundane warfare, but a devotee is not inclined to hear them. The topics of the warfare in which the Lord engages do not concern the war of death but the war against the chain of *māyā* which obliges one to accept repeated birth and death. In other words, one who takes delight in hearing the war topics of the Lord is relieved from the chains of birth and death. Foolish people are suspicious of Kṛṣṇa's taking part in the Battle of Kurukṣetra, not knowing that His taking part insured liberation for all who were present on the battlefield. It is said by Bhīṣmadeva that all who were present on the Battlefield of Kurukṣetra attained their original spiritual existences after death. Therefore, hearing the war topics of the Lord is as good as any other devotional service.

TEXT 6

यथोत्तानपदः पुत्रो मुनिना गीतयार्भकः ।
मृत्योः कृत्वैव मूर्ध्न्यङ्‌घ्रिमारुरोह हरेः पदम् ॥ ६ ॥

yayottānapadaḥ putro
muninā gītayārbhakaḥ
mṛtyoḥ kṛtvaiva mūrdhny aṅghrim
āruroha hareḥ padam

yayā—by which; *uttānapadaḥ*—of King Uttānapāda; *putraḥ*—son; *muninā*—by the sage; *gītayā*—being sung; *arbhakaḥ*—a child; *mṛtyoḥ*—of death; *kṛtvā*—placing; *eva*—certainly; *mūrdhni*—on the head; *aṅghrim*—feet; *āruroha*—ascended; *hareḥ*—of the Personality of Godhead; *padam*—to the abode.

TRANSLATION

By hearing these topics from the sage [Nārada], the son of King Uttānapāda [Dhruva] was enlightened regarding the Personality of

Godhead, and he ascended to the abode of the Lord, placing his feet over the head of death.

PURPORT

While quitting his body, Mahārāja Dhruva, the son of King Uttānapāda, was attended by personalities like Sunanda and others, who received him in the kingdom of God. He left this world at an early age, as a young boy, although he had attained the throne of his father and had several children of his own. Because he was due to quit this world, death was waiting for him. He did not care for death, however, and even with his present body he boarded a spiritual airplane and went directly to the planet of Viṣṇu because of his association with the great sage Nārada, who had spoken to him the narration of the pastimes of the Lord.

TEXT 7

अथात्रापीतिहासोऽयं श्रुतो मे वर्णितः पुरा ।
ब्रह्मणा देवदेवेन देवानामनुपृच्छताम् ॥ ७ ॥

athātrāpītihāso 'yaṁ
śruto me varṇitaḥ purā
brahmaṇā deva-devena
devānām anupṛcchatām

atha—now; *atra*—in this matter; *api*—also; *itihāsaḥ*—history; *ayam*—this; *śrutaḥ*—heard; *me*—by me; *varṇitaḥ*—described; *purā*—years ago; *brahmaṇā*—by Brahmā; *deva-devena*—the foremost of the demigods; *devānām*—by the demigods; *anupṛcchatām*—asking.

TRANSLATION

This history of the fight between the Lord as a boar and the demon Hiraṇyākṣa was heard by me in a year long ago as it was described by the foremost of the demigods, Brahmā, when he was questioned by the other demigods.

His Divine Grace A. C. Bhaktivedanta Swami Prabhupāda
Founder-*Ācārya* of the International Society for Krishna Consciousness

PLATE ONE

Lord Śrī Kṛṣṇa performed the *rāsa* dance, a completely spiritual pastime, ir the company of the *gopīs,* the cowherd damsels of Vṛndāvana. Kṛṣṇa, the supreme mystic, expanded Himself into many forms and stood beside each *gopī*. Yet as He began dancing in their midst, each *gopī* thought that Kṛṣṇa was dancing with her alone. Above that wonderful dance flew many air-planes carrying the denizens of the heavenly planets, who were very eager tc see the wonderful dance of Kṛṣṇa with the *gopīs* and who sang and showered

flowers on the dancers. As the *gopīs* and Kṛṣṇa danced together, Kṛṣṇa appeared like a greenish sapphire locket in the midst of a golden necklace decorated with valuable stones. *(p. 24)*

PLATE TWO

When the Lord appeared as Lord Kṛṣṇa, He lifted the Govardhana Hill as an umbrella to protect His devotees from a torrential downpour of rain. The Lord can lift millions of Govardhana Hills by His simple desire; He does not need to lift a hill with his hand. But He imitates the ordinary living entity by lifting, and at the same time He exhibits His supernatural power. *(p. 26)*

PLATE THREE

At the time of the devastation at the end of Brahmā's day, the fire of time blazes over the three worlds, and everything becomes silent. The sun and moon disappear, and a great fire emanates from the mouths of Saṅkarṣaṇa, Ananta, the serpent bed of the Personality of Godhead. As hurricane winds blow violently, the seas overflow and inundate the three worlds with water. *(pp. 108–110)*

PLATE FOUR

The four-headed Brahmā, the first created living being, created the four great sages Sanaka, Sanandana, Sanātana and Sanat-kumāra, who eternally appear to be children. The sages were all unwilling to adopt materialistic activities, and therefore when Brahmā ordered them to generate progeny, they refused. This disobedience angered Lord Brahmā, and although he tried to control his anger and not express it, he was unable to do so. Thus his anger came out from between his eyebrows as a child of mixed blue and red. This child was Rudra (Lord Śiva), the incarnation of anger. *(pp. 124–127)*

PLATE FIVE

The post of Brahmā, the first created living being, the engineer of the universal creation, is the highest responsible post in the universe. In the material world, Brahmā is the complete representation of the Supreme Personality of Godhead. He is therefore invested with multifarious energies, from which all the demigods are manifested. The qualities of nescience, the great sages, sacrificial paraphernalia, social duties, the Vedic hymns, the arts and sciences, the letters of the alphabet—these and many other aspects of the cosmic manifestation were generated from the body and mind of Lord Brahmā. *(pp. 121–162)*

FEAR of DEATH
ANGER AFTER FRUSTRATION
SENSE of FALSE OWNERSHIP
PURANAS
MEDICAL SCIENCE
KRATU
ATRI
ATHARVA
PULASTYA
VASISTHA
ANGIRA
NĀRADA
PULAHA
KARDAMA
ya-ra-la-va
sa-r-gā-ma-pa-dha-ni
ka...ma

PLATE SIX

While the sage Kaśyapa was meditating in trance, his wife Diti, afflicted by sexual desire, begged him for sexual intercourse. "O lotus-eyed one," she said, "kindly bless me by fulfilling my desire. When someone in distress approaches a great person, his pleas should never go in vain." Although the time was inappropriate and inauspicious, she caught hold of the clothing of the great sage, just like a shameless public prostitute. *(pp. 225–246)*

PLATE SEVEN

The four Kumāras, great sages appearing like children, directly saw the Su preme Personality of Godhead in the spiritual world, the kingdom of God He was formerly visible only within their hearts in ecstatic trance, but nov He actually became visible to their eyes. The Lord was accompanied b His own associates, who bore paraphernalia like an umbrella and a fan. Al though the sages were impersonalists, their minds changed when they sav the beautiful transcendental features of the Lord. After seeing the face o

he Lord, the sages were fully satisfied, and when they wanted to see Him urther, they looked upon the nails of His lotus feet, which resembled rubies. As they viewed the Lord's transcendental body again and again, they finally chieved meditation on the Lord's personal feature. *(pp. 314–322)*

TEXT 8

दितिर्दाक्षायणी क्षत्तर्मारीचं कश्यपं पतिम् ।
अपत्यकामा चकमे सन्ध्यायां हृच्छयार्दिता ॥ ८ ॥

ditir dākṣāyaṇī kṣattar
mārīcaṁ kaśyapaṁ patim
apatya-kāmā cakame
sandhyāyāṁ hṛc-chayārditā

ditiḥ—Diti; *dākṣāyaṇī*—the daughter of Dakṣa; *kṣattaḥ*—O Vidura; *mārīcam*—the son of Marīci; *kaśyapam*—Kaśyapa; *patim*—her husband; *apatya-kāmā*—desirous of having a child; *cakame*—longed for; *sandhyāyām*—in the evening; *hṛt-śaya*—by sex desires; *arditā*—distressed.

TRANSLATION

Diti, daughter of Dakṣa, being afflicted with sex desire, begged her husband, Kaśyapa, the son of Marīci, to have intercourse with her in the evening in order to beget a child.

TEXT 9

इष्ट्वाग्निजिह्वं पयसा पुरुषं यजुषां पतिम् ।
निम्लोचत्यर्क आसीनमग्न्यगारे समाहितम् ॥ ९ ॥

iṣṭvāgni-jihvaṁ payasā
puruṣaṁ yajuṣāṁ patim
nimlocaty arka āsīnam
agny-agāre samāhitam

iṣṭvā—after worshiping; *agni*—fire; *jihvam*—tongue; *payasā*—by oblation; *puruṣam*—unto the Supreme Person; *yajuṣām*—of all sacrifices; *patim*—master; *nimlocati*—while setting; *arke*—the sun; *āsīnam*—sitting; *agni-agāre*—in the sacrificial hall; *samāhitam*—completely in trance.

TRANSLATION

The sun was setting, and the sage was sitting in trance after offering oblations to the Supreme Personality of Godhead, Viṣṇu, whose tongue is the sacrificial fire.

PURPORT

Fire is considered to be the tongue of the Personality of Godhead Viṣṇu, and oblations of grains and clarified butter offered to the fire are thus accepted by Him. That is the principle of all sacrifices, of which Lord Viṣṇu is the master. In other words, the satisfaction of Lord Viṣṇu includes the satisfaction of all demigods and other living beings.

TEXT 10

दितिरुवाच
एष मां त्वत्कृते विद्वन् काम आत्तशरासनः ।
दुनोति दीनां विक्रम्य रम्भामिव मतङ्गजः ॥१०॥

ditir uvāca
eṣa māṁ tvat-kṛte vidvan
kāma ātta-śarāsanaḥ
dunoti dīnāṁ vikramya
rambhām iva mataṅgajaḥ

ditiḥ uvāca—beautiful Diti said; *eṣaḥ*—all these; *mām*—unto me; *tvat-kṛte*—for you; *vidvan*—O learned one; *kāmaḥ*—Cupid; *ātta-śarāsanaḥ*—taking his arrows; *dunoti*—distresses; *dīnām*—poor me; *vikramya*—attacking; *rambhām*—banana tree; *iva*—like; *matam-gajaḥ*—mad elephant.

TRANSLATION

In that place the beautiful Diti expressed her desire: O learned one, Cupid is taking his arrows and distressing me forcibly, as a mad elephant troubles a banana tree.

PURPORT

Beautiful Diti, seeing her husband absorbed in trance, began to speak loudly, not attempting to attract him by bodily expressions. She frankly said that her whole body was distressed by sex desire because of her husband's presence, just as a banana tree is troubled by a mad elephant. It was not natural for her to agitate her husband when he was in trance, but she could not control her strong sexual appetite. Her sex desire was like a mad elephant, and therefore it was the prime duty of her husband to give her all protection by fulfilling her desire.

TEXT 11

तद्भवान्दह्यमानायां सपत्नीनां समृद्धिभिः ।
प्रजावतीनां भद्रं ते मय्यायुङ्क्तामनुग्रहम् ॥११॥

tad bhavān dahyamānāyāṁ
sa-patnīnāṁ samṛddhibhiḥ
prajāvatīnāṁ bhadraṁ te
mayy āyuṅktām anugraham

tat—therefore; *bhavān*—your good self; *dahyamānāyām*—being distressed; *sa-patnīnām*—of the co-wives; *samṛddhibhiḥ*—by the prosperity; *prajā-vatīnām*—of those who have children; *bhadram*—all prosperity; *te*—unto you; *mayi*—unto me; *āyuṅktām*—do unto me, in all respects; *anugraham*—favor.

TRANSLATION

Therefore you should be kind towards me by showing me complete mercy. I desire to have sons, and I am much distressed by seeing the opulence of my co-wives. By performing this act, you will become happy.

PURPORT

In *Bhagavad-gītā* sexual intercourse for begetting children is accepted as righteous. A person sexually inclined for simple sense gratification, however, is unrighteous. In Diti's appeal to her husband for sex, it was not exactly that she was afflicted by sex desires, but she desired sons. Since she had no sons, she felt poorer than her co-wives. Therefore Kaśyapa was supposed to satisfy his bona fide wife.

TEXT 12

भर्तर्याप्तोरुमानानां लोकानाविशते यशः ।
पतिर्भवद्विधो यासां प्रजया ननु जायते ॥१२॥

bhartary āptorumānānāṁ
lokān āviśate yaśaḥ
patir bhavad-vidho yāsāṁ
prajayā nanu jāyate

bhartari—by the husband; *āpta-urumānānām*—of those who are beloved; *lokān*—in the world; *āviśate*—spreads; *yaśaḥ*—fame; *patiḥ*—husband; *bhavat-vidhaḥ*—like your good self; *yāsām*—of those whose; *prajayā*—by children; *nanu*—certainly; *jāyate*—expands.

TRANSLATION

A woman is honored in the world by the benediction of her husband, and a husband like you will become famous by having children because you are meant for the expansion of living entities.

PURPORT

According to Ṛṣabhadeva, one should not become a father or mother unless one is confident that he can beget children whom he can deliver from the clutches of birth and death. Human life is the only opportunity to get out of the material scene, which is full of the miseries of birth, death, old age and diseases. Every human being should be given the opportunity to take advantage of his human form of life, and a father like Kaśyapa is supposed to beget good children for the purpose of liberation.

TEXT 13

पुरा पिता नो भगवान्दक्षो दुहितृवत्सलः ।
कं वृणीत वरं वत्सा इत्यपृच्छत नः पृथक् ॥१३॥

purā pitā no bhagavān
dakṣo duhitṛ-vatsalaḥ
kaṁ vṛṇīta varaṁ vatsā
ity apṛcchata naḥ pṛthak

purā—in days long ago; *pitā*—father; *naḥ*—our; *bhagavān*—the most opulent; *dakṣaḥ*—Dakṣa; *duhitṛ-vatsalaḥ*—affectionate to his daughters; *kam*—unto whom; *vṛṇīta*—you want to accept; *varam*—your husband; *vatsāḥ*—O my children; *iti*—thus; *apṛcchata*—inquired; *naḥ*—us; *pṛthak*—separately.

TRANSLATION

In days long ago, our father, the most opulent Dakṣa, who was affectionate to his daughters, asked each of us separately whom we would prefer to select as our husband.

PURPORT

It appears from this verse that free selection of a husband was allowed by the father, but not by free association. The daughters were asked separately to submit their selection of a husband who was famous for his acts and personality. The ultimate selection depended on the choice of the father.

TEXT 14

स विदित्वात्मजानां नो भावं सन्तानभावनः ।
त्रयोदशाददात्तासां यास्ते शीलमनुव्रताः ॥१४॥

sa viditvātmajānāṁ no
bhāvaṁ santāna-bhāvanaḥ
trayodaśādadāt tāsāṁ
yās te śīlam anuvratāḥ

saḥ—Dakṣa; *viditvā*—understanding; *ātma-jānām*—of the daughters; *naḥ*—our; *bhāvam*—indication; *santāna*—children; *bhāvanaḥ*—well-wisher; *trayodaśa*—thirteen; *adadāt*—handed over; *tāsām*—of all of them; *yāḥ*—those who are; *te*—your; *śīlam*—behavior; *anuvratāḥ*—all faithful.

TRANSLATION

Our well-wishing father, Dakṣa, after knowing our intentions, handed over thirteen of his daughters unto you, and since then we have all been faithful.

PURPORT

Generally the daughters were too shy to express their opinions before their father, but the father would accept the daughters' intentions through someone else, such as a grandmother to whom the grandchildren had free access. King Dakṣa collected the opinions of his daughters and thus handed over thirteen to Kaśyapa. Every one of Diti's sisters was a mother of children. Therefore, since she was equally faithful to the same husband, why should she remain without children?

TEXT 15

अथ मे कुरु कल्याणं कामं कमललोचन ।
आर्तोपसर्पणं भूमन्नमोघं हि महीयसि ॥१५॥

atha me kuru kalyāṇaṁ
kāmaṁ kamala-locana
ārtopasarpaṇaṁ bhūmann
amoghaṁ hi mahīyasi

atha—therefore; *me*—unto me; *kuru*—kindly do; *kalyāṇam*—benediction; *kāmam*—desire; *kamala-locana*—O lotus-eyed one; *ārta*—of the distressed; *upasarpaṇam*—the approaching; *bhūman*—O great one; *amogham*—without failure; *hi*—certainly; *mahīyasi*—to a great person.

TRANSLATION

O lotus-eyed one, kindly bless me by fulfilling my desire. When someone in distress approaches a great person, his pleas should never go in vain.

PURPORT

Diti knew well that her request might be rejected because of the untimely situation, but she pleaded that when there is an emergency or a distressful condition, there is no consideration of time or situation.

TEXT 16

इति तां वीर मारीचः कृपणां बहुभाषिणीम् ।
प्रत्याहानुनयन् वाचा प्रवृद्धानङ्गकश्मलाम् ॥१६॥

iti tāṁ vīra mārīcaḥ
kṛpaṇāṁ bahu-bhāṣiṇīm
pratyāhānunayan vācā
pravṛddhānaṅga-kaśmalām

iti—thus; *tām*—unto her; *vīra*—O hero; *mārīcaḥ*—the son of Marīci (Kaśyapa); *kṛpaṇām*—unto the poor; *bahu-bhāṣiṇīm*—too talkative; *pratyāha*—replied; *anunayan*—pacifying; *vācā*—by words; *pravṛddha*—highly agitated; *anaṅga*—lust; *kaśmalām*—contaminated.

TRANSLATION

O hero [Vidura], Diti, being thus afflicted by the contamination of lust, and therefore poor and talkative, was pacified by the son of Marīci in suitable words.

PURPORT

When a man or woman is afflicted by the lust of sex desire, it is to be understood as sinful contamination. Kaśyapa was engaged in his spiritual activities, but he did not have sufficient strength to refuse his wife, who was thus afflicted. He could have refused her with strong words expressing impossibility, but he was not as spiritually strong as Vidura. Vidura is addressed here as a hero because no one is stronger in self-control than a devotee of the Lord. It appears that Kaśyapa was already inclined to have sexual enjoyment with his wife, and because he was not a strong man he tried to dissuade her only with pacifying words.

TEXT 17

एष तेऽहं विधास्यामि प्रियं भीरु यदिच्छसि ।
तस्याः कामं न कः कुर्यात्सिद्धिस्त्रैवर्गिकी यतः ॥१७॥

eṣa te 'haṁ vidhāsyāmi
priyaṁ bhīru yad icchasi

tasyāḥ kāmaṁ na kaḥ kuryāt
siddhis traivargikī yataḥ

eṣaḥ—this; *te*—your request; *aham*—I; *vidhāsyāmi*—shall execute; *priyam*—very dear; *bhīru*—O afflicted one; *yat*—what; *icchasi*—you are desiring; *tasyāḥ*—her; *kāmam*—desires; *na*—not; *kaḥ*—who; *kuryāt*—would perform; *siddhiḥ*—perfection of liberation; *traivargikī*—three; *yataḥ*—from whom.

TRANSLATION

O afflicted one, I shall forthwith gratify whatever desire is dear to you, for who else but you is the source of the three perfections of liberation?

PURPORT

The three perfections of liberation are religiosity, economic development and sense gratification. For a conditioned soul, the wife is considered to be the source of liberation because she offers her service to the husband for his ultimate liberation. Conditional material existence is based on sense gratification, and if someone has the good fortune to get a good wife, he is helped by the wife in all respects. If one is disturbed in his conditional life, he becomes more and more entangled in material contamination. A faithful wife is supposed to cooperate with her husband in fulfilling all material desires so that he can then become comfortable and execute spiritual activities for the perfection of life. If, however, the husband is progressive in spiritual advancement, the wife undoubtedly shares in his activities, and thus both the wife and the husband profit in spiritual perfection. It is essential, therefore, that girls as well as boys be trained to discharge spiritual duties so that at the time of cooperation both will be benefited. The training of the boy is *brahmacarya*, and the training of the girl is chastity. A faithful wife and spiritually trained *brahmacārī* are a good combination for advancement of the human mission.

TEXT 18

सर्वाश्रमानुपादाय स्वाश्रमेण कलत्रवान् ।
व्यसनार्णवमत्येति जलयानैर्यथार्णवम् ॥१८॥

sarvāśramān upādāya
svāśrameṇa kalatravān
vyasanārṇavam atyeti
jala-yānair yathārṇavam

sarva—all; *āśramān*—social orders; *upādāya*—completing; *sva*—own; *āśrameṇa*—by the social orders; *kalatra-vān*—a person living with a wife; *vyasana-arṇavam*—the dangerous ocean of material existence; *atyeti*—one can cross over; *jala-yānaiḥ*—with seagoing vessels; *yathā*—as; *arṇavam*—the ocean.

TRANSLATION

As one can cross over the ocean with seagoing vessels, one can cross the dangerous situation of the material ocean by living with a wife.

PURPORT

There are four social orders for cooperation in the endeavor for liberation from material existence. The orders of *brahmacarya*, or pious student life, household life with a wife, retired life and renounced life all depend for successful advancement on the householder who lives with a wife. This cooperation is essential for the proper functioning of the institution of the four social orders and the four spiritual orders of life. This Vedic *varṇāśrama* system is generally known as the caste system. The man who lives with a wife has a great responsibility in maintaining the members of the other social orders—the *brahmacārīs*, *vānaprasthas* and *sannyāsīs*. Except for the *gṛhasthas*, or the householders, everyone is supposed to engage in the spiritual advancement of life, and therefore the *brahmacārī*, the *vānaprastha* and the *sannyāsī* have very little time to earn a livelihood. They therefore collect alms from the *gṛhasthas*, and thus they secure the bare necessities of life and cultivate spiritual understanding. By helping the other three sections of society cultivate spiritual values, the householder also makes advancement in spiritual life. Ultimately every member of society automatically becomes spiritually advanced and easily crosses the ocean of nescience.

TEXT 19

यामाहुरात्मनो ह्यर्धं श्रेयस्कामस्य मानिनि ।
यस्यां स्वधुरमध्यस्य पुमांश्चरति विज्वरः ॥१९॥

yām āhur ātmano hy ardhaṁ
śreyas-kāmasya mānini
yasyāṁ sva-dhuram adhyasya
pumāṁś carati vijvaraḥ

yām—the wife who; *āhuḥ*—is said; *ātmanaḥ*—of the body; *hi*—thus; *ardham*—half; *śreyaḥ*—welfare; *kāmasya*—of all desires; *mānini*—O respectful one; *yasyām*—in whom; *sva-dhuram*—all responsibilities; *adhyasya*—entrusting; *pumān*—a man; *carati*—moves; *vijvaraḥ*—without anxiety.

TRANSLATION

O respectful one, a wife is so helpful that she is called the better half of a man's body because of her sharing in all auspicious activities. A man can move without anxiety entrusting all responsibilities to his wife.

PURPORT

By the Vedic injunction, the wife is accepted as the better half of a man's body because she is supposed to be responsible for discharging half of the duties of the husband. A family man has a responsibility to perform five kinds of sacrifices, called *pañca-yajña,* in order to get relief from all kinds of unavoidable sinful reaction incurred in the course of his affairs. When a man becomes qualitatively like the cats and dogs, he forgets his duties in cultivating spiritual values, and thus he accepts his wife as a sense gratificatory agency. When the wife is accepted as a sense gratificatory agency, personal beauty is the main consideration, and as soon as there is a break in personal sense gratification, there is disruption or divorce. But when husband and wife aim at spiritual advancement by mutual cooperation, there is no consideration of personal beauty or the disruption of so-called love. In the material world there is no question of love. Marriage is actually a duty performed in mutual cooperation as directed in the authoritative scriptures for spiritual advancement. Therefore marriage is essential in order to avoid the life of cats and dogs, who are not meant for spiritual enlightenment.

TEXT 20

यामाश्रित्येन्द्रियारातीन्दुर्जयानितराश्रमैः ।
वयं जयेम हेलाभिर्दस्यून्दुर्गपतिर्यथा ॥२०॥

yām āśrityendriyārātīn
durjayān itarāśramaiḥ
vayaṁ jayema helābhir
dasyūn durga-patir yathā

yām—whom; *āśritya*—taking shelter of; *indriya*—senses; *arātīn*—enemies; *durjayān*—difficult to conquer; *itara*—other than the householders; *āśramaiḥ*—by orders of society; *vayam*—we; *jayema*—can conquer; *helābhiḥ*—easily; *dasyūn*—invading plunderers; *durga-patiḥ*—a fort commander; *yathā*—as.

TRANSLATION

As a fort commander very easily conquers invading plunderers, by taking shelter of a wife one can conquer the senses, which are unconquerable in the other social orders.

PURPORT

Of the four orders of human society—the student, or *brahmacārī* order, the householder, or *gṛhastha* order, the retired, or *vānaprastha* order, and the renounced, or *sannyāsī* order—the householder is on the safe side. The bodily senses are considered plunderers of the fort of the body. The wife is supposed to be the commander of the fort, and therefore whenever there is an attack on the body by the senses, it is the wife who protects the body from being smashed. The sex demand is inevitable for everyone, but one who has a fixed wife is saved from the onslaught of the sense enemies. A man who possesses a good wife does not create a disturbance in society by corrupting virgin girls. Without a fixed wife, a man becomes a debauchee of the first order and is a nuisance in society—unless he is a trained *brahmacārī*, *vānaprastha* or *sannyāsī*. Unless there is rigid and systematic training of the *brahmacārī* by the expert spiritual master, and unless the student is obedient, it is sure that the so-called *brahmacārī* will fall prey to the attack of sex. There are so many instances of falldown, even for great *yogīs* like Viśvāmitra. A *gṛhastha* is saved, however, because of his faithful wife. Sex life is the cause of material bondage, and therefore it is prohibited in three *āśramas* and is allowed only in the *gṛhastha-āśrama*. The *gṛhastha* is responsible for producing first-quality *brahmacārīs*, *vānaprasthas* and *sannyāsīs*.

TEXT 21

न वयं प्रभवस्तां त्वामनुकर्तुं गृहेश्वरि ।
अप्यायुषा वा कार्त्स्न्येन ये चान्ये गुणगृध्नवः ॥२१॥

na vayaṁ prabhavas tāṁ tvām
anukartuṁ gṛheśvari
apy āyuṣā vā kārtsnyena
ye cānye guṇa-gṛdhnavaḥ

na—never; *vayam*—we; *prabhavaḥ*—are able; *tām*—that; *tvām*—unto you; *anukartum*—do the same; *gṛha-īśvari*—O queen of the home; *api*—in spite of; *āyuṣā*—by duration of life; *vā*—or (in the next life); *kārtsnyena*—entire; *ye*—who; *ca*—also; *anye*—others; *guṇa-gṛdhnavaḥ*—those who are able to appreciate qualities.

TRANSLATION

O queen of the home, we are not able to act like you, nor could we repay you for what you have done, even if we worked for our entire life or even after death. To repay you is not possible, even for those who are admirers of personal qualities.

PURPORT

So much glorification of a woman by her husband indicates that he is henpecked or is talking lightly in joke. Kaśyapa meant that householders living with wives enjoy the heavenly blessings of sense enjoyment and at the same time have no fear of going down to hell. The man in the renounced order of life has no wife and may be driven by sex desire to seek another woman or another's wife and thus go to hell. In other words, the so-called man of the renounced order, who has left his house and wife, goes to hell if he again desires sexual pleasure, knowingly or unknowingly. In that way the householders are on the side of safety. Therefore husbands as a class cannot repay their debt to women either in this life or in the next. Even if they engage themselves in repaying the women throughout their whole lives, it is still not possible. Not all husbands are as able to appreciate the good qualities of their wives, but even though one is able to appreciate these qualities, it is still not possible to repay the debt to the wife. Such extraordinary praises by a husband for his wife are certainly in the mode of joking.

TEXT 22

अथापि काममेतं ते प्रजात्यै करवाण्यलम् ।
यथा मां नातिरोचन्ति मुहूर्तं प्रतिपालय ॥२२॥

athāpi kāmam etaṁ te
prajātyai karavāṇy alam
yathā māṁ nātirocanti
muhūrtaṁ pratipālaya

atha api—even though (it is not possible); *kāmam*—this sex desire; *etam*—as it is; *te*—your; *prajātyai*—for the sake of children; *karavāṇi*—let me do; *alam*—without delay; *yathā*—as; *mām*—unto me; *na*—may not; *atirocanti*—reproach; *muhūrtam*—a few seconds; *pratipālaya*—wait for.

TRANSLATION

Even though it is not possible to repay you, I shall satisfy your sex desire immediately for the sake of begetting children. But you must wait for only a few seconds so that others may not reproach me.

PURPORT

The henpecked husband may not be able to repay his wife for all the benefits that he derives from her, but as for begetting children by fulfilling sexual desire, it is not at all difficult for any husband unless he is thoroughly impotent. This is a very easy task for a husband under normal conditions. In spite of Kaśyapa's being very eager, he requested her to wait for a few seconds so that others might not reproach him. He explains his position as follows.

TEXT 23

एषा घोरतमा वेला घोराणां घोरदर्शना ।
चरन्ति यस्यां भूतानि भूतेशानुचराणि ह ॥२३॥

eṣā ghoratamā velā
ghorāṇāṁ ghora-darśanā
caranti yasyāṁ bhūtāni
bhūteśānucarāṇi ha

eṣā—this time; *ghora-tamā*—most horrible; *velā*—period; *ghorāṇām*—of the horrible; *ghora-darśanā*—horrible looking; *caranti*—move; *yasyām*—in which; *bhūtāni*—ghosts; *bhūta-īśa*—the lord of the ghosts; *anucarāṇi*—constant companions; *ha*—indeed.

TRANSLATION

This particular time is most inauspicious because at this time the horrible-looking ghosts and constant companions of the lord of the ghosts are visible.

PURPORT

Kaśyapa has already told his wife Diti to wait for a while, and now he warns her that failure to consider the particular time will result in punishment from the ghosts and evil spirits who move during this time, along with their master, Lord Rudra.

TEXT 24

एतस्यां साध्वि सन्ध्यायां भगवान् भूतभावनः ।
परीतो भूतपर्षद्भिर्वृषेणाटति भूतराट् ॥२४॥

etasyāṁ sādhvi sandhyāyāṁ
bhagavān bhūta-bhāvanaḥ

parīto bhūta-parṣadbhir
vṛṣeṇāṭati bhūtarāṭ

etasyām—in this period; *sādhvi*—O chaste one; *sandhyāyām*—at the junction of day and night (evening); *bhagavān*—the Personality of God; *bhūta-bhāvanaḥ*—the well-wisher of the ghostly characters; *parītaḥ*—surrounded by; *bhūta-parṣadbhiḥ*—by ghostly companions; *vṛṣeṇa*—on the back of the bull carrier; *aṭati*—travels; *bhūta-rāṭ*—the king of the ghosts.

TRANSLATION

Lord Śiva, the king of the ghosts, sitting on the back of his bull carrier, travels at this time, accompanied by ghosts who follow him for their welfare.

PURPORT

Lord Śiva, or Rudra, is the king of the ghosts. Ghostly characters worship Lord Śiva to be gradually guided toward a path of self-realization. Māyāvādī philosophers are mostly worshipers of Lord Śiva, and Śrīpāda Śaṅkarācārya is considered to be the incarnation of Lord Śiva for preaching godlessness to the Māyāvādī philosophers. Ghosts are bereft of a physical body because of their grievously sinful acts, such as suicide. The last resort of the ghostly characters in human society is to take shelter of suicide, either material or spiritual. Material suicide causes loss of the physical body, and spiritual suicide causes loss of the individual identity. Māyāvādī philosophers desire to lose their individuality and merge into the impersonal spiritual *brahmajyoti* existence. Lord Śiva, being very kind to the ghosts, sees that although they are condemned, they get physical bodies. He places them into the wombs of women who indulge in sexual intercourse regardless of the restrictions on time and circumstance. Kaśyapa wanted to impress this fact upon Diti so that she might wait for a while.

TEXT 25

श्मशानचक्रानिलधूलिधूम्र-
विकीर्णविद्योतजटाकलापः

भस्मावगुण्ठामलरुक्मदेहो
देवस्त्रिभिः पश्यति देवरस्ते ॥२५॥

śmaśāna-cakrānila-dhūli-dhūmra-
vikīrṇa-vidyota-jaṭā-kalāpaḥ
bhasmāvaguṇṭhāmala-rukma-deho
devas tribhiḥ paśyati devaras te

śmaśāna—burning crematorium; *cakra-anila*—whirlwind; *dhūli*—dust; *dhūmra*—smoky; *vikīrṇa-vidyota*—thus smeared over beauty; *jaṭā-kalāpaḥ*—bunches of matted hair; *bhasma*—ashes; *avaguṇṭha*—covered by; *amala*—stainless; *rukma*—reddish; *dehaḥ*—body; *devaḥ*—the demigod; *tribhiḥ*—with three eyes; *paśyati*—sees; *devaraḥ*—younger brother of the husband; *te*—your.

TRANSLATION

Lord Śiva's body is reddish, and he is unstained, but he is covered with ashes. His hair is dusty from the whirlwind dust of the burning crematorium. He is the younger brother of your husband, and he sees with his three eyes.

PURPORT

Lord Śiva is not an ordinary living entity, nor is he in the category of Viṣṇu, or the Supreme Personality of Godhead. He is far more powerful than any living entity up to the standard of Brahmā, yet he is not on an equal level with Viṣṇu. Since he is almost like Lord Viṣṇu, Śiva can see past, present and future. One of his eyes is like the sun, another is like the moon, and his third eye, which is between his eyebrows, is like fire. He can generate fire from his middle eye, and he is able to vanquish any powerful living entity, including Brahmā, yet he does not live pompously in a nice house, etc., nor does he possess any material properties, although he is master of the material world. He lives mostly in the crematorium, where dead bodies are burnt, and the whirlwind dust of the crematorium is his bodily dress. He is unstained by material contamination. Kaśyapa took him as his younger brother because the youngest sister of Diti (Kaśyapa's wife) was married to Lord Śiva. The husband of one's sister is considered one's brother. By that social relationship, Lord Śiva happened to be the younger brother of Kaśyapa. Kaśyapa warned his wife that because Lord Śiva would see their sex indulgence, the time was not appropriate. Diti might argue that they would enjoy sex life in a private place, but Kaśyapa reminded her that Lord Śiva has three eyes, called the sun, moon and fire, and one cannot escape his vigilance any more than one can escape Viṣṇu. Although seen by the police, a criminal is sometimes not immediately punished; the police wait for the proper time to apprehend him. The forbidden time for sexual intercourse would be noted by Lord Śiva, and Diti would meet with proper punishment by giving birth to a child of ghostly character or a godless impersonalist. Kaśyapa foresaw this, and thus he warned his wife Diti.

TEXT 26

न यस्य लोके स्वजनः परो वा
नात्यादृतो नोत कश्चिद्विगर्ह्यः ।
वयं व्रतैर्यच्चरणापविद्धा-
माशास्महेऽजां बत भुक्तभोगाम् ॥२६॥

na yasya loke sva-janaḥ paro vā
nātyādṛto nota kaścid vigarhyaḥ
vayaṁ vratair yac-caraṇāpaviddhām
āśāsmahe 'jāṁ bata bhukta-bhogām

na—never; *yasya*—of whom; *loke*—in the world; *sva-janaḥ*—kinsman; *paraḥ*—unconnected; *vā*—nor; *na*—neither; *ati*—greater; *ādṛtaḥ*—favorable; *na*—not; *uta*—or; *kaścit*—anyone; *vigarhyaḥ*—criminal; *vayam*—we; *vrataiḥ*—by vows; *yat*—whose; *caraṇa*—feet; *apaviddhām*—rejected; *āśāsmahe*—respectfully worship; *ajām*—*mahā-prasāda; bata*—certainly; *bhukta-bhogām*—remnants of foodstuff.

TRANSLATION

Lord Śiva regards no one as his relative, yet there is no one who is not connected with him; he does not regard anyone as very

favorable or abominable. We respectfully worship the remnants of his foodstuff, and we vow to accept what is rejected by him.

PURPORT

Kaśyapa informed his wife that just because Lord Śiva happened to be his brother-in-law, that should not encourage her in her offense towards him. Kaśyapa warned her that actually Lord Śiva is not connected with anyone, nor is anyone his enemy. Since he is one of the three controllers of the universal affairs, he is equal to everyone. His greatness is incomparable because he is a great devotee of the Supreme Personality of Godhead. It is said that among all the devotees of the Personality of Godhead, Lord Śiva is the greatest. Thus the remnants of foodstuff left by him are accepted by other devotees as *mahā-prasāda*, or great spiritual foodstuff. The remnants of foodstuff offered to Lord Kṛṣṇa are called *prasāda*, but when the same *prasāda* is eaten by a great devotee like Lord Śiva, it is called *mahā-prasāda*. Lord Śiva is so great that he does not care for the material prosperity for which every one of us is so eager. Pārvatī, who is the powerful material nature personified, is under his full control as his wife, yet he does not use her even to build a residential house. He prefers to remain without shelter, and his great wife also agrees to live with him humbly. People in general worship goddess Durgā, the wife of Lord Śiva, for material prosperity, but Lord Śiva engages her in his service without material desire. He simply advises his great wife that of all kinds of worship, the worship of Viṣṇu is the highest, and greater than that is the worship of a great devotee or anything in relation with Viṣṇu.

TEXT 27

यस्यानवद्याचरितं मनीषिणो
गृणन्त्यविद्यापटलं बिभित्सवः ।
निरस्तसाम्यातिशयोऽपि यत्स्वयं
पिशाचचर्यामचरद्गतिः सताम् ॥२७॥

yasyānavadyācaritaṁ manīṣiṇo
gṛṇanty avidyā-paṭalaṁ bibhitsavaḥ
nirasta-sāmyātiśayo 'pi yat svayaṁ
piśāca-caryām acarad gatiḥ satām

yasya—whose; *anavadya*—unimpeachable; *ācaritam*—character; *manīṣiṇaḥ*—great sages; *gṛṇanti*—follow; *avidyā*—nescience; *paṭalam*—mass; *bibhitsavaḥ*—desiring to dismantle; *nirasta*—nullified; *sāmya*—equality; *atiśayaḥ*—greatness; *api*—in spite of; *yat*—as; *svayam*—personally; *piśāca*—devil; *caryām*—activities; *acarat*—performed; *gatiḥ*—destination; *satām*—of the devotees of the Lord.

TRANSLATION

Although no one in the material world is equal to or greater than Lord Śiva, and although his unimpeachable character is followed by great souls to dismantle the mass of nescience, he nevertheless remains as if a devil to give salvation to all devotees of the Lord.

PURPORT

Lord Śiva's uncivilized, devilish characteristics are never abominable because he teaches the sincere devotees of the Lord how to practice detachment from material enjoyment. He is called Mahādeva, or the greatest of all demigods, and no one is equal to or greater than him in the material world. He is almost equal with Lord Viṣṇu. Although he always associates with Māyā, Durgā, he is above the reactionary stage of the three modes of material nature, and although he is in charge of devilish characters in the mode of ignorance, he is not affected by such association.

TEXT 28

हसन्ति यस्याचरितं हि दुर्भगाः
स्वात्मन्-रतस्याविदुषः समीहितम् ।
यैर्वस्त्रमाल्याभरणानुलेपनैः
श्वभोजनं स्वात्मतयोपलालितम् ॥२८॥

hasanti yasyācaritaṁ hi durbhagāḥ
svātman-ratasyāviduṣaḥ samīhitam
yair vastra-mālyābharaṇānulepanaiḥ
śva-bhojanaṁ svātmatayopalālitam

hasanti—laugh at; *yasya*—whose; *ācaritam*—activity; *hi*—certainly; *durbhagāḥ*—the unfortunate; *sva-ātman*—in the self; *ratasya*—of one engaged; *aviduṣaḥ*—not knowing; *samīhitam*—his purpose; *yaiḥ*—by whom; *vastra*—clothing; *mālya*—garlands; *ābharaṇa*—ornaments; *anu*—such luxurious; *lepanaiḥ*—with ointments; *śva-bhojanam*—eatable by the dogs; *sva-ātmatayā*—as if the self; *upalālitam*—fondled.

TRANSLATION

Unfortunate, foolish persons, not knowing that he is engaged in his own self, laugh at him. Such foolish persons engage in maintaining the body—which is eatable by dogs—with dresses, ornaments, garlands and ointments.

PURPORT

Lord Śiva never accepts any luxurious dress, garland, ornament or ointment. But those who are addicted to the decoration of the body, which is finally eatable by dogs, very luxuriously maintain it as the self. Such persons do not understand Lord Śiva, but they approach him for luxurious material comforts. There are two kinds of devotees of Lord Śiva. One class is the gross materialist seeking only bodily comforts from Lord Śiva, and the other class desires to become one with him. They are mostly impersonalists and prefer to chant *śivo 'ham*, "I am Śiva," or "After liberation I shall become one with Lord Śiva." In other words, the *karmīs* and *jñānīs* are generally devotees of Lord Śiva, but they do not properly understand his real purpose in life. Sometimes so-called devotees of Lord Śiva imitate him in using poisonous intoxicants. Lord Śiva once swallowed an ocean of poison, and thus his throat became blue. The imitation Śivas try to follow him by indulging in poisons, and thus they are ruined. The real purpose of Lord Śiva is to serve the Soul of the soul, Lord Kṛṣṇa. He desires that all luxurious articles, such as nice garments, garlands, ornaments and cosmetics, be given to Lord Kṛṣṇa only, because Kṛṣṇa is the real enjoyer. He refuses to accept such luxurious items himself because they are only meant for Kṛṣṇa. However, since they do not know this purpose of Lord Śiva, foolish persons either laugh at him or profitlessly try to imitate him.

TEXT 29

ब्रह्मादयो यत्कृतसेतुपाला
यत्कारणं विश्वमिदं च माया ।
आज्ञाकरी यस्य पिशाचचर्या
अहो विभूम्नश्चरितं विडम्बनम् ॥२९॥

brahmādayo yat-kṛta-setu-pālā
yat-kāraṇaṁ viśvam idaṁ ca māyā
ājñā-karī yasya piśāca-caryā
aho vibhūmnaś caritaṁ viḍambanam

brahma-ādayaḥ—demigods like Brahmā; *yat*—whose; *kṛta*—activities; *setu*—religious rites; *pālāḥ*—observers; *yat*—one who is; *kāraṇam*—the origin of; *viśvam*—the universe; *idam*—this; *ca*—also; *māyā*—material energy; *ājñā-karī*—order carrier; *yasya*—whose; *piśāca*—devilish; *caryā*—activity; *aho*—O my lord; *vibhūmnaḥ*—of the great; *caritam*—character; *viḍambanam*—simply imitation.

TRANSLATION

Demigods like Brahmā also follow the religious rites observed by him. He is the controller of the material energy, which causes the creation of the material world. He is great, and therefore his devilish characteristics are simply imitation.

PURPORT

Lord Śiva is the husband of Durgā, the controller of the material energy. Durgā is personified material energy, and Lord Śiva, being her husband, is the controller of the material energy. He is also the incarnation of the mode of ignorance and one of the three deities representing the Supreme Lord. As His representative, Lord Śiva is identical with the Supreme Personality of Godhead. He is very great, and his renunciation of all material enjoyment is an ideal example of how one should be materially unattached. One should therefore follow in his footsteps and be unattached to matter, not imitate his uncommon acts like drinking poison.

TEXT 30

मैत्रेय उवाच
सैवं संविदिते भर्त्रा मन्मथोन्मथितेन्द्रिया ।
जग्राह वासो ब्रह्मर्षेर्वृषलीव गतत्रपा ॥३०॥

maitreya uvāca
saivaṁ saṁvidite bhartrā
manmathonmathitendriyā
jagrāha vāso brahmarṣer
vṛṣalīva gata-trapā

maitreyaḥ uvāca—Maitreya said; *sā*—she; *evam*—thus; *saṁvidite*—in spite of being informed; *bhartrā*—by her husband; *manmatha*—by Cupid; *unmathita*—being pressed; *indriyā*—senses; *jagrāha*—caught hold of; *vāsaḥ*—clothing; *brahma-ṛṣeḥ*—of the great *brāhmaṇa*-sage; *vṛṣalī*—public prostitute; *iva*—like; *gata-trapā*—without shame.

TRANSLATION

Maitreya said: Diti was thus informed by her husband, but she was pressed by Cupid for sexual satisfaction. She caught hold of the clothing of the great brāhmaṇa-sage, just like a shameless public prostitute.

PURPORT

The difference between a married wife and a public prostitute is that one is restrained in sex life by the rules and regulations of the scriptures, whereas the other is unrestricted in sex life and is conducted solely by the strong sex urge. Although very enlightened, Kaśyapa, the great sage, became a victim of his prostitute wife. Such is the strong force of material energy.

TEXT 31

स विदित्वाथ भार्यायास्तं निर्बन्धं विकर्मणि ।
नत्वा दिष्टाय रहसि तयाथोपविवेश हि ॥३१॥

sa viditvātha bhāryāyās
taṁ nirbandhaṁ vikarmaṇi

natvā diṣṭāya rahasi
tayāthopaviveśa hi

saḥ—he; *viditvā*—understanding; *atha*—thereupon; *bhāryāyāḥ*—of the wife; *tam*—that; *nirbandham*—obstinacy; *vikarmaṇi*—in the forbidden act; *natvā*—offering obeisances; *diṣṭāya*—unto worshipable fate; *rahasi*—in a secluded place; *tayā*—with her; *atha*—thus; *upaviveśa*—lay; *hi*—certainly.

TRANSLATION

Understanding his wife's purpose, he was obliged to perform the forbidden act, and thus after offering his obeisances unto worshipable fate, he lay with her in a secluded place.

PURPORT

It appears from the talks of Kaśyapa with his wife that he was a worshiper of Lord Śiva, and although he knew that Lord Śiva would not be pleased with him for such a forbidden act, he was obliged to act by his wife's desire, and thus he offered his obeisances unto fate. He knew that the child born of such untimely sexual intercourse would certainly not be a good child, but could not protect himself because he was too obligated to his wife. In a similar case, however, when Ṭhākura Haridāsa was tempted by a public prostitute at the dead of night, he avoided the allurement because of his perfection in Kṛṣṇa consciousness. That is the difference between a Kṛṣṇa conscious person and others. Kaśyapa Muni was greatly learned and enlightened, and he knew all the rules and regulations of systematic life, yet he failed to protect himself from the attack of sex desire. Ṭhākura Haridāsa was not born of a *brāhmaṇa* family, nor was he himself *brāhmaṇa*, yet he could protect himself from such an attack due to his being Kṛṣṇa conscious. Ṭhākura Haridāsa used to chant the holy name of the Lord three hundred thousand times daily.

TEXT 32

अथोपस्पृश्य सलिलं प्राणानायम्य वाग्यतः ।
ध्यायञ्जजाप विरजं ब्रह्म ज्योतिः सनातनम् ॥३२॥

athopaspṛśya salilaṁ
prāṇān āyamya vāg-yataḥ
dhyāyañ jajāpa virajaṁ
brahma jyotiḥ sanātanam

atha—thereafter; *upaspṛśya*—touching or taking bath in water; *salilam*—water; *prāṇān āyamya*—practicing trance; *vāk-yataḥ*—controlling speech; *dhyāyan*—meditating; *jajāpa*—chanted within the mouth; *virajam*—pure; *brahma*—Gāyatrī hymns; *jyotiḥ*—effulgence; *sanātanam*—eternal.

TRANSLATION

Thereafter the brāhmaṇa took his bath in the water and controlled his speech by practicing trance, meditating on the eternal effulgence and chanting the holy Gāyatrī hymns within his mouth.

PURPORT

As one has to take bath after using the toilet, so one has to wash himself with water after sexual intercourse, especially when at a forbidden time. Kaśyapa Muni meditated on the impersonal *brahmajyoti* by chanting the Gāyatrī *mantra* within his mouth. When a Vedic *mantra* is chanted within the mouth so that only the chanter can hear, the chanting is called *japa.* But when such *mantras* are chanted loudly, it is called *kīrtana.* The Vedic hymn Hare Kṛṣṇa, Hare Kṛṣṇa, Kṛṣṇa Kṛṣṇa, Hare Hare/ Hare Rāma, Hare Rāma, Rāma Rāma, Hare Hare can be chanted both softly to oneself or loudly; therefore it is called the *mahā-mantra,* or the great hymn.

Kaśyapa Muni appears to be an impersonalist. Comparing his character with that of Ṭhākura Haridāsa as referred to above, it is clear that the personalist is stronger in sense control than the impersonalist. This is explained in *Bhagavad-gītā* as *paraṁ dṛṣṭvā nivartate;* i.e., one ceases to accept lower grade things when one is situated in a superior condition. One is supposed to be purified after taking bath and chanting Gāyatrī, but the *mahā-mantra* is so powerful that one can chant loudly or softly, in any condition, and he is protected from all the evils of material existence.

TEXT 33

दितिस्तु व्रीडिता तेन कर्मावद्येन भारत ।
उपसङ्गम्य विप्रर्षिमधोमुख्यभ्यभाषत ॥३३॥

ditis tu vrīḍitā tena
karmāvadyena bhārata
upasaṅgamya viprarṣim
adho-mukhy abhyabhāṣata

ditiḥ—Diti, the wife of Kaśyapa; *tu*—but; *vrīḍitā*—ashamed; *tena*—by that; *karma*—act; *avadyena*—faulty; *bhārata*—O son of the Bharata family; *upasaṅgamya*—going nearer to; *vipra-ṛṣim*—the *brāhmaṇa*-sage; *adhaḥ-mukhī*—with her face lowered; *abhyabhāṣata*—politely said.

TRANSLATION

O son of the Bharata family, Diti, after this, went nearer to her husband, her face lowered because of her faulty action. She spoke as follows.

PURPORT

When one is ashamed of an abominable action, one naturally becomes down-faced. Diti came to her senses after the abominable sexual intercourse with her husband. Such sexual intercourse is condemned as prostitution. In other words, sex life with one's wife is equal to prostitution if the regulations are not properly followed.

TEXT 34

दितिरुवाच
न मे गर्भमिमं ब्रह्मन् भूतानामृषभोऽवधीत् ।
रुद्रः पतिर्हि भूतानां यस्याकरवमंहसम् ॥३४॥

ditir uvāca
na me garbham imaṁ brahman
bhūtānām ṛṣabho 'vadhīt

rudraḥ patir hi bhūtānāṁ
yasyākaravam aṁhasam

ditiḥ uvāca—the beautiful Diti said; *na*—not; *me*—my; *garbham*—pregnancy; *imam*—this; *brahman*—O *brāhmaṇa; bhūtānām*—of all living entities; *ṛṣabhaḥ*—the noblest of all living entities; *avadhīt*—let him kill; *rudraḥ*—Lord Śiva; *patiḥ*—master; *hi*—certainly; *bhūtānām*—of all living entities; *yasya*—whose; *akaravam*—I have done; *aṁhasam*—offense.

TRANSLATION

The beautiful Diti said: My dear brāhmaṇa, kindly see that my embryo is not killed by Lord Śiva, the lord of all living entities, because of the great offense I have committed against him.

PURPORT

Diti was conscious of her offense and was anxious to be excused by Lord Śiva. Lord Śiva has two popular names, Rudra and Āśutoṣa. He is very prone to anger as well as quickly pacified. Diti knew that because of his being quickly angered he might spoil the pregnancy she had so unlawfully achieved. But because he was also Āśutoṣa, she implored her *brāhmaṇa*-husband to help her in pacifying Lord Śiva, for her husband was a great devotee of Lord Śiva. In other words, Lord Śiva might have been angry with Diti because she obliged her husband to transgress the law, but he would not refuse her husband's prayer. Therefore the application for excuse was submitted through her husband. She prayed to Lord Śiva as follows.

TEXT 35

नमो रुद्राय महते देवायोग्राय मीढुषे ।
शिवाय न्यस्तदण्डाय धृतदण्डाय मन्यवे ॥३५॥

namo rudrāya mahate
devāyogrāya mīḍhuṣe
śivāya nyasta-daṇḍāya
dhṛta-daṇḍāya manyave

namaḥ—all obeisances unto; *rudrāya*—unto the angry Lord Śiva; *mahate*—unto the great; *devāya*—unto the demigod; *ugrāya*—unto the ferocious; *mīḍhuṣe*—unto the fulfiller of all material desires; *śivāya*—unto the all-auspicious; *nyasta-daṇḍāya*—unto the forgiving; *dhṛta-daṇḍāya*—unto the immediate chastiser; *manyave*—unto the angry.

TRANSLATION

Let me offer my obeisances unto the angry Lord Śiva, who is simultaneously the very ferocious great demigod and the fulfiller of all material desires. He is all-auspicious and forgiving, but his anger can immediately move him to chastise.

PURPORT

Diti prayed for the mercy of Lord Śiva very cleverly. She prayed: "The lord can cause me to cry, but if he likes he can also stop my crying because he is Āśutoṣa. He is so great that if he likes he can immediately destroy my pregnancy, but by his mercy he can also fulfill my desire that my pregnancy not be spoiled. Because he is all-auspicious, it is not difficult for him to excuse me from being punished, although he is now ready to punish me because I have moved his great anger. He appears like a man, but he is the lord of all men."

TEXT 36

स नः प्रसीदतां भामो भगवानुर्वनुग्रहः ।
व्याधस्याप्यनुकम्प्यानां स्त्रीणां देवः सतीपतिः ॥३६॥

sa naḥ prasīdatāṁ bhāmo
bhagavān urv-anugrahaḥ
vyādhasyāpy anukampyānāṁ
strīṇāṁ devaḥ satī-patiḥ

saḥ—he; *naḥ*—with us; *prasīdatām*—be pleased; *bhāmaḥ*—brother-in-law; *bhagavān*—the personality of all opulences; *uru*—very great; *anugrahaḥ*—merciful; *vyādhasya*—of the hunter; *api*—also; *anukampyānām*—of the objects of mercy; *strīṇām*—of the women;

devaḥ—the worshipable lord; *satī-patiḥ*—the husband of Satī (the chaste).

TRANSLATION

Let him be pleased with us, since he is my brother-in-law, the husband of my sister Satī. He is also the worshipable lord of all women. He is the personality of all opulences and can show mercy towards women, who are excused even by the uncivilized hunters.

PURPORT

Lord Śiva is the husband of Satī, one of the sisters of Diti. Diti invoked the pleasure of her sister Satī so that Satī would request her husband to excuse her. Besides that, Lord Śiva is the worshipable lord of all women. He is naturally very kind towards women, on whom even the uncivilized hunters also show their mercy. Since Lord Śiva is himself associated with women, he knows very well their defective nature, and he might not take very seriously Diti's unavoidable offense, which occurred due to her faulty nature. Every virgin girl is supposed to be a devotee of Lord Śiva. Diti remembered her childhood worship of Lord Śiva and begged his mercy.

TEXT 37

मैत्रेय उवाच

स्वसर्गस्याशिषं लोक्यामाशासानां प्रवेपतीम् ।
निवृत्तसन्ध्यानियमो भार्यामाह प्रजापतिः ॥३७॥

maitreya uvāca
sva-sargasyāśiṣaṁ lokyām
āśāsānāṁ pravepatīm
nivṛtta-sandhyā-niyamo
bhāryām āha prajāpatiḥ

maitreyaḥ uvāca—the great sage Maitreya said; *sva-sargasya*—of her own children; *āśiṣam*—welfare; *lokyām*—in the world; *āśāsānām*—desiring; *pravepatīm*—while trembling; *nivṛtta*—averted from;

sandhyā-niyamaḥ—the rules and regulations of evening; *bhāryām*—unto the wife; *āha*—said; *prajāpatiḥ*—the progenitor.

TRANSLATION

Maitreya said: The great sage Kaśyapa thus addressed his wife, who was trembling because of fear that her husband was offended. She understood that he had been dissuaded from his daily duties of offering evening prayers, yet she desired the welfare of her children in the world.

TEXT 38

कश्यप उवाच
अप्रायत्यादात्मनस्ते दोषान्मौहूर्तिकादुत ।
मन्निदेशातिचारेण देवानां चातिहेलनात् ॥३८॥

kaśyapa uvāca
aprāyatyād ātmanas te
doṣān mauhūrtikād uta
man-nideśāticāreṇa
devānāṁ cātihelanāt

kaśyapaḥ uvāca—the learned *brāhmaṇa* Kaśyapa said; *aprāyatyāt*—because of the pollution; *ātmanaḥ*—of the mind; *te*—your; *doṣāt*—because of defilement; *mauhūrtikāt*—in terms of the moment; *uta*—also; *mat*—my; *nideśa*—direction; *aticāreṇa*—being too neglectful; *devānām*—of the demigods; *ca*—also; *atihelanāt*—being too apathetic.

TRANSLATION

The learned Kaśyapa said: Because of your mind's being polluted, because of defilement of the particular time, because of your negligence of my directions, and because of your being apathetic to the demigods, everything was inauspicious.

PURPORT

The conditions for having good progeny in society are that the husband should be disciplined in religious and regulative principles and the wife should be faithful to the husband. In *Bhagavad-gītā* (7.11) it is said that sexual intercourse according to religious principles is a representation of Kṛṣṇa consciousness. Before engaging in sexual intercourse, both the husband and the wife must consider their mental condition, the particular time, the husband's direction, and obedience to the demigods. According to Vedic society, there is a suitable auspicious time for sex life, which is called the time for *garbhādhāna*. Diti neglected all the principles of scriptural injunction, and therefore, although she was very anxious for auspicious children, she was informed that her children would not be worthy to be the sons of a *brāhmaṇa*. There is a clear indication herein that a *brāhmaṇa*'s son is not always a *brāhmaṇa*. Personalities like Rāvaṇa and Hiraṇyakaśipu were actually born of *brāhmaṇas*, but they were not accepted as *brāhmaṇas* because their fathers did not follow the regulative principles for their birth. Such children are called demons, or Rākṣasas. There were only one or two Rākṣasas in the previous ages due to negligence of the disciplinary methods, but during the age of Kali there is no discipline in sex life. How, then, can one expect good children? Certainly unwanted children cannot be a source of happiness in society, but through the Kṛṣṇa consciousness movement they can be raised to the human standard by chanting the holy name of God. That is the unique contribution of Lord Caitanya to human society.

TEXT 39

भविष्यतस्तवाभद्रावभद्रे जाठराधमौ ।
लोकान् सपालांस्त्रींश्चण्डि मुहुराक्रन्दयिष्यतः ॥३९॥

bhaviṣyatas tavābhadrāv
abhadre jāṭharādhamau
lokān sa-pālāṁs trīṁś caṇḍi
muhur ākrandayiṣyataḥ

bhaviṣyataḥ—will take birth; *tava*—your; *abhadrau*—two contemptuous sons; *abhadre*—O unlucky one; *jāṭhara-adhamau*—born of a condemned womb; *lokān*—all planets; *sa-pālān*—with their rulers; *trīn*—three; *caṇḍi*—haughty one; *muhuḥ*—constantly; *ākrandayiṣyataḥ*—will cause lamentation.

TRANSLATION

O haughty one, you will have two contemptuous sons born of your condemned womb. Unlucky woman, they will cause constant lamentation to all the three worlds!

PURPORT

Contemptuous sons are born of the condemned womb of their mother. In *Bhagavad-gītā* (1.40) it is said, "When there is deliberate negligence of the regulative principles of religious life, the women as a class become polluted, and as a result there are unwanted children." This is especially true for boys; if the mother is not good, there cannot be good sons. The learned Kaśyapa could foresee the character of the sons who would be born of the condemned womb of Diti. The womb was condemned because of the mother's being too sexually inclined and thus transgressing all the laws and injunctions of the scriptures. In a society where such women are predominant, one should not expect good children.

TEXT 40

प्राणिनां हन्यमानानां दीनानामकृतागसाम् ।
स्त्रीणां निगृह्यमाणानां कोपितेषु महात्मसु ॥४०॥

prāṇinām hanyamānānām
dīnānām akṛtāgasām
strīṇām nigṛhyamāṇānām
kopiteṣu mahātmasu

prāṇinām—when the living entities; *hanyamānānām*—being killed; *dīnānām*—of the poor; *akṛta-āgasām*—of the faultless; *strīṇām*—of the women; *nigṛhyamāṇānām*—being tortured; *kopiteṣu*—being enraged; *mahātmasu*—when the great souls.

TRANSLATION

They will kill poor, faultless living entities, torture women and enrage the great souls.

PURPORT

Demoniac activities are predominant when innocent, faultless living entities are killed, women are tortured, and the great souls engaged in Kṛṣṇa consciousness are enraged. In a demoniac society, innocent animals are killed to satisfy the tongue, and women are tortured by unnecessary sexual indulgence. Where there are women and meat, there must be liquor and sex indulgence. When these are prominent in society, by God's grace one can expect a change in the social order by the Lord Himself or by His bona fide representative.

TEXT 41

तदा विश्वेश्वरः क्रुद्धो भगवाल्लोकभावनः ।
हनिष्यत्यवतीर्यासौ यथाद्रीन् शतपर्वधृक् ॥४१॥

tadā viśveśvaraḥ kruddho
bhagavāl loka-bhāvanaḥ
haniṣyaty avatīryāsau
yathādrīn śataparva-dhṛk

tadā—at that time; *viśva-īśvaraḥ*—the Lord of the universe; *kruddhaḥ*—in great anger; *bhagavān*—the Supreme Personality of Godhead; *loka-bhāvanaḥ*—desiring the welfare of the people in general; *haniṣyati*—will kill; *avatīrya*—descending Himself; *asau*—He; *yathā*—as if; *adrīn*—the mountains; *śata-parva-dhṛk*—the controller of the thunderbolt (Indra).

TRANSLATION

At that time the Lord of the universe, the Supreme Personality of Godhead, who is the well-wisher of all living entities, will descend and kill them, just as Indra smashes the mountains with his thunderbolts.

PURPORT

As stated in *Bhagavad-gītā* (4.8), the Lord descends as an incarnation to deliver the devotees and kill the miscreants. The Lord of the universe and of everything would appear to kill the sons of Diti because of their offending the devotees of the Lord. There are many agents of the Lord, such as Indra, Candra, Varuṇa, goddess Durgā, and Kālī, who can chastise any formidable miscreants in the world. The example of mountains being smashed by a thunderbolt is very appropriate. The mountain is considered the most strongly built body within the universe, yet it can be easily smashed by the arrangement of the Supreme Lord. The Supreme Personality of Godhead does not need to descend in order to kill any strongly built body; He comes down just for the sake of His devotees. Everyone is subject to the miseries offered by material nature, but because the activities of miscreants, such as killing innocent people and animals or torturing women, are harmful to everyone and are therefore a source of pain for the devotees, the Lord comes down. He descends only to give relief to His ardent devotees. The killing of the miscreant by the Lord is also the mercy of the Lord towards the miscreant, although apparently the Lord takes the side of the devotee. Since the Lord is absolute, there is no difference between His activities of killing the miscreants and favoring the devotees.

TEXT 42

दितिरुवाच

वधं भगवता साक्षात्सुनाभोदारबाहुना ।
आशासे पुत्रयोर्मह्यं मा क्रुद्धाद्ब्राह्मणात्प्रभो ॥४२॥

ditir uvāca
vadhaṁ bhagavatā sākṣāt
sunābhodāra-bāhunā
āśāse putrayor mahyaṁ
mā kruddhād brāhmaṇād prabho

ditiḥ uvāca—Diti said; *vadham*—the killing; *bhagavatā*—by the Supreme Personality of Godhead; *sākṣāt*—directly; *sunābha*—with His Sudarśana weapon; *udāra*—very magnanimous; *bāhunā*—by the arms; *āśāse*—I desire; *putrayoḥ*—of the sons; *mahyam*—of mine; *mā*—never be it so; *kruddhāt*—by the rage; *brāhmaṇāt*—of the *brāhmaṇas*; *prabho*—O my husband.

TRANSLATION

Diti said: It is very good that my sons will be magnanimously killed by the arms of the Personality of Godhead with His Sudarśana weapon. O my husband, may they never be killed by the wrath of the brāhmaṇa-devotees.

PURPORT

When Diti heard from her husband that the great souls would be angered by the activities of her sons, she was very anxious. She thought that her sons might be killed by the wrath of the *brāhmaṇas.* The Lord does not appear when the *brāhmaṇas* become angry at someone, because the wrath of a *brāhmaṇa* is sufficient in itself. He certainly appears, however, when His devotee simply becomes sorry. A devotee of the Lord never prays to the Lord to appear for the sake of the troubles the miscreants cause for him, and he never bothers Him by asking for protection. Rather, the Lord is anxious to give protection to the devotees. Diti knew well that the killing of her sons by the Lord would also be His mercy, and therefore she says that the wheel and arms of the Lord are magnanimous. If someone is killed by the wheel of the Lord and is thus fortunate enough to see the arms of the Lord, that is sufficient for his liberation. Such good fortune is not achieved even by the great sages.

TEXT 43

न ब्रह्मदण्डदग्धस्य न भूतभयदस्य च ।
नारकाश्चानुगृह्णन्ति यां यां योनिमसौ गतः ॥४३॥

na brahma-daṇḍa-dagdhasya
na bhūta-bhayadasya ca
nārakāś cānugṛhṇanti
yāṁ yāṁ yonim asau gataḥ

na—never; *brahma-daṇḍa*—punishment by a *brāhmaṇa; dagdhasya*—of one who is so punished; *na*—neither; *bhūta-bhaya-dasya*—of one who is always fearful to the living entities; *ca*—also; *nārakāḥ*—those condemned to hell; *ca*—also; *anugṛhṇanti*—do any favor; *yām*

yām—whichever; *yonim*—species of life; *asau*—the offender; *gataḥ*—goes.

TRANSLATION

A person who is condemned by a brāhmaṇa or is always fearful to other living entities is not favored either by those who are already in hell or by those in the species in which he is born.

PURPORT

A practical example of a condemned species of life is the dog. Dogs are so condemned that they never show any sympathy to their contemporaries.

TEXTS 44–45

कश्यप उवाच

कृतशोकानुतापेन सद्यः प्रत्यवमर्शनात् ।
भगवत्युरुमानाच्च भवे मय्यपि चादरात् ॥४४॥
पुत्रस्यैव च पुत्राणां भवितैकः सतां मतः ।
गास्यन्ति यद्यशः शुद्धं भगवद्यशसा समम् ॥४५॥

kaśyapa uvāca
kṛta-śokānutāpena
sadyaḥ pratyavamarśanāt
bhagavaty uru-mānāc ca
bhave mayy api cādarāt

putrasyaiva ca putrāṇāṁ
bhavitaikaḥ satāṁ mataḥ
gāsyanti yad-yaśaḥ śuddhaṁ
bhagavad-yaśasā samam

kaśyapaḥ uvāca—the learned Kaśyapa said; *kṛta-śoka*—having lamented; *anutāpena*—by penitence; *sadyaḥ*—immediately; *pratyavamarśanāt*—by proper deliberation; *bhagavati*—unto the Supreme Personality of Godhead; *uru*—great; *mānāt*—adoration; *ca*—and;

bhave—unto Lord Śiva; *mayi api*—unto me also; *ca*—and; *ādarāt*—by respect; *putrasya*—of the son; *eva*—certainly; *ca*—and; *putrāṇām*—of the sons; *bhavitā*—shall be born; *ekaḥ*—one; *satām*—of the devotees; *mataḥ*—approved; *gāsyanti*—will broadcast; *yat*—of whom; *yaśaḥ*—recognition; *śuddham*—transcendental; *bhagavat*—of the Personality of Godhead; *yaśasā*—with recognition; *samam*—equally.

TRANSLATION

The learned Kaśyapa said: Because of your lamentation, penitence and proper deliberation, and also because of your unflinching faith in the Supreme Personality of Godhead and your adoration for Lord Śiva and me, one of the sons [Prahlāda] of your son [Hiraṇyakaśipu] will be an approved devotee of the Lord, and his fame will be broadcast equally with that of the Personality of Godhead.

TEXT 46

योगैर्हेमेव दुर्वर्णं भावयिष्यन्ति साधवः ।
निर्वैरादिभिरात्मानं यच्छीलमनुवर्तितुम् ॥४६॥

yogair hemeva durvarṇaṁ
bhāvayiṣyanti sādhavaḥ
nirvairādibhir ātmānaṁ
yac-chīlam anuvartitum

yogaiḥ—by the rectifying processes; *hema*—gold; *iva*—like; *durvarṇam*—inferior quality; *bhāvayiṣyanti*—will purify; *sādhavaḥ*—saintly persons; *nirvaira-ādibhiḥ*—by practice of freedom from animosity, etc.; *ātmānam*—the self; *yat*—whose; *śīlam*—character; *anuvartitum*—to follow in the footsteps.

TRANSLATION

In order to follow in his footsteps, saintly persons will try to emulate his character by practicing freedom from animosity, just as the purifying processes rectify gold of inferior quality.

PURPORT

Yoga practice, the process of purifying one's existential identity, is based mainly on self-control. Without self-control one cannot practice freedom from animosity. In the conditional state, every living being is envious of another living being, but in the liberated state there is an absence of animosity. Prahlāda Mahārāja was tortured by his father in so many ways, yet after the death of his father he prayed for his father's liberation by the Supreme Personality of Godhead. He did not ask any benediction that he might have asked, but he prayed that his atheistic father might be liberated. He never cursed any of the persons who engaged in torturing him at the instigation of his father.

TEXT 47

यत्प्रसादादिदं विश्वं प्रसीदति यदात्मकम् ।
स स्वदृग्भगवान् यस्य तोष्यतेऽनन्यया दृशा ॥४७॥

yat-prasādād idaṁ viśvaṁ
prasīdati yad-ātmakam
sa sva-dṛg bhagavān yasya
toṣyate 'nanyayā dṛśā

yat—by whose; *prasādāt*—mercy of; *idam*—this; *viśvam*—universe; *prasīdati*—becomes happy; *yat*—whose; *ātmakam*—because of His omnipotence; *saḥ*—He; *sva-dṛk*—taking special care for His devotees; *bhagavān*—the Supreme Personality of Godhead; *yasya*—whose; *toṣyate*—becomes pleased; *ananyayā*—without deviation; *dṛśā*—by intelligence.

TRANSLATION

Everyone will be pleased with him because the Personality of Godhead, the supreme controller of the universe, is always satisfied with a devotee who does not wish for anything beyond Him.

PURPORT

The Supreme Personality of Godhead is situated everywhere as the Supersoul, and He can dictate to anyone and everyone as He likes. The would-be grandson of Diti, who was predicted to be a great devotee, would be liked by everyone, even by the enemies of his father, because he would have no other vision besides the Supreme Personality of Godhead. A pure devotee of the Lord sees the presence of his worshipable Lord everywhere. The Lord reciprocates in such a way that all living entities in whom the Lord is dwelling as the Supersoul also like a pure devotee because the Lord is present in their hearts and can dictate to them to be friendly to His devotee. There are many instances in history wherein even the most ferocious animal became friendly to a pure devotee of the Lord.

TEXT 48

स वै महाभागवतो महात्मा
महानुभावो महतां महिष्ठः ।
प्रवृद्धभक्त्या ह्यनुभाविताशये
निवेश्य वैकुण्ठमिमं विहास्यति ॥४८॥

sa vai mahā-bhāgavato mahātmā
mahānubhāvo mahatāṁ mahiṣṭhaḥ
pravṛddha-bhaktyā hy anubhāvitāśaye
niveśya vaikuṇṭham imaṁ vihāsyati

saḥ—he; *vai*—certainly; *mahā-bhāgavataḥ*—the topmost devotee; *mahā-ātmā*—expanded intelligence; *mahā-anubhāvaḥ*—expanded influence; *mahatām*—of the great souls; *mahiṣṭhaḥ*—the greatest; *pravṛddha*—well matured; *bhaktyā*—by devotional service; *hi*—certainly; *anubhāvita*—being situated in the *anubhāva* stage of ecstasy; *āśaye*—in the mind; *niveśya*—entering; *vaikuṇṭham*—in the spiritual sky; *imam*—this (material world); *vihāsyati*—will quit.

TRANSLATION

That topmost devotee of the Lord will have expanded intelligence and expanded influence and will be the greatest of the great souls. Due to matured devotional service, he will certainly be situated in transcendental ecstasy and will enter the spiritual sky after quitting this material world.

PURPORT

There are three stages of transcendental development in devotional service, which are technically called *sthāyi-bhāva, anubhāva* and *mahābhāva.* Continual perfect love of Godhead is called *sthāyi-bhāva,* and when it is performed in a particular type of transcendental relationship it is called *anubhāva.* But the stage of *mahābhāva* is visible amongst the personal pleasure potential energies of the Lord. It is understood that the grandson of Diti, namely Prahlāda Mahārāja, would constantly meditate on the Lord and reiterate His activities. Because he would constantly remain in meditation, he would easily transfer himself to the spiritual world after quitting his material body. Such meditation is still more conveniently performed by chanting and hearing the holy name of the Lord. This is especially recommended in this age of Kali.

TEXT 49

अलम्पटः शीलधरो गुणाकरो
हृष्टः परर्द्ध्या व्यथितो दुःखितेषु ।
अभूतशत्रुर्जगतः शोकहर्ता
नैदाघिकं तापमिवोडुराजः ॥४९॥

alampaṭaḥ śīla-dharo guṇākaro
hṛṣṭaḥ pararddhyā vyathito duḥkhiteṣu
abhūta-śatrur jagataḥ śoka-hartā
naidāghikaṁ tāpam ivoḍurājaḥ

alampaṭaḥ—virtuous; *śīla-dharaḥ*—qualified; *guṇa-ākaraḥ*—reservoir of all good qualities; *hṛṣṭaḥ*—jolly; *para-ṛddhyā*—by others' happiness; *vyathitaḥ*—distressed; *duḥkhiteṣu*—in others' unhappiness; *abhūta-śatruḥ*—without enemies; *jagataḥ*—of all the universe; *śoka-hartā*—destroyer of lamentation; *naidāghikam*—due to the summer sun; *tāpam*—distress; *iva*—likened; *uḍu-rājaḥ*—the moon.

TRANSLATION

He will be a virtuously qualified reservoir of all good qualities; he will be jolly and happy in others' happiness, distressed in

others' distress, and will have no enemies. He will be a destroyer of the lamentation of all the universes, like the pleasant moon after the summer sun.

PURPORT

Prahlāda Mahārāja, the exemplary devotee of the Lord, had all the good qualities humanly possible. Although he was the emperor of this world, he was not profligate. Beginning from his childhood he was the reservoir of all good qualities. Without enumerating those qualities, it is said here summarily that he was endowed with all good qualities. That is the sign of a pure devotee. The most important characteristic of a pure devotee is that he is not *lampaṭa*, or licentious, and another quality is that he is always eager to mitigate the miseries of suffering humanity. The most obnoxious misery of a living entity is his forgetfulness of Kṛṣṇa. A pure devotee, therefore, always tries to evoke everyone's Kṛṣṇa consciousness. This is the panacea for all miseries.

TEXT 50

अन्तर्बहिश्चामलमब्जनेत्रं
स्वपूरुषेच्छानुगृहीतरूपम् ।
पौत्रस्तव श्रीललनाललामं
द्रष्टा स्फुरत्कुण्डलमण्डिताननम् ॥५०॥

antar bahiś cāmalam abja-netraṁ
sva-pūruṣecchānugṛhīta-rūpam
pautras tava śrī-lalanā-lalāmaṁ
draṣṭā sphurat-kuṇḍala-maṇḍitānanam

antaḥ—within; *bahiḥ*—without; *ca*—also; *amalam*—spotless; *abja-netram*—lotus eyes; *sva-pūruṣa*—own devotee; *icchā-anugṛhīta-rūpam*—accepting form according to desire; *pautraḥ*—grandchild; *tava*—your; *śrī-lalanā*—beautiful goddess of fortune; *lalāmam*—decorated; *draṣṭā*—will see; *sphurat-kuṇḍala*—with brilliant earrings; *maṇḍita*—decorated; *ānanam*—face.

TRANSLATION

Your grandson will be able to see, inside and outside, the Supreme Personality of Godhead, whose wife is the beautiful goddess of fortune. The Lord can assume the form desired by the devotee, and His face is always beautifully decorated with earrings.

PURPORT

It is predicted herewith that the grandson of Diti, Prahlāda Mahārāja, would not only see the Personality of Godhead within himself by meditation but would also be able to see Him personally with his eyes. This direct vision is possible only for one who is highly elevated in Kṛṣṇa consciousness, for the Lord is not possible to see with material eyes. The Supreme Personality of Godhead has multifarious eternal forms such as Kṛṣṇa, Baladeva, Saṅkarṣaṇa, Aniruddha, Pradyumna, Vāsudeva, Nārāyaṇa, Rāma, Nṛsiṁha, Varāha and Vāmana, and the devotee of the Lord knows all those Viṣṇu forms. A pure devotee becomes attached to one of the eternal forms of the Lord, and the Lord is pleased to appear before him in the form desired. A devotee does not imagine something whimsical about the form of the Lord, nor does he ever think that the Lord is impersonal and can assume a form desired by the nondevotee. The nondevotee has no idea of the form of the Lord, and thus he cannot think of any one of the above-mentioned forms. But whenever a devotee sees the Lord, he sees Him in a most beautifully decorated form, accompanied by His constant companion the goddess of fortune, who is eternally beautiful.

TEXT 51

मैत्रेय उवाच

श्रुत्वा भागवतं पौत्रममोदत दितिर्भृशम् ।
पुत्रयोश्च वधं कृष्णाद्विदित्वासीन्महामनाः ॥५१॥

maitreya uvāca
śrutvā bhāgavataṁ pautram
amodata ditir bhṛśam
putrayoś ca vadhaṁ kṛṣṇād
viditvāsīn mahā-manāḥ

maitreyaḥ uvāca—the sage Maitreya said; *śrutvā*—by hearing; *bhāgavatam*—to be a great devotee of the Lord; *pautram*—grandson; *amodata*—took pleasure; *ditiḥ*—Diti; *bhṛśam*—very greatly; *putrayoḥ*—of two sons; *ca*—also; *vadham*—the killing; *kṛṣṇāt*—by Kṛṣṇa; *viditvā*—knowing this; *āsīt*—became; *mahā-manāḥ*—highly pleased in mind.

TRANSLATION

The sage Maitreya said: Hearing that her grandson would be a great devotee and that her sons would be killed by Kṛṣṇa, Diti was highly pleased in mind.

PURPORT

Diti was very aggrieved to learn that because of her untimely pregnancy her sons would be demons and would fight with the Lord. But when she heard that her grandson would be a great devotee and that her two sons would be killed by the Lord, she was very satisfied. As the wife of a great sage and the daughter of a great Prajāpati, Dakṣa, she knew that being killed by the Personality of Godhead is a great fortune. Since the Lord is absolute, His acts of violence and nonviolence are both on the absolute platform. There is no difference in such acts of the Lord. Mundane violence and nonviolence have nothing to do with the Lord's acts. A demon killed by Him attains the same result as one who attains liberation after many, many births of penance and austerity. The word *bhṛśam* is significant herein because it indicates that Diti was pleased beyond her expectations.

Thus end the Bhaktivedanta purports of the Third Canto, Fourteenth Chapter, of the Śrīmad-Bhāgavatam, *entitled "Pregnancy of Diti in the Evening."*

CHAPTER FIFTEEN

Description of the Kingdom of God

TEXT 1

मैत्रेय उवाच
प्राजापत्यं तु तत्तेजः परतेजोहनं दितिः ।
दधार वर्षाणि शतं शङ्कमाना सुरार्दनात् ॥ १ ॥

maitreya uvāca
prājāpatyaṁ tu tat tejaḥ
para-tejo-hanaṁ ditiḥ
dadhāra varṣāṇi śataṁ
śaṅkamānā surārdanāt

maitreyaḥ uvāca—the sage Maitreya said; *prājāpatyam*—of the great Prajāpati; *tu*—but; *tat tejaḥ*—his powerful semen; *para-tejaḥ*—others' prowess; *hanam*—troubling; *ditiḥ*—Diti (Kaśyapa's wife); *dadhāra*—bore; *varṣāṇi*—years; *śatam*—hundred; *śaṅkamānā*—being doubtful; *sura-ardanāt*—disturbing to the demigods.

TRANSLATION

Śrī Maitreya said: My dear Vidura, Diti, the wife of the sage Kaśyapa, could understand that the sons within her womb would be a cause of disturbance to the demigods. As such, she continuously bore the powerful semen of Kaśyapa Muni, which was meant to give trouble to others, for one hundred years.

PURPORT

The great sage Śrī Maitreya was explaining to Vidura the activities of the demigods, including Lord Brahmā. When Diti heard from her husband that the sons she bore within her abdomen would be causes of disturbances to the demigods, she was not very happy. There are two classes of men—devotees and nondevotees. Nondevotees are called demons, and devotees are called demigods. No sane man or woman can tolerate the nondevotees' giving trouble to devotees. Diti, therefore, was reluctant to give birth to her babies; she waited for one hundred years so that at least she could save the demigods from the disturbance for that period.

TEXT 2

लोके तेनाहतालोके लोकपाला हतौजसः ।
न्यवेदयन् विश्वसृजे ध्वान्तव्यतिकरं दिशाम् ॥ २ ॥

loke tenāhatāloke
loka-pālā hataujasaḥ
nyavedayan viśva-sṛje
dhvānta-vyatikaraṁ diśām

loke—within this universe; *tena*—by the force of the pregnancy of Diti; *āhata*—being devoid of; *āloke*—light; *loka-pālāḥ*—the demigods of various planets; *hata-ojasaḥ*—whose prowess was diminished; *nyavedayan*—asked; *viśva-sṛje*—Brahmā; *dhvānta-vyatikaram*—expansion of darkness; *diśām*—in all directions.

TRANSLATION

By the force of the pregnancy of Diti, the light of the sun and moon was impaired in all the planets, and the demigods of various planets, being disturbed by that force, asked the creator of the universe, Brahmā, "What is this expansion of darkness in all directions?"

PURPORT

It appears from this verse of *Śrīmad-Bhāgavatam* that the sun is the source of light for all the planets in the universe. The modern scientific theory which states that there are many suns in each universe is not supported by this verse. It is understood that in each universe there is only one sun, which supplies light to all the planets. In *Bhagavad-gītā* the moon is also stated to be one of the stars. There are many stars, and when we see them glittering at night we can understand that they are reflectors of light; just as moonlight is a reflection of sunlight, other planets also reflect sunlight, and there are many other planets which cannot be seen by our naked eyes. The demoniac influence of the sons in the womb of Diti expanded darkness throughout the universe.

TEXT 3

देवा ऊचुः
तम एतद्विभो वेत्थ संविग्ना यद्वयं भृशम् ।
न ह्यव्यक्तं भगवतः कालेनास्पृष्टवर्त्मनः ॥ ३ ॥

devā ūcuḥ
tama etad vibho vettha
saṁvignā yad vayaṁ bhṛśam
na hy avyaktaṁ bhagavataḥ
kālenāspṛṣṭa-vartmanaḥ

devāḥ ūcuḥ—the demigods said; *tamaḥ*—darkness; *etat*—this; *vibho*—O great one; *vettha*—you know; *saṁvignāḥ*—very anxious; *yat*—because; *vayam*—we; *bhṛśam*—very much; *na*—not; *hi*—because; *avyaktam*—unmanifest; *bhagavataḥ*—of You (the Supreme Personality of Godhead); *kālena*—by time; *aspṛṣṭa*—untouched; *vartmanaḥ*—whose way.

TRANSLATION

The fortunate demigods said: O great one, just see this darkness, which you know very well and which is causing us anxieties. Because the influence of time cannot touch you, there is nothing unmanifest before you.

PURPORT

Brahmā is addressed herein as Vibhu and as the Personality of Godhead. He is the Supreme Personality of Godhead's incarnation of the mode of passion in the material world. He is nondifferent, in the representative sense, from the Supreme Personality of Godhead, and therefore the influence of time cannot affect him. The influence of time, which manifests as past, present and future, cannot touch higher personalities like Brahmā and other demigods. Sometimes demigods and great sages who have attained such perfection are called *tri-kāla-jña.*

TEXT 4

देवदेव जगद्धातर्लोकनाथशिखामणे ।
परेषामपरेषां त्वं भूतानामसि भाववित् ॥ ४ ॥

deva-deva jagad-dhātar
lokanātha-śikhāmaṇe
pareṣām apareṣāṁ tvaṁ
bhūtānām asi bhāva-vit

deva-deva—O god of the demigods; *jagat-dhātaḥ*—O sustainer of the universe; *lokanātha-śikhāmaṇe*—O head jewel of all the demigods in other planets; *pareṣām*—of the spiritual world; *apareṣām*—of the material world; *tvam*—you; *bhūtānām*—of all living entities; *asi*—are; *bhāva-vit*—knowing the intentions.

TRANSLATION

O god of the demigods, sustainer of the universe, head jewel of all the demigods in other planets, you know the intentions of all living entities, in both the spiritual and material worlds.

PURPORT

Because Brahmā is almost on an equal footing with the Personality of Godhead, he is addressed here as the god of the demigods, and because he is the secondary creator of this universe, he is addressed as the sustainer of the universe. He is the head of all the demigods, and therefore he is addressed here as the head jewel of the demigods. It is not difficult for him to understand everything which is happening in both the spiritual and material worlds. He knows everyone's heart and everyone's intentions. Therefore he was requested to explain this incident. Why was the pregnancy of Diti causing such anxieties all over the universe?

TEXT 5

नमो विज्ञानवीर्याय माययेदमुपेयुषे ।
गृहीतगुणभेदाय नमस्तेऽव्यक्तयोनये ॥ ५ ॥

namo vijñāna-vīryāya
māyayedam upeyuṣe
gṛhīta-guṇa-bhedāya
namas te 'vyakta-yonaye

namaḥ—respectful obeisances; *vijñāna-vīryāya*—O original source of strength and scientific knowledge; *māyayā*—by the external energy; *idam*—this body of Brahmā; *upeyuṣe*—having obtained; *gṛhīta*—accepting; *guṇa-bhedāya*—the differentiated mode of passion; *namaḥ te*—offering obeisances unto you; *avyakta*—unmanifested; *yonaye*—source.

TRANSLATION

O original source of strength and scientific knowledge, all obeisances unto you! You have accepted the differentiated mode of passion from the Supreme Personality of Godhead. With the help of external energy you are born of the unmanifested source. All obeisances unto you!

PURPORT

The *Vedas* are the original scientific knowledge for all departments of understanding, and this knowledge of the *Vedas* was first impregnated into the heart of Brahmā by the Supreme Personality of Godhead. Therefore Brahmā is the original source of all scientific knowledge. He is born directly from the transcendental body of Garbhodakaśāyī Viṣṇu, who is never seen by any creature of this material universe and therefore always remains unmanifested. Brahmā is stated here to be born of the unmanifested. He is the incarnation of the mode of passion in material nature, which is the separated, external energy of the Supreme Lord.

TEXT 6

ये त्वानन्येन भावेन भावयन्त्यात्मभावनम् ।
आत्मनि प्रोतभुवनं परं सदसदात्मकम् ॥ ६ ॥

ye tvānanyena bhāvena
bhāvayanty ātma-bhāvanam
ātmani prota-bhuvanaṁ
paraṁ sad-asad-ātmakam

ye—those who; *tvā*—on you; *ananyena*—without deviation; *bhāvena*—with devotion; *bhāvayanti*—meditate; *ātma-bhāvanam*—who generates all living entities; *ātmani*—within your self; *prota*—linked; *bhuvanam*—all the planets; *param*—the supreme; *sat*—effect; *asat*—cause; *ātmakam*—generator.

TRANSLATION

O lord, all these planets exist within your self, and all the living entities are generated from you. Therefore you are the cause of this universe, and anyone who meditates upon you without deviation attains devotional service.

TEXT 7

तेषां सुपक्वयोगानां जितश्वासेन्द्रियात्मनाम् ।
लब्धयुष्मत्प्रसादानां न कुतश्चित्पराभवः ॥ ७ ॥

teṣāṁ supakva-yogānāṁ
jita-śvāsendriyātmanām
labdha-yuṣmat-prasādānāṁ
na kutaścit parābhavaḥ

teṣām—of them; *su-pakva-yogānām*—who are mature mystics; *jita*—controlled; *śvāsa*—breath; *indriya*—the senses; *ātmanām*—the mind; *labdha*—attained; *yuṣmat*—your; *prasādānām*—mercy; *na*—not; *kutaścit*—anywhere; *parābhavaḥ*—defeat.

TRANSLATION

There is no defeat in this material world for persons who control the mind and senses by controlling the breathing process and

who are therefore experienced, mature mystics. This is because by such perfection in yoga they have attained your mercy.

PURPORT

The purpose of yogic performances is explained here. It is said that an experienced mystic attains full control of the senses and the mind by controlling the breathing process. Therefore, controlling the breathing process is not the ultimate aim of *yoga*. The real purpose of yogic performances is to control the mind and the senses. Anyone who has such control is to be understood to be an experienced, mature mystic *yogī*. It is indicated herein that a *yogī* who has control over the mind and senses has the actual benediction of the Lord, and he has no fear. In other words, one cannot attain the mercy and benediction of the Supreme Lord until one is able to control the mind and the senses. This is actually possible when one fully engages in Kṛṣṇa consciousness. A person whose senses and mind are always engaged in the transcendental service of the Lord has no possibility of engaging in material activities. The devotees of the Lord are not defeated anywhere in the universe. It is stated, *nārāyaṇa-parāḥ sarve:* one who is *nārāyaṇa-para*, or a devotee of the Supreme Personality of Godhead, is not afraid anywhere, whether he is sent to hell or promoted to heaven (*Bhāg.* 6.17.28).

TEXT 8

यस्य वाचा प्रजाः सर्वा गावस्तन्त्येव यन्त्रिताः ।
हरन्ति बलिमायत्तास्तस्मै मुख्याय ते नमः ॥ ८ ॥

yasya vācā prajāḥ sarvā
gāvas tantyeva yantritāḥ
haranti balim āyattās
tasmai mukhyāya te namaḥ

yasya—of whom; *vācā*—by the Vedic directions; *prajāḥ*—living entities; *sarvāḥ*—all; *gāvaḥ*—bulls; *tantyā*—by a rope; *iva*—as; *yantritāḥ*—are directed; *haranti*—offer, take away; *balim*—presentation, ingredients for worship; *āyattāḥ*—under control; *tasmai*—unto him; *mukhyāya*—unto the chief person; *te*—unto you; *namaḥ*—respectful obeisances.

TRANSLATION

All the living entities within the universe are conducted by the Vedic directions, as a bull is directed by the rope attached to its nose. No one can violate the rules laid down in the Vedic literatures. To the chief person, who has contributed the Vedas, we offer our respect!

PURPORT

The Vedic literatures are the laws of the Supreme Personality of Godhead. One cannot violate the injunctions given in the Vedic literatures any more than one can violate the state laws. Any living creature who wants real benefit in life must act according to the direction of the Vedic literature. The conditioned souls who have come to this material world for material sense gratification are regulated by the injunctions of the Vedic literature. Sense gratification is just like salt. One cannot take too much or too little, but one must take some salt in order to make one's foodstuff palatable. Those conditioned souls who have come to this material world should utilize their senses according to the direction of the Vedic literature, otherwise they will be put into a more miserable condition of life. No human being or demigod can enact laws like those of the Vedic literature because the Vedic regulations are prescribed by the Supreme Lord.

TEXT 9

स त्वं विधत्स्व शं भूमंस्तमसा लुप्तकर्मणाम् ।
अदभ्रदयया दृष्ट्या आपन्नानर्हसीक्षितुम् ॥ ९ ॥

sa tvaṁ vidhatsva śaṁ bhūmaṁs
tamasā lupta-karmaṇām
adabhra-dayayā dṛṣṭyā
āpannān arhasīkṣitum

saḥ—he; *tvam*—you; *vidhatsva*—perform; *śam*—good fortune; *bhūman*—O great lord; *tamasā*—by the darkness; *lupta*—have been suspended; *karmaṇām*—of prescribed duties; *adabhra*—magnanimous, without reservation; *dayayā*—mercy; *dṛṣṭyā*—by your glance; *āpannān*—us, the surrendered; *arhasi*—are able; *īkṣitum*—to see.

TRANSLATION

The demigods prayed to Brahmā: Please look upon us mercifully, for we have fallen into a miserable condition; because of the darkness, all our work has been suspended.

PURPORT

Because of complete darkness throughout the universe, the regular activities and engagements of all the different planets were suspended. In the North and South Poles of this planet there are sometimes no divisions of day and night; similarly, when the sunlight does not approach the different planets within the universe, there is no distinction between day and night.

TEXT 10

एष देव दितेर्गर्भ ओजः काश्यपमर्पितम् ।
दिशस्तिमिरयन् सर्वा वर्धतेऽग्निरिवैधसि ॥१०॥

eṣa deva diter garbha
ojaḥ kāśyapam arpitam
diśas timirayan sarvā
vardhate 'gnir ivaidhasi

eṣaḥ—this; *deva*—O lord; *diteḥ*—of Diti; *garbhaḥ*—womb; *ojaḥ*—semen; *kāśyapam*—of Kaśyapa; *arpitam*—deposited; *diśaḥ*—directions; *timirayan*—causing complete darkness; *sarvāḥ*—all; *vardhate*—overloads; *agniḥ*—fire; *iva*—as; *edhasi*—fuel.

TRANSLATION

As fuel overloads a fire, so the embryo created by the semen of Kaśyapa in the womb of Diti has caused complete darkness throughout the universe.

PURPORT

The darkness throughout the universe is explained herewith as being caused by the embryo created in the womb of Diti by the semen of Kaśyapa.

TEXT 11

मैत्रेय उवाच

स प्रहस्य महाबाहो भगवान् शब्दगोचरः ।
प्रत्याचष्टात्मभूर्देवान् प्रीणन् रुचिरया गिरा ॥११॥

maitreya uvāca
sa prahasya mahā-bāho
bhagavān śabda-gocaraḥ
pratyācaṣṭātma-bhūr devān
prīṇan ruciraya girā

maitreyaḥ uvāca—Maitreya said; *saḥ*—he; *prahasya*—smiling; *mahā-bāho*—O mighty-armed (Vidura); *bhagavān*—the possessor of all opulences; *śabda-gocaraḥ*—who is understood by transcendental sound vibration; *pratyācaṣṭa*—replied; *ātma-bhūḥ*—Lord Brahmā; *devān*—the demigods; *prīṇan*—satisfying; *rucirayā*—with sweet; *girā*—words.

TRANSLATION

Śrī Maitreya said: Thus Lord Brahmā, who is understood by transcendental vibration, tried to satisfy the demigods, being pleased with their words of prayer.

PURPORT

Brahmā could understand the misdeeds of Diti, and therefore he smiled at the whole situation. He replied to the demigods present there in words they could understand.

TEXT 12

ब्रह्मोवाच

मानसा मे सुता युष्मत्पूर्वजाः सनकादयः ।
चेरुर्विहायसा लोकाल्लोकेषु विगतस्पृहाः ॥१२॥

brahmovāca
mānasā me sutā yuṣmat-
pūrvajāḥ sanakādayaḥ
cerur vihāyasā lokāl
lokeṣu vigata-spṛhāḥ

brahmā uvāca—Lord Brahmā said; *mānasāḥ*—born from the mind; *me*—my; *sutāḥ*—sons; *yuṣmat*—than you; *pūrva-jāḥ*—born previously; *sanaka-ādayaḥ*—headed by Sanaka; *ceruḥ*—traveled; *vihāyasā*—by traveling in outer space or flying in the sky; *lokān*—to the material and spiritual worlds; *lokeṣu*—among the people; *vigata-spṛhāḥ*—without any desire.

TRANSLATION

Lord Brahmā said: My four sons Sanaka, Sanātana, Sanandana and Sanat-kumāra, who were born from my mind, are your predecessors. Sometimes they travel throughout the material and spiritual skies without any definite desire.

PURPORT

When we speak of desire we refer to desire for material sense gratification. Saintly persons like Sanaka, Sanātana, Sanandana and Sanat-kumāra have no material desire, but sometimes they travel all over the universe, out of their own accord, to preach devotional service.

TEXT 13

त एकदा भगवतो वैकुण्ठस्यामलात्मनः ।
ययुर्वैकुण्ठनिलयं सर्वलोकनमस्कृतम् ॥१३॥

ta ekadā bhagavato
vaikuṇṭhasyāmalātmanaḥ
yayur vaikuṇṭha-nilayaṁ
sarva-loka-namaskṛtam

te—they; *ekadā*—once upon a time; *bhagavataḥ*—of the Supreme Personality of Godhead; *vaikuṇṭhasya*—of Lord Viṣṇu; *amala-ātmanaḥ*—being freed from all material contamination; *yayuḥ*—entered;

vaikuṇṭha-nilayam—the abode named Vaikuṇṭha; *sarva-loka*—by the residents of all the material planets; *namaskṛtam*—worshiped.

TRANSLATION

After thus traveling all over the universes, they also entered into the spiritual sky, for they were freed from all material contamination. In the spiritual sky there are spiritual planets known as Vaikuṇṭhas, which are the residence of the Supreme Personality of Godhead and His pure devotees and are worshiped by the residents of all the material planets.

PURPORT

The material world is full of cares and anxieties. In any one of the planets, beginning from the highest down to the lowest, Pātāla, every living creature must be full of cares and anxieties because in the material planets one cannot live eternally. The living entities, however, are actually eternal. They want an eternal home, an eternal residence, but because of accepting a temporal abode in the material world, they are naturally full of anxiety. In the spiritual sky the planets are called Vaikuṇṭha because the residents of these planets are free from all anxieties. For them there is no question of birth, death, old age and diseases, and therefore they are not anxious. On the other hand, the residents of the material planets are always afraid of birth, death, disease and old age, and therefore they are full of anxieties.

TEXT 14

वसन्ति यत्र पुरुषाः सर्वे वैकुण्ठमूर्तयः ।
येऽनिमित्तनिमित्तेन धर्मेणाराधयन् हरिम् ॥१४॥

vasanti yatra puruṣāḥ
sarve vaikuṇṭha-mūrtayaḥ
ye 'nimitta-nimittena
dharmeṇārādhayan harim

vasanti—they live; *yatra*—where; *puruṣāḥ*—persons; *sarve*—all; *vaikuṇṭha-mūrtayaḥ*—having a four-handed form similar to that of the

Supreme Lord, Viṣṇu; *ye*—those Vaikuṇṭha persons; *animitta*—without desire for sense gratification; *nimittena*—caused by; *dharmeṇa*—by devotional service; *ārādhayan*—continuously worshiping; *harim*—unto the Supreme Personality of Godhead.

TRANSLATION

In the Vaikuṇṭha planets all the residents are similar in form to the Supreme Personality of Godhead. They all engage in devotional service to the Lord without desires for sense gratification.

PURPORT

The residents and the form of living in Vaikuṇṭha are described in this verse. The residents are all like the Supreme Personality of Godhead Nārāyaṇa. In the Vaikuṇṭha planets Kṛṣṇa's plenary feature as four-handed Nārāyaṇa is the predominating Deity, and the residents of Vaikuṇṭhaloka are also four-handed, just contrary to our conception here in the material world. Nowhere in the material world do we find a human being with four hands. In Vaikuṇṭhaloka there is no occupation but the service of the Lord, and this service is not rendered with a purpose. Although every service has a particular result, the devotees never aspire for the fulfillment of their own desires; their desires are fulfilled by rendering transcendental loving service to the Lord.

TEXT 15

यत्र चाद्यः पुमानास्ते भगवान् शब्दगोचरः ।
सत्त्वं विष्टभ्य विरजं स्वानां नो मृडयन् वृषः ॥१५॥

yatra cādyaḥ pumān āste
bhagavān śabda-gocaraḥ
sattvaṁ viṣṭabhya virajaṁ
svānāṁ no mṛḍayan vṛṣaḥ

yatra—in the Vaikuṇṭha planets; *ca*—and; *ādyaḥ*—original; *pumān*—person; *āste*—is there; *bhagavān*—the Supreme Personality of Godhead; *śabda-gocaraḥ*—understood through the Vedic literature; *sattvam*—the mode of goodness; *viṣṭabhya*—accepting; *virajam*—

uncontaminated; *svānām*—of His own associates; *naḥ*—us; *mṛḍayan*—increasing happiness; *vṛṣaḥ*—the personification of religious principles.

TRANSLATION

In the Vaikuṇṭha planets is the Supreme Personality of Godhead, who is the original person and who can be understood through the Vedic literature. He is full of the uncontaminated mode of goodness, with no place for passion or ignorance. He contributes religious progress for the devotees.

PURPORT

The kingdom of the Supreme Personality of Godhead in the spiritual sky cannot be understood by any process other than hearing from the description of the *Vedas.* No one can go see it. In this material world also, one who is unable to pay to go to a far distant place by motorized conveyances can only understand about that place from authentic books. Similarly, the Vaikuṇṭha planets in the spiritual sky are beyond this material sky. The modern scientists who are trying to travel in space are having difficulty going even to the nearest planet, the moon, to say nothing of the highest planets within the universe. There is no possibility that they can go beyond the material sky, enter the spiritual sky and see for themselves the spiritual planets, Vaikuṇṭha. Therefore, the kingdom of God in the spiritual sky can be understood only through the authentic descriptions of the *Vedas* and *Purāṇas.*

In the material world there are three modes of material qualities—goodness, passion and ignorance—but in the spiritual world there is no trace of the modes of passion and ignorance; there is only the mode of goodness, which is uncontaminated by any tinge of ignorance or passion. In the material world, even if a person is completely in goodness, he is sometimes subject to be polluted by tinges of the modes of ignorance and passion. But in the Vaikuṇṭha world, the spiritual sky, only the mode of goodness in its pure form exists. The Lord and His devotees reside in the Vaikuṇṭha planets, and they are of the same transcendental quality, namely, *śuddha-sattva,* the mode of pure goodness. The Vaikuṇṭha planets are very dear to the Vaiṣṇavas, and for the progressive march of the

Vaiṣṇavas toward the kingdom of God, the Lord Himself helps His devotees.

TEXT 16

यत्र नैःश्रेयसं नाम वनं कामदुघैर्द्रुमैः ।
सर्वर्तुश्रीभिर्विभ्राजत्कैवल्यमिव मूर्तिमत् ॥१६॥

yatra naiḥśreyasaṁ nāma
vanaṁ kāma-dughair drumaiḥ
sarvartu-śrībhir vibhrājat
kaivalyam iva mūrtimat

yatra—in the Vaikuṇṭha planets; *naiḥśreyasam*—auspicious; *nāma*—named; *vanam*—forests; *kāma-dughaiḥ*—yielding desire; *drumaiḥ*—with trees; *sarva*—all; *ṛtu*—seasons; *śrībhiḥ*—with flowers and fruits; *vibhrājat*—splendid; *kaivalyam*—spiritual; *iva*—as; *mūrtimat*—personal.

TRANSLATION

In those Vaikuṇṭha planets there are many forests which are very auspicious. In those forests the trees are desire trees, and in all seasons they are filled with flowers and fruits because everything in the Vaikuṇṭha planets is spiritual and personal.

PURPORT

In the Vaikuṇṭha planets the land, the trees, the fruits and flowers and the cows—everything—is completely spiritual and personal. The trees are desire trees. On this material planet the trees can produce fruits and flowers according to the order of material energy, but in the Vaikuṇṭha planets the trees, the land, the residents and the animals are all spiritual. There is no difference between the tree and the animal or the animal and the man. Here the word *mūrtimat* indicates that everything has a spiritual form. Formlessness, as conceived by the impersonalists, is refuted in this verse; in the Vaikuṇṭha planets, although everything is spiritual, everything has a particular form. The trees and the men have form, and because all of them, although differently formed, are spiritual, there is no difference between them.

TEXT 17

वैमानिकाः सललनाश्चरितानि शश्वद्
गायन्ति यत्र शमलक्षपणानि भर्तुः ।
अन्तर्जलेऽनुविकसन्मधुमाधवीनां
गन्धेन खण्डितधियोऽप्यनिलं क्षिपन्तः ॥१७॥

vaimānikāḥ sa-lalanāś caritāni śaśvad
gāyanti yatra śamala-kṣapaṇāni bhartuḥ
antar-jale 'nuvikasan-madhu-mādhavīnām
gandhena khaṇḍita-dhiyo 'py anilaṁ kṣipantaḥ

vaimānikāḥ—flying in their airplanes; *sa-lalanāḥ*—along with their wives; *caritāni*—activities; *śaśvat*—eternally; *gāyanti*—sing; *yatra*—in those Vaikuṇṭha planets; *śamala*—all inauspicious qualities; *kṣapaṇāni*—devoid of; *bhartuḥ*—of the Supreme Lord; *antaḥ-jale*—in the midst of the water; *anuvikasat*—blossoming; *madhu*—fragrant, laden with honey; *mādhavīnām*—of the *mādhavī* flowers; *gandhena*—by the fragrance; *khaṇḍita*—disturbed; *dhiyaḥ*—minds; *api*—even though; *anilam*—breeze; *kṣipantaḥ*—deriding.

TRANSLATION

In the Vaikuṇṭha planets the inhabitants fly in their airplanes, accompanied by their wives and consorts, and eternally sing of the character and activities of the Lord, which are always devoid of all inauspicious qualities. While singing the glories of the Lord, they deride even the presence of the blossoming mādhavī flowers, which are fragrant and laden with honey.

PURPORT

It appears from this verse that the Vaikuṇṭha planets are full of all opulences. There are airplanes in which the inhabitants travel in the spiritual sky with their sweethearts. There is a breeze carrying the fragrance of blossoming flowers, and this breeze is so nice that it also carries the honey of the flowers. The inhabitants of Vaikuṇṭha, however, are so interested in glorifying the Lord that they do not like the disturbance of such a nice breeze while they are chanting the Lord's glories. In other words, they are pure devotees. They consider glorification of the Lord more important than their own sense gratification. In the Vaikuṇṭha planets there is no question of sense gratification. To smell the fragrance of a blossoming flower is certainly very nice, but it is simply for sense gratification. The inhabitants of Vaikuṇṭha give first preference to the service of the Lord, not their own sense gratification. Serving the Lord in transcendental love yields such transcendental pleasure that, in comparison, sense gratification is counted as insignificant.

TEXT 18

पारावतान्यभृतसारसचक्रवाक-
दात्यूहहंसशुकतित्तिरिबर्हिणां यः ।
कोलाहलो विरमतेऽचिरमात्रमुच्चै-
र्भृङ्गाधिपे हरिकथामिव गायमाने ॥१८॥

pārāvatānyabhṛta-sārasa-cakravāka-
dātyūha-haṁsa-śuka-tittiri-barhiṇāṁ yaḥ
kolāhalo viramate 'cira-mātram uccair
bhṛṅgādhipe hari-kathām iva gāyamāne

pārāvata—pigeons; *anyabhṛta*—cuckoo; *sārasa*—crane; *cakravāka*—*cakravāka;* *dātyūha*—gallinule; *haṁsa*—swan; *śuka*—parrot; *tittiri*—partridge; *barhiṇām*—of the peacock; *yaḥ*—which; *kolāhalaḥ*—tumult; *viramate*—stops; *acira-mātram*—temporarily; *uccaiḥ*—loudly; *bhṛṅga-adhipe*—king of the bumblebees; *hari-kathām*—the glories of the Lord; *iva*—as; *gāyamāne*—while singing.

TRANSLATION

When the king of bees hums in a high pitch, singing the glories of the Lord, there is a temporary lull in the noise of the pigeon, the cuckoo, the crane, the cakravāka, the swan, the parrot, the partridge and the peacock. Such transcendental birds stop their own singing simply to hear the glories of the Lord.

PURPORT

This verse reveals the absolute nature of Vaikuṇṭha. There is no difference between the birds there and the human residents. The situation in the spiritual sky is that everything is spiritual and variegated. Spiritual variegatedness means that everything is animate. There is nothing inanimate. Even the trees, the ground, the plants, the flowers, the birds and the beasts are all on the level of Kṛṣṇa consciousness. The special feature of Vaikuṇṭhaloka is that there is no question of sense gratification. In the material world even an ass enjoys his sound vibration, but in the Vaikuṇṭhas such nice birds as the peacock, the *cakravāka* and the cuckoo prefer to hear the vibration of the glories of the Lord from the bees. The principles of devotional service, beginning with hearing and chanting, are very prominent in the Vaikuṇṭha world.

TEXT 19

मन्दारकुन्दकुरबोत्पलचम्पकार्ण-
पुन्नागनागबकुलाम्बुजपारिजाताः ।
गन्धेऽर्चिते तुलसिकाभरणेन तस्या
यस्मिंस्तपः सुमनसो बहु मानयन्ति ॥१९॥

mandāra-kunda-kurabotpala-campakārṇa-
punnāga-nāga-bakulāmbuja-pārijātāḥ
gandhe 'rcite tulasikābharaṇena tasyā
yasmiṁs tapaḥ sumanaso bahu mānayanti

mandāra—*mandāra; kunda*—*kunda; kuraba*—*kuraba; utpala*—*utpala; campaka*—*campaka; arṇa*—*arṇa* flower; *punnāga*—*punnāga; nāga*—*nāgakeśara; bakula*—*bakula; ambuja*—lily; *pārijātāḥ*—*pārijāta; gandhe*—fragrance; *arcite*—being worshiped; *tulasikā*—*tulasī; ābharaṇena*—with a garland; *tasyāḥ*—of her; *yasmin*—in which Vaikuṇṭha; *tapaḥ*—austerity; *su-manasaḥ*—good minded, Vaikuṇṭha minded; *bahu*—very much; *mānayanti*—glorify.

TRANSLATION

Although flowering plants like the mandāra, kunda, kurabaka, utpala, campaka, arṇa, punnāga, nāgakeśara, bakula, lily and pāri-

jāta are full of transcendental fragrance, they are still conscious of the austerities performed by tulasī, for tulasī is given special preference by the Lord, who garlands Himself with tulasī leaves.

PURPORT

The importance of *tulasī* leaves is very clearly mentioned here. *Tulasī* plants and their leaves are very important in devotional service. Devotees are recommended to water the *tulasī* tree every day and collect the leaves to worship the Lord. One time an atheistic *svāmī* remarked, "What is the use of watering the *tulasī* plant? It is better to water eggplant. By watering the eggplant one can get some fruits, but what is the use of watering the *tulasī*?" These foolish creatures, unacquainted with devotional service, sometimes play havoc with the education of people in general.

The most important thing about the spiritual world is that there is no envy among the devotees there. This is true even among the flowers, which are all conscious of the greatness of *tulasī*. In the Vaikuṇṭha world entered by the four Kumāras, even the birds and flowers are conscious of service to the Lord.

TEXT 20

यत्संकुलं हरिपदानतिमात्रदृष्टै-
वैंदूर्यमारकतहेममयैर्विमानैः ।
येषां बृहत्कटितटाः स्मितशोभिमुख्यः
कृष्णात्मनां न रज आदधुरुत्स्मयाद्यैः ॥२०॥

yat saṅkulaṁ hari-padānati-mātra-dṛṣṭair
vaidūrya-mārakata-hema-mayair vimānaiḥ
yeṣāṁ bṛhat-kaṭi-taṭāḥ smita-śobhi-mukhyaḥ
kṛṣṇātmanāṁ na raja ādadhur utsmayādyaiḥ

yat—that Vaikuṇṭha abode; *saṅkulam*—is pervaded; *hari-pada*—at the two lotus feet of Hari, the Supreme Personality of Godhead; *ānati*—by obeisances; *mātra*—simply; *dṛṣṭaiḥ*—are obtained; *vaidūrya*—lapis lazuli; *mārakata*—emeralds; *hema*—gold; *mayaiḥ*—made of; *vimānaiḥ*—with airplanes; *yeṣām*—of those passengers; *bṛhat*—large; *kaṭi-taṭāḥ*—hips; *smita*—smiling; *śobhi*—beautiful; *mukhyaḥ*—faces; *kṛṣṇa*—in Kṛṣṇa; *ātmanām*—whose minds are absorbed; *na*—not;

rajaḥ—sex desire; *ādadhuḥ*—stimulate; *utsmaya-ādyaiḥ*—by intimate friendly dealings, laughing and joking.

TRANSLATION

The inhabitants of Vaikuṇṭha travel in their airplanes made of lapis lazuli, emerald and gold. Although crowded by their consorts, who have large hips and beautiful smiling faces, they cannot be stimulated to passion by their mirth and beautiful charms.

PURPORT

In the material world, opulences are achieved by materialistic persons by dint of their labor. One cannot enjoy material prosperity unless he works very hard to achieve it. But the devotees of the Lord who are residents of Vaikuṇṭha have the opportunity to enjoy a transcendental situation of jewels and emeralds. Ornaments made of gold bedecked with jewels are achieved not by working hard but by the benediction of the Lord. In other words, devotees in the Vaikuṇṭha world, or even in this material world, cannot be poverty-stricken, as is sometimes supposed. They have ample opulences for enjoyment, but they need not labor to achieve them. It is also stated that in the Vaikuṇṭha world the consorts of the residents are many, many times more beautiful than we can find in this material world, even in the higher planets. It is specifically mentioned here that a woman's large hips are very attractive and they stimulate man's passion, but the wonderful feature of Vaikuṇṭha is that although the women have large hips and beautiful faces and are decorated with ornaments of emeralds and jewels, the men are so absorbed in Kṛṣṇa consciousness that the beautiful bodies of the women cannot attract them. In other words, there is enjoyment of the association of the opposite sex, but there is no sexual relationship. The residents of Vaikuṇṭha have a better standard of pleasure, so there is no need of sex pleasure.

TEXT 21

श्री रूपिणी क्वणयती चरणारविन्दं
लीलाम्बुजेन हरिसद्मनि मुक्तदोषा ।

संलक्ष्यते स्फटिककुड्य उपेतहेम्नि
सम्मार्जतीव यदनुग्रहणेऽन्ययत्नः ॥२१॥

śrī rūpiṇī kvaṇayatī caraṇāravindaṁ
līlāmbujena hari-sadmani mukta-doṣā
saṁlakṣyate sphaṭika-kuḍya upeta-hemni
sammārjatīva yad-anugrahaṇe 'nya-yatnaḥ

śrī—Lakṣmī, the goddess of fortune; *rūpiṇī*—assuming a beautiful form; *kvaṇayatī*—tinkling; *caraṇa-aravindam*—lotus feet; *līlā-ambujena*—playing with a lotus flower; *hari-sadmaṇi*—the house of the Supreme Personality; *mukta-doṣā*—freed from all faults; *saṁlakṣyate*—becomes visible; *sphaṭika*—crystal; *kuḍye*—walls; *upeta*—mixed; *hemni*—gold; *sammārjatī iva*—appearing like a sweeper; *yat-anugrahaṇe*—to receive her favor; *anya*—others'; *yatnaḥ*—very much careful.

TRANSLATION

The ladies in the Vaikuṇṭha planets are as beautiful as the goddess of fortune herself. Such transcendentally beautiful ladies, their hands playing with lotuses and their leg bangles tinkling, are sometimes seen sweeping the marble walls, which are bedecked at intervals with golden borders, in order to receive the grace of the Supreme Personality of Godhead.

PURPORT

In the *Brahma-saṁhitā* it is stated that the Supreme Lord, Govinda, is always served in His abode by many, many millions of goddesses of fortune. *Lakṣmī-sahasra-śata-sambhrama-sevyamānam.* These millions and trillions of goddesses of fortune who reside in the Vaikuṇṭha planets are not exactly consorts of the Supreme Personality of Godhead, but are the wives of the devotees of the Lord and also engage in the service of the Supreme Personality of Godhead. It is stated here that in the Vaikuṇṭha planets the houses are made of marble. Similarly, in the *Brahma-saṁhitā* it is stated that the ground on the Vaikuṇṭha planets is made of touchstone. Thus there is no need to sweep the stone in Vaikuṇṭha, for there is hardly any dust on it, but still, in order to satisfy the Lord, the ladies there always engage in dusting the marble walls. Why? The reason is that they are eager to achieve the grace of the Lord by doing so.

It is also stated here that in the Vaikuṇṭha planets the goddesses of fortune are faultless. Generally the goddess of fortune does not remain steadily in one place. Her name is Cañcalā, which means "one who is not steady." We find, therefore, that a man who is very rich may become the poorest of the poor. Another example is Rāvaṇa. Rāvaṇa took away Lakṣmī, Sītājī, to his kingdom, and instead of being happy by the grace of Lakṣmī, his family and his kingdom were vanquished. Thus Lakṣmī in the house of Rāvaṇa is Cañcalā, or unsteady. Men of Rāvaṇa's class want Lakṣmī only, without her husband, Nārāyaṇa; therefore they become unsteady due to Lakṣmījī. Materialistic persons find fault on the part of Lakṣmī, but in Vaikuṇṭha Lakṣmījī is fixed in the service of the Lord. In spite of her being the goddess of fortune, she cannot be happy without the grace of the Lord. Even the goddess of fortune needs the Lord's grace in order to be happy, yet in the material world even Brahmā, the highest created being, seeks the favor of Lakṣmī for happiness.

TEXT 22

वापीषु विद्रुमतटास्वमलामृताप्सु
प्रेष्यान्विता निजवने तुलसीभिरीशम् ।
अभ्यर्चती स्वलकमुन्नसमीक्ष्य वक्त्र-
मुच्छेषितं भगवतेत्यमताङ्ग यच्छ्रीः ॥२२॥

vāpīṣu vidruma-taṭāsv amalāmṛtāpsu
preṣyānvitā nija-vane tulasībhir īśam
abhyarcatī svalakam unnasam īkṣya vaktram
ucchesitaṁ bhagavatety amatāṅga yac-chrīḥ

vāpīṣu—in the ponds; *vidruma*—made of coral; *taṭāsu*—banks; *amala*—transparent; *amṛta*—nectarean; *apsu*—water; *preṣyā-anvitā*—surrounded by maidservants; *nija-vane*—in her own garden; *tulasībhiḥ*—with *tulasī; īśam*—the Supreme Lord; *abhyarcatī*—worship; *su-alakam*—with her face decorated with *tilaka; unnasam*—raised nose; *īkṣya*—by seeing; *vaktram*—face; *ucchesitam*—being kissed;

bhagavatā—by the Supreme Lord; *iti*—thus; *amata*—thought; *aṅga*—O demigods; *yat-śrīḥ*—whose beauty.

TRANSLATION

The goddesses of fortune worship the Lord in their own gardens by offering tulasī leaves on the coral-paved banks of transcendental reservoirs of water. While offering worship to the Lord, they can see on the water the reflection of their beautiful faces with raised noses, and it appears that they have become more beautiful because of the Lord's kissing their faces.

PURPORT

Generally, when a woman is kissed by her husband, her face becomes more beautiful. In Vaikuṇṭha also, although the goddess of fortune is naturally as beautiful as can be imagined, she nevertheless awaits the kissing of the Lord to make her face more beautiful. The beautiful face of the goddess of fortune appears in ponds of transcendental crystal water when she worships the Lord with *tulasī* leaves in her garden.

TEXT 23

यन्न व्रजन्त्यघभिदो रचनानुवादा-
च्छृण्वन्ति येऽन्यविषयाः कुकथा मतिघ्नीः ।
यास्तु श्रुता हतभगैर्नृभिरात्तसारा-
स्तांस्तान् क्षिपन्त्यशरणेषु तमःसु हन्त ॥२३॥

yan na vrajanty agha-bhido racanānuvādāc
chṛṇvanti ye 'nya-viṣayāḥ kukathā mati-ghnīḥ
yās tu śrutā hata-bhagair nṛbhir ātta-sārās
tāṁs tān kṣipanty aśaraṇeṣu tamaḥsu hanta

yat—Vaikuṇṭha; *na*—never; *vrajanti*—approach; *agha-bhidaḥ*—of the vanquisher of all kinds of sins; *racanā*—of the creation; *anuvādāt*—than narrations; *śṛṇvanti*—hear; *ye*—those who; *anya*—other; *viṣayāḥ*—subject matter; *ku-kathāḥ*—bad words; *mati-ghnīḥ*—killing intelligence; *yāḥ*—which; *tu*—but; *śrutāḥ*—are heard; *hata-bhagaiḥ*—

unfortunate; *nṛbhiḥ*—by men; *ātta*—taken away; *sārāḥ*—values of life; *tān tān*—such persons; *kṣipanti*—are thrown; *aśaraṇeṣu*—devoid of all shelter; *tamaḥsu*—in the darkest part of material existence; *hanta*—alas.

TRANSLATION

It is very much regrettable that unfortunate people do not discuss the description of the Vaikuṇṭha planets but engage in topics which are unworthy to hear and which bewilder one's intelligence. Those who give up the topics of Vaikuṇṭha and take to talk of the material world are thrown into the darkest region of ignorance.

PURPORT

The most unfortunate persons are the impersonalists, who cannot understand the transcendental variegatedness of the spiritual world. They are afraid to talk about the beauty of the Vaikuṇṭha planets because they think that variegatedness must be material. Such impersonalists think that the spiritual world is completely void, or, in other words, that there is no variegatedness. This mentality is described here as *ku-kathā mati-ghnīḥ,* "intelligence bewildered by unworthy words." The philosophies of voidness and of the impersonal situation of the spiritual world are condemned here because they bewilder one's intelligence. How can the impersonalist and the void philosopher think of this material world, which is full of variegatedness, and then say that there is no variegatedness in the spiritual world? It is said that this material world is the perverted reflection of the spiritual world, so unless there is variegatedness in the spiritual world, how can there be temporary variegatedness in the material world? That one can transcend this material world does not imply that there is no transcendental variegatedness.

Here in the *Bhāgavatam,* in this verse particularly, it is stressed that people who try to discuss and understand the real spiritual nature of the spiritual sky and the Vaikuṇṭhas are fortunate. The variegatedness of the Vaikuṇṭha planets is described in relation to the transcendental pastimes of the Lord. But instead of trying to understand the spiritual abode and the spiritual activities of the Lord, people are more interested in politics and economic developments. They hold many conventions, meetings and discussions to solve the problems of this worldly situation, where they can remain for only a few years, but they are not interested in understanding the spiritual situation of the Vaikuṇṭha world. If they are at all fortunate, they become interested in going back home, back to Godhead, but unless they understand the spiritual world, they rot in this material darkness continuously.

TEXT 24

येऽभ्यर्थितामपि च नो नृगतिं प्रपन्ना
ज्ञानं च तत्त्वविषयं सहधर्मं यत्र ।
नाराधनं भगवतो वितरन्त्यमुष्य
सम्मोहिता विततया बत मायया ते ॥२४॥

ye 'bhyarthitām api ca no nṛ-gatiṁ prapannā
jñānaṁ ca tattva-viṣayaṁ saha-dharmaṁ yatra
nārādhanaṁ bhagavato vitaranty amuṣya
sammohitā vitatayā bata māyayā te

ye—those persons; *abhyarthitām*—desired; *api*—certainly; *ca*—and; *naḥ*—by us (Brahmā and the other demigods); *nṛ-gatim*—the human form of life; *prapannāḥ*—have attained; *jñānam*—knowledge; *ca*—and; *tattva-viṣayam*—subject matter about the Absolute Truth; *saha-dharmam*—along with religious principles; *yatra*—where; *na*—not; *ārādhanam*—worship; *bhagavataḥ*—of the Supreme Personality of Godhead; *vitaranti*—perform; *amuṣya*—of the Supreme Lord; *sammohitāḥ*—being bewildered; *vitatayā*—all-pervading; *bata*—alas; *māyayā*—by the influence of the illusory energy; *te*—they.

TRANSLATION

Lord Brahmā said: My dear demigods, the human form of life is of such importance that we also desire to have such life, for in the human form one can attain perfect religious truth and knowledge. If one in this human form of life does not understand the Supreme Personality of Godhead and His abode, it is to be understood that he is very much affected by the influence of external nature.

PURPORT

Brahmājī condemns very vehemently the condition of the human being who does not take interest in the Personality of Godhead and His transcendental abode, Vaikuṇṭha. The human form of life is desired even by Brahmājī. Brahmā and other demigods have much better material bodies than human beings, yet the demigods, including Brahmā, nevertheless desire to attain the human form of life because it is specifically meant for the living entity who can attain transcendental knowledge and religious perfection. It is not possible to go back to Godhead in one life, but in the human form one should at least understand the goal of life and begin Kṛṣṇa consciousness. It is said that the human form is a great boon because it is the most suitable boat for crossing over the nescience ocean. The spiritual master is considered to be the most able captain in that boat, and the information from the scriptures is the favorable wind for floating over the ocean of nescience. The human being who does not take advantage of all these facilities in this life is committing suicide. Therefore one who does not begin Kṛṣṇa consciousness in the human form of life loses his life to the influence of the illusory energy. Brahmā regrets the situation of such a human being.

TEXT 25

यच्च व्रजन्त्यनिमिषामृषभानुवृत्त्या
दूरेयमा ह्युपरि नः स्पृहणीयशीलाः ।
भर्तुर्मिथः सुयशसः कथनानुराग-
वैक्लव्यबाष्पकलया पुलकीकृताङ्गाः ॥२५॥

yac ca vrajanty animiṣām ṛṣabhānuvṛttyā
dūre yamā hy upari naḥ spṛhaṇīya-śīlāḥ
bhartur mithaḥ suyaśasaḥ kathanānurāga-
vaiklavya-bāṣpa-kalayā pulakī-kṛtāṅgāḥ

yat—Vaikuṇṭha; *ca*—and; *vrajanti*—go; *animiṣām*—of the demigods; *ṛṣabha*—chief; *anuvṛttyā*—following in the footsteps; *dūre*—keeping at a distance; *yamāḥ*—regulative principles; *hi*—certainly; *upari*—above; *naḥ*—us; *spṛhaṇīya*—to be desired; *śīlāḥ*—good qualities; *bhartuḥ*—of the Supreme Lord; *mithaḥ*—for one another; *suyaśasaḥ*—glories; *kathana*—by discussions, discourses; *anurāga*—attraction; *vaiklavya*—ecstasy; *bāṣpa-kalayā*—tears in the eyes; *pulakīkṛta*—shivering; *aṅgāḥ*—bodies.

TRANSLATION

Persons whose bodily features change in ecstasy and who breathe heavily and perspire due to hearing the glories of the Lord are promoted to the kingdom of God, even though they do not care for meditation and other austerities. The kingdom of God is above the material universes, and it is desired by Brahmā and other demigods.

PURPORT

It is clearly stated herein that the kingdom of God is above the material universes. Just as there are many hundreds of thousands of higher planets above this earth, so there are many millions and billions of spiritual planets belonging to the spiritual sky. Brahmājī states herein that the spiritual kingdom is above the kingdom of the demigods. One can enter the kingdom of the Supreme Lord only when one is highly developed in desirable qualities. All good qualities develop in the person of a devotee. It is stated in *Śrīmad-Bhāgavatam*, Fifth Canto, Eighteenth Chapter, verse 12, that anyone who is Kṛṣṇa conscious is endowed with all the good qualities of the demigods. In the material world the qualities of the demigods are highly appreciated, just as, even in our experience, the qualities of a gentleman are more highly appreciated than the qualities of a man in ignorance or in a lower condition of life. The qualities of the demigods in the higher planets are far superior to the qualities of the inhabitants of this earth.

Brahmājī confirms herewith that only persons who have developed the desirable qualities can enter into the kingdom of God. In the *Caitanya-caritāmṛta*, the devotee's desirable qualities are described to be twenty-six in number. They are stated as follows: He is very kind; he does not quarrel with anyone; he accepts Kṛṣṇa consciousness as the highest goal of life; he is equal to everyone; no one can find fault in his character; he is magnanimous, mild and always clean, internally and externally; he does not profess to possess anything in this material world; he is a benefactor to all living entities; he is peaceful and is a soul completely surrendered to Kṛṣṇa; he has no material desire to fulfill; he is meek and humble, always steady, and has conquered the sensual activities; he does not eat more than required to maintain body and soul together; he is never mad after material identity; he is respectful to all others and does not demand respect for himself; he is very grave, very compassionate and very friendly; he is poetic; he is expert in all activities, and he is silent in nonsense. Similarly, in *Śrīmad-Bhāgavatam*, Third Canto, Twenty-fifth Chapter, verse 21, the qualifications of a saintly person are mentioned. It is said there that a saintly person eligible to enter into the kingdom of God is very tolerant and very kind to all living entities. He is not partial; he is kind both to human beings and to animals. He is not such a fool that he will kill a goat Nārāyaṇa to feed a human Nārāyaṇa, or *daridra-nārāyaṇa.* He is very kind to all living entities; therefore he has no enemy. He is very peaceful. These are the qualities of persons who are eligible to enter into the kingdom of God. That such a person gradually becomes liberated and enters the kingdom of God is confirmed in *Śrīmad-Bhāgavatam*, Fifth Canto, Fifth Chapter, verse 2. The *Śrīmad-Bhāgavatam*, Second Canto, Third Chapter, verse 24, also states that if a person does not cry or exhibit bodily changes after chanting the holy name of God without offense, it is to be understood that he is hardhearted and that therefore his heart does not change even after he chants the holy name of God, Hare Kṛṣṇa. These bodily changes can take place due to ecstasy when we offenselessly chant the holy names of God: Hare Kṛṣṇa, Hare Kṛṣṇa, Kṛṣṇa Kṛṣṇa, Hare Hare/ Hare Rāma, Hare Rāma, Rāma Rāma, Hare Hare.

It may be noted that there are ten offenses we should avoid. The first offense is to decry persons who try in their lives to broadcast the glories of the Lord. People must be educated in understanding the glories of the Supreme; therefore the devotees who engage in preaching the glories of the Lord are never to be decried. It is the greatest offense. Furthermore, the holy name of Viṣṇu is the most auspicious name, and His pastimes are also nondifferent from the holy name of the Lord. There are many foolish persons who say that one can chant Hare Kṛṣṇa or chant the name of Kālī or Durgā or Śiva because they are all the same. If one thinks that the holy name of the Supreme Personality of Godhead and the names and activities of the demigods are on the same level, or if one accepts the holy name of Viṣṇu to be a material sound vibration, that is also an offense. The third offense is to think of the spiritual master who spreads the glories of the Lord as an ordinary human being. The fourth offense is to consider the Vedic literatures, such as the *Purāṇas* or other transcendentally revealed scriptures, to be ordinary books of knowledge. The fifth offense is to think that devotees have given artificial importance to the holy name of God. The actual fact is that the Lord is nondifferent from His name. The highest realization of spiritual value is to chant the holy name of God, as prescribed for the age—Hare Kṛṣṇa, Hare Kṛṣṇa, Kṛṣṇa Kṛṣṇa, Hare Hare/ Hare Rāma, Hare Rāma, Rāma Rāma, Hare Hare. The sixth offense is to give some interpretation on the holy name of God. The seventh offense is to act sinfully on the strength of chanting the holy name of God. It is understood that one can be freed from all sinful reaction simply by chanting the holy name of God, but if one thinks that he is therefore at liberty to commit all kinds of sinful acts, that is a symptom of offense. The eighth offense is to equate the chanting of Hare Kṛṣṇa with other spiritual activities, such as meditation, austerity, penance or sacrifice. They cannot be equated at any level. The ninth offense is to specifically glorify the importance of the holy name before persons who have no interest. The tenth offense is to be attached to the misconception of possessing something, or to accept the body as one's self, while executing the process of spiritual cultivation.

When one is free from all ten of these offenses in chanting the holy name of God, he develops the ecstatic bodily features called *pulakāśru*. *Pulaka* means "symptoms of happiness," and *aśru* means "tears in the eyes." The symptoms of happiness and tears in the eyes must appear in a person who has chanted the holy name offenselessly. Here in this verse it is stated that those who have actually developed the symptoms of happiness and tears in the eyes by chanting the glories of the Lord are eligible to enter the kingdom of God. In the *Caitanya-caritāmṛta* it is said that if one does not develop these symptoms while chanting Hare Kṛṣṇa, it is to be understood that he is still offensive. *Caitanya-caritāmṛta* suggests a nice remedy in this connection. There it is said in verse 31, Chapter Eight, of *Ādi-līlā*, that if anyone takes shelter of Lord Caitanya and just chants the holy name of the Lord, Hare Kṛṣṇa, he becomes freed from all offenses.

TEXT 26

तद्विश्वगुर्वधिकृतं भुवनैकवन्द्यं
दिव्यं विचित्रविबुधाग्र्यविमानशोचिः ।
आपुः परां मुदमपूर्वमुपेत्य योग-
मायाबलेन मुनयस्तदथो विकुण्ठम् ॥२६॥

tad viśva-gurv-adhikṛtaṁ bhuvanaika-vandyaṁ
divyaṁ vicitra-vibudhāgrya-vimāna-śociḥ
āpuḥ parāṁ mudam apūrvam upetya yoga-
māyā-balena munayas tad atho vikuṇṭham

tat—then; *viśva-guru*—by the teacher of the universe, the Supreme Personality of Godhead; *adhikṛtam*—predominated; *bhuvana*—of the planets; *eka*—alone; *vandyam*—worthy to be worshiped; *divyam*—spiritual; *vicitra*—highly decorated; *vibudha-agrya*—of the devotees (who are the best of the learned); *vimāna*—of the airplanes; *śociḥ*—illuminated; *āpuḥ*—attained; *parām*—the highest; *mudam*—happiness; *apūrvam*—unprecedented; *upetya*—having attained; *yoga-māyā*—by spiritual potency; *balena*—by the influence; *munayaḥ*—the sages; *tat*—Vaikuṇṭha; *atho*—that; *vikuṇṭham*—Viṣṇu.

TRANSLATION

Thus the great sages, Sanaka, Sanātana, Sanandana and Sanat-kumāra, upon reaching the above-mentioned Vaikuṇṭha in the spiritual world by dint of their mystic yoga performance, perceived unprecedented happiness. They found that the spiritual sky was illuminated by highly decorated airplanes piloted by the best devotees of Vaikuṇṭha and was predominated by the Supreme Personality of Godhead.

PURPORT

The Supreme Personality of Godhead is one without a second. He is above everyone. No one is equal to Him, nor is anyone greater than Him. Therefore He is described here as *viśva-guru.* He is the prime living entity of the entire material and spiritual creation and is *bhuvanaika-van-*

dyam, the only worshipable personality in the three worlds. The airplanes in the spiritual sky are self-illuminated and are piloted by great devotees of the Lord. In other words, in the Vaikuṇṭha planets there is no scarcity of the things which are available in the material world; they are available, but they are more valuable because they are spiritual and therefore eternal and blissful. The sages felt an unprecedented happiness because Vaikuṇṭha was not predominated by an ordinary man. The Vaikuṇṭha planets are predominated by expansions of Kṛṣṇa, who are differently named as Madhusūdana, Mādhava, Nārāyaṇa, Pradyumna, etc. These transcendental planets are worshipable because the Personality of Godhead personally rules them. It is said here that the sages reached the transcendental spiritual sky by dint of their mystic power. That is the perfection of the *yoga* system. The breathing exercises and disciplines to keep health in proper order are not the ultimate goals of *yoga* perfection. The *yoga* system as generally understood is *aṣṭāṅga-yoga*, or *siddhi*, eightfold perfection in *yoga*. By dint of perfection in *yoga* one can become lighter than the lightest and heavier than the heaviest; one can go wherever he likes and can achieve opulences as he likes. There are eight such perfections. The *ṛṣis*, the four Kumāras, reached Vaikuṇṭha by becoming lighter than the lightest and thus passing over the space of the material world. Modern mechanical space vehicles are unsuccessful because they cannot go to the highest region of this material creation, and they certainly cannot enter the spiritual sky. But by perfection of the *yoga* system one not only can travel through material space, but can surpass material space and enter the spiritual sky. We learn this fact also from an incident concerning Durvāsā Muni and Mahārāja Ambarīṣa. It is understood that in one year Durvāsā Muni traveled everywhere and went into the spiritual sky to meet the Supreme Personality of Godhead, Nārāyaṇa. By present standards, scientists calculate that if one could travel at the speed of light, it would take forty thousand years to reach the highest planet of this material world. But the *yoga* system can carry one without limitation or difficulty. The word *yogamāyā* is used in this verse. *Yoga-māyā-balena vikuṇṭham.* The transcendental happiness exhibited in the spiritual world and all other spiritual manifestations there are made possible by the influence of *yogamāyā*, the internal potency of the Supreme Personality of Godhead.

TEXT 27

तस्मिन्नतीत्य मुनयः षडसज्जमानाः
कक्षाः समानवयसावथ सप्तमायाम् ।
देवावचक्षत गृहीतगदौ परार्ध्य-
केयूरकुण्डलकिरीटविटङ्कवेषौ ॥२७॥

tasminn atītya munayaḥ ṣaḍ asajjamānāḥ
kakṣāḥ samāna-vayasāv atha saptamāyām
devāv acakṣata gṛhīta-gadau parārdhya-
keyūra-kuṇḍala-kirīṭa-viṭaṅka-veṣau

tasmin—in that Vaikuṇṭha; *atītya*—after passing through; *munayaḥ*—the great sages; *ṣaṭ*—six; *asajjamānāḥ*—without being much attracted; *kakṣāḥ*—walls; *samāna*—equal; *vayasau*—age; *atha*—thereafter; *saptamāyām*—at the seventh gate; *devau*—two Vaikuṇṭha doormen; *acakṣata*—saw; *gṛhīta*—carrying; *gadau*—maces; *para-ardhya*—most valuable; *keyūra*—bracelets; *kuṇḍala*—earrings; *kirīṭa*—helmets; *viṭaṅka*—beautiful; *veṣau*—garments.

TRANSLATION

After passing through the six entrances of Vaikuṇṭha-purī, the Lord's residence, without feeling astonishment at all the decorations, they saw at the seventh gate two shining beings of the same age, armed with maces and adorned with most valuable jewelry, earrings, diamonds, helmets, garments, etc.

PURPORT

The sages were so eager to see the Lord within Vaikuṇṭha-purī that they did not care to see the transcendental decorations of the six gates which they passed by one after another. But at the seventh door they found two doormen of the same age. The significance of the doormen's being of the same age is that in the Vaikuṇṭha planets there is no old age, so one cannot distinguish who is older than whom. The inhabitants of Vaikuṇṭha are decorated like the Supreme Personality of Godhead, Nārāyaṇa, with *śaṅkha, cakra, gadā* and *padma* (conch, wheel, club and lotus).

TEXT 28

मत्तद्विरेफवनमालिकया निवीतौ
विन्यस्तयासितचतुष्टयबाहुमध्ये ।
वक्त्रं भ्रुवा कुटिलया स्फुटनिर्गमाभ्यां
रक्तेक्षणेन च मनाग्रभसं दधानौ ॥२८॥

matta-dvirepha-vanamālikayā nivītau
vinyastayāsita-catuṣṭaya-bāhu-madhye
vaktraṁ bhruvā kuṭilayā sphuṭa-nirgamābhyām
raktekṣaṇena ca manāg rabhasaṁ dadhānau

matta—intoxicated; *dvi-repha*—bees; *vana-mālikayā*—with a garland of fresh flowers; *nivītau*—hanging on the neck; *vinyastayā*—placed around; *asita*—blue; *catuṣṭaya*—four; *bāhu*—hands; *madhye*—between; *vaktram*—face; *bhruvā*—with their eyebrows; *kuṭilayā*—arched; *sphuṭa*—snorting; *nirgamābhyām*—breathing; *rakta*—reddish; *īkṣaṇena*—with eyes; *ca*—and; *manāk*—somewhat; *rabhasam*—agitated; *dadhānau*—glanced over.

TRANSLATION

The two doormen were garlanded with fresh flowers which attracted intoxicated bees and which were placed around their necks and between their four blue arms. From their arched eyebrows, discontented nostrils and reddish eyes, they appeared somewhat agitated.

PURPORT

Their garlands attracted swarms of bees because they were garlands of fresh flowers. In the Vaikuṇṭha world everything is fresh, new and transcendental. The inhabitants of Vaikuṇṭha have bodies of bluish color and four hands like Nārāyaṇa.

TEXT 29

द्वार्येतयोर्निविविशुर्मिषतोरपृष्ट्वा
पूर्वा यथा पुरटवज्रकपाटिका याः ।

सर्वत्र तेऽविषमया मुनयः स्वदृष्ट्या
ये सञ्चरन्त्यविहता विगताभिशङ्काः ॥२९॥

dvāry etayor niviviśur miṣator apṛṣṭvā
pūrvā yathā puraṭa-vajra-kapāṭikā yāḥ
sarvatra te 'viṣamayā munayaḥ sva-dṛṣṭyā
ye sañcaranty avihatā vigatābhiśaṅkāḥ

dvāri—in the door; *etayoḥ*—both doorkeepers; *niviviśuḥ*—entered; *miṣatoḥ*—while seeing; *apṛṣṭvā*—without asking; *pūrvāḥ*—as before; *yathā*—as; *puraṭa*—made of gold; *vajra*—and diamond; *kapāṭikāḥ*—the doors; *yāḥ*—which; *sarvatra*—everywhere; *te*—they; *aviṣamayā*—without any sense of discrimination; *munayaḥ*—the great sages; *sva-dṛṣṭyā*—out of their own will; *ye*—who; *sañcaranti*—move; *avihatāḥ*—without being checked; *vigata*—without; *abhiśaṅkāḥ*—doubt.

TRANSLATION

The great sages, headed by Sanaka, had opened doors everywhere. They had no idea of "ours" and "theirs." With open minds, they entered the seventh door out of their own will, just as they had passed through the six other doors, which were made of gold and diamonds.

PURPORT

The great sages—namely, Sanaka, Sanātana, Sanandana and Sanatkumāra—although very old in years, maintained themselves eternally as small children. They were not at all duplicitous, and they entered the doors exactly as little children enter places without any idea of what it is to trespass. That is a child's nature. A child can enter any place, and no one checks him. Indeed, a child is generally welcome in his attempts to go places, but if it so happens that a child is checked from entering a door, he naturally becomes very sorry and angry. That is the nature of a child. In this case, the same thing happened. The childlike saintly personalities entered all the six doors of the palace, and no one checked them; therefore when they attempted to enter the seventh door and were forbidden by the doormen, who checked them with their sticks, they naturally became very angry and sorrowful. An ordinary child would cry, but because these were not ordinary children, they immediately made preparations to punish the doormen, for the doormen had committed a great offense. Even to this day a saintly person is never checked from entering anyone's door in India.

TEXT 30

तान् वीक्ष्य वातरशनांश्चतुरः कुमारान्
वृद्धान्दशार्धवयसो विदितात्मतत्त्वान् ।
वेत्रेण चास्खलयतामतदर्हणांस्तौ
तेजो विहस्य भगवत्प्रतिकूलशीलौ ॥३०॥

tān vīkṣya vāta-raśanāṁś caturaḥ kumārān
vṛddhān daśārdha-vayaso viditātma-tattvān
vetreṇa cāskhalayatām atad-arhaṇāṁs tau
tejo vihasya bhagavat-pratikūla-śīlau

tān—them; *vīkṣya*—after seeing; *vāta-raśanān*—naked; *caturaḥ*—four; *kumārān*—boys; *vṛddhān*—aged; *daśa-ardha*—five years; *vayasaḥ*—appearing as of the age; *vidita*—had realized; *ātma-tattvān*—the truth of the self; *vetreṇa*—with their staffs; *ca*—also; *askhalayatām*—forbade; *a-tat-arhaṇān*—not deserving such from them; *tau*—those two porters; *tejaḥ*—glories; *vihasya*—disregarding the etiquette; *bhagavat-pratikūla-śīlau*—having a nature displeasing to the Lord.

TRANSLATION

The four boy-sages, who had nothing to cover their bodies but the atmosphere, looked only five years old, even though they were the oldest of all living creatures and had realized the truth of the self. But when the porters, who happened to possess a disposition quite unpalatable to the Lord, saw the sages, they blocked their way with their staffs, despising their glories, although the sages did not deserve such treatment at their hands.

PURPORT

The four sages were the first-born sons of Brahmā. Therefore all other living entities, including Lord Śiva, are born later and are therefore younger than the four Kumāras. Although they looked like five-year-old boys and traveled naked, the Kumāras were older than all other living creatures and had realized the truth of the self. Such saints were not to be forbidden to enter the kingdom of Vaikuṇṭha, but by chance the doormen objected to their entrance. This was not fitting. The Lord is always anxious to serve sages like the Kumāras, but in spite of knowing this fact, the doormen, astonishingly and outrageously, prohibited them from entering.

TEXT 31

ताभ्यां मिषत्स्वनिमिषेषु निषिध्यमानाः
स्वर्हत्तमा ह्यपि हरेः प्रतिहारपाभ्याम् ।
ऊचुः सुहृत्तमदिदृक्षितभङ्ग ईष-
त्कामानुजेन सहसा त उपप्लुताक्षाः ॥३१॥

tābhyāṁ miṣatsv animiṣeṣu niṣidhyamānāḥ
svarhattamā hy api hareḥ pratihāra-pābhyām
ūcuḥ suhṛttama-didṛkṣita-bhaṅga īṣat
kāmānujena sahasā ta upaplutākṣāḥ

tābhyām—by those two porters; *miṣatsu*—while looking on; *animiṣeṣu*—demigods living in Vaikuṇṭha; *niṣidhyamānāḥ*—being forbidden; *su-arhattamāḥ*—by far the fittest persons; *hi api*—although; *hareḥ*—of Hari, the Supreme Personality of Godhead; *pratihāra-pābhyām*—by the two doorkeepers; *ūcuḥ*—said; *suhṛt-tama*—most beloved; *didṛkṣita*—eagerness to see; *bhaṅge*—hindrance; *īṣat*—slight; *kāma-anujena*—by the younger brother of lust (anger); *sahasā*—suddenly; *te*—those great sages; *upapluta*—agitated; *akṣāḥ*—eyes.

TRANSLATION

When the Kumāras, although by far the fittest persons, were thus forbidden entrance by the two chief doorkeepers of Śrī Hari

while other divinities looked on, their eyes suddenly turned red because of anger due to their great eagerness to see their most beloved master, Śrī Hari, the Personality of Godhead.

PURPORT

According to the Vedic system, a *sannyāsī*, a person in the renounced order of life, is dressed in saffron-colored garments. This saffron dress is practically a passport for the mendicant and *sannyāsī* to go anywhere. The *sannyāsī*'s duty is to enlighten people in Kṛṣṇa consciousness. Those in the renounced order of life have no other business but preaching the glories and supremacy of the Supreme Personality of Godhead. Therefore the Vedic sociological conception is that a *sannyāsī* should not be restricted; he is allowed to go anywhere and everywhere he wants, and he is not refused any gift he might demand from a householder. The four Kumāras came to see the Supreme Personality of Godhead Nārāyaṇa. The word *suhṛttama*, "best of all friends," is important. As Lord Kṛṣṇa states in the *Bhagavad-gītā*, He is the best friend of all living entities. *Suhṛdaṁ sarva-bhūtānām*. No one can be a greater well-wishing friend to any living entity than the Supreme Personality of Godhead. He is so kindly disposed towards everyone that in spite of our completely forgetting our relationship with the Supreme Lord, He comes Himself—sometimes personally, as Lord Kṛṣṇa appeared on this earth, and sometimes as His devotee, as did Lord Caitanya Mahāprabhu—and sometimes He sends His bona fide devotees to reclaim all the fallen souls. Therefore, He is the greatest well-wishing friend of everyone, and the Kumāras wanted to see Him. The doorkeepers should have known that the four sages had no other business, and therefore to restrict them from entering the palace was not apt.

In this verse it is figuratively stated that the younger brother of desire suddenly appeared in person when the sages were forbidden to see their most beloved Personality of Godhead. The younger brother of desire is anger. If one's desire is not fulfilled, the younger brother, anger, follows. Here we can mark that even great saintly persons like the Kumāras were also angry, but they were not angry for their personal interests. They were angry because they were forbidden to enter the palace to see the Personality of Godhead. Therefore the theory that in the perfectional stage one should not have anger is not supported in this verse. Anger will continue even in the liberated stage. These four mendicant brothers, the Kumāras, were considered liberated persons, but still they were angry because they were restricted in their service to the Lord. The difference between the anger of an ordinary person and that of a liberated person is that an ordinary person becomes angry because his sense desires are not being fulfilled, whereas a liberated person like the Kumāras becomes angry when restricted in the discharge of duties for serving the Supreme Personality of Godhead.

In the previous verse it has been clearly mentioned that the Kumāras were liberated persons. *Viditātma-tattva* means "one who understands the truth of self-realization." One who does not understand the truth of self-realization is called ignorant, but one who understands the self, the Superself, their interrelation, and activities in self-realization is called *viditātma-tattva.* Although the Kumāras were already liberated persons, they nevertheless became angry. This point is very important. Becoming liberated does not necessitate losing one's sensual activities. Sense activities continue even in the liberated stage. The difference is, however, that sense activities in liberation are accepted only in connection with Kṛṣṇa consciousness, whereas sense activities in the conditioned stage are enacted for personal sense gratification.

TEXT 32

मुनय ऊचुः
को वामिहैत्य भगवत्परिचर्ययोच्चै-
स्तद्धर्मिणां निवसतां विषमः स्वभावः ।
तस्मिन् प्रशान्तपुरुषे गतविग्रहे वां
को वात्मवत्कुहकयोः परिशङ्कनीयः ॥३२॥

munaya ūcuḥ
ko vām ihaitya bhagavat-paricaryayoccais
tad-dharmiṇāṁ nivasatāṁ viṣamaḥ svabhāvaḥ
tasmin praśānta-puruṣe gata-vigrahe vāṁ
ko vātmavat kuhakayoḥ pariśaṅkanīyaḥ

munayaḥ—the great sages; *ūcuḥ*—said; *kaḥ*—who; *vām*—you two; *iha*—in Vaikuṇṭha; *etya*—having attained; *bhagavat*—of the Supreme

Personality of Godhead; *paricaryayā*—by the service; *uccaiḥ*—having been developed by past pious actions; *tat-dharmiṇām*—of the devotees; *nivasatām*—dwelling in Vaikuṇṭha; *viṣamaḥ*—discordant; *sva-bhāvaḥ*—mentality; *tasmin*—in the Supreme Lord; *praśānta-puruṣe*—without anxieties; *gata-vigrahe*—without any enemy; *vām*—of you two; *kaḥ*—who; *vā*—or; *ātma-vat*—like yourselves; *kuhakayoḥ*—maintaining duplicity; *pariśaṅkanīyaḥ*—not becoming trustworthy.

TRANSLATION

The sages said: Who are these two persons who have developed such a discordant mentality even though they are posted in the service of the Lord in the highest position and are expected to have developed the same qualities as the Lord? How are these two persons living in Vaikuṇṭha? Where is the possibility of an enemy's coming into this kingdom of God? The Supreme Personality of Godhead has no enemy. Who could be envious of Him? Probably these two persons are imposters; therefore they suspect others to be like themselves.

PURPORT

The difference between the inhabitants of a Vaikuṇṭha planet and those of a material planet is that in Vaikuṇṭha all the residents engage in the service of the Lord Himself and are equipped with all His good qualities. It has been analyzed by great personalities that when a conditioned soul is liberated and becomes a devotee, about seventy-nine percent of all the good qualities of the Lord develop in his person. Therefore in the Vaikuṇṭha world there is no question of enmity between the Lord and the residents. Here in this material world the citizens may be inimical to the chief executives or heads of state, but in Vaikuṇṭha there is no such mentality. One is not allowed to enter Vaikuṇṭha unless he has completely developed the good qualities. The basic principle of goodness is to accept subordination to the Supreme Personality of Godhead. The sages, therefore, were surprised to see that the two doormen who checked them from entering the palace were not exactly like the residents of Vaikuṇṭhaloka. It may be said that a doorman's duty is to determine who should be allowed to enter the palace and who should not. But that is not relevant in this matter because no one is allowed to enter the Vaikuṇṭha planets unless he has developed one hundred percent his mentality of devotional service to the Supreme Lord. No enemy of the Lord can enter Vaikuṇṭhaloka. The Kumāras concluded that the only reason for the doormen's checking them was that the doormen themselves were imposters.

TEXT 33

न ह्यन्तरं भगवतीह समस्तकुक्षा-
वात्मानमात्मनि नभो नभसीव धीराः ।
पश्यन्ति यत्र युवयोः सुरलिङ्गिनोः किं
व्युत्पादितं ह्युदरभेदि भयं यतोऽस्य ॥३३॥

na hy antaraṁ bhagavatīha samasta-kukṣāv
ātmānam ātmani nabho nabhasīva dhīrāḥ
paśyanti yatra yuvayoḥ sura-liṅginoḥ kiṁ
vyutpāditaṁ hy udara-bhedi bhayaṁ yato 'sya

na—not; *hi*—because; *antaram*—distinction; *bhagavati*—in the Supreme Personality of Godhead; *iha*—here; *samasta-kukṣau*—everything is within the abdomen; *ātmānam*—the living entity; *ātmani*—in the Supersoul; *nabhaḥ*—the small quantity of air; *nabhasi*—within the whole air; *iva*—as; *dhīrāḥ*—the learned; *paśyanti*—see; *yatra*—in whom; *yuvayoḥ*—of you two; *sura-liṅginoḥ*—dressed like inhabitants of Vaikuṇṭha; *kim*—how; *vyutpāditam*—awakened, developed; *hi*—certainly; *udara-bhedi*—distinction between the body and the soul; *bhayam*—fearfulness; *yataḥ*—wherefrom; *asya*—of the Supreme Lord.

TRANSLATION

In the Vaikuṇṭha world there is complete harmony between the residents and the Supreme Personality of Godhead, just as there is complete harmony within space between the big and the small skies. Why then is there a seed of fear in this field of harmony? These two persons are dressed like inhabitants of Vaikuṇṭha, but wherefrom can their disharmony come into existence?

PURPORT

Just as there are different departments in each state in this material world—the civil department and the criminal department—so, in God's creation, there are two departments of existence. As in the material world we find that the criminal department is far, far smaller than the civil department, so this material world, which is considered the criminal department, is one fourth of the entire creation of the Lord. All living entities who are residents of the material universes are considered to be more or less criminals because they do not wish to abide by the order of the Lord or they are against the harmonious activities of God's will. The principle of creation is that the Supreme Lord, the Personality of Godhead, is by nature joyful, and He becomes many in order to enhance His transcendental joy. The living entities like ourselves, being part and parcel of the Supreme Lord, are meant to satisfy the senses of the Lord. Thus, whenever there is a discrepancy in that harmony, immediately the living entity is entrapped by *māyā*, or illusion.

The external energy of the Lord is called the material world, and the kingdom of the internal energy of the Lord is called Vaikuṇṭha, or the kingdom of God. In the Vaikuṇṭha world there is no disharmony between the Lord and the residents. Therefore God's creation in the Vaikuṇṭha world is perfect. There is no cause of fear. The entire kingdom of God is such a completely harmonious unit that there is no possibility of enmity. Everything there is absolute. Just as there are many physiological constructions within the body yet they work in one order for the satisfaction of the stomach, and just as in a machine there are hundreds and thousands of parts yet they run in harmony to fulfill the function of the machine, in the Vaikuṇṭha planets the Lord is perfect, and the inhabitants also perfectly engage in the service of the Lord.

The Māyāvādī philosophers, the impersonalists, interpret this verse of *Śrīmad-Bhāgavatam* to mean that the small sky and the big sky are one, but this idea cannot stand. The example of the big sky and the small skies is also applicable within a person's body. The big sky is the body itself, and the intestines and other parts of the body occupy the small sky. Each and every part of the body has individuality, even though occupying a small part of the total body. Similarly, the whole creation is the body of the Supreme Lord, and we created beings, or anything that is created, are but a small part of that body. The parts of the body are never equal to the whole. This is never possible. In *Bhagavad-gītā* it is said that the living entities, who are parts and parcels of the Supreme Lord, are eternally parts and parcels. According to the Māyāvādī philosophers, the living entity in illusion considers himself part and parcel although he is actually one and the same as the supreme whole. This theory is not valid. The oneness of the whole and the part is in their quality. The qualitative oneness of the small and large portions of the sky does not imply that the small sky becomes the big sky.

There is no cause for the politics of divide and rule in the Vaikuṇṭha planets; there is no fear, because of the united interests of the Lord and the residents. *Māyā* means disharmony between the living entities and the Supreme Lord, and Vaikuṇṭha means harmony between them. Actually all living entities are provided for and maintained by the Lord because He is the supreme living entity. But foolish creatures, although actually under the control of the supreme living entity, defy His existence, and that state is called *māyā*. Sometimes they deny that there is such a being as God. They say, "Everything is void." And sometimes they deny Him in a different way: "There may be a God, but He has no form." Both these conceptions arise from the rebellious condition of the living entity. As long as this rebellious condition prevails, the material world will continue in disharmony.

Harmony or disharmony is realized because of the law and order of a particular place. Religion is the law and order of the Supreme Lord. In the *Śrīmad Bhagavad-gītā* we find that religion means devotional service, or Kṛṣṇa consciousness. Kṛṣṇa says, "Give up all other religious principles and simply become a soul surrendered unto Me." This is religion. When one is fully conscious that Kṛṣṇa is the supreme enjoyer and Supreme Lord and one acts accordingly, that is real religion. Anything which goes against this principle is not religion. Kṛṣṇa therefore says: "Just give up all other religious principles." In the spiritual world this religious principle of Kṛṣṇa consciousness is maintained in harmony, and therefore that world is called Vaikuṇṭha. If the same principles can be adopted here, wholly or partially, then it is also Vaikuṇṭha. So it is with any society, such as the International Society for Krishna Consciousness: If the members of the International Society for Krishna Consciousness, putting faith in Kṛṣṇa as the center, live in harmony according to the order and principles of *Bhagavad-gītā,* then they are living in Vaikuṇṭha, not in this material world.

TEXT 34

तद्वाममुष्य परमस्य विकुण्ठभर्तुः
कर्तुं प्रकृष्टमिह धीमहि मन्दधीभ्याम् ।
लोकानितो व्रजतमन्तरभावदृष्ट्या
पापीयसस्त्रय इमे रिपवोऽस्य यत्र ॥३४॥

tad vām amuṣya paramasya vikuṇṭha-bhartuḥ
kartuṁ prakṛṣṭam iha dhīmahi manda-dhībhyām
lokān ito vrajatam antara-bhāva-dṛṣṭyā
pāpīyasas traya ime ripavo 'sya yatra

tat—therefore; *vām*—unto these two; *amuṣya*—of Him; *paramasya*—the Supreme; *vikuṇṭha-bhartuḥ*—the Lord of Vaikuṇṭha; *kartum*—to bestow; *prakṛṣṭam*—benefit; *iha*—in the matter of this offense; *dhīmahi*—let us consider; *manda-dhībhyām*—those whose intelligence is not very nice; *lokān*—to the material world; *itaḥ*—from this place (Vaikuṇṭha); *vrajatam*—go; *antara-bhāva*—duality; *dṛṣṭyā*—on account of seeing; *pāpīyasaḥ*—sinful; *trayaḥ*—three; *ime*—these; *ripavaḥ*—enemies; *asya*—of a living entity; *yatra*—where.

TRANSLATION

Therefore let us consider how these two contaminated persons should be punished. The punishment should be apt, for thus benefit can eventually be bestowed upon them. Since they find duality in the existence of Vaikuṇṭha life, they are contaminated and should be removed from this place to the material world, where the living entities have three kinds of enemies.

PURPORT

The reason why pure souls come into the existential circumstances of the material world, which is considered to be the criminal department of the Supreme Lord, is stated in *Bhagavad-gītā,* Seventh Chapter, verse 27. It is stated that as long as a living entity is pure, he is in complete harmony with the desires of the Supreme Lord, but as soon as he becomes impure he is in disharmony with the desires of the Lord. By contamination he is forced to transfer to this material world, where the living entities have three enemies, namely desire, anger and lust. These three enemies force the living entities to continue material existence, and when one is free from them he is eligible to enter the kingdom of God. One should not, therefore, be angry in the absence of an opportunity for sense gratification, and one should not be lusty to acquire more than necessary. In this verse it is clearly stated that the two doormen should be sent into the material world, where criminals are allowed to reside. Since the basic principles of criminality are sense gratification, anger and unnecessary lust, persons conducted by these three enemies of the living entity are never promoted to Vaikuṇṭhaloka. People should learn *Bhagavad-gītā* and accept the Supreme Personality of Godhead, Kṛṣṇa, as the Lord of everything; they should practice satisfying the senses of the Supreme Lord instead of trying to satisfy their own senses. Training in Kṛṣṇa consciousness will help one be promoted to Vaikuṇṭha.

TEXT 35

तेषामितीरितमुभाववधार्य घोरं
तं ब्रह्मदण्डमनिवारणमस्त्रपूगैः ।
सद्यो हरेरनुचरावुरु बिभ्यतस्तत्-
पादग्रहावपततामतिकातरेण ॥३५॥

teṣām itīritam ubhāv avadhārya ghoraṁ
taṁ brahma-daṇḍam anivāraṇam astra-pūgaiḥ
sadyo harer anucarāv uru bibhyatas tat-
pāda-grahāv apatatām atikātareṇa

teṣām—of the four Kumāras; *iti*—thus; *īritam*—uttered; *ubhau*—both doorkeepers; *avadhārya*—understanding; *ghoram*—terrible; *tam*—that; *brahma-daṇḍam*—curse of a *brāhmaṇa; anivāraṇam*—not able to be counteracted; *astra-pūgaiḥ*—by any kind of weapon; *sadyaḥ*—at once; *hareḥ*—of the Supreme Lord; *anucarau*—devotees; *uru*—very much; *bibhyataḥ*—became fearful; *tat-pāda-grahau*—

grasping their feet; *apatatām*—fell down; *ati-kātareṇa*—in great anxiety.

TRANSLATION

When the doormen of Vaikuṇṭhaloka, who were certainly devotees of the Lord, found that they were going to be cursed by the brāhmaṇas, they at once became very much afraid and fell down at the feet of the brāhmaṇas in great anxiety, for a brāhmaṇa's curse cannot be counteracted by any kind of weapon.

PURPORT

Although, by chance, the doormen committed a mistake by checking the *brāhmaṇas* from entering the gate of Vaikuṇṭha, they were at once aware of the gravity of the curse. There are many kinds of offenses, but the greatest offense is to offend a devotee of the Lord. Because the doormen were also devotees of the Lord, they were able to understand their mistake and were terrified when the four Kumāras were ready to curse them.

TEXT 36

भूयादघोनि भगवद्भिरकारि दण्डो
यो नौ हरेत सुरहेलनमप्यशेषम् ।
मा वोऽनुतापकलया भगवत्स्मृतिघ्नो
मोहो भवेदिह तु नौ व्रजतोरधोऽधः ॥३६॥

bhūyād aghoni bhagavadbhir akāri daṇḍo
yo nau hareta sura-helanam apy aśeṣam
mā vo 'nutāpa-kalayā bhagavat-smṛti-ghno
moho bhaved iha tu nau vrajator adho 'dhaḥ

bhūyāt—let it be; *aghoni*—for the sinful; *bhagavadbhiḥ*—by you; *akāri*—was done; *daṇḍaḥ*—punishment; *yaḥ*—that which; *nau*—in relation to us; *hareta*—should destroy; *sura-helanam*—disobeying great demigods; *api*—certainly; *aśeṣam*—unlimited; *mā*—not; *vaḥ*—of you; *anutāpa*—repentance; *kalayā*—by a little; *bhagavat*—of the Supreme Personality of Godhead; *smṛti-ghnaḥ*—destroying the memory of;

mohaḥ—illusion; *bhavet*—should be; *iha*—in the foolish species of life; *tu*—but; *nau*—of us; *vrajatoḥ*—who are going; *adhaḥ adhaḥ*—down to the material world.

TRANSLATION

After being cursed by the sages, the doormen said: It is quite apt that you have punished us for neglecting to respect sages like you. But we pray that due to your compassion at our repentance, the illusion of forgetting the Supreme Personality of Godhead will not come upon us as we go progressively downward.

PURPORT

To a devotee, any heavy punishment is tolerable but the one which effects forgetfulness of the Supreme Lord. The doormen, who were also devotees, could understand the punishment meted out to them, for they were conscious of the great offense they had committed by not allowing the sages to enter Vaikuṇṭhaloka. In the lowest species of life, including the animal species, forgetfulness of the Lord is very prominent. The doormen were aware that they were going to the criminal department of the material world, and they expected that they might go to the lowest species and forget the Supreme Lord. They prayed, therefore, that this might not happen in the lives they were going to accept because of the curse. In *Bhagavad-gītā*, Sixteenth Chapter, verses 19 and 20, it is said that those who are envious of the Lord and His devotees are thrown into the species of abominable life; life after life such fools are unable to remember the Supreme Personality of Godhead, and therefore they continue going down and down.

TEXT 37

एवं तदैव भगवानरविन्दनाभः
स्वानां विबुध्य सदतिक्रममार्यहृद्यः ।
तस्मिन् ययौ परमहंसमहामुनीना-
मन्वेषणीयचरणौ चलयन् सहश्रीः ॥३७॥

evaṁ tadaiva bhagavān aravinda-nābhaḥ
svānāṁ vibudhya sad-atikramam ārya-hṛdyaḥ

tasmin yayau paramahaṁsa-mahā-munīnām
anveṣaṇīya-caraṇau calayan saha-śrīḥ

evam—thus; *tadā eva*—at that very moment; *bhagavān*—the Supreme Personality of Godhead; *aravinda-nābhaḥ*—with a lotus growing from His navel; *svānām*—of His own servants; *vibudhya*—learned about; *sat*—to the great sages; *atikramam*—the insult; *ārya*—of the righteous; *hṛdyaḥ*—the delight; *tasmin*—there; *yayau*—went; *paramahaṁsa*—recluses; *mahā-munīnām*—by the great sages; *anveṣaṇīya*—which are worthy to be sought; *caraṇau*—the two lotus feet; *calayan*—walking; *saha-śrīḥ*—with the goddess of fortune.

TRANSLATION

At that very moment, the Lord, who is called Padmanābha because of the lotus grown from His navel and who is the delight of the righteous, learned about the insult offered by His own servants to the saints. Accompanied by His spouse, the goddess of fortune, He went to the spot on those very feet sought for by recluses and great sages.

PURPORT

In *Bhagavad-gītā* the Lord declares that His devotees cannot be vanquished at any time. The Lord could understand that the quarrel between the doormen and the sages was taking a different turn, and therefore He instantly came out of His place and went to the spot to stop further aggravation so that His devotees, the doormen, might not be vanquished for good.

TEXT 38

तं त्वागतं प्रतिहृतौपयिकं स्वपुम्भि-
स्तेऽचक्षताक्षविषयं स्वसमाधिभाग्यम् ।
हंसश्रियोर्व्यजनयोः शिववायुलोल-
च्छुभ्रातपत्रशशिकेसरशीकराम्बुम् ॥३८॥

taṁ tv āgataṁ pratihṛtaupayikaṁ sva-pumbhis
te 'cakṣatākṣa-viṣayaṁ sva-samādhi-bhāgyam

haṁsa-śriyor vyajanayoḥ śiva-vāyu-lolac-
chubhrātapatra-śaśi-kesara-śīkarāmbum

tam—Him; *tu*—but; *āgatam*—coming forward; *pratihṛta*—carried; *aupayikam*—the paraphernalia; *sva-pumbhiḥ*—by His own associates; *te*—the great sages (the Kumāras); *acakṣata*—saw; *akṣa-viṣayam*—now a subject matter for seeing; *sva-samādhi-bhāgyam*—visible simply by ecstatic trance; *haṁsa-śriyoḥ*—as beautiful as white swans; *vyajanayoḥ*—the *cāmaras* (bunches of white hair); *śiva-vāyu*—favorable winds; *lolat*—moving; *śubhra-ātapatra*—the white umbrella; *śaśi*—the moon; *kesara*—pearls; *śīkara*—drops; *ambum*—water.

TRANSLATION

The sages, headed by Sanaka Ṛṣi, saw that the Supreme Personality of Godhead, Viṣṇu, who was formerly visible only within their hearts in ecstatic trance, had now actually become visible to their eyes. As He came forward, accompanied by His own associates bearing all paraphernalia, such as an umbrella and a cāmara fan, the white bunches of hair moved very gently, like two swans, and due to their favorable breeze the pearls garlanding the umbrella also moved, like drops of nectar falling from the white full moon or ice melting due to a gust of wind.

PURPORT

In this verse we find the word *acakṣatākṣa-viṣayam.* The Supreme Lord cannot be seen by ordinary eyes, but He now became visible to the eyesight of the Kumāras. Another significant word is *samādhi-bhāgyam.* Meditators who are very fortunate can see the Viṣṇu form of the Lord within their hearts by following the yogic process. But to see Him face to face is a different matter. This is only possible for pure devotees. The Kumāras, therefore, upon seeing the Lord coming forward with His associates, who were holding an umbrella and a *cāmara* fan, were struck with wonder that they were seeing the Lord face to face. It is said in the *Brahma-saṁhitā* that devotees, being elevated in love of God, always see Śyāmasundara, the Supreme Personality of Godhead, within their hearts. But when they are mature, the same God is visible before them face to face. For ordinary persons the Lord is not visible; however, when one can understand the significance of His holy name and one engages himself in the devotional service of the Lord, beginning with the tongue, by chanting and tasting *prasāda*, then gradually the Lord reveals Himself. Thus the devotee constantly sees the Lord within his heart, and, in a more mature stage, one can see the same Lord directly, as we see everything else.

TEXT 39

कृत्स्नप्रसादसुमुखं स्पृहणीयधाम
स्नेहावलोककलया हृदि संस्पृशन्तम् ।
श्यामे पृथावुरसि शोभितया श्रिया स्व-
श्चूडामणिं सुभगयन्तमिवात्मधिष्ण्यम् ॥३९॥

kṛtsna-prasāda-sumukhaṁ spṛhaṇīya-dhāma
snehāvaloka-kalayā hṛdi saṁspṛśantam
śyāme pṛthāv urasi śobhitayā śriyā svaś-
cūḍāmaṇiṁ subhagayantam ivātma-dhiṣṇyam

kṛtsna-prasāda—blessing everyone; *su-mukham*—auspicious face; *spṛhaṇīya*—desirable; *dhāma*—shelter; *sneha*—affection; *avaloka*—looking upon; *kalayā*—by expansion; *hṛdi*—within the heart; *saṁspṛśantam*—touching; *śyāme*—unto the Lord with blackish color; *pṛthau*—broad; *urasi*—chest; *śobhitayā*—being decorated; *śriyā*—goddess of fortune; *svaḥ*—heavenly planets; *cūḍā-maṇim*—summit; *subhagayantam*—spreading good fortune; *iva*—like; *ātma*—the Supreme Personality of Godhead; *dhiṣṇyam*—abode.

TRANSLATION

The Lord is the reservoir of all pleasure. His auspicious presence is meant for everyone's benediction, and His affectionate smiling and glancing touch the core of the heart. The Lord's beautiful bodily color is blackish, and His broad chest is the resting place of the goddess of fortune, who glorifies the entire spiritual world, the summit of all heavenly planets. Thus it appeared that the Lord was personally spreading the beauty and good fortune of the spiritual world.

PURPORT

When the Lord came, He was pleased with everyone; therefore it is stated here, *kṛtsna-prasāda-sumukham.* The Lord knew that even the offensive doormen were His pure devotees, although by chance they committed an offense at the feet of other devotees. To commit an offense against a devotee is very dangerous in devotional service. Lord Caitanya therefore said that an offense to a devotee is just like a mad elephant run loose; when a mad elephant enters a garden, it tramples all the plants. Similarly, an offense unto the feet of a pure devotee murders one's position in devotional service. On the part of the Lord there was no offended mood because He does not accept any offense created by His sincere devotee. But a devotee should be very cautious of committing offenses at the feet of another devotee. The Lord, being equal to all, and being especially inclined to His devotee, looked as mercifully at the offenders as at the offended. This attitude of the Lord was due to His unlimited quantity of transcendental qualities. His cheerful attitude towards the devotees was so pleasing and heart-touching that His very smile was attractive for them. That attraction was glorious not only for all the higher planets of this material world, but beyond, for the spiritual world also. Generally a human being has no idea of what the constitutional position is in the higher material planets, which are far better constituted in regard to all paraphernalia, yet the Vaikuṇṭha planet is so pleasing and so celestial that it is compared to the middle jewel or locket in a necklace of jewels.

In this verse the words *spṛhaṇīya-dhāma* indicate that the Lord is the reservoir of all pleasure because He has all the transcendental qualities. Although only some of these are aspired for by persons who hanker after the pleasure of merging in the impersonal Brahman, there are other aspirants who want to associate with the Lord personally as His servants. The Lord is so kind that He gives shelter to everyone—both impersonalists and devotees. He gives shelter to the impersonalists in His impersonal Brahman effulgence, whereas He gives shelter to the devotees in His personal abodes known as the Vaikuṇṭhalokas. He is especially inclined to His devotee; He touches the core of the heart of the devotee simply by smiling and glancing over him. The Lord is always served in the Vaikuṇṭhaloka by many hundreds and thousands of goddesses of fortune, as stated by the *Brahma-saṁhitā* (*lakṣmī-sahasra-śata-sam-*

bhrama-sevyamānam). In this material world, one is glorified if he is favored even a pinch by the goddess of fortune, so we can simply imagine how glorified is the kingdom of God in the spiritual world, where many hundreds and thousands of goddesses of fortune engage in the direct service of the Lord. Another feature of this verse is that it openly declares where the Vaikuṇṭhalokas are situated. They are situated as the summit of all the heavenly planets, which are above the sun globe, at the upper limit of the universe, and are known as Satyaloka, or Brahmaloka. The spiritual world is situated beyond the universe. Therefore it is stated here that the spiritual world, Vaikuṇṭhaloka, is the summit of all planetary systems.

TEXT 40

पीतांशुके पृथुनितम्बिनि विस्फुरन्त्या
काञ्च्यालिभिर्विरुतया वनमालया च ।
वल्गुप्रकोष्ठवलयं विनतासुतांसे
विन्यस्तहस्तमितरेण धुनानमब्जम् ॥४०॥

pītāṁśuke pṛthu-nitambini visphurantyā
kāñcyālibhir virutayā vana-mālayā ca
valgu-prakoṣṭha-valayaṁ vinatā-sutāṁse
vinyasta-hastam itareṇa dhunānam abjam

pīta-aṁśuke—covered with a yellow cloth; *pṛthu-nitambini*—on His large hips; *visphurantyā*—shining brightly; *kāñcyā*—with a girdle; *alibhiḥ*—by the bees; *virutayā*—humming; *vana-mālayā*—with a garland of fresh flowers; *ca*—and; *valgu*—lovely; *prakoṣṭha*—wrists; *valayam*—bracelets; *vinatā-suta*—of Garuḍa, the son of Vinatā; *aṁse*—on the shoulder; *vinyasta*—rested; *hastam*—one hand; *itareṇa*—with another hand; *dhunānam*—being twirled; *abjam*—a lotus flower.

TRANSLATION

He was adorned with a girdle that shone brightly on the yellow cloth covering His large hips, and He wore a garland of fresh flowers which was distinguished by humming bees. His lovely

wrists were graced with bracelets, and He rested one of His hands on the shoulder of Garuḍa, His carrier, and twirled a lotus with another hand.

PURPORT

Here is a full description of the Personality of Godhead as personally experienced by the sages. The Lord's personal body was covered with yellow robes, and His waist was thin. In Vaikuṇṭha, whenever there is a flower garland on the chest of the Personality of Godhead or any one of His associates, it is described that the humming bees are there. All these features were very beautiful and attractive for the devotees. One of the Lord's hands rested on His carrier, Garuḍa, and in another hand He twirled a lotus flower. These are personal characteristics of the Personality of Godhead, Nārāyaṇa.

TEXT 41

विद्युत्क्षिपन्मकरकुण्डलमण्डनार्ह-
गण्डस्थलोन्नसमुखं मणिमत्किरीटम्।
दोर्दण्डषण्डविवरे हरता परार्ध्य-
हारेण कन्धरगतेन च कौस्तुभेन ॥४१॥

vidyut-kṣipan-makara-kuṇḍala-maṇḍanārha-
gaṇḍa-sthalonnasa-mukhaṁ maṇimat-kirīṭam
dor-daṇḍa-ṣaṇḍa-vivare haratā parārdhya-
hāreṇa kandhara-gatena ca kaustubhena

vidyut—lightning; *kṣipat*—outshining; *makara*—alligator shaped; *kuṇḍala*—earrings; *maṇḍana*—decoration; *arha*—as it fits; *gaṇḍa-sthala*—cheeks; *unnasa*—prominent nose; *mukham*—countenance; *maṇi-mat*—gem-studded; *kirīṭam*—crown; *doḥ-daṇḍa*—of His four stout arms; *ṣaṇḍa*—group; *vivare*—between; *haratā*—charming; *para-ardhya*—by the most precious; *hāreṇa*—necklace; *kandhara-gatena*—adorning His neck; *ca*—and; *kaustubhena*—by the Kaustubha jewel.

TRANSLATION

His countenance was distinguished by cheeks that enhanced the beauty of His alligator-shaped pendants, which outshone light-

ning. His nose was prominent, and His head was covered with a gem-studded crown. A charming necklace hung between His stout arms, and His neck was adorned with the gem known by the name Kaustubha.

TEXT 42

अत्रोपसृष्टमिति चोत्स्मितमिन्दिरायाः
स्वानां धिया विरचितं बहुसौष्ठवाढ्यम् ।
मह्यं भवस्य भवतां च भजन्तमङ्गं
नेमुर्निरीक्ष्य नवितृप्तदृशो मुदा कैः ॥४२॥

atropasṛṣṭam iti cotsmitam indirāyāḥ
svānāṁ dhiyā viracitaṁ bahu-sauṣṭhavāḍhyam
mahyaṁ bhavasya bhavatāṁ ca bhajantam aṅgaṁ
nemur nirīkṣya na vitṛpta-dṛśo mudā kaiḥ

atra—here, in the matter of the beauty; *upasṛṣṭam*—curbed down; *iti*—thus; *ca*—and; *utsmitam*—the pride of her beauty; *indirāyāḥ*—of the goddess of fortune; *svānām*—of His own devotees; *dhiyā*—by intelligence; *viracitam*—meditated on; *bahu-sauṣṭhava-āḍhyam*—very beautifully decorated; *mahyam*—of me; *bhavasya*—of Lord Śiva; *bhavatām*—of all of you; *ca*—and; *bhajantam*—worshiped; *aṅgam*—the figure; *nemuḥ*—bowed down; *nirīkṣya*—after seeing; *na*—not; *vitṛpta*—satiated; *dṛśaḥ*—eyes; *mudā*—joyously; *kaiḥ*—by their heads.

TRANSLATION

The exquisite beauty of Nārāyaṇa, being many times magnified by the intelligence of His devotees, was so attractive that it defeated the pride of the goddess of fortune in being the most beautiful. My dear demigods, the Lord who thus manifested Himself is worshipable by me, by Lord Śiva and by all of you. The sages regarded Him with unsated eyes and joyously bowed their heads at His lotus feet.

PURPORT

The beauty of the Lord was so enchanting that it could not be sufficiently described. The goddess of fortune is supposed to be the most beautiful sight within the spiritual and material creations of the Lord; she has a sense of being the most beautiful, yet her beauty was defeated when the Lord appeared. In other words, the beauty of the goddess of fortune is secondary in the presence of the Lord. In the words of Vaiṣṇava poets, it is said that the Lord's beauty is so enchanting that it defeats hundreds of thousands of Cupids. He is therefore called Madana-mohana. It is also described that the Lord sometimes becomes mad after the beauty of Rādhārāṇī. Poets describe that under those circumstances, although Lord Kṛṣṇa is Madana-mohana, He becomes Madana-dāha, or enchanted by the beauty of Rādhārāṇī. Actually the Lord's beauty is superexcellent, surpassing even the beauty of Lakṣmī in Vaikuṇṭha. The devotees of the Lord in the Vaikuṇṭha planets want to see the Lord as the most beautiful, but the devotees in Gokula or Kṛṣṇaloka want to see Rādhārāṇī as more beautiful than Kṛṣṇa. The adjustment is that the Lord, being *bhakta-vatsala*, or one who wants to please His devotees, assumes such features so that devotees like Lord Brahmā, Lord Śiva and other demigods may be pleased. Here also, for the devotee-sages, the Kumāras, the Lord appeared in His most beautiful feature, and they continued to see Him without satiation and wanted to continue seeing Him more and more.

TEXT 43

तस्यारविन्दनयनस्य पदारविन्द-
किञ्जल्कमिश्रतुलसीमकरन्दवायुः ।
अन्तर्गतः स्वविवरेण चकार तेषां
सङ्क्षोभमक्षरजुषामपि चित्ततन्वोः ॥४३॥

tasyāravinda-nayanasya padāravinda-
kiñjalka-miśra-tulasī-makaranda-vāyuḥ
antar-gataḥ sva-vivareṇa cakāra teṣāṁ
saṅkṣobham akṣara-juṣām api citta-tanvoḥ

tasya—of Him; *aravinda-nayanasya*—of the lotus-eyed Lord; *pada-aravinda*—of the lotus feet; *kiñjalka*—with the toes; *miśra*—mixed; *tulasī*—the *tulasī* leaves; *makaranda*—fragrance; *vāyuḥ*—breeze; *an-*

taḥ-gataḥ—entered within; *sva-vivareṇa*—through their nostrils; *cakāra*—made; *teṣām*—of the Kumāras; *saṅkṣobham*—agitation for change; *akṣara-juṣām*—attached to impersonal Brahman realization; *api*—even though; *citta-tanvoḥ*—in both mind and body.

TRANSLATION

When the breeze carrying the aroma of tulasī leaves from the toes of the lotus feet of the Personality of Godhead entered the nostrils of those sages, they experienced a change both in body and in mind, even though they were attached to the impersonal Brahman understanding.

PURPORT

It appears from this verse that the four Kumāras were impersonalists or protagonists of the philosophy of monism, becoming one with the Lord. But as soon as they saw the Lord's features, their minds changed. In other words, the impersonalist who feels transcendental pleasure in striving to become one with the Lord is defeated when he sees the beautiful transcendental features of the Lord. Because of the fragrance of His lotus feet, carried by the air and mixed with the aroma of *tulasī*, their minds changed; instead of becoming one with the Supreme Lord, they thought it wise to be devotees. Becoming a servitor of the lotus feet of the Lord is better than becoming one with the Lord.

TEXT 44

ते वा अमुष्य वदनासितपद्मकोश-
मुद्वीक्ष्य सुन्दरतराधरकुन्दहासम् ।
लब्धाशिषः पुनरवेक्ष्य तदीयमङ्घ्रि-
द्वन्द्वं नखारुणमणिश्रयणं निदध्युः ॥४४॥

te vā amuṣya vadanāsita-padma-kośam
udvīkṣya sundaratarādhara-kunda-hāsam
labdhāśiṣaḥ punar avekṣya tadīyam aṅghri-
dvandvaṁ nakhāruṇa-maṇi-śrayaṇaṁ nidadhyuḥ

te—those sages; *vai*—certainly; *amuṣya*—of the Supreme Personality of Godhead; *vadana*—face; *asita*—blue; *padma*—lotus; *kośam*—inside; *udvīkṣya*—after looking up; *sundara-tara*—more beautiful; *adhara*—lips; *kunda*—jasmine flower; *hāsam*—smiling; *labdha*—achieved; *āśiṣaḥ*—aims of life; *punaḥ*—again; *avekṣya*—looking down; *tadīyam*—His; *aṅghri-dvandvam*—pair of lotus feet; *nakha*—nails; *aruṇa*—red; *maṇi*—rubies; *śrayaṇam*—shelter; *nidadhyuḥ*—meditated.

TRANSLATION

The Lord's beautiful face appeared to them like the inside of a blue lotus, and the Lord's smile appeared to be a blossoming jasmine flower. After seeing the face of the Lord, the sages were fully satisfied, and when they wanted to see Him further, they looked upon the nails of His lotus feet, which resembled rubies. Thus they viewed the Lord's transcendental body again and again, and so they finally achieved meditation on the Lord's personal feature.

TEXT 45

पुंसां गतिं मृगयतामिह योगमार्गै-
ध्यार्नास्पदं बहु मतं नयनाभिरामम् ।
पौंस्नं वपुर्दर्शयानमनन्यसिद्धै-
रौत्पत्तिकैः समगृणन् युतमष्टभोगैः ॥४५॥

puṁsāṁ gatiṁ mṛgayatām iha yoga-mārgair
dhyānāspadaṁ bahu-mataṁ nayanābhirāmam
pauṁsnaṁ vapur darśayānam ananya-siddhair
autpattikaiḥ samagṛṇan yutam aṣṭa-bhogaiḥ

puṁsām—of those persons; *gatim*—liberation; *mṛgayatām*—who are searching; *iha*—here in this world; *yoga-mārgaiḥ*—by the process of *aṣṭāṅga-yoga; dhyāna-āspadam*—object of meditation; *bahu*—by the great *yogīs; matam*—approved; *nayana*—eyes; *abhirāmam*—pleasing; *pauṁsnam*—human; *vapuḥ*—form; *darśayānam*—displaying; *ananya*—not by others; *siddhaiḥ*—perfected; *autpattikaiḥ*—eternally present; *samagṛṇan*—praised; *yutam*—the Supreme Personality of Godhead, who is endowed; *aṣṭa-bhogaiḥ*—with eight kinds of achievement.

TRANSLATION

This is the form of the Lord which is meditated upon by the followers of the yoga process, and it is pleasing to the yogīs in meditation. It is not imaginary but factual, as proved by great yogīs. The Lord is full in eight kinds of achievement, but for others these achievements are not possible in full perfection.

PURPORT

The success of the *yoga* process is very nicely described here. It is specifically mentioned that the form of the Lord as four-handed Nārāyaṇa is the object of meditation for the followers of *yoga-mārga*. In the modern age there are so many so-called *yogīs* who do not target their meditation on the four-handed Nārāyaṇa form. Some of them try to meditate on something impersonal or void, but that is not approved by the great *yogīs* who follow the standard method. The real *yoga-mārga* process is to control the senses, sit in a solitary and sanctified place and meditate on the four-handed form of Nārāyaṇa, decorated as described in this chapter as He appeared before the four sages. This Nārāyaṇa form is Kṛṣṇa's expansion; therefore the Kṛṣṇa consciousness movement which is now spreading is the real, topmost process of *yoga* practice.

Kṛṣṇa consciousness is the highest *yoga* performance by trained devotional *yogīs*. Despite all the allurement of *yoga* practice, the eight kinds of yogic perfections are hardly achievable by the common man. But here it is described that the Lord, who appeared before the four sages, is Himself full of all eight of those perfections. The highest *yoga-mārga* process is to concentrate the mind twenty-four hours a day on Kṛṣṇa. This is called Kṛṣṇa consciousness. The *yoga* system, as described in *Śrīmad-Bhāgavatam* and *Bhagavad-gītā* or as recommended in the Patañjali *yoga* process, is different from the nowadays-practiced *haṭha-yoga* as it is generally understood in the Western countries. Real *yoga* practice is to control the senses and, after such control is established, to concentrate the mind on the Nārāyaṇa form of the Supreme Personality of Godhead,

Śrī Kṛṣṇa. Lord Kṛṣṇa is the original Personality of Godhead, and all the other Viṣṇu forms—with four hands decorated with conch, lotus, club and wheel—are plenary expansions of Kṛṣṇa. In *Bhagavad-gītā* it is recommended that one meditate upon the form of the Lord. To practice concentration of the mind, one has to sit with the head and the back in a straight line, and one must practice in a secluded place, sanctified by a sacred atmosphere. The *yogī* should observe the rules and regulations of *brahmacarya*—to strictly live a life of self-restraint and celibacy. One cannot practice *yoga* in a congested city, living a life of extravagancy, including unrestricted sex indulgence and adultery of the tongue. *Yoga* practice necessitates controlling the senses, and the beginning of sense control is to control the tongue. One who can control the tongue can also have control over the other senses. One cannot allow the tongue to take all kinds of forbidden food and drink and at the same time advance in the practice of *yoga*. It is a very regrettable fact that many unauthorized so-called *yogīs* come to the Western countries and exploit people's inclination towards *yoga* practice. Such unauthorized *yogīs* even dare to say publicly that one can indulge in the habit of drinking and at the same time practice meditation.

Five thousand years ago Lord Kṛṣṇa recommended *yoga* practice to Arjuna, but Arjuna frankly expressed his inability to follow the stringent rules and regulations of the *yoga* system. One should be very practical in every field of activities and should not waste his valuable time in practicing useless gymnastic feats in the name of *yoga*. Real *yoga* is to search out the four-handed Supersoul within one's heart and see Him perpetually in meditation. Such continued meditation is called *samādhi*, and the object of this meditation is the four-handed Nārāyaṇa, with bodily decorations as described in this chapter of *Śrīmad-Bhāgavatam*. If, however, one wants to meditate upon something void or impersonal, it will take a very long time before he achieves success in *yoga* practice. We cannot concentrate our mind on something void or impersonal. Real *yoga* is to fix the mind on the form of the Lord, the four-handed Nārāyaṇa who is sitting in everyone's heart.

By meditation one can understand that God is seated within one's heart. Even if one does not know it, God is seated within the heart of everyone. Not only is He seated in the heart of the human being, but He is also within the hearts of cats and dogs. *Bhagavad-gītā* certifies this fact by the declaration of the Lord, *īśvaraḥ sarva-bhūtānāṁ hṛd-deśe*. The *īśvara*, the supreme controller of the world, is seated in the heart of everyone. Not only is He in everyone's heart, but He is also present within the atom. No place is vacant or devoid of the presence of the Lord. That is the statement of *Īśopaniṣad*. God is present everywhere, and His right of proprietorship applies to everything. The feature of the Lord by which He is present everywhere is called Paramātmā. *Ātmā* means the individual soul, and Paramātmā means the individual Supersoul; both *ātmā* and Paramātmā are individual persons. The difference between *ātmā* and Paramātmā is that the *ātmā*, or the soul, is present only in a particular body, whereas the Paramātmā is present everywhere. In this connection, the example of the sun is very nice. An individual person may be situated in one place, but the sun, even though a similar individual entity, is present on the head of every individual person. In *Bhagavad-gītā* this is explained. Therefore even though the qualities of all entities, including the Lord, are equal, the Supersoul is different from the individual soul by quantitative power of expansion. The Lord, or the Supersoul, can expand Himself into millions of different forms, whereas the individual soul cannot do so.

The Supersoul, being seated in everyone's heart, can witness everyone's activities—past, present and future. In the *Upaniṣads* the Supersoul is described as being seated with the individual soul as friend and witness. As a friend, the Lord is always anxious to get back His friend, the individual soul, and bring him back home, back to Godhead. As a witness He is the bestower of all benedictions, and He endows each individual with the result of his actions. The Supersoul gives the individual soul all facilities to achieve whatever he desires to enjoy in this material world. Suffering is a reaction to the living entity's propensity to try to lord it over the material world. But the Lord instructs His friend, the individual soul, who is also His son, to give up all other engagements and simply surrender unto Him for perpetual bliss and an eternal life full of knowledge. This is the last instruction of *Bhagavad-gītā*, the most authorized and widely read book on all varieties of *yoga*. Thus the last word of *Bhagavad-gītā* is the last word in the perfection of *yoga*.

It is stated in *Bhagavad-gītā* that a person who is always absorbed in Kṛṣṇa consciousness is the topmost *yogī*. What is Kṛṣṇa consciousness? As the individual soul is present by his consciousness throughout his entire body, so the Supersoul, or Paramātmā, is present throughout the whole creation by superconsciousness. This superconscious energy is imitated by the individual soul, who has limited consciousness. I can understand what is going on within my limited body, but I cannot feel what is going on in another's body. I am present throughout my body by my consciousness, but my consciousness is not present in another's body. The Supersoul, or Paramātmā, however, being present everywhere and within everyone, is also conscious of everyone's existence. The theory that the soul and the Supersoul are one is not acceptable because it is not confirmed by authoritative Vedic literature. The individual soul's consciousness cannot act in superconsciousness. This superconsciousness can be achieved, however, by dovetailing individual consciousness with the consciousness of the Supreme. This dovetailing process is called surrender, or Kṛṣṇa consciousness. From the teachings of *Bhagavad-gītā* we learn very clearly that Arjuna, in the beginning, did not want to fight with his brothers and relatives, but after understanding *Bhagavad-gītā* he dovetailed his consciousness with the superconsciousness of Kṛṣṇa. He was then in Kṛṣṇa consciousness.

A person in full Kṛṣṇa consciousness acts by the dictation of Kṛṣṇa. In the beginning of Kṛṣṇa consciousness, dictation is received through the transparent medium of the spiritual master. When one is sufficiently trained and acts in submissive faith and love for Kṛṣṇa under the direction of the bona fide spiritual master, the dovetailing process becomes more firm and accurate. This stage of devotional service by the devotee in Kṛṣṇa consciousness is the most perfect stage of the *yoga* system. At this stage, Kṛṣṇa, or the Supersoul, dictates from within, while from without the devotee is helped by the spiritual master, who is the bona fide representative of Kṛṣṇa. From within He helps the devotee as *caitya*, for He is seated within the heart of everyone. Understanding that God is seated within everyone's heart is not, however, sufficient. One has to be acquainted with God from both within and without, and one must take dictation from within and without to act in Kṛṣṇa consciousness. This is the highest perfectional stage of the human form of life and the topmost perfection of all *yoga*.

For a perfect *yogī*, there are eight kinds of superachievements: one can become lighter than air, one can become smaller than the atom, one can become bigger than a mountain, one can achieve whatever he desires, one can control like the Lord, and so on. But when one rises to the perfectional stage of receiving dictation from the Lord, that is greater than any stage of material achievements above mentioned. The breathing exercise of the *yoga* system which is generally practiced is just the beginning. Meditation on the Supersoul is just another step forward. But to obtain direct contact with the Supersoul and take dictation from Him is the highest perfectional stage. The breathing exercises of meditation practice were very difficult even five thousand years ago, otherwise Arjuna would not have rejected the proposal of Kṛṣṇa that he adopt this system. This age of Kali is called the fallen age. In this age, people in general are short-living and very slow to understand self-realization or spiritual life; they are mostly unfortunate, and therefore if someone is a little bit interested in self-realization he is likely to be misguided by so many frauds. The only way to realize the perfect stage of *yoga* is to follow the principles of *Bhagavad-gītā* as practiced by Lord Caitanya. This is the simplest and highest perfection of *yoga* practice. Lord Caitanya demonstrated this Kṛṣṇa consciousness *yoga* system in a practical manner simply by chanting the holy name of Kṛṣṇa, as prescribed in the *Vedānta*, *Śrīmad-Bhāgavatam*, *Bhagavad-gītā*, and many important *Purāṇas*.

The largest number of Indians follow this *yoga* process, and in the United States it is gradually spreading in many cities. It is very easy and practical for this age, especially for those who are serious about success in *yoga*. No other process of *yoga* can be successful in this age. The meditation process was possible in the golden age, Satya-yuga, because people in that age used to live for hundreds of thousands of years. If one wants success in practical *yoga* practice, it is advised that he take to the chanting of Hare Kṛṣṇa, Hare Kṛṣṇa, Kṛṣṇa Kṛṣṇa, Hare Hare/ Hare Rāma, Hare Rāma, Rāma Rāma, Hare Hare, and he will actually feel himself making progress. In *Bhagavad-gītā* this practice of Kṛṣṇa consciousness is prescribed as *rāja-vidyā*, or the king of all erudition.

Those who have taken to this most sublime *bhakti-yoga* system, who practice devotional service in transcendental love of Kṛṣṇa, can testify to its happy and easy execution. The four sages Sanaka, Sanātana, Sanandana and Sanat-kumāra also became attracted by the features of the Lord and the transcendental aroma of the dust of His lotus feet, as already described in verse 43.

Yoga necessitates controlling the senses, and *bhakti-yoga*, or Kṛṣṇa consciousness, is the process of purifying the senses. When the senses are purified, they are automatically controlled. One cannot stop the activities of the senses by artificial means, but if one purifies the senses by engaging in the service of the Lord, the senses not only can be controlled from rubbish engagement, but can be engaged in the Lord's transcendental service, as aspired to by the four sages Sanaka, Sanātana, Sanandana and Sanat-kumāra. Kṛṣṇa consciousness is not, therefore, a manufactured concoction of the speculative mind. It is the process enjoined in *Bhagavad-gītā* (9.34): *man-manā bhava mad-bhakto mad-yājī māṁ namaskuru.*

TEXT 46

कुमारा ऊचुः

योऽन्तर्हितो हृदि गतोऽपि दुरात्मनां त्वं
सोऽद्यैव नो नयनमूलमनन्त राद्धः ।
यर्ह्येव कर्णविवरेण गुहां गतो नः
पित्रानुवर्णितरहा भवदुद्भवेन ॥४६॥

kumārā ūcuḥ
yo 'ntarhito hṛdi gato 'pi durātmanāṁ tvaṁ
so 'dyaiva no nayana-mūlam ananta rāddhaḥ
yarhy eva karṇa-vivareṇa guhāṁ gato naḥ
pitrānuvarṇita-rahā bhavad-udbhavena

kumārāḥ ūcuḥ—the Kumāras said; *yaḥ*—He who; *antarhitaḥ*—not manifested; *hṛdi*—in the heart; *gataḥ*—is seated; *api*—even though; *durātmanām*—to the rascals; *tvam*—You; *saḥ*—He; *adya*—today; *eva*—certainly; *naḥ*—of us; *nayana-mūlam*—face to face; *ananta*—O unlimited one; *rāddhaḥ*—attained; *yarhi*—when; *eva*—certainly; *karṇa-vivareṇa*—through the ears; *guhām*—intelligence; *gataḥ*—have attained; *naḥ*—our; *pitrā*—by our father; *anuvarṇita*—described; *rahāḥ*—mysteries; *bhavat-udbhavena*—by Your appearance.

TRANSLATION

The Kumāras said: Our dear Lord, You are not manifested to rascals, even though You are seated within the heart of everyone.

But as far as we are concerned, we see You face to face, although You are unlimited. The statements we have heard about You from our father, Brahmā, through the ears have now been actually realized by Your kind appearance.

PURPORT

The so-called *yogīs* who concentrate their mind or meditate upon the impersonal or void are described here. This verse of *Śrīmad-Bhāgavatam* describes persons who are expected to be very expert *yogīs* engaged in meditation but who do not find the Supreme Personality of Godhead seated within the heart. These persons are described here as *durātmā*, which means a person who has a very crooked heart, or a less intelligent person, just opposite to a *mahātmā*, which means one who has a broad heart. Those so-called *yogīs* who, although engaged in meditation, are not broad hearted cannot find the four-handed Nārāyaṇa form, even though He is seated within their heart. Although the first realization of the Supreme Absolute Truth is impersonal Brahman, one should not remain satisfied with experiencing the impersonal effulgence of the Supreme Lord. In the *Īśopaniṣad* also, the devotee prays that the glaring effulgence of Brahman may be removed from his eyes so that he can see the real, personal feature of the Lord and thus satisfy himself fully. Similarly, although the Lord is not visible in the beginning because of His glaring bodily effulgence, if a devotee sincerely wants to see Him, the Lord is revealed to him. It is said in *Bhagavad-gītā* that the Lord cannot be seen by our imperfect eyes, He cannot be heard by our imperfect ears, and He cannot be experienced by our imperfect senses; but if one engages in devotional service with faith and devotion, then God reveals Himself.

Here the four sages Sanat-kumāra, Sanātana, Sanandana and Sanaka are described as actually sincere devotees. Although they had heard from their father, Brahmā, about the personal feature of the Lord, only the impersonal feature—Brahman—was revealed to them. But because they were sincerely searching for the Lord, they finally saw His personal feature directly, which corresponded with the description given by their father. They thus became fully satisfied. Here they express their gratitude because although they were foolish impersonalists in the beginning, by the grace of the Lord they could now have the good fortune to see His personal feature. Another significant aspect of this verse is that the sages describe their experience of hearing from their father, Brahmā, who was born of the Lord directly. In other words, the disciplic succession from the Lord to Brahmā and from Brahmā to Nārada and from Nārada to Vyāsa, and so on, is accepted here. Because the Kumāras were sons of Brahmā, they had the opportunity to learn Vedic knowledge from the disciplic succession of Brahmā, and therefore, in spite of their impersonalist beginnings, they became, in the end, direct seers of the personal feature of the Lord.

TEXT 47

तं त्वां विदाम भगवन् परमात्मतत्त्वं
सत्त्वेन सम्प्रति रतिं रचयन्तमेषाम् ।
यत्तेऽनुतापविदितैर्दृढभक्तियोगै-
रुद्ग्रन्थयो हृदि विदुर्मुनयो विरागाः ॥४७॥

taṁ tvāṁ vidāma bhagavan param ātma-tattvaṁ
sattvena samprati ratiṁ racayantam eṣām
yat te 'nutāpa-viditair dṛḍha-bhakti-yogair
udgranthayo hṛdi vidur munayo virāgāḥ

tam—Him; *tvām*—You; *vidāma*—we know; *bhagavan*—O Supreme Personality of Godhead; *param*—the Supreme; *ātma-tattvam*—Absolute Truth; *sattvena*—by Your form of pure goodness; *samprati*—now; *ratim*—love of God; *racayantam*—creating; *eṣām*—of all of them; *yat*—which; *te*—Your; *anutāpa*—mercy; *viditaiḥ*—understood; *dṛḍha*—unflinching; *bhakti-yogaiḥ*—through devotional service; *udgranthayaḥ*—without attachment, free from material bondage; *hṛdi*—in the heart; *viduḥ*—understood; *munayaḥ*—great sages; *virāgāḥ*—not interested in material life.

TRANSLATION

We know that You are the Supreme Absolute Truth, the Personality of Godhead, who manifests His transcendental form in the uncontaminated mode of pure goodness. This transcendental, eternal form of Your personality can be understood only by Your

mercy, through unflinching devotional service, by great sages whose hearts have been purified in the devotional way.

PURPORT

The Absolute Truth can be understood in three features—impersonal Brahman, localized Paramātmā, and Bhagavān, the Supreme Personality of Godhead. Here it is admitted that the Supreme Personality of Godhead is the last word in understanding the Absolute Truth. Even though the four Kumāras were instructed by their great learned father, Brahmā, they could not actually understand the Absolute Truth. They could only understand the Supreme Absolute Truth when they personally saw the Personality of Godhead with their own eyes. In other words, if one sees or understands the Supreme Personality of Godhead, the other two features of the Absolute Truth—namely impersonal Brahman and localized Paramātmā—are also automatically understood. Therefore the Kumāras confirm: "You are the ultimate Absolute Truth." The impersonalist may argue that since the Supreme Personality of Godhead was so nicely decorated, He was therefore not the Absolute Truth. But here it is confirmed that all the variegatedness of the absolute platform is constituted of *śuddha-sattva,* pure goodness. In the material world, any quality—goodness, passion or ignorance—is contaminated. Even the quality of goodness here in the material world is not free from tinges of passion and ignorance. But in the transcendental world, only pure goodness, without any tinge of passion or ignorance, exists; therefore the form of the Supreme Personality of Godhead and His variegated pastimes and paraphernalia are all pure *sattva-guṇa.* Such variegatedness in pure goodness is exhibited eternally by the Lord for the satisfaction of the devotee. The devotee does not want to see the Supreme Personality of Absolute Truth in voidness or impersonalism. In one sense, absolute transcendental variegatedness is meant only for the devotees, not for others, because this distinct feature of transcendental variegatedness can be understood only by the mercy of the Supreme Lord and not by mental speculation or the ascending process. It is said that one can understand the Supreme Personality of Godhead when one is even slightly favored by Him; otherwise, without His mercy, a man may speculate for thousands of years and not understand what is actually the Absolute Truth.

This mercy can be perceived by the devotee when he is completely freed from contamination. It is stated, therefore, that only when all contamination is rooted out and the devotee is completely detached from material attractions can he receive this mercy of the Lord.

TEXT 48

नात्यन्तिकं विगणयन्त्यपि ते प्रसादं
किम्वन्यदर्पितभयं भ्रुव उन्नयैस्ते ।
येऽङ्ग त्वदङ्घ्रिशरणा भवतः कथायाः
कीर्तन्यतीर्थयशसः कुशला रसज्ञाः ॥४८॥

nātyantikaṁ vigaṇayanty api te prasādaṁ
kimv anyad arpita-bhayaṁ bhruva unnayais te
ye 'ṅga tvad-aṅghri-śaraṇā bhavataḥ kathāyāḥ
kīrtanya-tīrtha-yaśasaḥ kuśalā rasa-jñāḥ

na—not; *ātyantikam*—liberation; *vigaṇayanti*—care for; *api*—even; *te*—those; *prasādam*—benedictions; *kim u*—what to speak; *anyat*—other material happinesses; *arpita*—given; *bhayam*—fearfulness; *bhruvaḥ*—of the eyebrows; *unnayaiḥ*—by the raising; *te*—Your; *ye*—those devotees; *aṅga*—O Supreme Personality of Godhead; *tvat*—Your; *aṅghri*—lotus feet; *śaraṇāḥ*—who have taken shelter; *bhavataḥ*—Your; *kathāyāḥ*—narrations; *kīrtanya*—worth chanting; *tīrtha*—pure; *yaśasaḥ*—glories; *kuśalāḥ*—very expert; *rasa-jñāḥ*—knowers of the mellows or humors.

TRANSLATION

Persons who are very expert and most intelligent in understanding things as they are engage in hearing narrations of the auspicious activities and pastimes of the Lord, which are worth chanting and worth hearing. Such persons do not care even for the highest material benediction, namely liberation, to say nothing of other less important benedictions like the material happiness of the heavenly kingdom.

PURPORT

The transcendental bliss enjoyed by the devotees of the Lord is completely different from the material happiness enjoyed by less intelligent persons. The less intelligent persons in the material world are engaged by the four principles of benediction called *dharma*, *artha*, *kāma* and *mokṣa*. Generally they prefer to take to religious life to achieve some material benediction, the purpose of which is to satisfy the senses. When, by that process, they become confused or frustrated in fulfilling the maximum amount of sense enjoyment, they try to become one with the Supreme, which is, according to their conception, *mukti*, or liberation. There are five kinds of liberation, the least important of which is called *sāyujya*, to become one with the Supreme. Devotees don't care for such liberation because they are actually intelligent. Nor are they inclined to accept any of the other four kinds of liberation, namely to live on the same planet as the Lord, to live with Him side by side as an associate, to have the same opulence, and to attain the same bodily features. They are concerned only with glorifying the Supreme Lord and His auspicious activities. Pure devotional service is *śravaṇaṁ kīrtanam.* Pure devotees, who take transcendental pleasure in hearing and chanting the glories of the Lord, do not care for any kind of liberation; even if they are offered the five liberations, they refuse to accept them, as stated in the *Bhāgavatam* in the Third Canto. Materialistic persons aspire for the sense enjoyment of heavenly pleasure in the heavenly kingdom, but devotees reject such material pleasure at once. The devotee does not even care for the post of Indra. A devotee knows that any pleasurable material position is subject to be annihilated at a certain point. Even if one reaches the post of Indra, Candra, or any other demigod, he must be dissolved at a certain stage. A devotee is never interested in such temporary pleasure. From Vedic scriptures it is understood that sometimes even Brahmā and Indra fall down, but a devotee in the transcendental abode of the Lord never falls. This transcendental stage of life, in which one feels transcendental pleasure in hearing the Lord's pastimes, is also recommended by Lord Caitanya. When Lord Caitanya was talking with Rāmānanda Rāya, there were varieties of suggestions offered by Rāmānanda regarding spiritual realization, but Lord Caitanya rejected all but one—that one should hear the glories of the Lord in association with pure devotees.

That is acceptable for everyone, especially in this age. One should engage himself in hearing from pure devotees about the activities of the Lord. That is considered the supreme benediction for mankind.

TEXT 49

कामं भवः स्ववृजिनैर्निरयेषु नः स्ता-
च्चेतोऽलिवद्यदि नु ते पदयो रमेत ।
वाचश्च नस्तुलसिवद्यदि तेऽङ्घ्रिशोभाः
पूर्येत ते गुणगणैर्यदि कर्णरन्ध्रः ॥४९॥

kāmaṁ bhavaḥ sva-vṛjinair nirayeṣu naḥ stāc
ceto 'livad yadi nu te padayo rameta
vācaś ca nas tulasivad yadi te 'ṅghri-śobhāḥ
pūryeta te guṇa-gaṇair yadi karṇa-randhraḥ

kāmam—as much as deserved; *bhavaḥ*—birth; *sva-vṛjinaiḥ*—by our own sinful activities; *nirayeṣu*—in low births; *naḥ*—our; *stāt*—let it be; *cetaḥ*—minds; *ali-vat*—like bees; *yadi*—if; *nu*—may be; *te*—Your; *padayoḥ*—at Your lotus feet; *rameta*—are engaged; *vācaḥ*—words; *ca*—and; *naḥ*—our; *tulasi-vat*—like the *tulasī* leaves; *yadi*—if; *te*—Your; *aṅghri*—at Your lotus feet; *śobhāḥ*—beautified; *pūryeta*—are filled; *te*—Your; *guṇa-gaṇaiḥ*—by transcendental qualities; *yadi*—if; *karṇa-randhraḥ*—the holes of the ears.

TRANSLATION

O Lord, we pray that You let us be born in any hellish condition of life, just as long as our hearts and minds are always engaged in the service of Your lotus feet, our words are made beautiful [by speaking of Your activities] just as tulasī leaves are beautified when offered unto Your lotus feet, and as long as our ears are always filled with the chanting of Your transcendental qualities.

PURPORT

The four sages now offer their humility to the Personality of Godhead because of their having been haughty in cursing two other devotees of the Lord. Jaya and Vijaya, the two doorkeepers who checked them from entering the Vaikuṇṭha planet, were certainly offenders, but as Vaiṣṇavas, the four sages should not have cursed them in anger. After the incident, they became conscious that they had done wrong by cursing the devotees of the Lord, and they prayed to the Lord that even in the hellish condition of life their minds might not be distracted from the engagement of service to the lotus feet of Lord Nārāyaṇa. Those who are devotees of the Lord are not afraid of any condition of life, provided there is constant engagement in the service of the Lord. It is said of the *nārāyaṇa-para*, or those who are devotees of Nārāyaṇa, the Supreme Personality of Godhead, *na kutaścana bibhyati* (*Bhāg*. 6.17.28). They are not afraid of entering a hellish condition, for since they are engaged in the transcendental loving service of the Lord, heaven or hell is the same for them. In material life both heaven and hell are one and the same because they are material; in either place there is no engagement in the Lord's service. Therefore those who are engaged in the service of the Lord see no distinction between heaven and hell; it is only the materialists who prefer one to the other.

These four devotees prayed to the Lord that although they might go to hell because they had cursed devotees, they might not forget the service of the Lord. The transcendental loving service of the Lord is performed in three ways—with the body, with the mind and with words. Here the sages pray that their words may always be engaged in glorifying the Supreme Lord. One may speak very nicely with ornamental language or one may be expert at controlled grammatical presentation, but if one's words are not engaged in the service of the Lord, they have no flavor and no actual use. The example is given here of *tulasī* leaves. The *tulasī* leaf is very useful even from the medicinal or antiseptic point of view. It is considered sacred and is offered to the lotus feet of the Lord. The *tulasī* leaf has numerous good qualities, but if it were not offered to the lotus feet of the Lord, *tulasī* could not be of much value or importance. Similarly, one may speak very nicely from the rhetorical or grammatical point of view, which may be very much appreciated by a materialistic audience, but if one's words are not offered to the service of the Lord, they are useless. The holes of the ears are very small and can be filled with any insignificant sound, so how can they receive as great a vibration as the glorification of the Lord? The answer is that the holes of the ears are like the sky. As the sky can never be filled up, the quality of the ear is such that one may go on pouring in vibrations of various kinds, yet it is capable of receiving more and more vibrations. A devotee is not afraid of going to hell if he has the opportunity to hear the glories of the Lord constantly. This is the advantage of chanting Hare Kṛṣṇa, Hare Kṛṣṇa, Kṛṣṇa Kṛṣṇa, Hare Hare/ Hare Rāma, Hare Rāma, Rāma Rāma, Hare Hare. One may be put in any condition, but God gives him the prerogative to chant Hare Kṛṣṇa. In any condition of life, if one goes on chanting he will never be unhappy.

TEXT 50

प्रादुश्चकर्थ यदिदं पुरुहूत रूपं
तेनेश निर्वृतिमवापुरलं दृशो नः ।
तस्मा इदं भगवते नम इद्विधेम
योऽनात्मनां दुरुदयो भगवान् प्रतीतः ॥५०॥

prāduścakartha yad idaṁ puruhūta rūpaṁ
teneśa nirvṛtim avāpur alaṁ dṛśo naḥ
tasmā idaṁ bhagavate nama id vidhema
yo 'nātmanāṁ durudayo bhagavān pratītaḥ

prāduścakartha—You have manifested; *yat*—which; *idam*—this; *puruhūta*—O greatly worshiped; *rūpam*—eternal form; *tena*—by that form; *īśa*—O Lord; *nirvṛtim*—satisfaction; *avāpuḥ*—obtained; *alam*—so much; *dṛśaḥ*—vision; *naḥ*—our; *tasmai*—unto Him; *idam*—this; *bhagavate*—unto the Supreme Personality of Godhead; *namaḥ*—obeisances; *it*—only; *vidhema*—let us offer; *yaḥ*—who; *anātmanām*—of those who are less intelligent; *durudayaḥ*—cannot be seen; *bhagavān*—the Supreme Personality of Godhead; *pratītaḥ*—has been seen by us.

TRANSLATION

O Lord, we therefore offer our respectful obeisances unto Your eternal form as the Personality of Godhead, which You have so kindly manifested before us. Your supreme, eternal form cannot be seen by unfortunate, less intelligent persons, but we are so much satisfied in our mind and vision to see it.

PURPORT

The four sages were impersonalists in the beginning of their spiritual life, but afterwards, by the grace of their father and spiritual master, Brahmā, they understood the eternal, spiritual form of the Lord and felt completely satisfied. In other words, the transcendentalists who aspire to the impersonal Brahman or localized Paramātmā are not fully satisfied and still hanker for more. Even if they are satisfied in their minds, still, transcendentally, their eyes are not satisfied. But as soon as such persons come to realize the Supreme Personality of Godhead, they are satisfied in all respects. In other words, they become devotees and want to see the form of the Lord continually. It is confirmed in the *Brahma-saṁhitā* that one who has developed transcendental love of Kṛṣṇa by smearing his eyes with the ointment of love sees constantly the eternal form of the Lord. The particular word used in this connection, *anātmanām*, signifies those who have no control over the mind and senses and who therefore speculate and want to become one with the Lord. Such persons cannot have the pleasure of seeing the eternal form of the Lord. For the impersonalists and the so-called *yogīs*, the Lord is always hidden by the curtain of *yogamāyā*. *Bhagavad-gītā* says that even when Lord Kṛṣṇa was seen by everyone while He was present on the surface of the earth, the impersonalists and the so-called *yogīs* could not see Him because they were devoid of devotional eyesight. The theory of the impersonalists and so-called *yogīs* is that the Supreme Lord assumes a particular form when He comes in touch with *māyā*, although actually He has no form. This very conception of the impersonalists and so-called *yogīs* checks them from seeing the Supreme Personality of Godhead as He is. The Lord, therefore, is always beyond the sight of such nondevotees. The four sages felt so much obliged to the Lord that they offered their respectful obeisances unto Him again and again.

Thus end the Bhaktivedanta purports of the Third Canto, Fifteenth Chapter, of the Śrīmad-Bhāgavatam, *entitled "Description of the Kingdom of God."*

PURPORT

The four sages were impersonalists in the beginning of their spiritual life, but afterwards, by the grace of their father and spiritual master, Brahmā, they understood the eternal, spiritual form of the Lord and felt completely satisfied. In other words, the transcendentalists who aspire to the impersonal Brahman or localized Paramātmā are not fully satisfied and still hanker for more. Even if they are satisfied in their minds, still, transcendentally, their eyes are not satisfied. But as soon as such persons come to realize the Supreme Personality of Godhead, they are satisfied in all respects. In other words, they become devotees and want to see the form of the Lord continually. It is confirmed in the *Brahma-saṁhitā* that one who has developed transcendental love of Kṛṣṇa by smearing his eyes with the ointment of love sees constantly the eternal form of the Lord. The particular word used in this connection, *a-jitendriya*, signifies those who have no control over the senses and who therefore speculate and want to become one with the Lord. Such persons cannot have the pleasure of seeing the eternal form of the Lord. For the impersonalists and the so-called yogīs, the Lord is always hidden by the curtain of yogamāyā. *Bhagavad-gītā* says that even when Lord Kṛṣṇa was seen by everyone while He was present on the surface of the earth, the impersonalists and the so-called yogīs could not see Him because they were devoid of devotional eyesight. The theory of the impersonalists and so-called yogīs is that the Supreme Lord assumes a particular form when He comes in touch with *māyā*, although actually He has no form. This very conception of the impersonalists and so-called yogīs checks them from seeing the Supreme Personality of Godhead as He is. The Lord, therefore, is always beyond the sight of such nondevotees. The four sages felt so much obliged to the Lord that they offered their respectful obeisances unto Him again and again.

Thus end the Bhaktivedanta purports of the Third Canto, Fifteenth Chapter, of the Śrīmad-Bhāgavatam, entitled "Description of the Kingdom of God."

CHAPTER SIXTEEN

The Two Doorkeepers of Vaikuṇṭha, Jaya and Vijaya, Cursed by the Sages

TEXT 1

ब्रह्मोवाच

इति तद् गृणतां तेषां मुनीनां योगधर्मिणाम् ।
प्रतिनन्द्य जगादेदं विकुण्ठनिलयो विभुः ॥ १ ॥

brahmovāca

iti tad gṛṇatāṁ teṣāṁ
munīnāṁ yoga-dharmiṇām
pratinandya jagādedaṁ
vikuṇṭha-nilayo vibhuḥ

brahmā uvāca—Lord Brahmā said; *iti*—thus; *tat*—speech; *gṛṇatām*—praising; *teṣām*—of them; *munīnām*—those four sages; *yoga-dharmiṇām*—engaged in linking with the Supreme; *pratinandya*—after congratulating; *jagāda*—said; *idam*—these words; *vikuṇṭha-nilayaḥ*—whose abode is bereft of anxiety; *vibhuḥ*—the Supreme Personality of Godhead.

TRANSLATION

Lord Brahmā said: After thus congratulating the sages for their nice words, the Supreme Personality of Godhead, whose abode is in the kingdom of God, spoke as follows.

TEXT 2

श्रीभगवानुवाच

एतौ तौ पार्षदौ मह्यं जयो विजय एव च ।
कदर्थीकृत्य मां यद्वो बह्वक्रातामतिक्रमम् ॥ २ ॥

śrī-bhagavān uvāca
etau tau pārṣadau mahyaṁ
jayo vijaya eva ca
kadarthī-kṛtya māṁ yad vo
bahv akrātām atikramam

śrī-bhagavān uvāca—the Supreme Personality of Godhead said; *etau*—these two; *tau*—they; *pārṣadau*—attendants; *mahyam*—of Mine; *jayaḥ*—named Jaya; *vijayaḥ*—named Vijaya; *eva*—certainly; *ca*—and; *kadarthī-kṛtya*—by ignoring; *mām*—Me; *yat*—which; *vaḥ*—against you; *bahu*—great; *akrātām*—have committed; *atikramam*—offense.

TRANSLATION

The Personality of Godhead said: These attendants of Mine, Jaya and Vijaya by name, have committed a great offense against you because of ignoring Me.

PURPORT

To commit an offense at the feet of a devotee of the Lord is a great wrong. Even when a living entity is promoted to Vaikuṇṭha, there is still the chance that he may commit offenses, but the difference is that when one is in a Vaikuṇṭha planet, even if by chance one commits an offense, he is protected by the Lord. This is the remarkable fact in the dealings of the Lord and the servitor, as seen in the present incident concerning Jaya and Vijaya. The word *atikramam* used herein indicates that in offending a devotee one neglects the Supreme Lord Himself.

By mistake the doormen held the sages from entering Vaikuṇṭhaloka, but because they were engaged in the transcendental service of the Lord, their annihilation was not expected by advanced devotees. The Lord's presence on the spot was very pleasing to the hearts of the devotees. The Lord understood that the trouble was due to His lotus feet not being seen by the sages, and therefore He wanted to please them by personally going there. The Lord is so merciful that even if there is some impediment for the devotee, He Himself manages matters in such a way that the devotee is not bereft of having audience at His lotus feet. There is a very good example in the life of Haridāsa Ṭhākura. When Caitanya Mahāprabhu was residing at Jagannātha Purī, Haridāsa Ṭhākura, who happened to be Muhammadan by birth, was with Him. In Hindu temples, especially in those days, no one but a Hindu was allowed to enter. Although Haridāsa Ṭhākura was the greatest of all Hindus in his behavior, he considered himself a Muhammadan and did not enter the temple. Lord Caitanya could understand his humility, and since he did not go to see the temple, Lord Caitanya Himself, who is nondifferent from Jagannātha, used to come and sit with Haridāsa Ṭhākura daily. Here in *Śrīmad-Bhāgavatam* we also find this same behavior of the Lord. His devotees were prevented from seeing His lotus feet, but the Lord Himself came to see them on the same lotus feet for which they aspired. It is also significant that He was accompanied by the goddess of fortune. The goddess of fortune is not to be seen by ordinary persons, but the Lord was so kind that although the devotees did not aspire for such an honor, He appeared before them with the goddess of fortune.

TEXT 3

यस्त्वेतयोर्धृतो दण्डो भवद्भिर्मामनुव्रतैः ।
स एवानुमतोऽस्माभिर्मुनयो देवहेलनात् ॥ ३ ॥

yas tv etayor dhṛto daṇḍo
bhavadbhir mām anuvrataiḥ
sa evānumato 'smābhir
munayo deva-helanāt

yaḥ—which; *tu*—but; *etayoḥ*—regarding both Jaya and Vijaya; *dhṛtaḥ*—has been given; *daṇḍaḥ*—punishment; *bhavadbhiḥ*—by you; *mām*—Me; *anuvrataiḥ*—devoted to; *saḥ*—that; *eva*—certainly; *anumataḥ*—is approved; *asmābhiḥ*—by Me; *munayaḥ*—O great sages; *deva*—against you; *helanāt*—because of an offense.

TRANSLATION

O great sages, I approve of the punishment that you who are devoted to Me have meted out to them.

TEXT 4

तद्वः प्रसादयाम्यद्य ब्रह्म दैवं परं हि मे ।
तद्धीत्यात्मकृतं मन्ये यत्स्वपुम्भिरसत्कृताः ॥ ४ ॥

tad vaḥ prasādayāmy adya
brahma daivaṁ paraṁ hi me
tad dhīty ātma-kṛtaṁ manye
yat sva-pumbhir asat-kṛtāḥ

tat—therefore; *vaḥ*—you sages; *prasādayāmi*—I am seeking your forgiveness; *adya*—just now; *brahma*—the *brāhmaṇas; daivam*—most beloved personalities; *param*—highest; *hi*—because; *me*—My; *tat*—that offense; *hi*—because; *iti*—thus; *ātma-kṛtam*—done by Me; *manye*—I consider; *yat*—which; *sva-pumbhiḥ*—by My own attendants; *asat-kṛtāḥ*—having been disrespected.

TRANSLATION

To Me, the brāhmaṇa is the highest and most beloved personality. The disrespect shown by My attendants has actually been displayed by Me because the doormen are My servitors. I take this to be an offense by Myself; therefore I seek your forgiveness for the incident that has arisen.

PURPORT

The Lord is always in favor of the *brāhmaṇas* and the cows, and therefore it is said, *go-brāhmaṇa-hitāya ca.* Lord Kṛṣṇa, or Viṣṇu, the Supreme Personality of Godhead, is also the worshipable Deity of the *brāhmaṇas.* In the Vedic literature, in the *ṛg-mantra* hymns of the *Ṛg Veda,* it is stated that those who are actually *brāhmaṇas* always look to the lotus feet of Viṣṇu: *oṁ tad viṣṇoḥ paramaṁ padaṁ sadā paśyanti sūrayaḥ.* Those who are qualified *brāhmaṇas* worship only the Viṣṇu form of the Supreme Personality of Godhead, which means Kṛṣṇa, Rāma and all Viṣṇu expansions. A so-called *brāhmaṇa* who is born in the family of *brāhmaṇas* but performs activities aimed against the Vaiṣṇavas cannot be accepted as a *brāhmaṇa,* because *brāhmaṇa* means Vaiṣṇava and Vaiṣṇava means *brāhmaṇa.* One who has become a devotee of the

Lord is also a *brāhmaṇa*. The formula is *brahma jānātīti brāhmaṇaḥ*. A *brāhmaṇa* is one who has understood Brahman, and a Vaiṣṇava is one who has understood the Personality of Godhead. Brahman realization is the beginning of realization of the Personality of Godhead. One who understands the Personality of Godhead also knows the impersonal feature of the Supreme, which is Brahman. Therefore one who becomes a Vaiṣṇava is already a *brāhmaṇa*. It should be noted that the glories of the *brāhmaṇa* described in this chapter by the Lord Himself refer to His devotee-*brāhmaṇa*, or the Vaiṣṇava. It should never be misunderstood that the so-called *brāhmaṇas* who are born in *brāhmaṇa* families but have no brahminical qualifications are referred to in this connection.

TEXT 5

यन्नामानि च गृह्णाति लोको भृत्ये कृतागसि ।
सोऽसाधुवादस्तत्कीर्तिं हन्ति त्वचमिवामयः ॥ ५ ॥

yan-nāmāni ca gṛhṇāti
loko bhṛtye kṛtāgasi
so 'sādhu-vādas tat-kīrtiṁ
hanti tvacam ivāmayaḥ

yat—of whom; *nāmāni*—the names; *ca*—and; *gṛhṇāti*—take; *lokaḥ*—people in general; *bhṛtye*—when a servant; *kṛta-āgasi*—has committed something wrong; *saḥ*—that; *asādhu-vādaḥ*—blame; *tat*—of that person; *kīrtim*—the reputation; *hanti*—destroys; *tvacam*—the skin; *iva*—as; *āmayaḥ*—leprosy.

TRANSLATION

A wrong act committed by a servant leads people in general to blame his master, just as a spot of white leprosy on any part of the body pollutes all of the skin.

PURPORT

A Vaiṣṇava, therefore, should be fully qualified. As stated in the *Bhāgavatam*, anyone who has become a Vaiṣṇava has developed all the good qualities of the demigods. There are twenty-six qualifications mentioned in the *Caitanya-caritāmṛta.* A devotee should always see that his Vaiṣṇava qualities increase with the advancement of his Kṛṣṇa consciousness. A devotee should be blameless because any offense by the devotee is a scar on the Supreme Personality of Godhead. The devotee's duty is to be always conscious in his dealings with others, especially with another devotee of the Lord.

TEXT 6

यस्यामृतामलयशःश्रवणावगाहः
सद्यः पुनाति जगदाश्वपचाद्विकुण्ठः ।
सोऽहं भवद्भ्य उपलब्धसुतीर्थकीर्ति-
श्छिन्द्यां स्वबाहुमपि वः प्रतिकूलवृत्तिम् ॥ ६ ॥

yasyāmṛtāmala-yaśaḥ-śravaṇāvagāhaḥ
sadyaḥ punāti jagad āśvapacād vikuṇṭhaḥ
so 'haṁ bhavadbhya upalabdha-sutīrtha-kīrtiś
chindyāṁ sva-bāhum api vaḥ pratikūla-vṛttim

yasya—of whom; *amṛta*—nectar; *amala*—uncontaminated; *yaśaḥ*—glories; *śravaṇa*—hearing; *avagāhaḥ*—entering into; *sadyaḥ*—immediately; *punāti*—purifies; *jagat*—the universe; *āśva-pacāt*—including even the dog-eaters; *vikuṇṭhaḥ*—without anxiety; *saḥ*—that person; *aham*—I am; *bhavadbhyaḥ*—from you; *upalabdha*—obtained; *sutīrtha*—the best place of pilgrimage; *kīrtiḥ*—the fame; *chindyām*—would cut off; *sva-bāhum*—My own arm; *api*—even; *vaḥ*—towards you; *pratikūla-vṛttim*—acting inimically.

TRANSLATION

Anyone in the entire world, even down to the caṇḍāla, who lives by cooking and eating the flesh of the dog, is immediately purified if he takes bath in hearing through the ear the glorification of My name, fame, etc. Now you have realized Me without doubt; therefore I will not hesitate to lop off My own arm if its conduct is found hostile to you.

PURPORT

Real purification can take place in human society if its members take to Kṛṣṇa consciousness. This is clearly stated in all Vedic literature. Anyone who takes to Kṛṣṇa consciousness in all sincerity, even if he is not very advanced in good behavior, is purified. A devotee can be recruited from any section of human society, although it is not expected that everyone in all segments of society is well behaved. As stated in this verse and in many places in *Bhagavad-gītā*, even if one is not born in a *brāhmaṇa* family, or even if he is born in a family of *caṇḍālas*, if he simply takes to Kṛṣṇa consciousness he is immediately purified. In *Bhagavad-gītā*, Ninth Chapter, verses 30–32, it is clearly stated that even though a man is not well behaved, if he simply takes to Kṛṣṇa consciousness he is understood to be a saintly person. As long as a person is in this material world he has two different relationships in his dealings with others—one relationship pertains to the body, and the other pertains to the spirit. As far as bodily affairs or social activities are concerned, although a person is purified on the spiritual platform, it is sometimes seen that he acts in terms of his bodily relationships. If a devotee born in the family of a *caṇḍāla* (the lowest caste) is sometimes found engaged in his habitual activities, he is not to be considered a *caṇḍāla*. In other words, a Vaiṣṇava should not be evaluated in terms of his body. The *śāstra* states that no one should think the Deity in the temple to be made of wood or stone, and no one should think that a person coming from a lower-caste family who has taken to Kṛṣṇa consciousness is still of the same low caste. These attitudes are forbidden because anyone who takes to Kṛṣṇa consciousness is understood to be fully purified. He is at least engaged in the process of purification, and if he sticks to the principle of Kṛṣṇa consciousness he will very soon be fully purified. The conclusion is that if one takes to Kṛṣṇa consciousness with all seriousness, he is to be understood as already purified, and Kṛṣṇa is ready to give him protection by all means. The Lord assures herein that He is ready to give protection to His devotee even if there is need to cut off part of His own body.

TEXT 7

यत्सेवया चरणपद्मपवित्ररेणुं
सद्यःक्षताखिलमलं प्रतिलब्धशीलम् ।

न श्रीर्विरक्तमपि मां विजहाति यस्याः
प्रेक्षालवार्थ इतरे नियमान् वहन्ति ॥ ७ ॥

yat-sevayā caraṇa-padma-pavitra-reṇuṁ
sadyaḥ kṣatākhila-malaṁ pratilabdha-śīlam
na śrīr viraktam api māṁ vijahāti yasyāḥ
prekṣā-lavārtha itare niyamān vahanti

yat—of whom; *sevayā*—by the service; *caraṇa*—feet; *padma*—lotus; *pavitra*—sacred; *reṇum*—the dust; *sadyaḥ*—immediately; *kṣata*—wiped out; *akhila*—all; *malam*—sins; *pratilabdha*—acquired; *śīlam*—disposition; *na*—not; *śrīḥ*—the goddess of fortune; *viraktam*—have no attachment; *api*—even though; *mām*—Me; *vijahāti*—leave; *yasyāḥ*—of the goddess of fortune; *prekṣā-lava-arthaḥ*—for obtaining a slight favor; *itare*—others, like Lord Brahmā; *niyamān*—sacred vows; *vahanti*—observe.

TRANSLATION

The Lord continued: Because I am the servitor of My devotees, My lotus feet have become so sacred that they immediately wipe out all sin, and I have acquired such a disposition that the goddess of fortune does not leave Me, even though I have no attachment for her and others praise her beauty and observe sacred vows to secure from her even a slight favor.

PURPORT

The relationship between the Lord and His devotee is transcendentally beautiful. As the devotee thinks that it is due to being a devotee of the Lord that he is elevated in all good qualities, so the Lord also thinks that it is because of His devotion to the servitor that all His transcendental glories have increased. In other words, as the devotee is always anxious to render service to the Lord, so the Lord is ever anxious to render service to the devotee. The Lord admits herein that although He certainly has the quality that anyone who receives a slight particle of the dust of His lotus feet becomes at once a great personality, this greatness is due to His affection for His devotee. It is because of this affection that the goddess of fortune does not leave Him and that not only one but many thousands of goddesses of fortune engage in His service. In the material world, simply to get a little favor from the goddess of fortune, people observe many rigid regulations of austerity and penance. The Lord cannot tolerate any inconvenience on the part of the devotee. He is therefore famous as *bhakta-vatsala.*

TEXT 8

नाहं तथाद्मि यजमानहविर्विताने
श्च्योतद्घृतप्लुतमदन् हुतभुङ्मुखेन ।
यद्ब्राह्मणस्य मुखतश्चरतोऽनुघासं
तुष्टस्य मय्यवहितैर्निजकर्मपाकैः ॥ ८ ॥

nāhaṁ tathādmi yajamāna-havir vitāne
ścyotad-ghṛta-plutam adan huta-bhuṅ-mukhena
yad brāhmaṇasya mukhataś carato 'nughāsaṁ
tuṣṭasya mayy avahitair nija-karma-pākaiḥ

na—not; *aham*—I; *tathā*—on the other hand; *admi*—I eat; *yajamāna*—by the sacrificer; *haviḥ*—the oblations; *vitāne*—in the sacrificial fire; *ścyotat*—pouring; *ghṛta*—ghee; *plutam*—mixed; *adan*—eating; *huta-bhuk*—the sacrificial fire; *mukhena*—by the mouth; *yat*—as; *brāhmaṇasya*—of the *brāhmaṇa; mukhataḥ*—from the mouth; *carataḥ*—acting; *anughāsam*—morsels; *tuṣṭasya*—satisfied; *mayi*—to Me; *avahitaiḥ*—offered; *nija*—own; *karma*—activities; *pākaiḥ*—by the results.

TRANSLATION

I do not enjoy the oblations offered by the sacrificers in the sacrificial fire, which is one of My own mouths, with the same relish as I do the delicacies overflowing with ghee which are offered to the mouths of the brāhmaṇas who have dedicated to Me the results of their activities and who are ever satisfied with My prasāda.

PURPORT

The devotee of the Lord, or the Vaiṣṇava, does not take anything without offering it to the Lord. Since a Vaiṣṇava dedicates all the results of his activities to the Lord, he does not taste anything eatable which is not first offered to Him. The Lord also relishes giving to the Vaiṣṇava's mouth all eatables offered to Him. It is clear from this verse that the Lord eats through the sacrificial fire and the *brāhmaṇa*'s mouth. So many articles—grains, ghee, etc.—are offered in sacrifice for the satisfaction of the Lord. The Lord accepts sacrificial offerings from the *brāhmaṇas* and devotees, and elsewhere it is stated that whatever is given for the *brāhmaṇas* and Vaiṣṇavas to eat is also accepted by the Lord. But here it is said that He accepts offerings to the mouths of *brāhmaṇas* and Vaiṣṇavas with even greater relish. The best example of this is found in the life of Advaita Prabhu in his dealings with Haridāsa Ṭhākura. Even though Haridāsa was born of a Muhammadan family, Advaita Prabhu offered him the first dish of *prasāda* after the performance of a sacred fire ceremony. Haridāsa Ṭhākura informed him that he was born of a Muhammadan family and asked why Advaita Prabhu was offering the first dish to a Muhammadan instead of an elevated *brāhmaṇa*. Out of his humbleness, Haridāsa condemned himself a Muhammadan, but Advaita Prabhu, being an experienced devotee, accepted him as a real *brāhmaṇa*. Advaita Prabhu asserted that by offering the first dish to Haridāsa Ṭhākura, he was getting the result of feeding one hundred thousand *brāhmaṇas*. The conclusion is that if one can feed a *brāhmaṇa* or Vaiṣṇava, it is better than performing hundreds of thousands of sacrifices. In this age, therefore, it is recommended that *harer nāma*—chanting the holy name of God—and pleasing the Vaiṣṇava are the only means to elevate oneself to spiritual life.

TEXT 9

येषां बिभर्म्यहमखण्डविकुण्ठयोग-
मायाविभूतिरमलाङ्घ्रिरजः किरीटैः ।
विप्रांस्तु को न विषहेत यदर्हणाम्भः
सद्यः पुनाति सहचन्द्रललामलोकान् ॥९॥

yeṣāṁ bibharmy aham akhaṇḍa-vikuṇṭha-yoga-
māyā-vibhūtir amalāṅghri-rajaḥ kirīṭaiḥ
viprāṁs tu ko na viṣaheta yad-arhaṇāmbhaḥ
sadyaḥ punāti saha-candra-lalāma-lokān

yeṣām—of the *brāhmaṇas; bibharmi*—I bear; *aham*—I; *akhaṇḍa*—unbroken; *vikuṇṭha*—unobstructed; *yoga-māyā*—internal energy; *vibhūtiḥ*—opulence; *amala*—pure; *aṅghri*—of the feet; *rajaḥ*—the dust; *kirīṭaiḥ*—on My helmet; *viprān*—the *brāhmaṇas; tu*—then; *kaḥ*—who; *na*—not; *viṣaheta*—carry; *yat*—of the Supreme Lord; *arhaṇa-ambhaḥ*—water which has washed the feet; *sadyaḥ*—at once; *punāti*—sanctifies; *saha*—along with; *candra-lalāma*—Lord Śiva; *lokān*—the three worlds.

TRANSLATION

I am the master of My unobstructed internal energy, and the water of the Ganges is the remnant left after My feet are washed. That water sanctifies the three worlds, along with Lord Śiva, who bears it on his head. If I can take the dust of the feet of the Vaiṣṇava on My head, who will refuse to do the same?

PURPORT

The difference between the internal and external energies of the Supreme Personality of Godhead is that in the internal energy, or in the spiritual world, all the opulences are undisturbed, whereas in the external or material energy, all the opulences are temporary manifestations. The Lord's supremacy is equal in both the spiritual and material worlds, but the spiritual world is called the kingdom of God, and the material world is called the kingdom of *māyā. Māyā* refers to that which is not actually fact. The opulence of the material world is a reflection. It is stated in *Bhagavad-gītā* that this material world is just like a tree whose roots are up and branches down. This means that the material world is the shadow of the spiritual world. Real opulence is in the spiritual world. In the spiritual world the predominating Deity is the Lord Himself, whereas in the material world there are many lords. That is the difference between the internal and external energies. The Lord says that although He is the predominating factor of the internal energy and although the material world is sanctified just by the water that has washed His feet, He has the greatest respect for the *brāhmaṇa* and the Vaiṣṇava. When the Lord Himself offers so much respect to the Vaiṣṇava and the *brāhmaṇa*, how can one deny such respect to such personalities?

TEXT 10

ये मे तनूर्द्विजवरान्दुहतीर्मदीया
भूतान्यलब्धशरणानि च भेदबुद्ध्या ।
द्रक्ष्यन्त्यघक्षतदृशो ह्यहिमन्यवस्तान्
गृध्रा रुषा मम कुषन्त्यधिदण्डनेतुः ॥१०॥

ye me tanūr dvija-varān duhatīr madīyā
bhūtāny alabdha-śaraṇāni ca bheda-buddhyā
drakṣyanty agha-kṣata-dṛśo hy ahi-manyavas tān
gṛdhrā ruṣā mama kuṣanty adhidaṇḍa-netuḥ

ye—which persons; *me*—My; *tanūḥ*—body; *dvija-varān*—the best of the *brāhmaṇas; duhatīḥ*—cows; *madīyāḥ*—relating to Me; *bhūtāni*—living entities; *alabdha-śaraṇāni*—defenseless; *ca*—and; *bheda-buddhyā*—considering as different; *drakṣyanti*—see; *agha*—by sin; *kṣata*—is impaired; *dṛśaḥ*—whose faculty of judgment; *hi*—because; *ahi*—like a snake; *manyavaḥ*—angry; *tān*—those same persons; *gṛdhrāḥ*—the vulturelike messengers; *ruṣā*—angrily; *mama*—My; *kuṣanti*—tear; *adhidaṇḍa-netuḥ*—of the superintendent of punishment, Yamarāja.

TRANSLATION

The brāhmaṇas, the cows and the defenseless creatures are My own body. Those whose faculty of judgment has been impaired by their own sin look upon these as distinct from Me. They are just like furious serpents, and they are angrily torn apart by the bills of the vulturelike messengers of Yamarāja, the superintendent of sinful persons.

PURPORT

The defenseless creatures, according to *Brahma-saṁhitā*, are the cows, *brāhmaṇas*, women, children and old men. Of these five, the *brāhmaṇas* and cows are especially mentioned in this verse because the Lord is always anxious about the benefit of the *brāhmaṇas* and the cows and is prayed to in this way. The Lord especially instructs, therefore, that no one should be envious of these five, especially the cows and *brāhmaṇas*. In some of the *Bhāgavatam* readings, the word *duhitṝḥ* is used instead of *duhatīḥ*. But in either case, the meaning is the same. *Duhatīḥ* means "cow," and *duhitṝḥ* can also be used to mean "cow" because the cow is supposed to be the daughter of the sun-god. Just as children are taken care of by the parents, women as a class should be taken care of by the father, husband or grown-up son. Those who are helpless must be taken care of by their respective guardians, otherwise the guardians will be subjected to the punishment of Yamarāja, who is appointed by the Lord to supervise the activities of sinful living creatures. The assistants, or messengers, of Yamarāja are likened here to vultures, and those who do not execute their respective duties in protecting their wards are compared to serpents. Vultures deal very seriously with serpents, and similarly the messengers will deal very seriously with neglectful guardians.

TEXT 11

ये ब्राह्मणान्मयि धिया क्षिपतोऽर्चयन्त-
स्तुष्यद्‌धृदः स्मितसुधोक्षितपद्मवक्त्राः।
वाण्यानुरागकलयात्मजवद् गृणन्तः
सम्बोधयन्त्यहमिवाहमुपाहृतस्तैः ॥११॥

ye brāhmaṇān mayi dhiyā kṣipato 'rcayantas
tuṣyad-dhṛdaḥ smita-sudhokṣita-padma-vaktrāḥ
vāṇyānurāga-kalayātmajavad gṛṇantaḥ
sambodhayanty aham ivāham upāhṛtas taiḥ

ye—which persons; *brāhmaṇān*—the *brāhmaṇas; mayi*—in Me; *dhiyā*—with intelligence; *kṣipataḥ*—uttering harsh words; *arcayantaḥ*—

respecting; *tuṣyat*—gladdened; *hṛdaḥ*—hearts; *smita*—smiling; *sudhā*—nectar; *ukṣita*—wet; *padma*—lotuslike; *vaktrāḥ*—faces; *vāṇyā*—with words; *anurāga-kalayā*—loving; *ātmaja-vat*—like a son; *gṛṇantaḥ*—praising; *sambodhayanti*—pacify; *aham*—I; *iva*—as; *aham*—I; *upāhṛtaḥ*—being controlled; *taiḥ*—by them.

TRANSLATION

On the other hand, they captivate My heart who are gladdened in heart and who, their lotus faces enlightened by nectarean smiles, respect the brāhmaṇas, even though the brāhmaṇas utter harsh words. They look upon the brāhmaṇas as My own Self and pacify them by praising them in loving words, even as a son would appease an angry father or as I am pacifying you.

PURPORT

It has been observed in many instances in the Vedic scriptures that when the *brāhmaṇas* or Vaiṣṇavas curse someone in an angry mood, the person who is cursed does not take it upon himself to treat the *brāhmaṇas* or Vaiṣṇavas in the same way. There are many examples of this. For instance, the sons of Kuvera, when cursed by the great sage Nārada, did not seek revenge in the same harsh way, but submitted. Here also, when Jaya and Vijaya were cursed by the four Kumāras, they did not become harsh towards them; rather, they submitted. That should be the way of treating *brāhmaṇas* and Vaiṣṇavas. One may sometimes be faced with a grievous situation created by a *brāhmaṇa*, but instead of meeting him with a similar mood, one should try to pacify him with a smiling face and mild treatment. *Brāhmaṇas* and Vaiṣṇavas should be accepted as earthly representatives of Nārāyaṇa. Nowadays some foolish persons have manufactured the term *daridra-nārāyaṇa*, indicating that the poor man should be accepted as the representative of Nārāyaṇa. But in Vedic literature we do not find that poor men should be treated as representatives of Nārāyaṇa. Of course, "those who are unprotected" are mentioned here, but the definition of this phrase is clear from the *śāstras*. The poor man should not be unprotected, but the *brāhmaṇa* should especially be treated as the representative of Nārāyaṇa and should be worshiped like Him. It is specifically said that to pacify the *brāhmaṇas*, one's face should be lotuslike. A lotuslike face is exhibited when one is adorned with love and affection. In this respect, the example of the father's being angry at the son and the son's trying to pacify the father with smiling and sweet words is very appropriate.

TEXT 12

तन्मे स्वभर्तुरवसायमलक्षमाणौ
युष्मद्व्यतिक्रमगतिं प्रतिपद्य सद्यः ।
भूयो ममान्तिकमितां तदनुग्रहो मे
यत्कल्पतामचिरतो भृतयोर्विवासः ॥ १२ ॥

tan me sva-bhartur avasāyam alakṣamāṇau
yuṣmad-vyatikrama-gatiṁ pratipadya sadyaḥ
bhūyo mamāntikam itāṁ tad anugraho me
yat kalpatām acirato bhṛtayor vivāsaḥ

tat—therefore; *me*—My; *sva-bhartuḥ*—of their master; *avasāyam*—the intention; *alakṣamāṇau*—not knowing; *yuṣmat*—against you; *vyatikrama*—offense; *gatim*—result; *pratipadya*—reaping; *sadyaḥ*—immediately; *bhūyaḥ*—again; *mama antikam*—near Me; *itām*—obtain; *tat*—that; *anugrahaḥ*—a favor; *me*—to Me; *yat*—which; *kalpatām*—let it be arranged; *aciratah*—not long; *bhṛtayoḥ*—of these two servants; *vivāsaḥ*—exile.

TRANSLATION

These servants of Mine have transgressed against you, not knowing the mind of their master. I shall therefore deem it a favor done to Me if you order that, although reaping the fruit of their transgression, they may return to My presence soon and the time of their exile from My abode may expire before long.

PURPORT

From this statement we can understand how anxious the Lord is to get his servitor back into Vaikuṇṭha. This incident, therefore, proves that those who have once entered a Vaikuṇṭha planet can never fall down. The case of Jaya and Vijaya is not a falldown; it is just an accident. The Lord is always anxious to get such devotees back again to the Vaikuṇṭha planets as soon as possible. It is to be assumed that there is no possibility of a misunderstanding between the Lord and the devotees, but when there are discrepancies or disruptions between one devotee and another, one has to suffer the consequences, although that suffering is temporary. The Lord is so kind to His devotees that He took all the responsibility for the doormen's offense and requested the sages to give them facilities to return to Vaikuṇṭha as soon as possible.

TEXT 13

ब्रह्मोवाच
अथ तस्योशतीं देवीमृषिकुल्यां सरस्वतीम् ।
नास्वाद्य मन्युदष्टानां तेषामात्माप्यतृप्यत ॥१३॥

brahmovāca
atha tasyośatīṁ devīm
ṛṣi-kulyāṁ sarasvatīm
nāsvādya manyu-daṣṭānāṁ
teṣām ātmāpy atṛpyata

brahmā—Lord Brahmā; *uvāca*—said; *atha*—now; *tasya*—of the Supreme Lord; *uśatīm*—lovely; *devīm*—shining; *ṛṣi-kulyām*—like a series of Vedic hymns; *sarasvatīm*—speech; *na*—not; *āsvādya*—hearing; *manyu*—anger; *daṣṭānām*—bitten; *teṣām*—of those sages; *ātmā*—the mind; *api*—even though; *atṛpyata*—satiated.

TRANSLATION

Brahmā continued: Even though the sages had been bitten by the serpent of anger, their souls were not satiated with hearing the Lord's lovely and illuminating speech, which was like a series of Vedic hymns.

TEXT 14

सतीं व्यादाय शृण्वन्तो लघ्वीं गुर्वर्थगह्वराम् ।
विगाह्यागाधगम्भीरां न विदुस्तच्चिकीर्षितम् ॥१४॥

satīṁ vyādāya śṛṇvanto
laghvīṁ gurv-artha-gahvarām
vigāhyāgādha-gambhīrāṁ
na vidus tac-cikīrṣitam

satīm—excellent; *vyādāya*—with attentive aural reception; *śṛṇvantaḥ*—hearing; *laghvīm*—properly composed; *guru*—momentous; *artha*—import; *gahvarām*—difficult to understand; *vigāhya*—pondering; *agādha*—deep; *gambhīrām*—grave; *na*—not; *viduḥ*—understand; *tat*—of the Supreme Lord; *cikīrṣitam*—the intention.

TRANSLATION

The Lord's excellent speech was difficult to comprehend because of its momentous import and its most profound significance. The sages heard it with wide-open ears and pondered it as well. But although hearing, they could not understand what He intended to do.

PURPORT

It should be understood that no one can surpass the Supreme Personality of Godhead in speaking. There is no difference between the Supreme Person and His speeches, for He stands on the absolute platform. The sages tried with wide-open ears to understand the words from the lips of the Supreme Lord, but although His speech was very concise and meaningful, the sages could not completely comprehend what He was saying. They could not even comprehend the purport of the speech or what the Supreme Lord wanted to do. Nor could they understand whether the Lord was angry or pleased with them.

TEXT 15

ते योगमाययारब्धपारमेष्ठ्यमहोदयम् ।
प्रोचुः प्राञ्जलयो विप्राः प्रहृष्टाः क्षुभितत्वचः ॥१५॥

te yoga-māyayārabdha-
pārameṣṭhya-mahodayam
procuḥ prāñjalayo viprāḥ
prahṛṣṭāḥ kṣubhita-tvacaḥ

te—those; *yoga-māyayā*—through His internal potency; *ārabdha*—had been revealed; *pārameṣṭhya*—of the Supreme Personality of Godhead; *mahā-udayam*—multiglories; *procuḥ*—spoke; *prāñjalayaḥ*—with folded hands; *viprāḥ*—the four *brāhmaṇas; prahṛṣṭāḥ*—extremely delighted; *kṣubhita-tvacaḥ*—hair standing on end.

TRANSLATION

The four brāhmaṇa-sages were nevertheless extremely delighted to behold Him, and they experienced a thrill throughout their bodies. They then spoke as follows to the Lord, who had revealed the multiglories of the Supreme Personality through His internal potency, yogamāyā.

PURPORT

The sages were almost too puzzled to speak before the Supreme Personality of Godhead for the first time, and the hairs of their bodies stood erect due to their extreme joy. The highest opulence in the material world is called *pārameṣṭhya*, the opulence of Brahmā. But that material opulence of Brahmā, who lives on the topmost planet within this material world, cannot compare to the opulence of the Supreme Lord because the transcendental opulence in the spiritual world is caused by *yogamāyā*, whereas the opulence in the material world is caused by *mahāmāyā*.

TEXT 16

ऋषय ऊचुः

न वयं भगवन् विद्मस्तव देव चिकीर्षितम् ।
कृतो मेऽनुग्रहश्चेति यदध्यक्षः प्रभाषसे ॥१६॥

ṛṣaya ūcuḥ
na vayaṁ bhagavan vidmas
tava deva cikīrṣitam
kṛto me 'nugrahaś ceti
yad adhyakṣaḥ prabhāṣase

ṛṣayaḥ—the sages; *ūcuḥ*—said; *na*—not; *vayam*—we; *bhagavan*—O Supreme Personality of Godhead; *vidmaḥ*—did know; *tava*—Your; *deva*—O Lord; *cikīrṣitam*—wish for us to do; *kṛtaḥ*—has been done;

me—unto Me; *anugrahaḥ*—favor; *ca*—and; *iti*—thus; *yat*—which; *adhyakṣaḥ*—the supreme ruler; *prabhāṣase*—You say.

TRANSLATION

The sages said: O Supreme Personality of Godhead, we are unable to know what You intend for us to do, for even though You are the supreme ruler of all, You speak in our favor as if we had done something good for You.

PURPORT

The sages could understand that the Supreme Personality of Godhead, who is above everyone, was speaking as if He were in the wrong; therefore it was difficult for them to understand the words of the Lord. They could understand, however, that the Lord was speaking in such a humble way just to show them His all-merciful favor.

TEXT 17

ब्रह्मण्यस्य परं दैवं ब्राह्मणाः किल ते प्रभो ।
विप्राणां देवदेवानां भगवानात्मदैवतम् ॥१७॥

brahmaṇyasya paraṁ daivaṁ
brāhmaṇāḥ kila te prabho
viprāṇāṁ deva-devānāṁ
bhagavān ātma-daivatam

brahmaṇyasya—of the supreme director of the brahminical culture; *param*—the highest; *daivam*—position; *brāhmaṇāḥ*—the *brāhmaṇas; kila*—for the teaching of others; *te*—Your; *prabho*—O Lord; *viprāṇām*—of the *brāhmaṇas; deva-devānām*—to be worshiped by the demigods; *bhagavān*—the Supreme Personality of Godhead; *ātma*—the self; *daivatam*—worshipable Deity.

TRANSLATION

O Lord, You are the supreme director of the brahminical culture. Your considering the brāhmaṇas to be in the highest position is Your example for teaching others. Actually You are the

supreme worshipable Deity, not only for the gods but for the brāhmaṇas also.

PURPORT

In the *Brahma-saṁhitā* it is clearly stated that the Supreme Personality of Godhead is the cause of all causes. There are undoubtedly many demigods, the chiefs of whom are Brahmā and Śiva. Lord Viṣṇu is the Lord of Brahmā and Śiva, not to speak of the *brāhmaṇas* in this material world. As mentioned in *Bhagavad-gītā*, the Supreme Lord is very favorable towards all activities performed according to brahminical culture, or the qualities of control of the senses and mind, cleanliness, forbearance, faith in scripture, and practical and theoretical knowledge. The Lord is the Supersoul of everyone. In *Bhagavad-gītā* it is said that the Lord is the source of all emanations; thus He is also the source of Brahmā and Śiva.

TEXT 18

त्वत्तः सनातनो धर्मो रक्ष्यते तनुभिस्तव ।
धर्मस्य परमो गुह्यो निर्विकारो भवान्मतः ॥१८॥

tvattaḥ sanātano dharmo
rakṣyate tanubhis tava
dharmasya paramo guhyo
nirvikāro bhavān mataḥ

tvattaḥ—from You; *sanātanaḥ*—eternal; *dharmaḥ*—occupation; *rakṣyate*—is protected; *tanubhiḥ*—by multimanifestations; *tava*—Your; *dharmasya*—of religious principles; *paramaḥ*—the supreme; *guhyaḥ*—objective; *nirvikāraḥ*—unchangeable; *bhavān*—You; *mataḥ*—in our opinion.

TRANSLATION

You are the source of the eternal occupation of all living entities, and by Your multimanifestations of Personalities of Godhead, You have always protected religion. You are the supreme objective of religious principles, and in our opinion You are inexhaustible and unchangeable eternally.

PURPORT

The statement in this verse *dharmasya paramo guhyaḥ* refers to the most confidential part of all religious principles. This is confirmed in *Bhagavad-gītā.* The conclusion of Lord Kṛṣṇa in His advice to Arjuna is: "Give up all other religious engagement and just surrender unto Me." This is the most confidential knowledge in executing religious principles. In the *Bhāgavatam* also it is stated that if one does not become Kṛṣṇa conscious after very rigidly executing one's specified religious duties, all his labor in following so-called religious principles is simply a waste of time. Here also the sages confirm the statement that the Supreme Lord, not the demigods, is the ultimate goal of all religious principles. There are many foolish propagandists who say that worship of the demigods is also a way to reach the supreme goal, but in the authorized statements of *Śrīmad-Bhāgavatam* and *Bhagavad-gītā* this is not accepted. *Bhagavad-gītā* says that one who worships a particular demigod can reach the demigod's planet, but one who worships the Supreme Personality of Godhead can enter into Vaikuṇṭha. Some propagandists say that regardless of what one does he will ultimately reach the supreme abode of the Personality of Godhead, but this is not valid. The Lord is eternal, the Lord's servitor is eternal, and the Lord's abode is also eternal. They are all described here as *sanātana,* or eternal. The result of devotional service, therefore, is not temporary, as is the achievement of heavenly planets by worshiping the demigods. The sages wanted to stress that although the Lord, out of His causeless mercy, says that He worships the *brāhmaṇas* and Vaiṣṇavas, actually the Lord is worshipable not only by the *brāhmaṇas* and Vaiṣṇavas but also by the demigods.

TEXT 19

तरन्ति ह्यञ्जसा मृत्युं निवृत्ता यदनुग्रहात् ।
योगिनः स भवान् किंस्विदनुगृह्येत यत्परैः ॥१९॥

taranti hy añjasā mṛtyuṁ
nivṛttā yad-anugrahāt
yoginaḥ sa bhavān kiṁ svid
anugṛhyeta yat paraiḥ

taranti—cross over; *hi*—because; *añjasā*—easily; *mṛtyum*—birth and death; *nivṛttāḥ*—ceasing all material desires; *yat*—Your; *anugrahāt*—by mercy; *yoginaḥ*—transcendentalists; *saḥ*—the Supreme Lord; *bhavān*—You; *kim svit*—never possible; *anugṛhyeta*—may be favored; *yat*—which; *paraiḥ*—by others.

TRANSLATION

Mystics and transcendentalists, by the mercy of the Lord, cross beyond nescience by ceasing all material desires. It is not possible, therefore, that the Supreme Lord can be favored by others.

PURPORT

Unless one is favored by the Supreme Lord, one cannot cross over the ocean of the nescience of repeated birth and death. Here it is stated that *yogīs* or mystics cross beyond nescience by the mercy of the Supreme Personality of Godhead. There are many kinds of mystics, such as the *karma-yogī, jñāna-yogī, dhyāna-yogī* and *bhakti-yogī*. The *karmīs* particularly search after the favor of the demigods, the *jñānīs* want to become one with the Supreme Absolute Truth, and the *yogīs* are satisfied simply by partial vision of the Supreme Personality of Godhead, Paramātmā, and ultimately by oneness with Him. But the *bhaktas*, the devotees, want to associate with the Supreme Personality of Godhead eternally and serve Him. It has already been admitted that the Lord is eternal, and those who want the favor of the Supreme Lord perpetually are also eternal. Therefore *yogīs* here means devotees. By the mercy of the Lord, devotees can easily pass beyond the nescience of birth and death and attain the eternal abode of the Lord. The Lord is therefore not in need of another's favor because no one is equal to or greater than Him. Actually, everyone needs the favor of the Lord for successful understanding of his human mission.

TEXT 20

यं वै विभूतिरुपयात्यनुवेलमन्यै-
रर्थार्थिभिः स्वशिरसा धृतपादरेणुः ।
धन्यार्पिताङ्घ्रितुलसीनवदामधाम्नो
लोकं मधुव्रतपतेरिव कामयाना ॥२०॥

yaṁ vai vibhūtir upayāty anuvelam anyair
arthārthibhiḥ sva-śirasā dhṛta-pāda-reṇuḥ
dhanyārpitāṅghri-tulasī-nava-dāma-dhāmno
lokaṁ madhuvrata-pater iva kāma-yānā

yam—whom; *vai*—certainly; *vibhūtiḥ*—Lakṣmī, the goddess of fortune; *upayāti*—waits upon; *anuvelam*—occasionally; *anyaiḥ*—by others; *artha*—material facility; *arthibhiḥ*—by those who desire; *sva-śirasā*—on their own heads; *dhṛta*—accepting; *pāda*—of the feet; *reṇuḥ*—the dust; *dhanya*—by the devotees; *arpita*—offered; *aṅghri*—at Your feet; *tulasī*—of *tulasī* leaves; *nava*—fresh; *dāma*—on the garland; *dhāmnaḥ*—having a place; *lokam*—the place; *madhu-vrata-pateḥ*—of the king of the bees; *iva*—like; *kāma-yānā*—is anxious to secure.

TRANSLATION

The goddess of fortune, Lakṣmī, the dust of whose feet is worn on the head by others, waits upon You, as appointed, for she is anxious to secure a place in the abode of the king of bees, who hovers on the fresh wreath of tulasī leaves offered at Your feet by some blessed devotee.

PURPORT

As previously described, *tulasī* has attained all superior qualities due to being placed at the lotus feet of the Lord. The comparison made here is very nice. As the king of bees hovers over the *tulasī* leaves offered to the lotus feet of the Lord, so Lakṣmī, the goddess who is sought by the demigods, *brāhmaṇas*, Vaiṣṇavas and everyone else, always engages in rendering service to the lotus feet of the Lord. The conclusion is that no one can be the benefactor of the Lord; everyone is actually the servant of the servant of the Lord.

TEXT 21

यस्तां विविक्तचरितैरनुवर्तमानां
नात्याद्रियत्परमभागवतप्रसङ्गः ।
स त्वं द्विजानुपथपुण्यरजःपुनीतः
श्रीवत्सलक्ष्म किमगा भगभाजनस्त्वम् ॥२१॥

yas tāṁ vivikta-caritair anuvartamānāṁ
nātyādriyat parama-bhāgavata-prasaṅgaḥ
sa tvaṁ dvijānupatha-puṇya-rajaḥ-punītaḥ
śrīvatsa-lakṣma kim agā bhaga-bhājanas tvam

yaḥ—who; *tām*—Lakṣmī; *vivikta*—completely pure; *caritaiḥ*—devotional services; *anuvartamānām*—serving; *na*—not; *atyādriyat*—attached; *parama*—the highest; *bhāgavata*—devotees; *prasaṅgaḥ*—attached; *saḥ*—the Supreme Lord; *tvam*—You; *dvija*—of the *brāhmaṇas; anupatha*—on the path; *puṇya*—sanctified; *rajaḥ*—dust; *punītaḥ*—purified; *śrīvatsa*—of Śrīvatsa; *lakṣma*—the mark; *kim*—what; *agāḥ*—You obtained; *bhaga*—all opulences or all good qualities; *bhājanaḥ*—the reservoir; *tvam*—You.

TRANSLATION

O Lord, You are exceedingly attached to the activities of Your pure devotees, yet You are never attached to the goddesses of fortune who constantly engage in Your transcendental loving service. How can You be purified, therefore, by the dust of the path traversed by the brāhmaṇas, and how can You be glorified or made fortunate by the marks of Śrīvatsa on Your chest?

PURPORT

It is said in the *Brahma-saṁhitā* that the Lord is always served by many hundreds of thousands of goddesses of fortune in His Vaikuṇṭha planet, yet because of His attitude of renunciation of all opulences, He is not attached to any one of them. The Lord has six opulences—unlimited wealth, unlimited fame, unlimited strength, unlimited beauty, unlimited knowledge and unlimited renunciation. All the demigods and other living entities worship Lakṣmī, the goddess of fortune, just to get her favor, yet the Lord is never attached to her because He can create an unlimited number of such goddesses for His transcendental service. The goddess of fortune, Lakṣmī, is sometimes envious of the *tulasī* leaves which are placed at the lotus feet of the Lord, for they remain fixed there and do not move, whereas Lakṣmījī, although stationed by the chest of the Lord, sometimes has to please other devotees who pray for her favor. Lakṣmījī sometimes has to go to satisfy her numerous devotees, but *tulasī* leaves never forsake their position, and the Lord therefore appreciates the service of the *tulasī* more than the service of Lakṣmī. When the Lord says, therefore, that it is due to the causeless mercy of the *brāhmaṇas* that Lakṣmījī does not leave Him, we can understand that Lakṣmījī is attracted by the opulence of the Lord, not by the *brāhmaṇas'* benedictions upon Him. The Lord is not dependent on anyone's mercy for His opulence; He is always self-sufficient. The Lord's statement that His opulence is due to the benediction of the *brāhmaṇas* and Vaiṣṇavas is only to teach others that they should offer respect to the *brāhmaṇas* and Vaiṣṇavas, the devotees of the Lord.

TEXT 22

धर्मस्य ते भगवतस्त्रियुग त्रिभिः स्वैः
पद्भिश्चराचरमिदं द्विजदेवतार्थम् ।
नूनं भृतं तदभिघाति रजस्तमश्च
सत्त्वेन नो वरदया तनुवा निरस्य ॥२२॥

dharmasya te bhagavatas tri-yuga tribhiḥ svaiḥ
padbhiś carācaram idaṁ dvija-devatārtham
nūnaṁ bhṛtaṁ tad-abhighāti rajas tamaś ca
sattvena no varadayā tanuvā nirasya

dharmasya—of the personification of all religion; *te*—of You; *bhagavataḥ*—of the Supreme Personality of Godhead; *tri-yuga*—You who are manifest in all three millenniums; *tribhiḥ*—by three; *svaiḥ*—Your own; *padbhiḥ*—feet; *cara-acaram*—animate and inanimate; *idam*—this universe; *dvija*—the twice-born; *devatā*—the demigods; *artham*—for the sake of; *nūnam*—however; *bhṛtam*—protected; *tat*—those feet; *abhighāti*—destroying; *rajaḥ*—the mode of passion; *tamaḥ*—the mode of ignorance; *ca*—and; *sattvena*—of pure goodness; *naḥ*—unto us; *vara-dayā*—bestowing all blessings; *tanuvā*—by Your transcendental form; *nirasya*—driving away.

TRANSLATION

O Lord, You are the personification of all religion. Therefore You manifest Yourself in three millenniums, and thus You protect

this universe, which consists of animate and inanimate beings. By Your grace, which is of pure goodness and is the bestower of all blessings, kindly drive away the elements of rajas and tamas for the sake of the demigods and twice-born.

PURPORT

The Lord is addressed in this verse as *tri-yuga*, or one who appears in three millenniums—namely the Satya, Dvāpara and Tretā *yugas*. He is not mentioned as appearing in the fourth millennium, or Kali-yuga. It is described in Vedic literature that in Kali-yuga He comes as *channa-avatāra*, or an incarnation, but He does not appear as a manifest incarnation. In the other *yugas*, however, the Lord is a manifest incarnation, and therefore he is addressed as *tri-yuga*, or the Lord who appears in three *yugas*.

Śrīdhara Svāmī describes *tri-yuga* as follows: *yuga* means "couple," and *tri* means "three." The Lord is manifested as three couples by His six opulences, or three couples of opulences. In that way He can be addressed as *tri-yuga*. The Lord is the personality of religious principles. In three millenniums religious principles are protected by three kinds of spiritual culture, namely austerity, cleanliness and mercy. The Lord is called *tri-yuga* in that way also. In the age of Kali these three requisites to spiritual culture are almost absent, but the Lord is so kind that in spite of Kali-yuga's being devoid of these three spiritual qualities, He comes and protects the people of this age in His covered incarnation as Lord Caitanya. Lord Caitanya is called "covered" because although He is Kṛṣṇa Himself, He presents Himself as a devotee of Kṛṣṇa, not directly Kṛṣṇa. The devotees pray to Lord Caitanya, therefore, to eliminate their stock of passion and ignorance, the most conspicuous assets of this *yuga*. In the Kṛṣṇa consciousness movement one cleanses himself of the modes of passion and ignorance by chanting the holy name of the Lord, Hare Kṛṣṇa, Hare Kṛṣṇa, as introduced by Lord Caitanya.

The four Kumāras were cognizant of their situation in the modes of passion and ignorance because, although in Vaikuṇṭha, they wanted to curse devotees of the Lord. Since they were conscious of their own weakness, they prayed to the Lord to remove their still-existing passion and ignorance. The three transcendental qualifications—cleanliness, austerity and mercy—are the qualifications of the twice-born and the demigods. Those who are not situated in the quality of goodness cannot accept these three principles of spiritual culture. For the Kṛṣṇa consciousness movement, therefore, there are three sinful activities which are prohibited—namely illicit sex, intoxication, and eating food other than the *prasāda* offered to Kṛṣṇa. These three prohibitions are based on the principles of austerity, cleanliness and mercy. Devotees are merciful because they spare the poor animals, and they are clean because they are free of contamination from unwanted foodstuff and unwanted habits. Austerity is represented by restricted sex life. These principles, indicated by the prayers of the four Kumāras, should be followed by the devotees who are engaged in Kṛṣṇa consciousness.

TEXT 23

न त्वं द्विजोत्तमकुलं यदिहात्मगोपं
गोप्ता वृषः स्वर्हणेन ससूनृतेन ।
तर्ह्येव नङ्क्ष्यति शिवस्तव देव पन्था
लोकोऽग्रहीष्यदृषभस्य हि तत्प्रमाणम् ॥२३॥

na tvaṁ dvijottama-kulaṁ yadi hātma-gopaṁ
goptā vṛṣaḥ svarhaṇena sa-sūnṛtena
tarhy eva naṅkṣyati śivas tava deva panthā
loko 'grahīṣyad ṛṣabhasya hi tat pramāṇam

na—not; *tvam*—You; *dvija*—of the twice-born; *uttama-kulam*—the highest class; *yadi*—if; *ha*—indeed; *ātma-gopam*—worthy to be protected by You; *goptā*—the protector; *vṛṣaḥ*—the best; *su-arhaṇena*—by worship; *sa-sūnṛtena*—along with mild words; *tarhi*—then; *eva*—certainly; *naṅkṣyati*—will be lost; *śivaḥ*—auspicious; *tava*—Your; *deva*—O Lord; *panthāḥ*—the path; *lokaḥ*—the people in general; *agrahīṣyat*—would accept; *ṛṣabhasya*—of the best; *hi*—because; *tat*—that; *pramāṇam*—authority.

TRANSLATION

O Lord, You are the protector of the highest of the twice-born. If You do not protect them by offering worship and mild words,

then certainly the auspicious path of worship will be rejected by people in general, who act on the strength and authority of Your Lordship.

PURPORT

In *Bhagavad-gītā* it is stated by the Lord Himself that the acts and character of great authorities are followed by people in general. Leaders of ideal character are therefore needed in society. Kṛṣṇa, the Supreme Personality of Godhead, appeared in this material world just to show the example of perfect authority, and people have to follow His path. The Vedic injunction is that one cannot understand the Absolute Truth simply by mental speculation or logical argument. One has to follow the authorities. *Mahājano yena gataḥ sa panthāḥ.* Great authorities should be followed; otherwise, if we simply depend on the scriptures, we are sometimes misled by rascals, or else we cannot understand or follow the different spiritual injunctions. The best path is to follow the authorities. The four *brāhmaṇa*-sages stated that Kṛṣṇa is naturally the protector of the cows and *brāhmaṇas: go-brāhmaṇa-hitāya ca.* When Kṛṣṇa was on this planet, He set a practical example. He was a cowherd boy, and He was very respectful to the *brāhmaṇas* and devotees.

It is also affirmed herein that the *brāhmaṇas* are the best of the twice-born. *Brāhmaṇas, kṣatriyas* and *vaiśyas* are all twice-born, but the *brāhmaṇas* are the best. When there is a fight between two persons, each of them protects the upper part of his body—the head, the arms and the belly. Similarly, for the actual advancement of human civilization, the best part of the social body, namely the *brāhmaṇas*, the *kṣatriyas* and *vaiśyas* (the intelligent class of men, the military class and the mercantile men) should be given special protection. Protection of the laborers should not be neglected, but special protection should be given to the upper orders. Of all classes of men, the *brāhmaṇas* and the Vaiṣṇavas should be given special protection. They should be worshiped. When their protection is performed, it is just like worshiping God. That is not exactly protection; it is a duty. One should worship the *brāhmaṇas* and Vaiṣṇavas by offering them all kinds of endowments and sweet words, and if one has no means to offer anything, he must at least use sweet words to pacify them. The Lord personally exhibited this behavior towards the Kumāras.

If this system is not introduced by the leaders, then human civilization will be lost. When there is no protection and special treatment for persons who are devotees of the Lord, who are highly intelligent in spiritual life, then the whole society is lost. The word *naṅkṣyati* indicates that such a civilization becomes spoiled and is annihilated. The kind of civilization recommended is called *deva-patha*, which means the "royal road of the demigods." Demigods are supposed to be fully fixed in devotional service, or Kṛṣṇa consciousness; that is the auspicious path that should be protected. If the authorities or the leaders of society do not give special respect to the *brāhmaṇas* and Vaiṣṇavas and do not offer them not only sweet words but all facilities, then the path of progress will be lost to human civilization. The Lord personally wanted to teach this, and therefore He offered so much praise to the Kumāras.

TEXT 24

तत्तेऽनभीष्टमिव सत्त्वनिधेर्विधित्सोः
क्षेमं जनाय निजशक्तिभिरुद्धृतारेः ।
नैतावता त्र्यधिपतेर्बत विश्वभर्तु-
स्तेजः क्षतं त्ववनतस्य स ते विनोदः ॥२४॥

tat te 'nabhīṣṭam iva sattva-nidher vidhitsoḥ
kṣemaṁ janāya nija-śaktibhir uddhṛtāreḥ
naitāvatā try-adhipater bata viśva-bhartus
tejaḥ kṣataṁ tv avanatasya sa te vinodaḥ

tat—that destruction of the path of auspiciousness; *te*—by You; *anabhīṣṭam*—is not liked; *iva*—as; *sattva-nidheḥ*—the reservoir of all goodness; *vidhitsoḥ*—desiring to do; *kṣemam*—good; *janāya*—for the people in general; *nija-śaktibhiḥ*—by Your own potencies; *uddhṛta*—destroyed; *areḥ*—the opposite element; *na*—not; *etāvatā*—by this; *tri-adhipateḥ*—of the proprietor of the three kinds of creations; *bata*—O Lord; *viśva-bhartuḥ*—the maintainer of the universe; *tejaḥ*—potency; *kṣatam*—reduced; *tu*—but; *avanatasya*—submissive; *saḥ*—that; *te*—Your; *vinodaḥ*—pleasure.

TRANSLATION

Dear Lord, You never want the auspicious path to be destroyed, for You are the reservoir of all goodness. Just to benefit people in general, You destroy the evil element by Your mighty potency. You are the proprietor of the three creations and the maintainer of the entire universe. Therefore Your potency is not reduced by Your submissive behavior. Rather, by submission You exhibit Your transcendental pastimes.

PURPORT

Lord Kṛṣṇa was never reduced in His position by becoming a cowherd boy or by offering respect to Sudāmā Brāhmaṇa or His other devotees like Nanda Mahārāja, Vasudeva, Mahārāja Yudhiṣṭhira and the Pāṇḍavas' mother, Kuntī. Everyone knew that He was the Supreme Personality of Godhead, Kṛṣṇa, yet His behavior was exemplary. The Supreme Personality of Godhead is *sac-cid-ānanda-vigraha;* His form is completely spiritual, full of bliss and knowledge, and it is eternal. Because the living entities are His parts and parcels, originally they also belong to the same quality of eternal form as the Lord, but when they come in contact with *māyā*, the material potency, due to their forgetfulness their existential constitution is covered. We should try to understand the appearance of Lord Kṛṣṇa in this spirit, as the Kumāras pray to Him. He is eternally a cowherd boy at Vṛndāvana, He is eternally the leader of the Battle of Kurukṣetra, and He is eternally the opulent prince of Dvārakā and the lover of the damsels of Vṛndāvana; all His appearances are meaningful because they show His real characteristics to the conditioned souls, who have forgotten their relationship with the Supreme Lord. He does everything for their benefit. The force exhibited in the Battle of Kurukṣetra by the desire of Kṛṣṇa and through the agency of Arjuna was also necessary because when people become too irreligious, force is required. Nonviolence in this respect is rascaldom.

TEXT 25

यं वानयोर्दममधीश भवान् विधत्ते
वृत्तिं नु वा तदनुमन्महि निर्व्यलीकम् ।

अस्मासु वा य उचितो ध्रियतां स दण्डो
येऽनागसौ वयमयुङ्क्ष्महि किल्बिषेण ॥२५॥

yaṁ vānayor damam adhīśa bhavān vidhatte
vṛttiṁ nu vā tad anumanmahi nirvyalīkam
asmāsu vā ya ucito dhriyatāṁ sa daṇḍo
ye 'nāgasau vayam ayuṅkṣmahi kilbiṣeṇa

yam—which; *vā*—or; *anayoḥ*—of both of them; *damam*—punishment; *adhīśa*—O Lord; *bhavān*—Your Lordship; *vidhatte*—awards; *vṛttim*—better existence; *nu*—certainly; *vā*—or; *tat*—that; *anumanmahi*—we accept; *nirvyalīkam*—without duplicity; *asmāsu*—to us; *vā*—or; *yaḥ*—whichever; *ucitaḥ*—is proper; *dhriyatām*—may be awarded; *saḥ*—that; *daṇḍaḥ*—punishment; *ye*—who; *anāgasau*—sinless; *vayam*—we; *ayuṅkṣmahi*—allotted; *kilbiṣeṇa*—with a curse.

TRANSLATION

O Lord, whatever punishment You wish to award to these two innocent persons or also to us we shall accept without duplicity. We understand that we have cursed two faultless persons.

PURPORT

The sages, the four Kumāras, now reject their cursing of the two doorkeepers, Jaya and Vijaya, because they are now conscious that persons who engage in the service of the Lord cannot be at fault at any stage. It is said that anyone who has implicit faith in the service of the Lord, or who actually engages in transcendental loving service, has all the good qualities of the demigods. Therefore, a devotee cannot be at fault. If sometimes it is found that he is in error by accident or by some temporary arrangement, that should not be taken very seriously. The cursing of Jaya and Vijaya is here repented. Now the Kumāras are thinking in terms of their position in the modes of passion and ignorance, and they are prepared to accept any kind of punishment from the Lord. In general, when dealing with devotees, we should not try to find faults. In *Bhagavad-gītā* also it is confirmed that the devotee who faithfully serves the Supreme Lord, even if found to commit a gross mistake, should be considered a *sādhu,* or saintly person. Due to former habits he may commit some wrong, but because he is engaged in the service of the Lord, that wrong should not be taken very seriously.

TEXT 26

श्रीभगवानुवाच
एतौ सुरेतरगतिं प्रतिपद्य सद्यः
संरम्भसम्भृतसमाध्यनुबद्धयोगौ ।
भूयः सकाशमुपयास्यत आशु यो वः
शापो मयैव निमितस्तदवेत विप्राः ॥२६॥

śrī-bhagavān uvāca
etau suretara-gatiṁ pratipadya sadyaḥ
saṁrambha-sambhṛta-samādhy-anubaddha-yogau
bhūyaḥ sakāśam upayāsyata āśu yo vaḥ
śāpo mayaiva nimitas tad aveta viprāḥ

śrī-bhagavān uvāca—the Supreme Personality of Godhead replied; *etau*—these two doorkeepers; *sura-itara*—demoniac; *gatim*—the womb; *pratipadya*—obtaining; *sadyaḥ*—quickly; *saṁrambha*—by anger; *sambhṛta*—intensified; *samādhi*—concentration of mind; *anubaddha*—firmly; *yogau*—united with Me; *bhūyaḥ*—again; *sakāśam*—to My presence; *upayāsyataḥ*—shall return; *āśu*—shortly; *yaḥ*—which; *vaḥ*—of you; *śāpaḥ*—curse; *mayā*—by Me; *eva*—alone; *nimitaḥ*—ordained; *tat*—that; *aveta*—know; *viprāḥ*—O *brāhmaṇas.*

TRANSLATION

The Lord replied: O brāhmaṇas, know that the punishment you inflicted on them was originally ordained by Me, and therefore they will fall to a birth in a demoniac family. But they will be firmly united with Me in thought through mental concentration intensified by anger, and they will return to My presence shortly.

PURPORT

The Lord stated that the punishment inflicted by the sages upon the doorkeepers Jaya and Vijaya was conceived by the Lord Himself. Without the Lord's sanction, nothing can happen. It is to be understood that there was a plan in the cursing of the Lord's devotees in Vaikuṇṭha, and His plan is explained by many stalwart authorities. The Lord sometimes desires to fight. The fighting spirit also exists in the Supreme Lord, otherwise how could fighting be manifested at all? Because the Lord is the source of everything, anger and fighting are also inherent in His personality. When He desires to fight with someone, He has to find an enemy, but in the Vaikuṇṭha world there is no enemy because everyone is engaged fully in His service. Therefore He sometimes comes to the material world as an incarnation in order to manifest His fighting spirit.

In *Bhagavad-gītā* (4.8) also it is said that the Lord appears just to give protection to the devotees and to annihilate the nondevotees. The nondevotees are found in the material world, not in the spiritual world; therefore, when the Lord wants to fight, He has to come to this world. But who will fight with the Supreme Lord? No one is able to fight with Him! Therefore, because the Lord's pastimes in the material world are always performed with His associates, not with others, He has to find some devotee who will play the part of an enemy. In *Bhagavad-gītā* the Lord says to Arjuna, "My dear Arjuna, both you and I have appeared many, many times in this material world, but you have forgotten, whereas I remember." Thus Jaya and Vijaya were selected by the Lord to fight with Him in the material world, and that was the reason the sages came to see Him and accidentally the doorkeepers were cursed. It was the Lord's desire to send them to the material world, not perpetually, but for some time. Therefore, just as on a theatrical stage someone takes the part of enemy to the proprietor of the stage, although the play is for a short time and there is no permanent enmity between the servant and the proprietor, so the *sura-janas* (devotees) were cursed by the sages to go to the *asura-jana*, or atheistic families. That a devotee should come into an atheistic family is surprising, but it is simply a show. After finishing their mock fighting, both the devotee and the Lord are again associated in the spiritual planets. That is very explicitly explained here. The conclusion is that no one falls from the spiritual world, or Vaikuṇṭha planet, for it is the eternal abode. But sometimes, as the Lord desires, devotees come into this material world as preachers or as atheists. In each case we must understand that there is a plan of the Lord. Lord Buddha, for example, was an incarnation, yet he preached atheism: "There is no God."

But actually there was a plan behind this, as explained in the *Bhāgavatam.*

TEXT 27

ब्रह्मोवाच

अथ ते मुनयो दृष्ट्वा नयनानन्दभाजनम् ।
वैकुण्ठं तदधिष्ठानं विकुण्ठं च स्वयंप्रभम् ॥२७॥

brahmovāca
atha te munayo dṛṣṭvā
nayanānanda-bhājanam
vaikuṇṭhaṁ tad-adhiṣṭhānaṁ
vikuṇṭhaṁ ca svayaṁ-prabham

brahmā uvāca—Lord Brahmā said; *atha*—now; *te*—those; *munayaḥ*—sages; *dṛṣṭvā*—after seeing; *nayana*—of the eyes; *ānanda*—pleasure; *bhājanam*—producing; *vaikuṇṭham*—the Vaikuṇṭha planet; *tat*—of Him; *adhiṣṭhānam*—the abode; *vikuṇṭham*—the Supreme Personality of Godhead; *ca*—and; *svayam-prabham*—self-illuminating.

TRANSLATION

Lord Brahmā said: After seeing the Lord of Vaikuṇṭha, the Supreme Personality of Godhead, in the self-illuminated Vaikuṇṭha planet, the sages left that transcendental abode.

PURPORT

The transcendental abode of the Supreme Personality of Godhead, as stated in *Bhagavad-gītā* and confirmed in this verse, is self-illuminated. In *Bhagavad-gītā* it is said that in the spiritual world there is no need of sun, moon or electricity. This indicates that all the planets there are self-illuminated, self-sufficient and independent; everything there is complete. Lord Kṛṣṇa says that once one goes to that Vaikuṇṭha planet, he never returns. The inhabitants of Vaikuṇṭha never return to the material world, but the incident of Jaya and Vijaya was a different case. They came to the material world for some time, and then they returned to Vaikuṇṭha.

TEXT 28

भगवन्तं परिक्रम्य प्रणिपत्यानुमान्य च ।
प्रतिजग्मुः प्रमुदिताः शंसन्तो वैष्णवीं श्रियम् ॥२८॥

bhagavantaṁ parikramya
praṇipatyānumānya ca
pratijagmuḥ pramuditāḥ
śaṁsanto vaiṣṇavīṁ śriyam

bhagavantam—the Supreme Personality of Godhead; *parikramya*—after circumambulating; *praṇipatya*—after offering obeisances; *anumānya*—after learning; *ca*—and; *pratijagmuḥ*—returned; *pramuditāḥ*—extremely delighted; *śaṁsantaḥ*—glorifying; *vaiṣṇavīm*—of the Vaiṣṇavas; *śriyam*—opulence.

TRANSLATION

The sages circumambulated the Supreme Lord, offered their obeisances and returned, extremely delighted at learning of the divine opulences of the Vaiṣṇava.

PURPORT

It is still a respectful practice to circumambulate the Lord in Hindu temples. Especially in Vaiṣṇava temples there is an arrangement for people to offer their respects to the Deity and circumambulate the temple at least three times.

TEXT 29

भगवाननुगावाह यातं मा भैष्टमस्तु शम् ।
ब्रह्मतेजः समर्थोऽपि हन्तुं नेच्छे मतं तु मे ॥२९॥

bhagavān anugāv āha
yātaṁ mā bhaiṣṭam astu śam
brahma-tejaḥ samartho 'pi
hantuṁ necche mataṁ tu me

bhagavān—the Supreme Personality of Godhead; *anugau*—to His two attendants; *āha*—said; *yātam*—depart from this place; *mā*—let there not be; *bhaiṣṭam*—fear; *astu*—let there be; *śam*—happiness; *brahma*—of a *brāhmaṇa; tejaḥ*—the curse; *samarthaḥ*—being able; *api*—even; *hantum*—to nullify; *na icche*—do not desire; *matam*—approved; *tu*—on the contrary; *me*—by Me.

TRANSLATION

The Lord then said to His attendants, Jaya and Vijaya: Depart this place, but fear not. All glories unto you. Though I am capable of nullifying the brāhmaṇas' curse, I would not do so. On the contrary, it has My approval.

PURPORT

As explained in connection with text 26, all the incidents that took place had the approval of the Lord. Ordinarily, there is no possibility that the four sages could be so angry with the doorkeepers, nor could the Supreme Lord neglect His two doorkeepers, nor can one come back from Vaikuṇṭha after once taking birth there. All these incidents, therefore, were designed by the Lord Himself for the sake of His pastimes in the material world. Thus He plainly says that it was done with His approval. Otherwise, it would have been impossible for inhabitants of Vaikuṇṭha to come back to this material world simply because of a brahminical curse. The Lord especially blesses the so-called culprits: "All glories unto you." A devotee, once accepted by the Lord, can never fall down. That is the conclusion of this incident.

TEXT 30

एतत्पुरैव निर्दिष्टं रमया क्रुद्धया यदा ।
पुरापवारिता द्वारि विशन्ती मय्युपारते ॥३०॥

etat puraiva nirdiṣṭaṁ
ramayā kruddhayā yadā
purāpavāritā dvāri
viśantī mayy upārate

etat—this departure; *purā*—formerly; *eva*—certainly; *nirdiṣṭam*—foretold; *ramayā*—by Lakṣmī; *kruddhayā*—furious; *yadā*—when; *purā*—previously; *apavāritā*—prevented; *dvāri*—at the gate; *viśantī*—entering; *mayi*—as I; *upārate*—was resting.

TRANSLATION

This departure from Vaikuṇṭha was foretold by Lakṣmī, the goddess of fortune. She was very angry because when she left My abode and then returned, you stopped her at the gate while I was sleeping.

TEXT 31

मयि संरम्भयोगेन निस्तीर्य ब्रह्महेलनम् ।
प्रत्येष्यतं निकाशं मे कालेनाल्पीयसा पुनः ॥३१॥

mayi saṁrambha-yogena
nistīrya brahma-helanam
pratyeṣyataṁ nikāśaṁ me
kālenālpīyasā punaḥ

mayi—unto Me; *saṁrambha-yogena*—by practice of mystic *yoga* in anger; *nistīrya*—being liberated from; *brahma-helanam*—the result of disobedience to the *brāhmaṇas; pratyeṣyatam*—will come back; *nikāśam*—near; *me*—Me; *kālena*—in due course of time; *alpīyasā*—very short; *punaḥ*—again.

TRANSLATION

The Lord assured the two Vaikuṇṭha inhabitants, Jaya and Vijaya: By practicing the mystic yoga system in anger, you will be cleansed of the sin of disobeying the brāhmaṇas and within a very short time return to Me.

PURPORT

The Supreme Personality of Godhead advised the two doorkeepers, Jaya and Vijaya, that by dint of *bhakti-yoga* in anger they would be delivered from the curses of the *brāhmaṇas*. Śrīla Madhva Muni remarks in this connection that by practicing *bhakti-yoga* one can become free from all sinful reactions. Even a *brahma-śāpa*, or curse by a *brāhmaṇa*, which cannot be overcome by any other means, can be overcome by *bhakti-yoga*.

One can practice *bhakti-yoga* in many *rasas*. There are twelve *rasas*, five primary and seven secondary. The five primary *rasas* constitute direct *bhakti-yoga*, but although the seven secondary *rasas* are indirect, they are also counted within *bhakti-yoga* if they are used in the service of the Lord. In other words, *bhakti-yoga* is all-inclusive. If one somehow or other becomes attached to the Supreme Personality of Godhead, he becomes engaged in *bhakti-yoga*, as described in *Śrīmad-Bhāgavatam* (10.29.15): *kāmaṁ krodhaṁ bhayam*. The *gopīs* were attracted to Kṛṣṇa by *bhakti-yoga* in a relationship of lusty desire (*kāma*). Similarly, Kaṁsa was attached to *bhakti-yoga* by dint of fear of his death. Thus *bhakti-yoga* is so powerful that even becoming an enemy of the Lord and always thinking of Him can deliver one very quickly. It is said, *viṣṇu-bhaktaḥ smṛto daiva āsuras tad-vipanyayaḥ:* "Devotees of Lord Viṣṇu are called demigods, whereas nondevotees are called *asuras*." But *bhakti-yoga* is so powerful that both demigods and *asuras* can derive its benefits if they always think of the Personality of Godhead. The basic principle of *bhakti-yoga* is to think of the Supreme Lord always. The Lord says in *Bhagavad-gītā* (18.65), *man-manā bhava mad-bhaktaḥ:* "Always think of Me." It doesn't matter which way one thinks; the very thought of the Personality of Godhead is the basic principle of *bhakti-yoga*.

In the material planets there are different grades of sinful activities, of which disrespecting a *brāhmaṇa* or a Vaiṣṇava is the most sinful. Here it is clearly stated that one can overcome even that grave sin simply by thinking of Viṣṇu, not even favorably but in anger. Thus even if those who are not devotees always think of Viṣṇu, they become free from all sinful activities. Kṛṣṇa consciousness is the highest form of thought. Lord Viṣṇu is thought of in this age by chanting Hare Kṛṣṇa, Hare Kṛṣṇa, Kṛṣṇa Kṛṣṇa, Hare Hare/ Hare Rāma, Hare Rāma, Rāma Rāma, Hare Hare. From the statements of the *Bhāgavatam* it appears that if one thinks of Kṛṣṇa, even as an enemy, that particular qualification—*thinking of Viṣṇu, or Kṛṣṇa*—cleanses one of all sins.

TEXT 32

द्वाःस्थावादिश्य भगवान् विमानश्रेणिभूषणम् ।
सर्वातिशयया लक्ष्म्या जुष्टं स्वं धिष्ण्यमाविशत् ॥३२॥

dvāḥsthāv ādiśya bhagavān
vimāna-śreṇi-bhūṣaṇam
sarvātiśayayā lakṣmyā
juṣṭaṁ svaṁ dhiṣṇyam āviśat

dvāḥ-sthau—to the doorkeepers; *ādiśya*—just directing them; *bhagavān*—the Supreme Personality of Godhead; *vimāna-śreṇi-bhūṣaṇam*—always decorated with first-class airplanes; *sarva-atiśayayā*—in every respect extensively opulent; *lakṣmyā*—opulences; *juṣṭam*—bedecked with; *svam*—His own; *dhiṣṇyam*—abode; *āviśat*—went back.

TRANSLATION

After thus speaking at the door of Vaikuṇṭha, the Lord returned to His abode, where there are many celestial airplanes and all-surpassing wealth and splendor.

PURPORT

It is clear from this verse that all the incidents took place at the entrance of Vaikuṇṭhaloka. In other words, the sages were not actually within Vaikuṇṭhaloka, but were at the gate. It could be asked, "How could they return to the material world if they entered Vaikuṇṭhaloka?" But factually they did not enter, and therefore they returned. There are many similar incidents where great *yogīs* and *brāhmaṇas*, by dint of their *yoga* practice, have gone from this material world to Vaikuṇṭhaloka—but they were not meant to stay there. They came back. It is also confirmed here that the Lord was surrounded by many Vaikuṇṭha airplanes. Vaikuṇṭhaloka is described here as having splendid opulence, far surpassing the splendor of this material world.

All other living creatures, including the demigods, are born of Brahmā, and Brahmā is born of Lord Viṣṇu. Kṛṣṇa states in *Bhagavad-gītā*, in the Tenth Chapter, *ahaṁ sarvasya prabhavaḥ:* Lord Viṣṇu is the origin of all manifestations in the material world. Those who know that Lord Viṣṇu is the origin of everything, who are conversant with the process of creation and who understand that Viṣṇu, or Kṛṣṇa, is the most worshipable object of all living entities, engage themselves in Viṣṇu worship as Vaiṣṇavas. The Vedic hymns also confirm this: *oṁ tad viṣṇoḥ paramaṁ padam.* The goal of life is to understand Viṣṇu. The *Bhāgavatam* also confirms this elsewhere. Foolish people, not knowing that Viṣṇu is the supreme worshipable object, create so many worshipable objects in this material world, and therefore they fall down.

TEXT 33

तौ तु गीर्वाणऋषभौ दुस्तराद्धरिलोकतः ।
हतश्रियौ ब्रह्मशापादभूतां विगतस्मयौ ॥३३॥

tau tu gīrvāṇa-ṛṣabhau
dustarād dhari-lokataḥ
hata-śriyau brahma-śāpād
abhūtāṁ vigata-smayau

tau—those two gatekeepers; *tu*—but; *gīrvāṇa-ṛṣabhau*—the best of the demigods; *dustarāt*—unable to be avoided; *hari-lokataḥ*—from Vaikuṇṭha, the abode of Lord Hari; *hata-śriyau*—diminished in beauty and luster; *brahma-śāpāt*—from the curse of a *brāhmaṇa; abhūtām*—became; *vigata-smayau*—morose.

TRANSLATION

But those two gatekeepers, the best of the demigods, their beauty and luster diminished by the curse of the brāhmaṇas, became morose and fell from Vaikuṇṭha, the abode of the Supreme Lord.

TEXT 34

तदा विकुण्ठधिषणात्तयोर्निपतमानयोः ।
हाहाकारो महानासीद्विमानाग्र्येषु पुत्रकाः ॥३४॥

tadā vikuṇṭha-dhiṣaṇāt
tayor nipatamānayoḥ
hāhā-kāro mahān āsīd
vimānāgryeṣu putrakāḥ

tadā—then; *vikuṇṭha*—of the Supreme Lord; *dhiṣaṇāt*—from the abode; *tayoḥ*—as both of them; *nipatamānayoḥ*—were falling; *hāhā-kāraḥ*—roaring in disappointment; *mahān*—great; *āsīt*—occurred; *vimāna-agryeṣu*—in the best of airplanes; *putrakāḥ*—O demigods.

TRANSLATION

Then, as Jaya and Vijaya fell from the Lord's abode, a great roar of disappointment arose from all the demigods, who were sitting in their splendid airplanes.

TEXT 35

तावेव ह्यधुना प्राप्तौ पार्षदप्रवरौ हरेः ।
दितेर्जठरनिर्विष्टं काश्यपं तेज उल्बणम् ॥३५॥

tāv eva hy adhunā prāptau
pārṣada-pravarau hareḥ
diter jaṭhara-nirviṣṭaṁ
kāśyapaṁ teja ulbaṇam

tau—those two doorkeepers; *eva*—certainly; *hi*—addressed; *adhunā*—now; *prāptau*—having gotten; *pārṣada-pravarau*—important associates; *hareḥ*—of the Supreme Personality of Godhead; *diteḥ*—of Diti; *jaṭhara*—womb; *nirviṣṭam*—entering; *kāśyapam*—of Kaśyapa Muni; *tejaḥ*—semen; *ulbaṇam*—very strong.

TRANSLATION

Lord Brahmā continued: Those two principal doorkeepers of the Personality of Godhead have now entered the womb of Diti, the powerful semen of Kaśyapa Muni having covered them.

PURPORT

Here is clear proof of how a living entity coming originally from Vaikuṇṭhaloka is encaged in material elements. The living entity takes shelter within the semen of a father, which is injected within the womb of a mother, and with the help of the mother's emulsified ovum the living entity grows a particular type of a body. In this connection it is to be remembered that the mind of Kaśyapa Muni was not in order when he conceived the two sons, Hiraṇyākṣa and Hiraṇyakaśipu. Therefore the semen he discharged was simultaneously extremely powerful and mixed with the quality of anger. It is to be concluded that while conceiving a child one's mind must be very sober and devotional. For this purpose the *Garbhādhāna-saṁskāra* is recommended in the Vedic scriptures. If the mind of the father is not sober, the semen discharged will not be very good. Thus the living entity, wrapped in the matter produced from the father and mother, will be demoniac like Hiraṇyākṣa and Hiraṇyakaśipu. The conditions of conception are to be carefully studied. This is a very great science.

TEXT 36

तयोरसुरयोरद्य तेजसा यमयोर्हि वः ।
आक्षिप्तं तेज एतर्हि भगवांस्तद्विधित्सति ॥३६॥

tayor asurayor adya
tejasā yamayor hi vaḥ
ākṣiptaṁ teja etarhi
bhagavāṁs tad vidhitsati

tayoḥ—of them; *asurayoḥ*—of the two *asuras; adya*—today; *tejasā*—by the prowess; *yamayoḥ*—of the twins; *hi*—certainly; *vaḥ*—of all you demigods; *ākṣiptam*—agitated; *tejaḥ*—power; *etarhi*—thus certainly; *bhagavān*—the Supreme Personality of Godhead; *tat*—that; *vidhitsati*—desires to do.

TRANSLATION

It is the prowess of these twin asuras [demons] that has disturbed you, for it has minimized your power. There is no remedy

within my power, however, for it is the Lord Himself who desires to do all this.

PURPORT

Although Hiraṇyakaśipu and Hiraṇyākṣa, formerly Jaya and Vijaya, became *asuras*, the demigods of this material world could not control them, and therefore Lord Brahmā said that neither he nor all the demigods could counteract the disturbance they created. They came within the material world by the order of the Supreme Personality of Godhead, and He alone could counteract such disturbances. In other words, although Jaya and Vijaya assumed the bodies of *asuras*, they remained more powerful than anyone, thus proving that the Supreme Personality of Godhead desired to fight because the fighting spirit is also within Him. He is the original in everything, but when He desires to fight He must fight with a devotee. Therefore by His desire only were Jaya and Vijaya cursed by the Kumāras. The Lord ordered the gatekeepers to go down to the material world to become His enemies so that He could fight with them and His fighting desires would be satisfied by the service of His personal devotees.

Brahmā showed the demigods that the situation created by the darkness, for which they were disturbed, was the desire of the Supreme Lord. He wanted to show that even though these two attendants were coming in the forms of demons, they were very powerful, greater than the demigods, who could not control them. No one can surpass the acts of the Supreme Lord. The demigods were also advised not to try to counteract this incident, because it was ordered by the Lord. Similarly, anyone who is ordered by the Lord to perform some action in this material world, especially preaching His glories, cannot be counteracted by anyone; the will of the Lord is executed under all circumstances.

TEXT 37

विश्वस्य यः स्थितिलयोद्भवहेतुराद्यो
योगेश्वरैरपि दुरत्ययययोगमायः ।
क्षेमं विधास्यति स नो भगवांस्त्र्यधीश-
स्तत्रास्मदीयविमृशेन कियानिहार्थः ॥३७॥

viśvasya yaḥ sthiti-layodbhava-hetur ādyo
yogeśvarair api duratyaya-yogamāyaḥ
kṣemaṁ vidhāsyati sa no bhagavāṁs tryadhīśas
tatrāsmadīya-vimṛśena kiyān ihārthaḥ

viśvasya—of the universe; *yaḥ*—who; *sthiti*—maintenance; *laya*—destruction; *udbhava*—creation; *hetuḥ*—the cause; *ādyaḥ*—the most ancient person; *yoga-īśvaraiḥ*—by the masters of *yoga; api*—even; *duratyaya*—cannot be easily understood; *yoga-māyaḥ*—His *yogamāyā* potency; *kṣemam*—good; *vidhāsyati*—will do; *saḥ*—He; *naḥ*—of us; *bhagavān*—the Supreme Personality of Godhead; *tri-adhīśaḥ*—the controller of the three modes of material nature; *tatra*—there; *asmadīya*—by our; *vimṛśena*—deliberation; *kiyān*—what; *iha*—on this subject; *arthaḥ*—purpose.

TRANSLATION

My dear sons, the Lord is the controller of the three modes of nature and is responsible for the creation, preservation and dissolution of the universe. His wonderful creative power, yoga-māyā, cannot be easily understood even by the masters of yoga. That most ancient person, the Personality of Godhead, will alone come to our rescue. What purpose can we serve on His behalf by deliberating on the subject?

PURPORT

When something is arranged by the Supreme Personality of Godhead, one should not be disturbed by it, even if it appears to be a reverse according to one's calculations. For example, sometimes we see that a powerful preacher is killed, or sometimes he is put into difficulty, just as Haridāsa Ṭhākura was. He was a great devotee who came into this material world to execute the will of the Lord by preaching the Lord's glories. But Haridāsa was punished at the hands of the Kazi by being beaten in twenty-two marketplaces. Similarly, Lord Jesus Christ was crucified, and Prahlāda Mahārāja was put through so many tribulations. The Pāṇḍavas, who were direct friends of Kṛṣṇa, lost their kingdom, their wife was insulted, and they had to undergo many severe tribulations. Seeing all these reverses affect devotees, one should not be disturbed; one should simply understand that in these matters there must be some plan of the Supreme Personality of Godhead. The *Bhāgavatam*'s conclusion is that a devotee is never disturbed by such reverses. He accepts even reverse conditions as the grace of the Lord. One who continues to serve the Lord even in reverse conditions is assured that he will go back to Godhead, back to the Vaikuṇṭha planets. Lord Brahmā assured the demigods that there was no use in talking about how the disturbing situation of darkness was taking place, since the actual fact was that it was ordered by the Supreme Lord. Brahmā knew this because he was a great devotee; it was possible for him to understand the plan of the Lord.

Thus end the Bhaktivedanta purports of the Third Canto, Sixteenth Chapter, of the Śrīmad-Bhāgavatam, *entitled "The Two Doorkeepers of Vaikuṇṭha, Jaya and Vijaya, Cursed by the Sages."*

Appendixes

The Author

His Divine Grace A. C. Bhaktivedanta Swami Prabhupāda appeared in this world in 1896 in Calcutta, India. He first met his spiritual master, Śrīla Bhaktisiddhānta Sarasvatī Gosvāmī, in Calcutta in 1922. Bhaktisiddhānta Sarasvatī, a prominent religious scholar and the founder of sixty-four Gauḍīya Maṭhas (Vedic institutes), liked this educated young man and convinced him to dedicate his life to teaching Vedic knowledge. Śrīla Prabhupāda became his student, and eleven years later (1933) at Allahabad he became his formally initiated disciple.

At their first meeting, in 1922, Śrīla Bhaktisiddhānta Sarasvatī Ṭhākura requested Śrīla Prabhupāda to broadcast Vedic knowledge through the English language. In the years that followed, Śrīla Prabhupāda wrote a commentary on the *Bhagavad-gītā*, assisted the Gauḍīya Maṭha in its work and, in 1944, without assistance, started an English fortnightly magazine, edited it, typed the manuscripts and checked the galley proofs. He even distributed the individual copies freely and struggled to maintain the publication. Once begun, the magazine never stopped; it is now being continued by his disciples in the West and is published in twelve languages.

Recognizing Śrīla Prabhupāda's philosophical learning and devotion, the Gauḍīya Vaiṣṇava Society honored him in 1947 with the title "Bhaktivedanta." In 1950, at the age of fifty-four, Śrīla Prabhupāda retired from married life, adopting the *vānaprastha* (retired) order to devote more time to his studies and writing. Śrīla Prabhupāda traveled to the holy city of Vṛndāvana, where he lived in very humble circumstances in the historic medieval temple of Rādhā-Dāmodara. There he engaged for several years in deep study and writing. He accepted the renounced order of life (*sannyāsa*) in 1959. At Rādhā-Dāmodara, Śrīla Prabhupāda began work on his life's masterpiece: a multivolume translation of and commentary on the eighteen-thousand-verse *Śrīmad-Bhāgavatam* (*Bhāgavata Purāṇa*). He also wrote *Easy Journey to Other Planets.*

After publishing three volumes of *Bhāgavatam*, Śrīla Prabhupāda came to the United States, in 1965, to fulfill the mission of his spiritual master. Since that time, His Divine Grace has written over sixty volumes of authoritative translations, commentaries and summary studies of the philosophical and religious classics of India.

In 1965, when he first arrived by freighter in New York City, Śrīla Prabhupāda was practically penniless. It was after almost a year of great difficulty that he established the International Society for Krishna Consciousness in July of 1966. Under his careful guidance, the Society has grown within a decade to a worldwide confederation of more than one hundred *āśramas*, schools, temples, institutes and farm communities.

In 1968, Śrīla Prabhupāda created New Vṛndāvana, an experimental Vedic community in the hills of West Virginia. Inspired by the success of New Vṛndāvana, now a thriving farm community of more than one thousand acres, his students have since founded several similar communities in the United States and abroad.

In 1972, His Divine Grace introduced the Vedic system of primary and secondary education in the West by founding the Gurukula school in Dallas, Texas. Since then, under his supervision, his disciples have established children's schools throughout the United States and the rest of the world. As of 1977, there are twenty *gurukula* schools worldwide, with the principal educational center now located in Vṛndāvana, India.

Śrīla Prabhupāda has also inspired the construction of several large international cultural centers in India. The center at Śrīdhāma Māyāpur in West Bengal is the site for a planned spiritual city, an ambitious project for which construction will extend over the next decade. In Vṛndāvana, India, is the magnificent Kṛṣṇa-Balarāma Temple and International Guesthouse. There are also major cultural and educational centers in Bombay and the holy city of Purī in Orissa. Other centers are planned in a dozen other important locations on the Indian subcontinent.

Śrīla Prabhupāda's most significant contribution, however, is his books. Highly respected by the academic community for their authoritativeness, depth and clarity, they are used as standard textbooks in numerous college courses. His writings have been translated into twenty-three languages. The Bhaktivedanta Book Trust, established in 1972 exclusively to publish the works of His Divine Grace, has thus become the world's largest publisher of books in the field of Indian religion and philosophy. Its principal project is the ongoing publication of Śrīla Prabhupāda's celebrated multivolume translation of and commentary on *Śrīmad-Bhāgavatam.*

In the past ten years, in spite of his advanced age, Śrīla Prabhupāda has circled the globe twelve times on lecture tours that have taken him to six continents. In spite of such a vigorous schedule, Śrīla Prabhupāda continues to write prolifically. His writings constitute a veritable library of Vedic philosophy, religion, literature and culture.

References

The purports of *Śrīmad-Bhāgavatam* are all confirmed by standard Vedic authorities. The following authentic scriptures are specifically cited in this volume:

Bhagavad-gītā, 2, 5, 7, 14, 18–19, 21, 23, 26, 27, 32, 45, 57, 71, 72, 113, 123, 130, 158, 167–168, 201, 205, 209, 210, 216, 248, 254, 255, 256, 303, 309–310, 312, 324–325, 328, 345, 371, 376, 377

Brahma-saṁhitā, 5, 7, 97, 116, 120, 287, 316–317

Bṛhan-nāradīya Purāṇa, 190

Caitanya-caritāmṛta, 295

Gopāla-tāpanī Upaniṣad, 24

Īśopaniṣad, 17

Ṛg Veda, 342

Śrīmad-Bhāgavatam, 16–17, 29–30, 72, 126, 131, 144, 151, 273, 293, 294, 335, 376

Viṣṇu-dharma, 196

Viṣṇu Purāṇa, 179

Glossary

A

Ācārya—a spiritual master who teaches by example.

Ārati—a ceremony for greeting the Lord with offerings of food, lamps, fans, flowers and incense.

Arcanā—the devotional process of Deity worship.

Āśrama—the four spiritual orders of life: celibate student, householder, retired life and renounced life.

Asuras—atheistic demons.

Avatāra—a descent of the Supreme Lord.

B

Bhagavad-gītā—the basic directions for spiritual life spoken by the Lord Himself.

Bhakta—a devotee.

Bhakti-yoga—linking with the Supreme Lord by devotional service.

Brahmacarya—celibate student life; the first order of Vedic spiritual life.

Brahman—the Absolute Truth; especially the impersonal aspect of the Absolute.

Brāhmaṇa—one wise in the *Vedas* who can guide society; the first Vedic social order.

Buddhi-yoga—the surrender of one's intelligence to the will of the Supreme.

D

Dharma—eternal occupational duty; religious principles.

E

Ekādaśī—a special fast day for increased remembrance of Kṛṣṇa, which comes on the eleventh day of both the waxing and waning moon.

G

Garbhādhāna-saṁskāra—Vedic purificatory ritual for obtaining good progeny; performed by husband and wife before child's conception.

Goloka (Kṛṣṇaloka)—the highest spiritual planet, containing Kṛṣṇa's personal abodes, Dvārakā, Mathurā and Vṛndāvana.

Gopīs—Kṛṣṇa's cowherd girl friends, His most confidential servitors.

Gṛhastha—regulated householder life; the second order of Vedic spiritual life.

Guru—a spiritual master.

H

Hare Kṛṣṇa mantra—*See: Mahā-mantra*

J

Jīva-tattva—the living entities, atomic parts of the Lord.

K

Kali-yuga (Age of Kali)—the present age, characterized by quarrel; it is last in the cycle of four and began five thousand years ago.

Karatālas—hand cymbals used in *kīrtana.*

Karma—fruitive action, for which there is always reaction, good or bad.

Karmī—a person satisfied with working hard for flickering sense gratification.

Kīrtana—chanting the glories of the Supreme Lord.

Kṛṣṇaloka—*See:* Goloka

Kṣatriya—a warrior or administrator; the second Vedic social order.

M

Mahā-mantra—the great chanting for deliverance:

Hare Kṛṣṇa, Hare Kṛṣṇa, Kṛṣṇa Kṛṣṇa, Hare Hare
Hare Rāma, Hare Rāma, Rāma Rāma, Hare Hare.

Mahāmāyā—the illusory material energy of the Lord.

Maṅgala-ārati—a predawn ceremony for greeting the Lord with offerings of food, lamps, fans, flowers and incense.

Mantra—a sound vibration that can deliver the mind from illusion.

Mathurā—Lord Kṛṣṇa's abode, surrounding Vṛndāvana, where He took birth and later returned to after performing His Vṛndāvana pastimes.

Māyā—illusion; forgetfulness of one's relationship with Kṛṣṇa.

Māyāvādīs—impersonal philosophers who say that the Lord cannot have a transcendental body.

Mṛdaṅga—a clay drum used for congregational chanting.

P

Paramparā—the chain of spiritual masters in disciplic succession.

Prajāpatis—the populators of the universe.

Prasāda—food spiritualized by being offered to the Lord.

S

Sac-cid-ānanda-vigraha—the Lord's transcendental form, which is eternal, full of knowledge and bliss.

Saṅkīrtana—public chanting of the names of God, the approved *yoga* process for this age.

Sannyāsa—renounced life; the fourth order of Vedic spiritual life.

Sarga—material creation.

Śāstras—revealed scriptures.

Śravaṇaṁ kīrtanaṁ viṣṇoḥ—the devotional processes of hearing and chanting about Lord Viṣṇu.

Śūdra—a laborer; the fourth of the Vedic social orders.

Svāmī—one who controls his mind and senses; title of one in the renounced order of life.

T

Tapasya—austerity; accepting some voluntary inconvenience for a higher purpose.

Tilaka—auspicious clay marks that sanctify a devotee's body as a temple of the Lord.

V

Vaikuṇṭha—the spiritual world.

Vaiṣṇava—a devotee of Lord Viṣṇu, Kṛṣṇa.

Vaiśyas—farmers and merchants; the third Vedic social order.

Vānaprastha—one who has retired from family life; the third order of Vedic spiritual life.

Varṇa—the four occupational divisions of society: the intellectual class, the administrative class, the mercantile class, and the laborer class.

Varṇāśrama—the Vedic social system of four social and four spiritual orders.

Vedas—the original revealed scriptures, first spoken by the Lord Himself.

Viṣṇu, Lord—Kṛṣṇa's expansion for the creation and maintenance of the material universes.

Vṛndāvana—Kṛṣṇa's personal abode, where He fully manifests His quality of sweetness.

Vyāsadeva—Kṛṣṇa's incarnation, at the end of Dvāpara-yuga, for compiling the *Vedas*.

Y

Yajña—an activity performed to satisfy either Lord Viṣṇu or the demigods.

Yogī—a transcendentalist who, in one way or another, is striving for union with the Supreme.

Yugas—ages in the life of a universe, occurring in a repeated cycle of four.

Sanskrit Pronunciation Guide

Vowels

अ a आ ā इ i ई ī उ u ऊ ū ऋ ṛ ॠ ṝ

ऌ ḷ ए e ऐ ai ओ o औ au

ं ṁ *(anusvāra)* ः ḥ *(visarga)*

Consonants

Gutturals:	क ka	ख kha	ग ga	घ gha	ङ ṅa
Palatals:	च ca	छ cha	ज ja	झ jha	ञ ña
Cerebrals:	ट ṭa	ठ ṭha	ड ḍa	ढ ḍha	ण ṇa
Dentals:	त ta	थ tha	द da	ध dha	न na
Labials:	प pa	फ pha	ब ba	भ bha	म ma
Semivowels:	य ya	र ra	ल la	व va	
Sibilants:	श śa	ष ṣa	स sa		
Aspirate:	ह ha	ऽ ' *(avagraha)* – the apostrophe			

The numerals are: ० -0 १-1 २-2 ३-3 ४-4 ५-5 ६-6 ७-7 ८-8 ९-9

The vowels above should be pronounced as follows:

a – like the *a* in org*a*n or the *u* in b*u*t
ā – like the *a* in f*a*r but held twice as long as short *a*
i – like the *i* in p*i*n
ī – like the *i* in p*i*que but held twice as long as short *i*

u – like the *u* in p*u*sh
ū – like the *u* in r*u*le but held twice as long as short *u*
ṛ – like the *ri* in *ri*m
ṝ – like *ree* in *ree*d
ḷ – like *l* followed by *ṛ* (*lṛ*)
e – like the *e* in th*e*y
ai – like the *ai* in *ai*sle
o – like the *o* in g*o*
au – like the *ow* in h*ow*
ṁ (*anusvāra*) – a resonant nasal like the *n* in the French word *bon*
ḥ (*visarga*) – a final *h*-sound: *aḥ* is pronounced like *aha; iḥ* like *ihi*

The vowels are written as follows after a consonant:

ा ā ि i ी ī ु u ू ū ृ ṛ ॄ ṝ े e ै ai ो o ौ au

For example: क ka का kā कि ki की kī कु ku कू kū

कृ kṛ कॄ kṝ के ke कै kai को ko कौ kau

The vowel "a" is implied after a consonant with no vowel symbol.

The symbol virāma (्) indicates that there is no final vowel: क्

The consonants are pronounced as follows:

k – as in *k*ite
kh – as in Ec*kh*art
g – as in *g*ive
gh – as in di*g-h*ard
ṅ – as in si*ng*
c – as in *ch*air
ch – as in staun*ch-h*eart
j – as in *j*oy
jh – as in he*dgeh*og
ñ – as in ca*ny*on
ṭ – as in *t*ub
ṭh – as in ligh*t-h*eart
ḍ – as in *d*ove
ḍha- as in re*d-h*ot
ṇ – as r*na* (prepare to say the *r* and say *na*)

Cerebrals are pronounced with tongue to roof of mouth, but the following dentals are pronounced with tongue against teeth:

t – as in *t*ub but with tongue against teeth
th – as in ligh*t-h*eart but with tongue against teeth

d – as in *d*ove but with tongue against teeth
dh – as in re*d-h*ot but with tongue against teeth
n – as in *n*ut but with tongue between teeth
p – as in *p*ine
ph – as in u*ph*ill (not *f*)
b – as in *b*ird
bh – as in ru*b-h*ard
m – as in *m*other
y – as in *y*es
r – as in *r*un
l – as in *l*ight
v – as in *v*ine
ś (palatal) – as in the *s* in the German word *sprechen*
ṣ (cerebral) – as the *sh* in *sh*ine
s – as in *s*un
h – as in *h*ome

Generally two or more consonants in conjunction are written together in a special form, as for example: क्ष kṣa त्र tra

There is no strong accentuation of syllables in Sanskrit, or pausing between words in a line, only a flowing of short and long (twice as long as the short) syllables. A long syllable is one whose vowel is long (ā, ī, ū, e, ai, o, au), or whose short vowel is followed by more than one consonant (including anusvāra and visarga). Aspirated consonants (such as kha and gha) count as only single consonants.

Index of Sanskrit Verses

This index constitutes a complete listing of the first and third lines of each of the Sanskrit poetry verses of this volume of *Śrīmad-Bhāgavatam*, arranged in English alphabetical order. The first column gives the Sanskrit transliteration, and the second and third columns, respectively, list the chapter-verse reference and page number for each verse.

U

V

General Index

Numerals in boldface type indicate references to translations of the verses of *Śrīmad-Bhāgavatam.*

A

Absolute Truth
knowledge about. *See:* Knowledge, spiritual
Lord killing miscreants as, 257, 266
Lord's mercy reveals, 331–332
process for knowing, 366
realization of, in stages, 329, 331
water from the Lord as, 211
See also: Kṛṣṇa, Lord; Reality vs. reflection; Spiritual world; Supreme Lord
Ācāryas (saintly authorities)
in Brahma-sampradāya, 175–176
See also: Disciplic succession; Spiritual master
Activities
of lowborn devotees, 345
See also: Duty; Pious activities; Sinful activity; Supreme Lord, pastimes of; Welfare activity
Adānta-gobhir viśatāṁ tamisraṁ
verse quoted, 29
Administrators, pride in, 44
See also: Government leaders; *Kṣatriyas*
Advaitam acyutam anādim ananta-rūpam
verse quoted, 5
Advaita Prabhu offered *prasāda* to Haridāsa, 348
Affection
of Lord for His servitors, 346–347
real object of, **57–58**
See also: Love; Supreme Lord, love for
Age, present. *See:* Kali-yuga
Agelessness in spiritual world, 298
Agni-hotra, 202
Ahaṁ sarvasya prabhavaḥ, 377
Ahaṅkāra defined, 130
Airplanes, spiritual, 224, **296,** 297
Ākūti, **166, 167**
Alcohol in demoniac society, 256
Alphabet, Sanskrit, 161
Anādir ādir govindaḥ
verse quoted, 120
Analogies
angry father & *brāhmaṇas,* **352**–353
big sky & Lord, **306**
blind men & modern leaders, 12
boat & human body, 292
captain & spiritual master, 292
crows & materialists, 2–3
dramatic actor & Lord, 25–26
fire in wood & Lord's existence, **47**
fire in wood & Lord's potency, **208**–209
flames & Kṛṣṇa's expansions, 7
flowers & Lord's face, **322**
elephant & offense, 316
fortress & body, 235
gold & identity, **260**
leprosy & offense, **343**
machine parts & living entities, 307
mad elephant & sex desire, **226**–227
miser & loveless soul, 58
nonpoisonous snake & devotee's wealth, 10
prison & material world, 307
razor's edge & spiritual path, 39
salt & sense gratification, 274
serpents & negligent persons, **350,** 351
sky & ear holes, 335–336
stage play & Lord's fighting pastime, 371
stomach & Lord, 307
sun & Lord, 150

B

Brahma-sampradāya list, 175–176
Brahma-śāpa defined, 376
Brahma-tejas defined, 39
Brahmins. *See: Brāhmaṇas*
Breathing process in *yoga*, **272–273**, 327
Bṛhan-nāradīya Purāṇa, Hare Kṛṣṇa *mantra* in, 190
Buddha, Lord, preached atheism, 371–372
Businessmen. *See: Vaiśyas*

C

Caitanya-caritāmṛta, cited on chanting the holy name, 295
Caitanya Mahāprabhu
 in Brahma-sampradāya, 175
 cited on offending devotees, 316
 contribution by, 254
 Haridāsa blessed by, 341
 as Kṛṣṇa concealed, 364
 as missionary, 22
 pleased by *saṅkīrtana*, 202
 with Rāmānanda Rāya, 333
 as savior, 295
 yoga process taught by, 327
Caitya defined, 326
Cakra defined, 298
Cāṇakya Paṇḍita, cited on time, 70
Cañcalā, 288
Caṇḍāla can become devotee, **344**, 345
"Caste system." *See:* Devotees, beyond bodily designation; *Varṇāśrama-dharma*
Cātur-varṇyaṁ mayā sṛṣṭam quoted, 158
Celibacy
 of *brahmacārīs*, 157
 in *yoga* practice, 324
Ceremonies. *See:* Sacrifice; Vedic rituals
Chaitanya. *See:* Caitanya Mahāprabhu
Channa-avatāra defined, 364
Chanting the holy names of the Lord
 ecstatic symptoms from, 294, 295
 via Hare Kṛṣṇa *mantra*, 190
 by Haridāsa Ṭhākura, 247
 as highest thought, 376
Chanting the holy names of the Lord
 in Kali-yuga, 263
 offenses in, effect of, 294–295
 as only way, 327
 progeny elevated by, 254
 purifying power of, 364
 two ways of, 248
 See also: Gāyatrī *mantra;* Hare Kṛṣṇa *mantra;* Supreme Lord, name of
Charity, householders must give, 211
 See also: Welfare activity
Chastity of good wife, 232, 235
Cheaters
 pseudo religionists as, 17
 teaching "*yoga*," 323, 324
Children
 innocence of, 300
 protection for, 351
 purpose for having, 178–179, 228
 qualification for conceiving, 380
 via sexual intercourse, 227, 254, 255
 See also: Marriage
Christ, Jesus, 382
City-life "*yoga*," 324
Civilization, human. *See:* Society, human; *Varṇāśrama-dharma;* Vedic culture
Cleanliness
 mandatory times for, 248
 in spiritual culture, 364–365
 See also: Purification
Comparisons. *See:* Analogies
Compassion
 of devotees, 11–13
 of Prahlāda, 261
Conditioned souls. *See:* Souls, conditioned
Consciousness
 of Brahmā, **270**
 pure condition of, **48**
 superconsciousness vs., 326
 See also: Knowledge; Kṛṣṇa consciousness; Soul
Cosmic manifestation. *See:* Creation, the material; Material world; Planets, material; Universe
Cowherd girls. *See: Gopīs;* Rādhārāṇī

F

Factories as hellish, 15
Faith in Lord's pastimes, 222
False ego
  foolishness of, 130
  origin & by-products of, **74**
Family life
  father-son relationship in, 174–178
  Kumāras rejected, **125**–126
  miseries from, 10
  in Vedic society, 156
  See also: Children; Householders; Marriage
Father-son relationship, 174–178
Fear
  cause & cure for, **9–10**
  of death, 122
  devotees beyond, 273, 335, 336
  used in Lord's service, 376
Fighting pastime of the Lord, 371, 381
Fire
  mantra to ignite, 209
  in sacrifice to Viṣṇu, **226**
Flowers, spiritual, **284–285**
Fog, Brahmā created, **149**
Food. *See:* Eating
Forgetting the Lord, 312
Forms of the Lord. *See:* Supreme Lord, forms of
Freedom. *See:* Independence; Liberation

G

Gadā defined, 298
Ganges River from Lord's lotus feet, 211, **349**
Garbhādhāna defined, 254
Garbhodaka Ocean
  planets rest in, 196
  size of, 183
Garbhodakaśāyī Viṣṇu
  Brahmā dreams about, 104
  Brahmā, Viṣṇu & Śiva from, 3
  enjoys *rāsa* with external energy, 24
  See also: Mahā-Viṣṇu; Supersoul; Supreme Lord
Gatekeepers of Vaikuṇṭha. *See:* Jaya & Vijaya
Gāyatrī *mantra*
  mahā-mantra vs., 248
  origin of, **160**
  in Vedic hymns, **200,** 201
Ghosts, characteristics of, 239
Glorifying the Lord. *See:* Supreme Lord, glorification of
Goal of life. *See:* Life, goal of
Go-brāhmaṇa-hitāya ca
  quoted, 342, 366
God. *See:* Absolute Truth; Kṛṣṇa, Lord; Nārāyaṇa, Lord; Supersoul; Supreme Lord; Viṣṇu, Lord
God consciousness. *See:* Kṛṣṇa consciousness
Goddess of fortune (Lakṣmī)
  doorkeepers angered, **375**
  Lord's beauty surpasses, **319,** 320
  in Lord's service, 346–347, **361**
  as Ramā, **37**
  rarely seen, 341
  tulasī surpasses, 362–363
  unsteady, 288
  in Vaikuṇṭha, 287, 288
Goddess of learning, 142–143
"Gods." *See:* Demigods
Gokula (Kṛṣṇaloka), Rādhā & Kṛṣṇa in, 320
Goodness
  qualities of, 293–294
  in spiritual world, 280, 331
Gopāla-tāpanī Upaniṣad, quoted on Kṛṣṇa and *gopīs,* 24
Gopīs
  as internal potency, 40
  lusty desires of, 376
  in *rāsa* dance, 24
Govardhana Hill, Lord lifted, 26
Government leaders
  compared to blind men, 12
  duty of, 180
  enmity toward, 305
  Kṛṣṇa exemplary for, 366
  mundane interests of, 290–291
  See also: Kṣatriyas; Varṇāśrama-dharma
Gṛhasthas. See: Householders; *Varṇāśrama-dharma*

I

J

L

U

V

W

Y

De 1990 es *Las horas completas* cuyo título hace referencia a las últimas de las horas canónicas (maitines, prima, tercia, nona, sexta, vísperas y completas) que rezan los sacerdotes seculares y los frailes.

Se narra un viaje divertido de cinco sacerdotes que van de excursión; salen de una ciudad, probablemente leonesa, para ir a merendar a un pueblo, cercano al suyo, con el sacerdote del pueblo. También en esta novela el realismo va unido a lo fantástico y no falta el humor. Los personajes viven en la imaginación lo que no pueden vivir en la vida real.

De su última novela *Expediente del náufrago* (1992) ha dicho el autor que

> es ante todo un espejo de la realidad en que vivimos; frente a la filosofía del escalador y el triunfador hago protagonistas a los perdedores, símbolos literarios de lo más digno y noble de la condición humana.

Un grupo de poetas desafortunados se unen en su aislamiento para buscar la obra de un poeta local, funcionario municipal y apenas conocido como poeta, Alejandro Saelices. La novela cuenta los trabajos del poeta, y también funcionario, Fermín Bustarga, para encontrar la obra de su antecesor, Saelices, de quien encontró, casualmente, algunos versos. Es también un relato sobre el mundo de la provincia y los personajes son los perdedores. Pero también es verdad que aunque Saelices se ve como un náufrago dice que

> el naufragio es una vicisitud que sólo pueden correr quienes navegan, aquellos que en la vida se adentran

como en el mar, (...) dispuestos a enmendar su aventura...» (págs. 19-20)

Sólo son derrotados por la vida aquellos que se lanzan a vivirla.

Prólogo

Tres cuentos y su marco

En los tres cuentos que ofrecemos está la montaña leonesa. Dos de ellos, *El difunto Ezequiel Montes* y *La familia de Villar* están localizados en ella. *El viaje de doña Saturnina* se desarrolla en un paisaje mediterráneo, pero la montaña leonesa está también.

Algunos rasgos del leonés aparecen en los cuentos y el marco rural explica el vocabulario un poco específico a veces. Pero son pocas las dificultades que ofrece y van aclaradas en las notas.

La montaña occidental leonesa es de una belleza indescriptible. A una parte de ella ha consagrado LMD su *Relato de Babia.*

La montaña leonesa tiene famosos puertos que la comunican con Asturias (Ver mapa en página 4). Son, entre ellos, famosos los de Mesa, Somiedo, Leitariegos y Pajares. Los ríos Sil, Luna y Omaña riegan la región. Ríos famosos por sus truchas. Son zonas de aprovechamiento con sus embalses que dan fuerza a las centrales eléctricas y agua a las tierras llanas.

La comarca de El Bierzo es la más rica. Zona rica en minerales, posee una de las mejores reservas de hierro de Europa. Tiene también yacimientos de carbón.

Las regiones de Babia y Omaña son pastoriles, mientras que Laciana es región minera. Villablino el pueblo natal de LMD es rico en yacimientos de carbón.

La Provincia de León cuenta con un paisaje variado. Los cuentos que presentamos podrían situarse en la zona noroccidental, el norte, con un paisaje muy parecido al de Asturias. Así parece ser el de Pobladura, el del pueblo de doña Saturnina (pág. 44) y el de El Villar de los Barrios antes de ser sumergido por las aguas. (pág. 38) El centro de la Provincia es un extenso páramo (pág. 4) y sus tierras ya se integran en la llanura de la tierra de campos: tierras llanas de trigales y viñedos. La tierra llana de los Campos góticos.

León es una Provincia muy rica en todo lo cultural. La memoria popular guarda leyendas relacionadas con el oro de los árabes y las hachas de piedra encontradas hablan de la cultura de los castros. La historia guarda la memoria de la estancia de los romanos y militares romanos fundaron la ciudad de León.

Tanto la ciudad como la provincia son poseedoras de auténticas joyas en el terreno del arte y no es sólo la Catedral de León la joya en la arquitectura, una de las más bellas joyas del arte gótico español. Están representados el arte visigótico y el arte mozárabe. Ya en la época visigótica aparece el arte románico vigilando los caminos de peregrinación, pues por León pasaba el Camino de Santiago.

En el siglo XIII el Reino de León se unió definitivamente al reino de Castilla y desde 1230 en que el rey castellano Fernando III el Santo accedió al trono leonés la historia de León y la de Castilla van unidas.

En 1983 las Cortes Generales aprobaron el Estatuto de

Autonomía y hoy Castilla y León forman una Comunidad con sus instituciones y símbolos propios.

El difunto Ezequiel Montes es uno de los cuentos recogidos en *Memorial de hierbas*.
Es la historia de un amor imposible. LMD ha hablado de su pasión por contar y en este relato se muestra como narrador consumado. Logra atrapar la atención del lector desde la primera página, de forma que el misterio que rodea la vida de Ezequiel va adensando la necesidad de seguir leyendo. Al terminar, el lector se queda admirado ante esta breve, bella y melancólica historia de amor imposible.

Como **marco** de esta historia íntima está la vida del pueblo y el pueblo mismo. Un pueblo de montaña por el que pasan las cuatro estaciones del año: el verano de mucho calor en que llega Ezequiel al pueblo, en un día 15 de agosto, el día de la festividad de la Asunción de la Virgen a los cielos, los veranos ocupados con las tareas de la siega, la recolección de las mieses; el otoño con las siembras; el invierno de «crudos y furiosos carámbanos», de nieve que en febrero está brillante y helada «con el resol y las heladas»; la primavera en la que Ezequiel va perdiendo las ganas de vivir.

La historia está narrada por un chico, cuando Ezequiel es ya recuerdo, y cuando han pasado seis años de la llegada de Ezequiel al pueblo. Pero el narrador recuerda la vida de Ezequiel en el pueblo, mientras éste vivió en él, y entonces este pasado aparece en el plano de la vida diaria, presente en el pasado. Para el lector se tra-ta de un pasado remoto y de un pasado próximo. Sobre el narrador-niño hay que pensar en el escritor LMD.

Las connotaciones de **tiempo** cronológico se dan espaciadas y, una vez leído el relato, el lector puede establecer la cronología y ordenar las claves que el autor ha ido dejando caer como anticipaciones que se perciben como tales solamente después de haber leído todo el relato. Entre estas claves a descifrar está la fecha de la llegada de Ezequiel al pueblo y el nombre de la señora de Pobladura. Pero no son éstas las únicas.

La familia de Villar es el relato más breve de los tres que he seleccionado.

El **marco** queda trazado dentro de una problemática de actualidad reciente: la de los pueblos sumergidos. En relación con los planteamientos económicos, el Gobierno decidió desalojar algunos pueblos leoneses para construir un embalse que diese agua a regiones más extensas y secas. Se trataba, según la Administración, de soluciones necesarias para poder dar agua a grandes zonas de la España seca. Estos pueblos desalojados quedaron sumergidos en las aguas del embalse. Los habitantes de muchos de ellos se resistieron y protestaron, otros aceptaron las nuevas tierras. Pero todos se sintieron arrancados de sus tierras y para muchos fue difícil el arraigo en otros lugares, pues no son solo los pueblos los que quedan anegados, sino una historia y una identidad. La prensa del momento recogió la problemática y las opiniones de algunos escritores, no solamente escritores leoneses. No es aquí el lugar para hablar de los problemas económicos y de reconversión industrial de la España de hoy, pero es interesante mencionarlo porque ello nos permite situar los relatos en el **tiempo**. El escritor Julio Llamazares, también leonés, nació en 1955 el el pueblo de Vergamián, hoy sumergido. No sé si tras El Villar de los Barrios se esconde un pueblo real pero lo que recoge esta joya de la narrativa de hoy es la problemática de muchos pueblos leoneses que han sido anegados por las aguas del pantano, lo que ha dado lugar a un debate político-social en los años 80 y aún en los primeros años de la década actual. LMD recoge esta problemática de una manera bien medida, con gran economía narrativa, con hondo lirismo también, sin ocultar la tragedia y dejando una puerta abierta al futuro, me parece a mí.

El Villar de los Barrios fue un pueblo de la montaña que quedó bajo las aguas del embalse y es fácil percibir la contenida emoción ante el recuerdo silencioso del pueblo verde en la hondonada del valle del que solo asoma sobre el agua la torre de la ermita «quieta en la superficie como antes había estado en el aire.» (página 38)

El viaje de doña Saturnina tiene como **marco** las tierras del sur de España. Pero la montaña leonesa está también presente en el relato pues desde ella recuerda doña Saturnina el mar visto en su lejano viaje de bodas y a ese mar va por segunda vez huyendo de los duros inviernos de la montaña. Doña Saturnina hace breves viajes al pueblo en el verano para arreglar sus asuntos económicos y el resto del tiempo lo pasa en el pensionado que regentan unas monjas y en el que está contenta. Pero su imaginación económica la lleva a emplear un dinero en un apartamento que alquila y al que viaja cada mes para cobrar el alquiler. En uno de estos viajes le ocurre algo inaudito. En la narración de la aventura de doña Saturnina no falta ni el suspenso ni el humor y al acabar el relato el lector ha descubierto que junto con el viaje habitual doña Saturnina ha hecho otro tipo de viaje inusual.

El *difunto* Ezequiel Montes

1

El difunto se llamaba Ezequiel Montes.

Aquí le recordamos por algunos detalles intrascendentes: el labio *leporino*, la *gorra visera* y un andar de *cangrejo* que *insinuaba* la dificultad de los pies planos. Tenía *trazas* de cazador, aunque no lo era, barbas *amaralladas* y los ojos saltones y *punzantes* como las *liebres*. Era mediano de estatura, alto de cuello, *atravesado* de nariz, *cargado de hombros* y corto de brazos. Parecía un *roble* viejo de los que se *cuartean* en la *Dehesa de Pobladura*.

Atrajo nuestra curiosidad cuando le vimos aparecer, hace unos seis años, por el *Teso de los Corredores*, un agosto caliente como pocos, la misma tarde del *día de Nuestra Señora*.

Estábamos bañándonos en la *charca* de la *huerga* y andábamos desnudos por los *juncos* pescando *ranas* y atrapando *gusarapas*, atareados en llenar una cazuela de *ancas* que luego nos prepararaban con *pimentón* y cebolla en la *cantina* de Cecilio.

El hombre nos preguntó por el nombre del pueblo, dejó la bolsa que traía a la espalda en el verde de la charca, quitó las botas, metió los pies en el agua y *lió* un cigarro.

Cuando fumaba, descubrimos con mayor *nitidez* la extrañeza del labio leporino y nuestra curiosidad nos *embebió* en una contemplación *descarada* que a él no parecía molestarle.

| Ver notas en página 56

Después se marchó hacia el pueblo *babeando la colilla* por encima de las barbas y *atascando* los pasos en el polvo del camino vecinal.

Recuerdo que vestía una *sahariana* comida por el sol y los sudores, pantalones de *mahón arremangados* encima de las botas y camisa *caqui* con tres botones saltados.

La gorra visera, de color *pajizo*, le rozaba el saliente de las orejas y se deslizaba hacia la frente dejando al aire un pequeño *mechón* de pelos *encanecidos*.

Por el pueblo hubo muchos comentarios con la llegada de Ezequiel. Cuando los hombres se enteraron de su intención de quedarse a vivir aquí, el *recelo* abrió paso a las más variadas sospechas y durante los primeros días todos nos mirábamos con *complicidad*.

En las cocinas se hablaba en secreto del extraño personaje cuyo labio producía especial *aversión*, sobre todo a las mujeres.

En casa de Cecilio alquiló una habitación y pagó un mes por adelantado. El cantinero contaba que era hombre de pocas palabras y que a él su dinero le parecía tan bueno como el de cualquiera.

Solía pasarse las mañanas sentado en un *escaño* de la cantina, bebiendo copas de *orujo* y escribiendo en papel de carta con una *estilográfica* de color marrón.

Por las tardes, después de la siesta, paseaba por el pueblo y se iba al *Soto* controlado por la mirada disimulada de todos y llevando los dedos de la mano derecha hasta el *vértice* de la visera cuando se cruzaba con alguien.

| Ver notas en página 57

Al cabo de una semana, su presencia era tan habitual y *anodina*, que estábamos acostumbrados, y el nombre de Ezequiel se mezclaba en las conversaciones para salpicar la gracia ajena de aquel labio imposible o los andares *desmadejados* que *suscitaban* las risas de las mozas.

Seguían causando sensación las barbas amaralladas y *lacias*, que le daban un aspecto de *sanroque*, y la gorra visera.

Nosotros le esperábamos por la tarde a la salida de la cantina e íbamos tras él por las *veredas* de las *norias* hasta el Soto, convencidos ya de que se trataba de un ser inofensivo y despreocupados del misterio de su presencia en el pueblo.

Un día, cuando el hombre llevaba casi un mes entre nosotros, le dijo a Cecilio que necesitaba los servicios de una persona de confianza para hacerle un *recado* muy importante. El cantinero se ofreció él mismo y Ezequiel le confió una carta muy abultada, de varias *cuartillas*, *lacrada* en un sobre azul. Le rogó que no hablase con nadie y que la entregara según sus órdenes y *aguardara* la respuesta.

La carta era para doña Chon, la señora de Pobladura.

Emérita, la mujer de Cecilio, apenas tuvo tiempo para correr de casa en casa comunicando el secreto de Ezequiel, y en seguida todos supimos que el cantinero había marchado con el *mensaje* para la señora y que Ezequiel aguardaba una respuesta sentado en el *rincón* del escaño y bebiendo más orujo que de costumbre.

Aquel día, cuando yo volví a casa con mi padre -ha-

| Ver notas en página 58

bíamos pasado la mañana *aricando remolacha*-, mi madre nos contó que el hombre del labio -ella siempre le llamaba así- era un enamorado de doña Chon, y que estaba en el pueblo para *concertarle* una entrevista.

Mi padre sacaba vino del *pellejo* para la botella y escupió la colilla de *cuarterón*; después, moviendo la cabeza, se quedó mirando el *chorro* morado que bajaba por el cuello de cristal y dijo:

– Pobre *desgraciado*.

Cecilio no trajo ninguna contestación a la carta de Ezequiel. A su regreso, el hombre estaba casi borracho y el cantinero, según contó después, pasó un mal rato para hacerle entender que doña Chon y su ama de llaves, la *tía* Enedina, le habían despedido de malos modos.

La única obsesión de Ezequiel era saber si al menos se habían *hecho cargo* de la carta. Cecilio tuvo que confesarle que la misma había sido destruida en su presencia por la propia señora que, además, le había recordado una pequeña deuda de trigo que el cantinero tenía con ella.

2

Tras este suceso, Ezequiel se hundió en una visible *consternación* y en el pueblo se le *toleraba* con mayores *contemplaciones orillando* las burlas del labio leporino y los andares *cadenciosos*.

Pasó un invierno tristón y *despegado*, consumiendo las reservas de orujo de Cecilio, *atascado* en largas borracheras nada ruidosas. Sólo en contadas ocasiones

| Ver notas en página 59

salía de la cantina y se animaba con nosotros persiguiendo los *pardales* en la nieve, o *corriendo* una liebre *desorientada* de las que se acercan al pueblo *deslumbradas* por los *reverberos*.

En la primavera empezó de nuevo a consumir las cuartillas con la estilográfica, se arregló las barbas y estrenó una camisa de colores *chillones* que le trajo de la ciudad el cobrador del *coche de línea*.

Cecilio comunicó a los amigos que Ezequiel *volvía a las andadas* y que aquella carta infinita, en la que estaba invirtiendo mes y medio, tendría la misma dirección que la anterior.

Él se negaba de *antemano* a *oficiar* de mensajero y solicitaba ayuda para cuando llegase el momento de volver con el recado a doña Chon.

Entre todos, siempre de espaldas a Ezequiel, convencieron a Mauricio, el *alguacil*, para que se hiciese cargo del mensaje cuando llegase el momento.

El asunto se estaba convirtiendo en un problema de todo el *vecindario*, y las mujeres comentaban la *obstinación* de aquel hombre y compadecían su ánimo a la vez que se informaban del número de cuartillas en que iba aumentando la carta, *haciendo cábalas* sobre la extraordinaria inspiración del amante.

Fue un viernes de junio cuando Ezequiel dio fin a la *misiva* y volvió a solicitar de Cecilio sus servicios.

El cantinero se disculpó y señaló a Mauricio como persona de entera confianza.

El hombre *accedió* y Mauricio marchó aquella tarde para Pobladura con el sobre azul lacrado y vigilado por

| Ver notas en página 60

la curiosidad de todos.

En la cantina, los hombres alargaron las *partidas* y los *chavales* nos sentamos en los *poyos* de la entrada disimulando un juego de *chapas* o *arracimados* en las ventanas para observar a Ezequiel, que consumía las copas de orujo en un *rito imperturbable* y *acelerado*.

Al anochecer regresó el alguacil, entró en la cantina con la gorra en las manos, se acercó a Ezequiel y le comunicó que su recado estaba cumplido.

El hombre le preguntó si traía alguna respuesta y Mauricio le dijo que sí y le entregó un sobre blanco pequeño y *manoseado*.

Lo abrió Ezequiel con extraordinaria paciencia y sacó una tarjeta amarillenta.

Nadie pudo ver lo que en ella estaba escrito.

Ezequiel la guardó en el bolsillo de la sahariana, suspiró y volvió a llenar su vaso consumiéndolo de un *sorbo*.

La atención de todos quedó *suspensa* en aquellos ojos saltones y *vivaces* que se fueron apagando lentamente.

3

Se pensaba en el pueblo que las cosas habrían cambiado de alguna manera y que Ezequiel tomaría una decisión.

Pero pasaron tres días de *obsesiva* curiosidad y nada había cambiado visiblemente en el *talante* y las costumbres del hombre.

Sus paseos siguieron *prodigándose* y sus estancias en la cantina continuaron en las mismas condiciones ape-

| Ver notas en página 60

gado a las copas de orujo, con *intermitentes arrebatos* sobre el *cartapacio* de las cuartillas, que en ocasiones rompía y tiraba al suelo convertidas en pedazos.

El verano, atareado en las *siegas* y la *cosecha*, nos alejó a todos de Ezequiel, que estaba convirtiéndose poco a poco en una figura *entrañable* y olvidada, como esas imágenes *imperceptibles* que se retiran de los altares y se guardan en la *sacristía*.

Sólo en ocasiones las mujeres, al verle pasar desde la *era*, compadecían el silencio y la creciente ruina de aquel hombre ensimismado, que contemplaba los pájaros en la *rastrojera* y dormía la siesta recostado en los *pilares de paja*.

Por noviembre tuvo un *achaque* que llegó a preocupar seriamente a Cecilio.

Una *tos abotargada y cadenciosa estremecía* la cantina y el orujo llenaba las horas amargas y dolientes del enfermo, cuyo rostro estaba empalideciendo hasta *tornar* blanco como la cal.

Emérita le convenció para que se quedara algunos días en la cama.

Ella nos informaba de las profundas melancolías de Ezequiel y todos celebramos con alegría su *recuperación*, cuando una mañana le vimos salir a la plaza con una manta sobre los hombros y atrapar un pardal *arrecido*.

Recuerdo aquel invierno *crudo* y furioso de *carámbanos* y nieve.

La noche de *San Silvestre* se reunieron los hombres del pueblo en casa de Cecilio y bebieron como locos.

| Ver notas en página 61

Ezequiel estaba alegre y se *exaltaba* con las historias de lobos que relatan los viejos recordando las mentiras de sus mayores en los *filandones* pasados.

La noche terminó en una borrachera colectiva, y los chavales y las mujeres quedamos durmiendo en las cocinas, *amedrentados* por aquel *bullicio* violento que rompía el silencio *exuberante* de la nevada, como si la excitación de nuestros padres fuera como un *presagio* del más absoluto de los abandonos.

Por febrero -la nieve estaba brillante con el resol y las heladas-, Ezequiel volvió a ensimismarse en el escaño, iniciando otra carta y orillando las tertulias de la cantina.

Todos esperábamos que, como siempre, su dedicación durara largo tiempo, pero quedamos sorprendidos al observar que al cabo de tres días ponía fin a la misiva y la preparaba cuidadosamente en el sobre lacrado.

Mauricio estaba convencido para repetir su labor de mensajero.

Cecilio esperaba con impaciencia las órdenes de Ezequiel.

Las mujeres se reunían en las cocinas obsesionadas por las noticias de la nueva obstinación, asegurando que aquel hombre había *perdido el juicio*.

Una extraña ansiedad nos dominaba a todos, porque Ezequiel había guardado la carta y parecía no tener intención de enviarla.

Cuatro días después, la mañana de un domingo que amaneció *arrebatada* por los presagios de la nieve, Ezequiel salió del pueblo y tomó el camino de Pobladura.

| Ver notas en página 62

Había *untado* las botas con *sebo* y llevaba puesta toda la ropa que tenía.

Por el *filo* de las ventanas y las puertas todo el mundo *espió* aquellos pasos *bamboleantes* e inseguros, y le vimos desaparecer con la visera *calada*, las manos en los bolsillos de la sahariana y la colilla apagada en el labio leporino.

Algunos propusieron seguirle, y Cecilio y mi padre marcharon tras él con la intención de tenerle vigilado a una distancia suficiente.

Fue un domingo *turbio* y desapacible.

La nieve *cedió* a un viento de locura y los *cierzos cuajaban* en el aire una saliva fría que se colaba por todas las rendijas.

Llegó la noche y la *ventisca* había crecido *enmarañada* por las violencias del *azote*, desgajando carámbanos de los *aleros* y amontonando la nieve en las paredes.

Un grupo de hombres *armados de faroles, estacas* y *palas*, salió después al camino y regresaron todos casi al amanecer con Ezequiel tendido en unas *parihuelas* cubierto con una manta.

Las barbas amaralladas tenían el *rigor* del hielo y hasta el labio leporino le bajaban dos *escamas* de nieve *cuajada* que contrastaban con el *fulgor* morado de la piel.

| Ver notas en página 63

4

El resto del invierno lo pasó el hombre en la cama bajo los cuidados de Emérita.

Poco antes de la primavera volvimos a verle y era aparente el enorme *decaimiento* de salud.

Se ayudaba con un bastón y caminaba en intermitentes *bandazos*, *sofocado* y ausente.

Las barbas le habían crecido derramadas hasta el pecho, los ojos *entibiecían* la *soñolencia* de una mirada que iba *atrofiándose* hasta *desaliñar el destello* de su vivacidad.

Se cubría con un *echarpe* de lana y arrastraba las botas haciendo círculos alrededor de la fuente de la plaza.

Al atardecer se sentaba en el poyo del pilón y quedaba adormecido.

En estas condiciones pasó su último año con nosotros.

Un día le pidió a Cecilio que le llevaran a la ciudad y solicitaran su internamiento en el *Asilo* de Ancianos.

Tramitaron la solicitud y al cabo de quince días había una plaza a su disposición.

Era -esto lo recuerdo con mayor nitidez que cualquier cosa- un trece de abril, cuando Ezequiel se marchó en la *furgoneta* de Cecilio, acompañado por mi padre y Emérita.

Yo estaba en el *juncal* de la huerga y el coche atravesó el camino vecinal *arremolinando* el polvo.

En el asiento trasero, Ezequiel iba adormecido, la go-

| Ver notas en página 63

rra visera caída sobre los ojos, las manos contenidas contra el pecho y la colilla amarillenta bailando en la *ranura* del labio leporino.

Cecilio conducía, y mi padre y Emérita, sentados a su lado, *apuraban* la serena tristeza del viaje con el gesto sombrío en el que se cumplen los *designios* irremediables.

Dos años después un telegrama nos anunciaba la muerte de Ezequiel en el Asilo. A su entierro fueron muchos hombres y mujeres del pueblo.

Y no tardamos en saber que, el mismo día de la noticia de su muerte, doña Chon, la señora de Pobladura, había encargado las *misas gregorianas* en su *memoria*, y que en sus distanciadas y raras salidas a la calle se la veía vestida de *luto riguroso*.

Entonces comenzaron a correr las más diversas versiones sobre la auténtica identidad del difunto, pero la última clave de aquellos misterios la encontró Cecilio en el bolsillo de un viejo pantalón de Ezequiel, un día en que haciendo limpieza en los *baúles* de las habitaciones aparecieron diversas *prendas* que le habían pertenecido.

Era una tarjeta *ribeteada* con el negro de las *esquelas*.

Llevaba escritos los nombres de doña Chon y Ezequiel *garrapateados* con tinta color *sepia*, y al lado dos corazones dibujados con *exhaustiva minuciosidad*.

En la otra cara de la tarjeta, apenas visible bajo las huellas amarillas, una frase de amor que relataba las esperanzas de un regreso, escrita con la misma *caligrafía* que el hombre había empleado en las cuartillas de sus cartas, y la anotación: En San Juan de Puertorrico

| Ver notas en página 64

a 20 de mayo de 1929.

Fue *a raíz de* aquel descubrimiento cuando los más viejos del pueblo recordaron la sombra *difuminada* de un primo de la señora, que había huido a las Américas después del oscuro suceso de la muerte violenta de don Baldomero Torres, el *hacendado pretendiente* familiar de doña Chon, cuya cabeza separada del cuerpo y con los ojos *fregados* en el barro de la *torrentera* apareció en un *barranquillo* del Teso de los Corredores.

| Ver notas en página 65

La familia de Villar

La familia de *Villar* vino a mi pueblo dos meses antes de que llegara el agua. El padre se llamaba Antonio, la madre, Enedina, y los hijos, Benito y Clara. *Arrendaron* seis *hectáreas* del *secano pedregoso* cerca de la carretara de Villamaniel y compraron una casa de *adobe* que estaba a las afueras del pueblo.

Era una casa abandonada, de las que se emplean para almacenar la paja y guardar las *mulas*. Trabajaron en ella hasta componerle las paredes, la retejaron y dividieron la vivienda con *tabiques* de *ladrillo*. Estuvieron casi un mes dedicados a la obra. Antonio y Benito aunando las labores de albañilería con el trabajo de la tierra: la limpieza de *cardos* y *cenizales*, el aricado de las hectáreas *yermas*, donde la rastrojera antigua había dejado el *vicio* de las *sebes* y la *retama* hasta colmar el abandono en un color pajizo *entreverado* por las *ronchas de matojo* y *amapolas*. Enedina y Clara *recalando* los tabiques y el adobe, amasando el cemento y acarreando los ladrillos desde la tejera de Villamaniel.

El *encalado* lucía en las paredes derechas, las tejas formaban una *comba* casi vertical, y bajo el corte de los aleros un *canalón* de *aluminio* salvaba el agua de la lluvia, derivando a los lados las *escorreduras* y preservando la fachada.

Para entonces la familia ya era conocida en el pueblo con el nombre de Villar y se les miraba con la simpatía que *reporta* el trabajo bien hecho.

| Ver notas en página 69

El rastrojo de sus hectáreas tenía el aspecto limpio y acabado y la tierra estaba abierta con un sudor distinto, preparada para la siembra y aguardando el agua.

Benito y Clara vinieron a la escuela y se ganaron enseguida nuestra amistad. No eran aquellos muchachos *taciturnos* y lejanos del principio, cuando la labor les tenía atados desde el amanecer a la noche. Jugábamos mezclados por el vacío de las eras, correteando hasta la huerga y las norias, o nos sentábamos en el cemento del *canal* tirando piedras al *hondón* de aquella *brecha* tan larga, que un día no lejano nos traería el agua desde el *pantano* de Los Barrios.

A Benito le llamábamos Villar, como los hombres a Antonio. Y a Clara la Villarina, como las mujeres a su madre.

El Villar de los Barrios había sido su pueblo en la montaña, uno de los que las aguas del pantano *anegaban al ser embalsadas*. La familia era de las pocas que bajaron al *páramo* dispuestas a establecerse en las tierras nuevas, como se llamaba al *erial* empobrecido de nuestra llanura, que habría de transformarse con la promesa del *regadío*.

Benito nos contaba que su pueblo era un *término* de prados verdes en la *hondonada* del valle, con casas de piedra y tejado de *losa*, ganado lechero, la iglesia de dos campanas y una *ermita* de San Roque donde se celebraba la *romería* de la fiesta mayor.

Decía que en el límite donde el valle se cerraba formando el *tajo* de dos peñas enormes habían construido el *dique de la presa*, y que las aguas embalsadas se lleva-

| Ver notas en página 70

ban al vientre trece pueblos enteros con las fincas y los bosques de *robledal* y *haya*. Del suyo sólo quedaría fuera del agua la punta de la torre de la ermita y las *chozas de la braña*.

A nosotros se nos hacía difícil imaginar la inmensidad del agua *surtida* por los ríos y los *neveros* que habría de crecer contenida en el dique de la presa, *batiendo* las paredes de los corrales y las casas hasta *rozar* los tejados y recubrirlos, y perderse en las profundidades las calles y las fuentes y el bosque con los árboles más altos, y el campanario asomando los ojos vacíos de las campanas y la punta de la torre quieta en la superficie como antes había estado en el aire.

Benito había visto el agua embalsada, y cuando recordaba el paisaje de su pueblo -el verdor de los *pastizales* en las *vegas*, la inundación que debería pudrir hasta las raíces más tiernas- se le quedaban los ojos fijos en la llanura *estéril*, y alargaban la mirada *postrados* ante nuestro asombro, como siguiendo la línea del canal que estaba vacío y reciente y llevaba como una dirección misteriosa hasta el mismo origen del pueblo *sepultado*.

Poco después del agua -aquella ansiedad prodigiosa que reverdecía los cultivos en la *estepa* desértica de nuestro páramo- vendría la luz eléctrica, y aprenderíamos a comprender el milagro de las *bombillas* olvidando la *lámpara de aceite* y el *carburo*.

Las líneas trazadas sobre los *postes* esqueléticos elevaban kilómetros de cable y *casquillos de jícaras*, donde los pájaros *mendigos* de nuestra tierra comenzaban a

| Ver notas en página 71

posarse, apenas *acobardados* por aquella invasión que cruzaba el cielo *raso* de la llanura facilitándoles el reposo de sus vuelos.

Fueron las mujeres del pueblo, enteradas por Enedina, quienes primero supieron que la familia de Villar había dejado un hijo muerto en las obras del pantano.

Era el hijo mayor y se llamaba Antonio como el padre.

Había formado parte de la *brigada* que *horadó* el túnel que daba paso al agua desde la presa a la *caída* de la Central Eléctrica. Un túnel escarbado en la piedra caliza, de cinco kilómetros. La brigada, compuesta por veinte hombres y un *capataz*, trabajó en la dureza de los *martillos mecánicos* y el polvo venenoso produjo la *quemazón de los pulmones*, provocando la muerte lenta de todos los obreros, retirados en el grado más alto de *silicosis*.

Antonio había muerto en un hospital de la ciudad quince días antes de la llegada de la familia a nuestro pueblo.

Nosotros tuvimos presente aquel extraño secreto y en los juegos con Benito y Clara, cuando íbamos a romper con los *tiradores* algunas de las jícaras que colgaban en el brazo de los postes, apurábamos la tristeza de *albergar* a los dos hermanos y animábamos el silencio de Benito intentando distraer el recuerdo de la desgracia.

A los dos meses, poco antes de la siembra, una mañana soleada de las que barren el cielo limpiando las *canículas*, vimos el milagro del agua *avasallando* el reseco paredón del canal.

| Ver notas en página 72

Todo el pueblo salió *alborozado* festejando la emocionada curiosidad del espectáculo.

Era un agua limpia y sedosa que se deslizaba ante nosotros arrastrando las *motas de pajuelas* y los residuos de polvo.

Los mozos abrieron las *compuertas* de las primeras *acequias* y los chavales corrimos exaltados y descalzos, pisando la superficie por donde se adentraba la mano líquida, que iba extendiéndose como una caricia sobre el cuerpo atrofiado de los *sequedales*.

A mediodía los campos estaban *encharcados* y brillantes y las *azadas* de los hombres intentaban atajar la locura de aquella bendición, *agolpando* los *guijarros* para controlar la dirección en los *surcos*.

En el atardecer hubo baile en las eras y estallaron *manojos* de cohetes que retumbaban de pueblo en pueblo, anunciando la señal de la alegría colectiva.

La familia de Villar recibió el agua en sus hectáreas de la carretera de Villamaniel y luego vinieron a las eras a compartir el vino y las *empanadas*.

Los hombres se llevaron a Antonio; las mujeres a Enedina, y nosotros recogimos a Clara y a Benito.

Estuvimos un tiempo buscando *varillas* de cohetes y después nos sentamos *a la vera* del canal con los pies desnudos en el agua.

Apenas sabíamos cómo pronunciar una palabra que *rescatara* el silencio de aquellos amigos que miraban entristecidos *el espejo bullente* y encajonado en las paredes, la misma fuerza *vertiginosa* y *fertilizante* que antes

| Ver notas en página 73

de llegar allí había acariciado la ruina de las paredes de su antigua casa, el surco tierno *anegado* en el *lodo* y la *podredumbre* de su viejo huerto, la *espadaña* de la ermita de San Roque.

Fue Benito quien de pronto salió de su *ensimismamiento* y se puso de pie alborozado por una extraordinaria alegría, y comenzando a desnudarse nos señaló el cuerpo *centelleante* de una *trucha* que se *arrazaba* moviendo la cola en la desorientación del canal.

Cuando nos dimos cuenta, se había lanzado al agua y *buceaba* en el *espejo terciado de polvo* y pajuelas, y al cabo de unos segundos sacaba la trucha prisionera sujetándola por las *agallas*.

El animal volteaba el cuerpo en las piedras y nosotros retrocedimos asombrados, mientras Benito le acariciaba el lomo y la dejaba morir cruzándole una *vara* entre la boca y las agallas.

Quedamos *extasiados* ante la hermosura de aquel animal desconocido y maravilloso, cuyas *escamas punteadas* de colores diminutos brillaban en el contraste de la tierra.

Entonces Benito tomó a Clara de la mano y sonrió contagiado por aquella excitación que provocaba nuestro asombro.

Después, recogiendo la trucha y mostrando el cuerpo *satinado* donde *reverberaban* las profundas *irisaciones*, nos dijo:

– Vamos todos a mi casa, veréis qué buenas estaban las truchas del Villar.

| Ver notas en página 73

El viaje de doña Saturnina

1

Doña Saturnina miraba el mar.

Su habitación de *pensionista* en la Casa del Espíritu Santo que *regentaban* las *Siervas* tenía una pequeña terraza, a modo de humilde *atalaya*, sobre la *fronda* de la *pinada* que se extendía hacia la estrecha franja de arena, donde las olas batían aquel pedazo privado de playa.

La Casa era un edificio moderno. Tres pisos dispuestos en una arquitectura veraniega salpicada por el encalado y los ladrillos desnudos.

Las Siervas habían destinado siete habitaciones del piso alto para acoger como pensionistas de pago a señoras de edad, viudas o solteras absolutas, que, disponiendo de *emolumentos* suficientes, quisiesen verse atendidas en un ambiente pacífico y religioso y dentro de la benigna atmósfera de aquel clima mediterráneo, tan propicio para olvidar los *rigores* del invierno y el temor de los *achaques*.

Doña Saturnina había encontrado el refugio de aquella Casa después de algunas andanzas poco satisfactorias por hoteles y alquileres.

Su médico *de cabecera* y el especialista le recomendaron la huida de los inviernos montañeses y ella tomó la decisión de buscar paz para los *bronquios* en la costa sureña, animada por el *perenne* recuerdo del sol, y dispuesta a abandonar los espacios cada vez más cansados e imposibles de la *casona solariega* del pueblo, donde

| Ver notas en página 76

desde la muerte de su esposo, don Celedonio, su vida se había convertido en un *desolado* y oscuro *calvario*.

Las rentas de doña Saturnina eran elevadas y fecundas.

Siempre se había distinguido por una imaginación económica fuera de lo común y un especial olfato para *dilucidar* los *trances* de sus *pleitos*.

Don Celedonio -más dado a la tramitación apacible de la existencia, con una *rústica* y filosófica visión del futuro- se había conformado con las rentas fáciles y suficientes, y la soberana afición a los animales domésticos, dejando siempre a la inteligencia de su esposa el *flujo de las inversiones* y las compraventas y el *menudeo* -que jamás llegó a entender- de aquellos enormes y amarillentos paquetes de *acciones*, con los que doña Saturnina viajaba a la capital, en el coche de línea *guareciéndolos* en la inocente *entraña del capazo*.

Un primer invierno en el sur la convenció de que aquella tierra, donde había encontrado por segunda vez el mar, desde su lejanísimo viaje de bodas, era la más *adecuada* para entretener sus últimos años. El sol resultaba una presencia casi constante y la temperatura nunca se *viciaba* con aquellos rigores de la montaña que, en los últimos tiempos, habían *minado* su salud en una *tediosa compilación* de *catarros* y *reumas*.

Desde entonces se situó en la costa, y los viajes al pueblo se redujeron a lo imprescindible, apenas unas semanas en pleno verano para practicar las oportunas liquidaciones y visitar a sus dos sobrinos, únicos parientes que le quedaban y con los que mantenía, a causa de sus mujeres, relaciones no muy afectivas.

| Ver notas en página 76

La vida de los hoteles en seguida comenzó a *hastiarle*. No era doña Saturnina persona capacitada para *administrar el ocio* entre el frío *desaliento* de tantos desconocidos.

Tampoco iba a serle posible orillar por completo sus inclinaciones de negociante, aunque se había prometido a sí misma *cortarse la coleta* en lo referente a esas aficiones.

La Casa del Espíritu Santo fue la verdadera tabla de salvación. Pero antes de llegar a ella, doña Saturnina se había sentido *fascinada* por la presencia de las hermosas *urbanizacions* costeras, el idílico reducto de aquellos pisos y apartamentos construidos con absoluta *prodigalidad* y llenos de ofertas tentadoras.

Sólo existía un punto de contención ante tantas tentaciones *inmobiliarias*. Doña Saturnina observaba la *insidiosa desfachatez* de los moradores: gente de idiomas confusos, costumbres aparatosas que herían las mínimas obligaciones del *recato*, *bulliciosos* y olvidadizos de los límites más lógicos de moralidad, rubios como el *centeno* o negros y morados como el *betún* y las *habas pintas*.

Sin embargo, doña Saturnina cedió a la tentación y localizó un bello apartamento en una *torre* marina que se abría a la playa rodeada de *macizos* de flores y pinos, programó la *transferencia* bancaria y *legalizó* el contrato *estampando* su firma con las abultadas deformaciones de sus *caracteres* gruesos y *jorobados*, que llenaron de asombro al *gerente* de la inmobiliaria.

Durante dos semanas, doña Saturnina recorrió las tiendas de muebles y los almacenes, y, al cabo de ese

| Ver notas en página 77

tiempo, el apartamento ofrecía el aspecto de una estancia *presuntuosa* y *desmedida*, *comido* el salón por un *aparador de nogal torneado*, y las habitaciones, por amplios *lechos* de *furiosos herrajes*.

Una vez instalado el apartamento, lo puso en manos de una *agencia* y, al cabo de unos días, le comunicaban que estaba alquilado y doña Saturnina contaba con la *sustanciosa* mensualidad que iba a permitirle *enjuagar* sus gastos con las Siervas y atender algunos caprichos menores.

La inversión y la renta le proporcionaron la orgullosa seguridad de que su imaginación económica aún no estaba en decadencia, y las Siervas recibieron un *donativo* especial de dos mil pesetas que doña Saturnina entregó a la *priora* en un sobre azul, asegurándole que era el cumplimiento de una *promesa* a *Santa Gema*.

2

Todos los fines de mes se acercaba la señora a su apartamento para *saldar* el *recibo* correspondiente.

Hacía el viaje en autobús y aprovechaba la tarde para efectuar algunas compras y merendar sus tres *pasteles de merengue* en una *confitería* a la que era *adicta* por la especial calidad de los productos. En teorías sobre el merengue, tenía doña Saturnina una sabiduría total, adquirida en su viajera y *acrisolada* fama de *repostera*. Para *hojaldres* y merengues -señalaban todas las amistades de la señora, conocedoras de esas habilidades-, los de Saturnina la de Celedonio.

| Ver notas en página 78

Fue precisamente en uno de esos fines de mes cuando la señora descubrió la *mala jugada* de su *inquilino*.

El portero del *inmueble* la informó que el alemán, nombre por el que ella le conocía, había desaparecido de la noche a la mañana hacía cinco días sin dejar ningún recado ni, por supuesto, la mensualidad.

El apartamento ofrecía el aspecto de una violenta *devastación* y, cuando doña Saturnina entró en él, sintió que sus nervios se alteraban.

– Esto parece una *cuadra* -dijo con *apesadumbrada consternación*.

Los muebles estaban desordenados y *maltrechos*; la *vajilla*, medio rota, y las ropas, convertidas en *amasijos* malolientes.

Hasta los tiestos de la terraza habían sido *cercenados* en sus plantas, y las paredes, cubiertas con diabólicos carteles, *brochazos* de *indecorosas* pinturas y ronchas y *descascarillados*.

El portero le explicaba que el alemán parecía llevar una vida alterada y loca. Por las noches siempre llegaba acompañado por un grupo de amigos y en más de una ocasión había tenido que llamarles al orden, porque daba la impresión de que en el apartamento se armaban unas fiestas *desmelenadas* y explosivas que provocaban molestias al vecindario.

Doña Saturnina *se santiguó* pensando que aquel desalmado había abusado de su ingenuidad y decidió que el próximo alquiler lo formalizaría ella personalmente después de estudiar con minuciosidad a los interesados.

Esa tarde compró una *bata* e *hizo acopio* de *detergentes*

| Ver notas en página 79

y *desinfectantes*, poniéndose *manos a la obra*, dispuesta a recobrar el aspecto limpio y ordenado de su propiedad.

Limpió suelos y paredes, recogió las sábanas *teñidas* de manchas que su sensibilidad repelía con un gesto de asco y distancia, tiró a la *basura* toda la *porquería* acumulada, la colección de botellas vacías que rodaban por el suelo debajo de las camas, los carteles *impúdicos*, la mayor parte de la vajilla, y llenó el *fregadero* con agua caliente y desinfectantes fregando los objetos que consideró aprovechables.

Hacia el anochecer se sentaba en el *tresillo* acalorada y *rota*, sintiendo un agudo dolor en los *riñones*, pero confiada de que el apartamento volvía a ser un lugar habitable y digno.

Descansó largo rato olfateando en la atmósfera para comprobar que el aire viciado de la cerrazón y la porquería comenzaba a aliviarse con la brisa, que durante toda la tarde había entrado por las ventanas abiertas *de par en par*.

Antes de marcharse -decidida aún a llegar con tiempo para comprar sus merengues y tomar el autobús-, secó las piezas de la vajilla colocándolas en el armario de la cocina.

Y fue entonces cuando descubrió en el armario una caja de lata llena de *tarritos* con diversas *esquelas* anunciadoras de *tomillo*, sal de *apio*, *barbacoa*, *nuez moscada* y *bicarbonato*.

Era una curiosa colección que doña Saturnina tomó entre las manos con señalada alegría, rememorando sus aficiones *culinarias* y el recuerdo de los sabores exóticos en las comidas en la casa de su *madrina*, una vieja

| Ver notas en página 80

señora con la que había convivido en su juventud y que tenía especial predilección por las especias.

Doña Saturnina decidió quedarse con el *modesto* tesoro.

A fin de cuentas, era una manera bastante *parca* de cobrarse la deuda del alemán.

En la confitería compró media docena de merengues pensando que esa noche, después de la cena, invitaría a su habitación a la *hermana* Veneranda para contarle los tristes sucesos del apartamento.

La hermana Veneranda era su monja preferida y tenía una particular predisposición para escuchar las historias de la señora.

En el autobús, de regreso a la Casa del Espíritu Santo, doña Saturnina recordó la *turbia* jugada del indecente inquilino y movió la cabeza *retrayendo* una sonrisa inteligente y prometedora.

– A mí no me la vuelve a jugar ningún *tunante* -se dijo con seguridad.

3

La hermana Veneranda *se hacía cruces* al escuchar la historia, y doña Saturnina *se explayaba* a sus anchas pintando un cuadro *apocalíptico*, entre la intermitente *degustación* de los merengues.

– Dios nos asista, doña Saturna -decía la hermana limpiándose los *carrillos* con la servilleta-, estamos rodeadas por los *secuaces de Pedro Botero*.

La tertulia finalizó al cabo de una hora, y la hermana le dio las buenas noches, agradeciéndola la atención

| Ver notas en página 81

4*

de los pasteles, que eran una de sus más *irredentas* debilidades.

La señora se fue a la cama y entre el sosiego de las sábanas encontró una decidida pacificación, porque los *trajines* de la tarde la habían dejado literalmente *baldada*.

Tardó bastante tiempo en dormirse. Parecía que el exceso de merengue le creaba una creciente pesadez de estómago y tuvo que levantarse dos veces a beber agua antes de *conciliar* el sueño.

A medianoche, la pesadez se había transformado en un agudo malestar, y doña Saturnina se despertó molesta y *abatida*, con el estómago totalmente revuelto.

– Seguro que el *dichoso* merengue estaba *revenido*-se confesó con malhumor.

Encendió la luz y se sentó en la cama *eructando* con dificultad.

El sueño arrastraba sus *párpados* medio cerrados por la presión de las *legañas*, y el ruido del mar llegaba a sus oídos acrecentando el nerviosismo del imperioso *insomnio*.

Un *ardor* profundo se concentraba en el estómago *deteriorado* y el recuerdo del merengue le provocaba asco.

– Maldito *empacho* -dijo pasándose una mano por el *vientre*.

Volvió a apagar la luz e intentó adormecerse con la cabeza recostada en la almohada.

Pero el ardor era insistente y el sueño le resultaba imposible.

Fue entonces cuando recordó el pequeño tesoro

| Ver notas en página 81

abandonado por el alemán en el armario de la cocina del apartamento y que ella se había apropiado. Entre los diversos tarritos había uno de bicarbonato y doña Saturnina saltó de la cama y buscó el tarrito en la caja de lata que había guardado en la maleta.

Llenó medio vaso de agua en el grifo del lavabo y vertió bastante cantidad de aquel polvillo blanquecino. Después se bebió el contenido de un trago y volvió a la cama.

Un sabor *ácido* tremendamente fuerte llenó su paladar provocando un eructo que le causó cierto alivio.

El ardor del estómago pareció compensarse en seguida y los ojos de doña Saturnina se cerraron buscando el sueño con *avidez*.

Reposaba en la cama con las manos recogidas sobre el *regazo* y al cabo de media hora sentía una poderosa *lucidez* que desataba su imaginación, en una especie de ensueño dulcificado y brillante.

El ardor había desaparecido por completo y ahora se transformaba en un marco benigno y acariciador que la despegaba de toda sensación de espacio y límites.

En un instante creyó estar flotando por la habitación *arrullada* en las *plácidas* salpicaduras del mar que entraba en sus oídos convertido en una música religiosa, que luego se *desleía* sobre el tranquilo *ronroneo* de una canción infantil entonada por algún coro misterioso, y sus ojos se abrieron a un juego de luces doradas y verdes que parecían arrastrar las *reverberantes* amanecidas en las montañas de su pueblo, las salvajes vegetaciones de los valles y los prados, el cristalino *escorzo* del río surcando las *florestas* de la vega hasta partirse en una

| Ver notas en página 82

violenta *cascada*, bajo cuyas aguas doña Saturnina sentía su cuerpo joven y desnudo salpicado por una feliz humedad que traspasaba y *refulgía* los cabellos rubios de sus quince años en una exaltada sensación purificadora y libérrima.

Un prodigioso estallido de colores estremeció su mirada y su rostro se *impregnó* de aquellas *iridiscentes* tonalidades uniéndose el cuerpo al vacío del *firmamento*, donde parecía extasiarse cabalgando por las nubes, subiendo y bajando en veloces *zagas* a través de los algodonosos infinitos, sobre las *crestas* rubias de los *alcores* y en el lecho etéreo de las canículas.

El cuerpo de doña Saturnina se debatía en la cama sudoroso y *febril*.

El viaje finalizó en un regreso a las primeras sensaciones del mar y la música, y la *conciencia* del tiempo estaba *trastocada* cuando sus ojos se abrieron en la habitación y se quedó mirando hacia la ventana por donde la luz del amanecer llegaba tibia y lechosa sin que ella tuviese la mínima referencia sobre lo que aquella luz presagiaba, adentrándose de nuevo en el sueño y perdiendo por completo toda *consciencia*.

Era casi mediodía cuando la despertó la hermana Veneranda.

Doña Saturnina sintió una pesadez de acero en los párpados y se incorporó en la cama bastante excitada.

Los recuerdos de la noche al contacto con la primera realidad le provocaron una sensación de decaimiento y *desasosiego*.

Su cabeza tenía todos los síntomas de una *espesa re-*

| Ver notas en página 82

saca y le dijo a la hermana que no se encontraba bien y que iba a quedarse en la cama.

– Los pasteles nos han traicionado, doña Saturnina -le confesó la hermana Veneranda-, porque yo también *he andado* toda la noche *de seguidillas*.

| Ver notas en página 83

El difunto Ezequiel Montes.
Página 19

el *difunto*, persona que está muerta
leporino, el labio superior de una persona que, por defecto de nacimiento, está partido como el de la *liebre* (viñeta en pág. 66)
la *gorra visera*, ver viñeta en pág. 66
el *cangrejo* (viñeta en pág. 66)
insinuar, aquí, poner de manifiesto
las *trazas*, aspecto, apariencia
amaralladas, enmarañadas, revueltas (fig.)
punzante, aquí, agudos, muy despiertos
atravesado de nariz, interpreto: que tiene la nariz un poco torcida, de nariz torcida
cargado de hombros, con la espalda inclinada hacia adelante, no recta
el *roble*, árbol de madera muy dura
cuartearse, aquí, que la cáscara del tronco se abre en pedazos, formando figuras; estas partes no necesariamente se caen
la *dehesa*, campo cercado, dedicado a *pasto* (=la hierba) de ganados y en algunos lugares a la cría de toros *de lidia* (=los que se llevan a las plazas para ser toreados)
el *teso*, la parte de alta de un *cerro* (=montaña muy baja) o la *colina* (= elevación del terreno menor que la de un monte, de forma suave) baja, con un llano en la parte alta
el *día de Nuestra Señora*, el 15 de agosto, día en que se celebra la fiesta religiosa de la *Asunción* (=subida) de la Virgen María al cielo, en cuerpo y alma según la tradición. Asunción es, en España nombre de mujer (María de la Asunción) y *Chon*, el nombre de la señora de Pobladura, es la forma cariñosa o familiar de Asunción. Se dice también «Nuestra Señora de agosto»
la *charca*, extensión de agua más o menos grande
la *huerga*, terreno *pantanoso* (=bajo y húmedo; leonesismo)
el *junco*, planta de tallo recto, fino y flexible de color verde y que crece en las orillas de los ríos o en lugares donde hay agua; el lugar

en el que hay muchos juncos es el *juncal*
la *rana* (el *anca); anca* (=la parte gruesa de la pata de atrás)
la *gusarapa*, cualquier tipo de animal en forma de *gusano* que vive en el agua (viñeta en pág. 66)
el *pimentón*, polvo que se saca de los *pimientos* rojos y que se utiliza para dar sabor y color a algunos alimentos (viñeta en pág. 67)
la *cantina*, especie de bar donde se venden comidas y alimentos y, en los pueblos, lugar de reunión de los hombres
liar un cigarro, envolver el tabaco en el papel especial para formar el cigarro
la *nitidez*, claridad
embeber, aquí, dejar concentrado, muy atento
descarado, fresco, atrevido

Página 22
babeando la colilla, la *colilla*, la parte última del cigarro, cuando éste ya está casi consumido; que llevaba *húmeda* (=mojada) de *baba* o *saliva*, líquido que tenemos en la boca, de color blanco y que sirve para ablandar la comida y tragarla fácilmente
atascar, quedar detenido, aquí: los pasos parecen quedar detenidos en el polvo y a causa de él
la *sahariana*, chaqueta amplia con grandes bolsillos que suele ajustarse al cuerpo con un cinturón
mahón (de la ciudad de Mahón, capital de la isla de Menorca, Baleares), tela muy fuerte y resistente; se emplea para ropa de trabajo
arremangar, remangar, subir hacia arriba, doblándolas o no, las mangas de la ropa; aquí, el borde de los pantalones
caqui, color entre marrón y verde como el de algunos trajes de los militares
pajizo, de color parecido al de la *paja*, tallo seco de trigo; color amarillento
el *mechón*, aquí, porción de pelo separada del resto; *encanecido*, gris o casi blanco, con *canas*, pelo gris o blanco
el *recelo*, temor, falta de confianza
la *complicidad*, hecho de ser *cómplice*, persona que ayuda a otra en un delito o en una mala acción; aquí, porque de una manera u otra

todos tenían sospechas, sin saber muy bien de qué, el miedo ante lo desconocido
la *aversión*, sentimiento de disgusto y *repugnancia*, disgusto y asco
el *escaño*, asiento de madera, como un banco grande con *respaldo*, una madera ancha para apoyar la espalda; es mueble propio de las casas de campo y está casi siempre en la cocina
el *orujo*, bebida fuerte, o *aguardiente* bebida que se fabrica de las uvas
la *estilográfica* (viñeta en pág. 66)
el *Soto*, lugar con árboles, sobre todo al lado de un río; en casi todos los pueblos hay un lugar que se llama así
el *vértice*, aquí la parte que sobresale de la gorra; lo que hace Ezequiel es una forma de saludo

Página 23
anodina, de poco interés
desmadejado, como sin ganas, cansado
suscitar, provocar, ser la causa de; las mozas se reían de su manera de andar
lacio, liso
sanroque, San Roque, santo y *patrón* (=que proteje) de muchos pueblos. Se le invoca como abogado de toda clase de epidemias y también como protector de los animales. Se le representa con un perro, recordando al que, estando el santo enfermo de la peste, le lamía las heridas. Nació en Montpellier (Francia) donde murió en 1327; de familia noble abandonó las riquezas, para ayudar en el norte de Italia a los *apestados* (=enfermos de peste); su fiesta se celebra el 3 de agosto
la *vereda*, camino estrecho
la *noria*, máquina que se emplea para sacar agua del río o de un pozo; tiene una rueda y en ella hay unos cubos llamados *cangilones* que recogen el agua y la llevan hacia arriba
el *recado*, lo que se dice o se pide a alguien para que se lo diga a otro; encargo
la *cuartilla*, hoja de papel que es la cuarta parte de un pliego; la cuartilla mide 20 por 15 cm.

lacrada, cerrada con el *lacre*, pasta, en general de color rojo, que, calentada, se usa para cerrar cartas o paquetes
aguardar, aquí, esperar
el *mensaje*, aquí lo que se comunica en la carta
el *rincón*, aquí, el lugar retirado donde está el escaño; también podrá pensarse que está sentado en el escaño, hacia uno de los lados de éste
aricar, trabajo del campo que consiste en *arar* (=mover la tierra con el *arado*) muy superficialmente; *arado* (viñeta en pág. 67); la *remolacha* (viñeta en pág. 67)

Página 24
concertarle, concertar, ponerse de acuerdo en algo; *le*: a doña Chon; concertar con ella, ponerse de acuerdo con ella para celebrar una entrevista
el *pellejo*, la piel de un animal, en la que, una vez preparada, se guarda el vino (viñeta en pág. 67)
el *cuarterón*, cuarta parte de una *libra* (en Castilla= 460 grs.); el tabaco que se compraba en paquetes cuyo peso era de un cuarterón
el *chorro*, aquí, el vino que sale del pellejo
desgraciado, aquí, ¡pobre hombre!
la *tía*, en los pueblos se llama así a muchas mujeres, aunque no sean de la familia; en vez de «la señora»
hacerse cargo, aquí, recibir, recoger
la *consternación*, tristeza y dolor muy grandes
tolerar, aguantar su presencia
la *contemplación*, aquí, consideración hacia él, a causa de su tristeza
orillar, dejar a un lado, no emplear
cadencioso, aquí, lentos y con un cierto ritmo, siempre iguales
despegado, alejado de todo, solitario
atascado, detenido, que no salía de las borracheras. Ver nota en página 57

Página 25

el *pardal*, pájaro muy pequeño (viñeta en pág. 67)
correr una liebre, corriendo detrás de la liebre, para ahuyentarla o para cogerla
desorientada, aquí, que no sabe por dónde ir porque la luz de los *reverberos* (= objeto de cristal o de metal sobre cuya superficie «reverbera» (= se refleja) la luz; también farola, farol, aquí: reflejos la *deslumbra*, no le permite ver nada
chillón, color muy fuerte y que llama mucho la atención
el *coche de línea*, coche grande que pasa, por lo general una vez al día, por los pueblos, y es usado como medio de transporte público
volver a las andadas, frase con la que se indica que una persona *reincide* (=cae de nuevo) en un vicio o en una mala costumbre. Aquí: vuelve a escribir una carta
de antemano, anticipadamente; antes de que le hubieran pedido *oficiar* (=hacer el oficio) de mensajero
el *alguacil*, funcionario que está a las órdenes del *alcalde*, persona que preside un *Ayuntamiento* (=grupo de personas que gobiernan en un pueblo o ciudad; el edificio en el que trabajan esas personas)
el *vecindario*, conjunto de *vecinos* (=habitantes) de una casa; aquí, del pueblo
la *obstinación*, hecho de querer hacer una cosa, pase lo que pase
hacer cábalas, aquí: tratar de adivinar algo sobre alguna cosa; suponer
la *misiva*, la carta
acceder, aquí: aceptó a Mauricio como mensajero

Página 26

la *partida*, se refiere al juego de *cartas* (=baraja española o naipes) (viñeta en pág. 67), habitual entre los hombres del pueblo; *partida* es también la serie de *jugadas* (=veces que le toca jugar a cada uno de los del grupo) que terminan cuando uno de ellos gana, «gana la partida»
el *chaval*, el chico, el muchacho
el *poyo*, banco de piedra u otro material que se construye arrimado a la pared; aquí, a la entrada de la cantina

las *chapas*, juego infantil que se hace con las *chapas* (=tapaderas) de las botellas
arracimados, aquí, fig. muy juntos y muy cerca unos de otros, como formando un *racimo* (viñeta en pág. 67)
rito imperturbable y acelerado, aquí: bebía una copa tras otra en una acto repetido siempre de la misma manera (=*rito*) sin que nada le quite la calma (=*imperturbable*) y cada vez de forma más rápida (=*acelerada*)
manoseado, aquí: viejo y un poco sucio, porque se ha tocado muchas veces con las manos
el *sorbo*, cantidad de líquido que se bebe de una sola vez
suspensa, quieta, sin decir nada
vivaces, vivos, despiertos; sing.: vivaz
obsesiva, aquí, curiosidad que no se puede dejar ni un solo momento
el *talante*, modo de ser de una persona; aquí, también modo de obrar, de vivir
prodigar, dar mucho de algo; aquí, que paseaba mucho
intermitentes arrebatos, *arrebatos*, aquí, *impulso* (=acción rápida, deseo) que le dan de repente, que se detienen y luego continúan para volver a detenerse y así repetidas veces (=*intermitente*)

Página 28
el *cartapacio*, carpeta en la que guarda las cuartillas
la *siega, la cosecha*, trabajos del campo que consisten en *segar* (=cortar) por ejemplo el trigo de los campos y recogerlo; la *cosecha* es tanto la recogida de los frutos como los frutos recogidos
entrañable, querida
imperceptible, aquí: que casi no se las ve, aunque están; no se les presta atención
la *sacristía*, lugar de las iglesias donde se guardan las ropas y los objetos que se usan en los actos de culto
la *era*, espacio de tierra limpia donde se separa el grano de la paja
la *rastrojera*, campo en el que han quedado restos (=*rastrojo*) de la *mies* (=los cereales- plantas- como el trigo) después de la siega

el *pilar*, aquí montón de paja; también montón de paja formado por *haces* (= el trigo recién segado que se puede coger en los brazos (= *brazada*) y que se ata); sing.: haz
el *achaque*, enfermedad no grave
la *tos abotargada* y *cadenciosa*, *tos*, expulsión ruidosa y violenta del aire de los *pulmones* (Ver figura en página 85); *abotargada*, aquí, pesada; *cadenciosa*, aquí, que se repite regularmente
estremecer, fig., hacer temblar
tornar, tornarse, volverse blanco como
la *recuperación*, el hecho de que está curado o casi curado
arrecido o *aterido*, casi *paralizado* (=que no puede moverse) por el frío y temblando
crudo, tiempo muy frío y desagradable
el *carámbano*, trozo de hielo largo y con punta que se forma al helarse el agua que va cayendo o goteando
San Silvestre, fue un *papa* (314-335) (= la autoridad suprema, la más alta en la Iglesia católica). Su fiesta se celebra el 31 de diciembre y coincide con la celebración de la fiesta del último día del año
exaltarse, aquí, excitarse, ponerse nervioso y muy contento

Página 29
el *filandón*, reunión en la que se cuentan historias (Ver página 6)
amedrentado, con mucho miedo
el *bullicio*, ruido que hace mucha gente reunida
exuberante, aquí, grande, profundo y solemne
el *presagio*, señal que anuncia algo que va a suceder; aquí, algo malo
perder el juicio, volverse loco, perder la razón
arrebatada, aquí, dominada, ocupada
untar, poner algo sobre una superficie, aquí, las botas, y extenderlo; aquí el *sebo*, grasa sólida que se saca de los animales. Limpió las botas

Página 30

el filo de, aquí, el espacio muy delgado que deja la puerta o la ventana al entreabrirla muy poco
espiar, vigilar, tratar de mirar sin ser visto
bamboleante, que se *balancea*, se mueve de un lado a otro repetidamente
calada, muy metida en la cabeza
turbio, aquí, no claro
ceder, dejar paso a
el *cierzo*, viento muy frío que sopla del norte; *cuajar*, convertir en sólido un líquido
la *ventisca*, tomenta de viento y nieve
enmarañada, enredada por la fuerza del viento o *azote*, golpe constante del viento
el *alero*, parte saliente del tejado (=*borde*) que sobresale de los muros; es allí donde, al gotear el agua, se forman los carámbanos
armados de, fig., aquí: que llevaban para servirse de ellos en caso de necesidad: el *farol*, la *estaca*, la *pala*, las *parihuelas* (viñeta en pág. 68)
el *rigor*, aquí, la dureza
la *escama*, aquí, capa muy fina de nieve, como las *escamas* de los peces (ver nota en página 74); *cuajada*, aquí que se ha puesto dura formando una capa sólida
el *fulgor*, brillo intenso

Página 31

el *decaimiento*, aquí: que la salud es más débil, debilitamiento
el *bandazo*, movimiento brusco, no suave, hacia un lado, como el que hace un barco
sofocado, aquí, con ahogo, que respira mal
entibiecían la soñolencia, soñolencia, estado inmediatamente anterior al sueño, entre el sueño y la vigilia, *entibiecer*, poner algo tibio o templado. Aquí fig.: atenuar, moderar la soñolencia, apariencia de cansancio
atrofiarse, aquí, que va perdiendo su fuerza y su brillo hasta

desaliñar, descomponer, desarreglar el *destello*, el brillo
echarpe, procede del francés, especie de manto largo y estrecho que se ponen las mujeres sobre los hombros
tramitar, hacer los *trámites* (=cada cosa que hay que hacer para resolver un asunto o para conseguir algo). Aquí el ingreso en el *Asilo* de Ancianos, centro en el que se recoge a los ancianos pobres
la *furgoneta*, vehículo más pequeño que un camión, para transportar y repartir mercancías
el *juncal*, ver nota en página 56
arremolinar, juntar en forma de *remolino* (=masa de polvo que gira muy deprisa). Aquí: juntando el polvo

Página 32
la *ranura*, aquí, el hueco que dejan las dos partes en que está partido el labio superior, labio leporino
apurar, aquí, consumir y sentir hasta el final
el *designio*, plan o idea que tiene alguien de hacer algo
la *misa gregoriana, misa*, la parte central del culto católico en la que se recuerda el hecho de que Jesucristo tomara la naturaleza humana y muriera por los hombres; las *gregorianas* son las misas que se dicen por los difuntos, durante treinta días seguidos y por lo común inmediatos al día del entierro
memoria, aquí, en recuerdo de Ezequiel
de *luto riguroso*, vestida completamente de negro. La ropa de color negro se viste como muestra de dolor por la muerte de una persona querida
el *baúl* (viñeta en página 68)
la *prenda*, cualquier cosa que ha pertenecido a alguien, ropa, como prendas de ropa
ribeteada, que tiene un borde negro (=*ribete*), como la *esquela*, tarjeta pequeña con borde negro que se envía para comunicar la muerte de alguien; también la noticia que aparece en los periódicos para comunicar lo mismo (viñeta en página 67)
garrapateado, aquí, mal escritos, con letra poco segura
sepia, color parecido al rosa anaranjado
la *minuciosidad*, cuidado y detalle; *exhaustiva*, muy completa y minuciosa

la *caligrafía*, aquí, la letra, la escritura
a raíz de, a partir de, después de

Página 33
difuminado, poco claro; poco marcado en el recuerdo; *difuminar* es término del dibujo y de la pintura, hacer que algo quede menos claro como las líneas y las sombras de un dibujo
el *hacendado*, que posee muchas tierras, terrateniente; también bienes y propiedades (=*hacienda*)
el *pretendiente*, hombre que intenta conquistar a una mujer, en general para casarse con ella
fregados en el barro, fregados, interpreto: vueltos hacia el barro, y pasados por él varias veces, hundidos; la cara casi hundida en el barro; el *barro*, tierra mezclada con agua, como lo que se forma cuando llueve
la *torrentera*, el *cauce* (=camino por donde corre el agua de los ríos) de un *torrente*, corriente de agua muy abundante y rápida que se forma cuando llueve mucho o cuando la nieve se deshace
el *barranquillo*, el *barranco* pequeño, cauce hecho por una corriente de agua o por otra cosa

Viñetas

la gorra visera

el labio leporino

la liebre

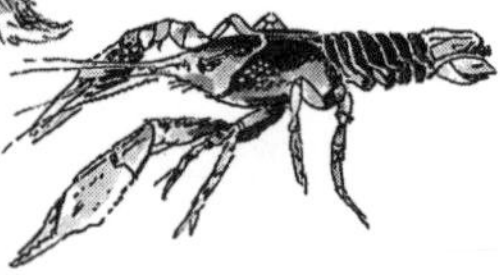

el cangrejo

la rana

el anca

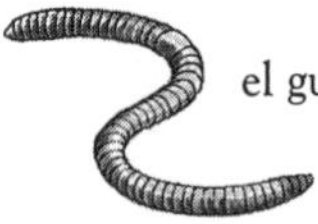

el gusano

la estilográfica

el arco iris

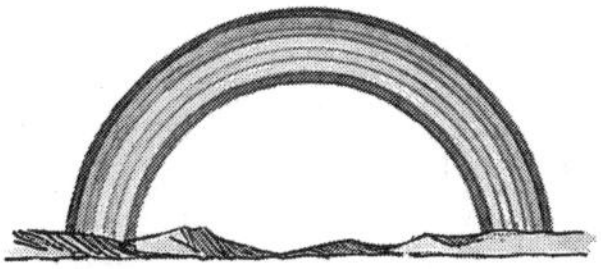

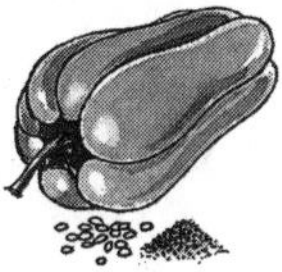

el pimiento

el ribete

el arado

el surco

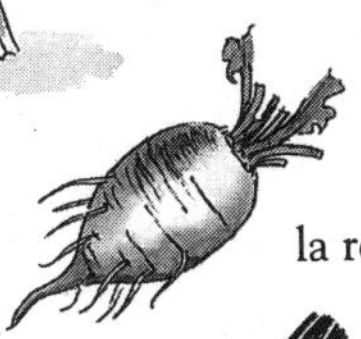

la remolacha

el pardal

el pellejo de vino

las cartas o naipes

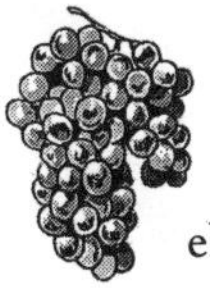

el racimo

5*

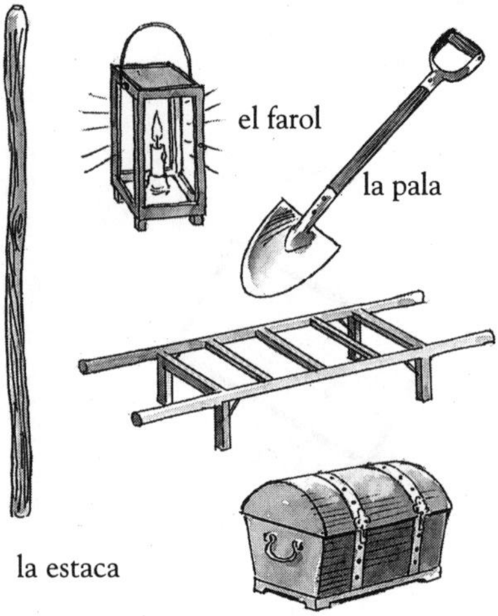
el farol
la pala
las parihuelas
la estaca
el baúl

La familia de Villar.
Página 34

Villar, el nombre del pueblo es Villar de los Barrios. No sé si el nombre corresponde a un pueblo real; pero en todo caso Villar puede ser cualquiera de los pueblos sumergidos. Ver Prólogo en página 17

arrendar, tomar *en arriendo*, tomar las tierras por un tiempo pagando por ello

la *hectárea*, medida de superficie que equivale a 100 áreas; y el área es la superficie de un cuadrado de 10 metros de lado

el *secano*, terreno para cultivos que no se riega y solo recibe el agua de la lluvia; *pedregoso*, que tiene muchas piedras y por lo tanto no es bueno para los cultivos

el *adobe*, mezcla de paja y barro en forma de *ladrillo* (viñeta en pág. 74) que se deja secar al aire y se usa en algunas construcciones, en general pobres o del campo

la *mula*, hembra del *mulo*, animal que resulta del cruce de caballo y asno

el *tabique*, pared delgada con que se dividen las habitaciones de una casa

el *cardo*, planta *silvestre* (=que nace y crece sin que se la cultive) con flores de colores intensos; los hay de muchas clases; el *cenizal*, lugar en el que crecen *cenizos*, planta silvestre con hojas dentadas y flores verdosas

yerma, que no produce nada

el *vicio*, frondosidad excesiva y que *perjudica* (=hace mal, impide) el crecimiento de la planta; hojas y plantas que se *pudren* (= se estropean, deshaciéndose; part.: podrido) y sirven de abono

las *sebes*, matas de monte bajo

la *retama*, arbusto que crece en las praderas con muchas ramas delgadas y flores pequeñas y amarillas

entreverado, que tiene mezcladas cosas diferentes; aquí, el color pajizo está mezclado con el color de las matas y el rojo de las *amapolas* (viñeta en pág. 74)

la *roncha de matojo*, *roncha*, aquí extensión redondeada, como una mancha grande; el *matojo*, planta de poca altura (sobre *mata*= planta de poca altura)

recalar, tapar o pintar con cal; el *encalado* es el resultado de *encalar*, pintar, para recubrir, con cal de modo que quede blanco
la *comba*, superficie curvada, no plana
el *canalón*, en los tejados, conducto que recoge el agua de lluvia que cae del tejado y la lleva hasta el suelo; del tejado al suelo es un tubo, al borde del tejado el tubo está cortado por la mitad horizontalmente; *aluminio*, metal de color gris y poco pesado
las *escorreduras*, el agua va del tejado al canalón que la recoge
reportar, dar, producir

Página 35
taciturno, que habla poco; callado y serio
el *canal*, aquí conducto artificial de agua, hecho de *cemento*, material de construcción en polvo, que mezclado con agua forma una masa que luego se endurece
el *hondón*, el fondo
la *brecha*, aquí, construcción de cemento que se hace en la tierra (como una *brecha*=herida); aquí, para hacer la conducción del agua
el *pantano*, *embalse* (=lago artificial) en el que el agua queda retenida por una *presa* (=muro que se construye para detener el agua) que *anega*, (de *anegar*, cubrir el agua) los terrenos o los pueblos al ser *embalsada*, recogida en el embalse. Ver ilustración en página 36-37
el *páramo*, terreno yermo y sin árboles
el *erial*, tierra o campo sin cultivar
el *regadío*, la posibilidad de regar, que convertirá el erial en terreno *fértil* (=que produce) para los cultivos que necesitan mucho riego. Ver nota a *secano* en página 69
el *término*, aquí lugar y también el *término municipal*, la *porción* (=parte) de un territorio sometido a la autoridad de un Ayuntamiento
la *hondonada*, la parte baja de un valle
la *losa*, aquí se refiere a la *pizarra* o *roca* de color gris o negro azulado formada por capas delgadas; se usa en la construcción para hacer tejados. Se dice tejados de *losa* y tejados de *pizarra*

la *ermita*, iglesia pequeña que suele estar en las afueras de los pueblos; en ella se celebra la *romería*, fiesta que se hace junto a la ermita el día de la fiesta del *patrón* (=santo protector) del lugar. Aquí: San Roque. Ver nota en página 58
el *tajo*, el corte, el lugar que dejan entre sí las dos *peñas* (=montes de piedra)
el *dique*, muro o pared para detener el agua de la *presa* o *embalse*, lago artificial en el que queda retenida o almacenada el agua de un río

Página 38
el *robledal*, lugar donde hay *robles*, el *roble*, árbol de madera muy dura
el *haya*, árbol muy alto que tiene la *corteza* (=la capa que cubre el tronco y las ramas) lisa y gris o blanca
la *choza*, vivienda hecha de piedra o de adobe y con el techo de paja; en ella se recogen los pastores que viven y cuidan sus ganados en la *braña*, lugar de pastos; en general está en algún montecillo donde hay agua y hierba
surtida por, aquí el agua que le daban los ríos
el *nevero*, lugar de la alta montaña que está cubierto de nieve todo el año
batiendo, golpeando
rozar, aquí llegar hasta el borde de los tejados
el *pastizal*, lugar o terreno con mucho pasto
la *vega*, terreno bajo, llano y rico, con hierba y por el que normalmente pasa un río
estéril, que no produce nada
los ojos... *postrados*, es una imagen: los ojos quietos, detenidos -porque pensaba en su pueblo sepultado bajo las aguas-; los otros niños están asombrados
sepultado, que queda debajo del agua; *sepultar* es *enterrar* (=poner bajo tierra) a las personas que mueren
la *estepa*, llanura extensa donde no crecen árboles; lo que crece allí puede hacerlo sin necesidad de agua

la *bombilla*, objeto que sirve para *iluminar* (=dar luz) formado por un globo de cristal que contiene un hilo metálico por el que pasa la corriente eléctrica
el *carburo*, producto que se emplea para alumbrar, lo usan los mineros; también la lámpara que se alimenta con carburo (viñeta en pág. 74)
el *poste*, palo en el que sostienen los *cables* (=hilo de metal protegido con una cubierta de plástico que se emplea para conducir la electricidad; el cable se sostiene en unos pequeños *casquillos de jícaras* o *aisladores*; el *aislador*, aparato de cristal o de porcelana con que se aíslan de sus soportes los cables que llevan la corriente eléctrica. Ver ilustración en página 36
mendigo, pobre; aquí fig.
acobardado, asustado, con miedo

Página 39
raso, limpio, sin nubes
la *brigada*, grupo de personas que se reúnen para hacer el mismo trabajo
horadar, abrir, hacer un agujero en algo atravesándolo
la *caída*, la parte de la Central Eléctrica a la que llega el agua
el *capataz*, persona que está al mando de los obreros y controla su trabajo
el *martillo mecánico*, martillo *perforador*, máquina que *perfora* (=hace un agujero) la piedra (viñeta en pág. 74)
la *quemazón*, acción y efecto de quemar
la *silicosis*, enfermedad producida por el polvo del *sílice* (=un mineral); ataca a los mineros y a los que trabajan con la piedra. Afecta la respiración y el polvo se asienta en los *pulmones* (viñeta en pág. 85)
el *tirador* (viñeta en pág. 75)
albergar, dar albergue, tener con ellos
la *canícula* parte del año en que hace más calor. En los países del Mediterráneo suele tomarse del 23 de julio al 2 de septiembre. También en plural: días que dura la canícula
avasallar, aquí dominar, pasar con fuerza
alborozado, con mucha alegría

Página 40

la *mota*, trozo muy pequeño, aquí de *pajuela*, dim. de paja

la *compuerta*, en la presa una *plancha* (=especie de puerta) que puede abrirse y cerrarse para dejar pasar el agua o *retenerla* (=no dejarla pasar)

la *acequia*, canal pequeño por donde va el agua; las acequias se hacen para conducir el agua del riego

el *sequedal*, lugar muy seco

encharcado, cubierto de agua, aquí del agua sobrante que no absorbe la tierra porque ya tiene bastante; el *charco*, agua detenida en un hoyo, más o menos profundo

la *azada* (viñeta en pág. 75)

agolpando, juntando los *guijarros*, piedras pequeñas y redondeadas

el *manojo*, conjunto de cosas, por lo general alargadas, que puede sujetarse con una mano que se cierra sobre ellas, aquí las *varillas* de los cohetes (viñeta en pág. 75)

la *empanada*, masa de pan, rellena por dentro con carne o con otros alimentos y que se cuece como el pan

a la vera de, loc. adv., junto a, al lado próximo

rescatar, aquí: librar, dejar libre al silencio para que hablaran y olvidaran la tristeza

el *espejo bullente*, imagen: el *espejo* (=el agua) *bullente* que se mueve de manera parecida al agua cuando hierve

vertiginosa, aquí, fuerza rápida y grande

fertilizante, que hace fértil, el *surco*, línea que se hace con el *arado* (viñeta en pág. 67) para labrar la tierra; *anegado*, hundido, en el *lodo*, barro

Página 41

la *podredumbre*, el resultado de *pudrirse*, estropearse y quedar inservible. Aquí: los productos del huerto se han estropeado (=*podrido*, part. de pudrir) bajo el agua. Ver nota a *vicio* en página 69

la *espadaña*, campanario de una sola pared donde se colocan las campanas

el *ensimismamiento*, estado de la persona muy concentrada en sus pensamientos

centelleante, que brilla y despide luz
la *trucha* (viñeta en pág. 75) con las *agallas* y las *escamas*
arrazar,voz leonesa; quedarse quieta
bucear, nadar por debajo del agua
el espejo *terciado*, el agua que lleva atravesadas pajuelas y polvo en su arrastre
la *vara*, aquí un palito muy delgado
extasiados, asombrados, con mucho gusto y admiración, como ante algo extraordinario
punteadas, con puntos muy pequeños de muchos colores
satinado, aquí, brillante
reverberar, brillar al recibir la luz. Ver nota a *reverbero* en pág. 60
la *irisación*, reflejos de luz con todos los colores del *arco iris* (viñeta en pág. 67)

El viaje de doña Saturnina.

Viñetas

la azada
el cohete
la varilla
la trucha
las agallas
la escama
el tirador

Página 44

pensionista, aquí, persona que vive en la Casa del E.S. y paga cierto dinero por su habitación, comida y otros servicios
regentar, dirigir
Siervas, orden religiosa femenina. Hay muchas órdenes religiosas femeninas que por humildad llevan el nombre de «Siervas» (=al servicio de)
la *atalaya*, lugar elevado desde el que se puede ver una gran extensión de tierra; aquí, de mar
la *fronda*, aquí el conjunto de hojas y ramas que forman la espesura de la *pinada*, lugar donde hay muchos pinos (viñeta en pág. 84)
los *emolumentos*, aquí, recursos económicos
los *rigores*, aquí, la dureza del invierno
los *achaques*, molestia o enfermedad poco grave, en general propia de la vejez
médico *de cabecera*, el que asiste de continuo al enfermo
los *bronquios*, ver figura en página 85
perenne, constante, que dura siempre o mucho tiempo
casona solariega, se dice de una casa muy grande, buena, noble y antigua; también se dice de la casa de los antepasados

Página 45

desolado, aquí, muy triste
el *calvario*, aquí, sufrimiento; Viene del Monte Calvario donde Jesucristo fue puesto en la cruz (=*crucificado)*
dilucidar, aclarar, poner en claro los *trances*, los momentos importantes, de sus *pleitos*: el *pleito*, enfrentamiento entre dos o más personas en el que decide un juez
rústica, propia del campo
el *flujo*, aquí, el movimiento de las *inversiones*, empleo del dinero de manera que produzca beneficios
el *menudeo, menudear*, hacer una cosa muchas veces
las *acciones*, en economía, cada una de las partes en que se divide el capital
guarecer, guardar, en la *entraña*, en lo más profundo del *capazo* (viñeta en pág. 84)
adecuada, propia y conveniente

viciarse, aquí: dañaba o perdía su bondad
minar, debilitar, destruir poco a poco
tediosa, aburrida y pesada
la *compilación*, reunión del *catarro* (=enfermedad no grave que produce tos), y el *reuma* (=enfermedad que produce dolores en las *articulaciones* y en los *músculos*). Ver figura en página 85

Página 46
hastiar, aburrir, causar; *le*: a ella
administrar el ocio, aquí: no sabe estar sin hacer nada; el *ocio*, estado de no hacer nada
el desaliento, falta de ánimo, desánimo
cortarse la coleta, dejar su oficio o apartarse de una afición o de una costumbre
fascinada, atraida su atención, deslumbrada
la *urbanización*, lugar formado por un conjunto de casas, que suelen ser parecidas, donde hay tiendas, parques y todo lo necesario para vivir en él
la *prodigalidad*, aquí, que habían construido muchos
la *inmobiliaria*, aquí, lo relacionado con la compra, venta y alquiler de casas
la *insidiosa desfachatez*, *insidiosa*, maliciosa y dañina; *desfachatez*, descaro, desvergüenza y falta de educación
el *recato*, todo lo que se debe hacer de manera decente
bulliciosos, que hacen mucho ruido
el *centeno*, planta de color amarillo, muy parecida al trigo y tiene los mismos usos (viñeta en pág. 84)
el *betún*, crema oscura que se usa para limpiar los zapatos
las *habas pintas*, el *haba*, fruto de una planta del mismo nombre, suelen ser blancas, amarillentas; las de color marrón o casi morado se llaman *pintas*; (viñeta en pág. 84)
la *torre*, el algunas partes de España se llama así a la casa de uno o dos pisos habitada, en general, por una sola familia; aquí, edificio de apartamentos
el *macizo*, grupo de plantas con flores en un parque o en un jardín
la *transferencia*, aquí, el hecho de que su dinero pase de ella a otra persona, en este caso la persona que vende el apartamento
legalizar, hacer todos los trámites que indica la ley; aquí, para com-

prar el apartamento
estampar, poner la firma; los *caracteres*, las letras, *jorobados*, no derechos, torcidos, ya sea por la edad o porque doña Saturnina no escribe muy bien
el *gerente*, persona que está al frente de los asuntos de la urbanización

Página 47
presuntuosa, aquí, una estancia demasiado lujosa y fuera de lugar; *desmedida*, exagerada, con un lujo no apropiado
comido, aquí fig., el aparador es demasiado grande en relación con el salón de manera que casi lo hace desaparecer, porque el mueble es el que domina; el *aparador*, mueble en el que se guarda todo lo relacionado con el servicio de la mesa; de *nogal*, de madera del árbol de ese nombre; *torneado*, de madera trabajada con figuras, no lisa; el *nogal* (viñeta en pág. 84)
el *lecho*, la cama; de *furiosos herrajes*, con adornos excesivos hechos en hierro
la *agencia,* aquí, la empresa encargada de alquilar apartamentos
sustanciosa, abundante
enjuagar, aquí fig. arreglar, aclarar con más libertad económica
el *donativo*, lo que se da; en general el dinero que se da para ayudar a personas que lo necesitan
la priora, la superiora del convento de monjas
la *promesa*, las personas piadosas piden ayuda a los santos y les prometen hacer, si les ayudan, alguna obra buena
Santa Gema, Santa Gema Galgani, joven italiana. Murió en Luca (Italia) en 1903
saldar, llevar el *recibo* (=el papel en el que va escrito el precio del alquiler) correspondiente a cada mes y cobrarlo
el *pastel de merengue*, dulce pequeño cuyo interior está relleno de *merengue*, crema dulce de color blanco hecha con leche y con azúcar
la *confitería*, lugar donde se hacen y se venden toda clase de dulces
ser adicta, aquí, que le gusta ir a ella
acrisolada, se dice de las cualidades que puestas a prueba salen me-

joradas. Aquí: fama probada de buena *repostera*, la mujer que hace dulces
el *hojaldre*, *masa* (=lo que resulta de mezclar agua o leche con harina) de algunos dulces en capas muy finas

Página 48
la *mala jugada*, aquí, mala acción
el *inquilino*, persona que vive en una casa alquilada, que no es suya y por la que paga el alquiler
el *inmueble*, edificio
la *devastación*, resultado de *devastar*, destruir por completo
la *cuadra*, lugar donde se tiene a los caballos y a otros animales de carga
apesadumbrada, aquí: triste, con pesar; la *consternación*, tristeza y dolor muy grandes
maltrecho, maltratados, rotos y estropeados
la *vajilla*, platos, tazas y otros utensilios en los que se sirve la comida
el *amasijo*, mezcla de cosas diferentes; aquí, ropas revueltas y en montón
cercenar, cortar
el *brochazo*, lo que se pinta con la *brocha* (viñeta en pág. 84) pero de una forma descuidada y no artística; *indecorosas pinturas*, pinturas no decentes
el *descascarillado*, aquí: la pared había perdido en algunas partes la pintura que la cubría
desmelenada, aquí fig., con mucho ruido y con mucho desorden
santiguarse, hacer la señal de la cruz desde la frente hasta el pecho y desde el hombro izquierdo hasta el derecho
la *bata*, vestido abierto y cómodo para hacer la limpieza
hacer acopio, reunir algo; aquí: los *detergentes*, jabón u otros productos para limpiar y los *desinfectantes*, productos que se usan para limpiar a fondo algo; en general, para las heridas
Página 49

ponerse manos a la obra, frase con la que se indica que se empieza a hacer alguna cosa, en general, con energía
teñir, hacer cambiar el color; también manchar
la *basura*, recipiente o lugar donde se echan las cosas que no sirven; las cosas mismas
la *porquería*, la suciedad
impúdico, aquí, no decente
el *fregadero*, la *pila* (=recipiente de piedra o de otro material que suele haber en las cocinas) en la que se lava o *friega* (de fregar) la vajilla
el *tresillo*, conjunto de sofá y dos sillones; también sofá en el que se pueden sentar tres personas
los *riñones*, ver figura en página 85
rota, fig., muy cansada
de par en par, loc. adv., significa que están abiertas enteramente
el *tarrito* dim. de *tarro* (viñeta en pág. 84); aparentemente los tarritos contienen *especias* (=hierbas que se usan, añadidas en pequeña cantidad, para dar sabor a los alimentos)
la *esquela*, aquí papel en el que va puesto el nombre de lo que contiene el tarro
el *tomillo*, el *apio*, la *nuez moscada* (viñeta en pág. 84)
la *barbacoa*, interpreto: el tarrito contiene especias para la *barbacoa*, asado de carne o pescado hecho al aire libre. Es voz antillana y nombre de la parrilla en la que se asa. Entre los indígenas es un conjunto de palos puestos sobre un hueco hecho en la tierra y sobre los que se pone la carne o el pescado
el *bicarbonato*, polvo blanco que se emplea en medicina para calmar la acidez del estómago u otras molestias; también se emplea en las tareas *culinarias* (=propias de la confección de las comidas)
la *madrina*, aquí, la mujer que lleva a la iglesia al niño a *bautizar* (=ponerle el nombre)

Página 50

modesto, aquí de poco valor
parca, sin exceso, moderada
la *hermana*, una categoría de monja dentro de los conventos; las monjas se llaman así entre ellas
turbia, aquí, sucia, poco clara
retrayendo ger. de retraer, aquí, una sonrisa no muy abierta, como para ella misma
tunante, fresco, sinvergüenza
hacerse cruces, mostrar extrañeza o admiración
explayarse, extenderse, alargarse mucho en hablar y contar con detalle
apocalíptico, como una gran catástrofe; de *Apocalipsis*, el fin del mundo
degustar, probar un alimento; aquí, comer
el *carrillo*, ver figura en página 85
secuaz, seguidor
Pedro Botero, el diablo, Satanás

Página 52

irredenta, que no se puede redimir; aquí: que no puede luchar contra ella
el *trajín*, mucha actividad y mucho trabajo
baldada, que tiene dolores por todo el cuerpo a causa de la limpieza y por lo que casi no puede moverse
conciliar el sueño, poder dormirse
abatida, triste y deprimida
dichoso, fig., aquí, molesto, que causa enfado o problemas
revenido, en mal estado, viejo
el *eructo*, de *eructar*, echar por la boca los gases del estómago
el *párpado*, ver figura en página 85
la *legaña*, sustancia que producen los párpados y que se seca a ambos lados de los ojos
el *insomnio*, el no poder dormir
el *ardor*, sensación de calor que se siente cuando duele el estómago

deteriorado, aquí, estropeado, enfermo
el *empacho*, molestia en el estómago (= la *indigestión*) causada por la comida; el *vientre*, ver figura en pág. 85

Página 53
ácido, muy amargo
la *avidez*, deseo muy grande
el *regazo*, parte del cuerpo de la mujer entre la cintura y las rodillas; especialmente cuando está sentada
la *lucidez*, claridad de pensamiento
arrullar, adormecer a un niño con canciones suaves; aquí, con un sonido agradable
plácido, tranquilo, sereno
desleírse, deshacerse, disolverse
el *ronroneo*, el ruido que hacen los gatos cuando están contentos
reverberante, aquí que reflejan la luz y brillan
el *escorzo*, la posición, la perspectiva
la *floresta*, bosque frondoso o lugar poblado de muchas plantas (=*vegetación*)

Página 54
la *cascada*, caída del agua de un río o de otra corriente desde la altura
refulgir, aquí, hacía brillar
impregnarse, empaparse, llenarse como cuando se moja una tela en agua
iridiscente, que muestra o refleja los colores del arco iris
el *firmamento*, el cielo, lugar en el que están las estrellas y los otros astros
las *zagas*, en movimiento de zig-zag: hacia un lado y hacia otro
la *cresta*, la parte alta de una montaña; aquí, del *alcor*, monte pequeño o colina
febril, con fiebre
la *conciencia*, aquí, la percepción del tiempo; no sabe en qué mo-

mento está; la *consciencia*, el conocimiento, la facultad de conocer
trastocar, cambiar el orden de las cosas, desordenar
el *desasosiego*, intranquilidad, malestar impreciso
la *resaca*, malestar que siente una persona por haber tomado el día anterior bebidas alcohólicas en exceso; *espesa*, muy fuerte, no ligera

Página 55
andar de seguidillas, en sentido fig. y fam.: andar con el vientre suelto o descompuesto; tener diarrea

Viñetas

el pino

el capazo

el centeno

el haba

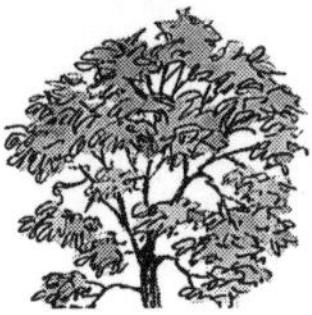

el nogal

el tarro

la brocha

el tomillo

el apio

la nuez moscada

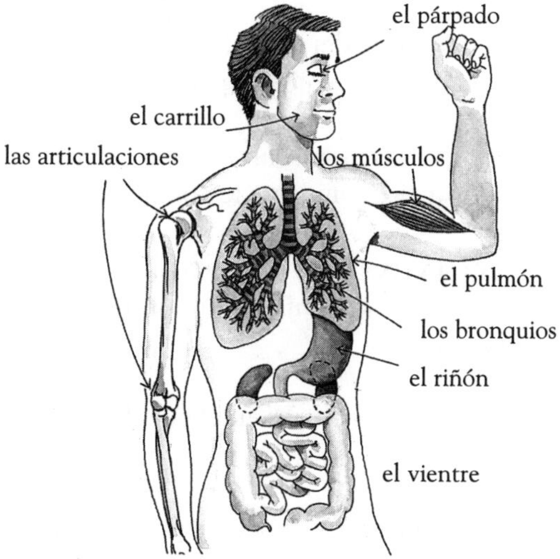
el párpado
el carrillo
las articulaciones
los músculos
el pulmón
los bronquios
el riñón
el vientre

ACTIVIDADES Y TAREAS

El difunto Ezequiel Montes

A) Comprensión

1. ¿Por qué dice el padre del narrador «¡Pobre desgraciado!» al referirse a Ezequiel? (página 24)

2. Explique por qué las mozas, al principio, se ríen de Ezequiel y por qué las mujeres le compadecen.

3. ¿Por qué sentían recelo en el pueblo ante Ezequiel y por qué los vecinos se miraban unos a otros con complicidad? (página 22)

4. Describa la vida de los chicos en el pueblo, durante el verano.

5. ¿Por qué cree usted que el sobre que recibe Ezequiel está manoseado y la tarjeta amarillenta? (página 26)

6. Haga una descripción de la vida del pueblo tal como se deduce de lo que el narrador cuenta.

7. Con cada uno de los nombres de animales que aparecen en la página 19 (cangrejo, rana,) y el que aparece en la página 25 (liebre) escriba dos frases, una empleando el nombre en su sentido propio y otra en el figurado.

B) Sobre los personajes

1. ¿Por qué cree usted que ha vuelto al pueblo Ezequiel?

2. ¿Qué cree usted que escribe Ezequiel en sus cartas a doña Chon?

3. ¿Por qué se emborracha? ¿Fue recibido por doña Chon cuando va él mismo a llevar la carta?

4. Haga un retrato de doña Chon tal como usted se la imagina o uno de Ezequiel.

5. ¿Amaba doña Chon a Ezequiel? Analice las diversas actitudes de la señora: a) rompe la primera carta, no contesta a la segunda más que con la que contiene la tarjeta amarillenta; b) se viste de luto a la muerte de Ezequiel y encarga misas por su alma.

6. ¿Qué papel juega Baldomero Torres en el relato?

C) General

1. ¿Le ha interesado el relato? Tanto si su respuesta es afirmativa como si es negativa razone y explique por qué.

2. Escriba una composición sobre la solidaridad de las gentes del pueblo hacia Ezequiel.

3. Escriba la carta que usted imagina que Ezequiel le escribe a doña Chon.

La familia de Villar

1. ¿Por qué parecían taciturnos Benito y Clara si no lo eran?

2. ¿Cuál es la tragedia de Antonio y Enedina? ¿Cómo reaccionan ante ella?

3. Comente las diferencias que hay entre los niños de un pueblo sin agua y los de un pueblo con ella?

4. ¿Qué supone la llegada del agua al pueblo? ¿Qué precio han tenido que pagar los habitantes de Villar? (Vea, además, Prólogo en página 17)

5. ¿Qué cambios tendrán lugar en el pueblo con la llegada del agua? Si tiene conocimientos sobre estos problemas escriba una composición sobre las diferencias entre la «España seca» y la «España húmeda».

6. Haga una descripción de Villar de los Barrios intentando presentar un pueblo de la «España húmeda».

7. Haga una composición con el título: **Un pueblo sumergido.**

8. Describa los sentimientos de Benito.

9. Comente la solidaridad del pueblo con los nuevos

habitantes, la familia de Villar. Hágalo en dos planos: a) el de los niños y b) el de los adultos. Comente después el problema de la integración en un nuevo ambiente.

10. Recoja los nombres de plantas y de árboles que aparecen en el relato y escriba una frase en la que entre cada uno de ellos.

El viaje de doña Saturnina

1. ¿Por qué se va doña Saturnina al sur?

2. Escriba una composición breve en la que comente los rasgos del carácter de doña Saturnina

3. ¿Qué hizo el alemán? ¿Cuál fue su comportamiento? ¿Por qué cree usted que desapareció?

4. ¿Qué le sucede a doña Saturnina? Describa su enfermedad.

5. ¿Qué fue lo que le hizo daño? ¿Fueron los merengues? ¿Qué le sucedió a la hermana Veneranda por comer los merengues? ¿Por qué le causaron los polvos del tarrito tantos trastornos a doña Saturnina?

6. Analice el sueño de doña Saturnina.

7. Comente los dos tipos de viaje que hace doña Saturnina.

8. ¿Qué cree usted que hará doña Saturnina cuando recupere la salud?

Sobre el libro en general

1. Si ha leído los tres relatos, tiene ahora una idea a) sobre un escritor leonés; b) sobre los pueblos leoneses y la problemática de algunos de ellos. Haga un trabajo, de manera oral o escrita, en el que compare la vida en la montaña leonesa y la vida en el sur de España.

2. ¿Cuál de los tres relatos le ha interesado más y por qué?

3. Haga sus comentarios sobre el **cuento español contemporáneo**. Puede apoyarse en los cuentos que conozca de otros autores españoles.

NOTAS